Horizon Chasers

Horizon Chasers

*The Lives and Adventures
of Richard Halliburton
and Paul Mooney*

GERRY MAX

McFarland & Company, Inc., Publishers
Jefferson, North Carolina, and London

Frontispiece: Paul Mooney, about 1929
(courtesy John Murphy Scott)

Quotations from *The Royal Road to Romance* by Richard Halliburton are reprinted with the permission of Scribner, an imprint of Simon & Schuster Adult Publishing Group. Copyright ©1925 by the Bobbs-Merrill Company; copyright renewed ©1953 by Wesley Halliburton.

Quotations from *Richard Halliburton: His Story of His Life's Adventures* by Richard Halliburton are reprinted with the permission of Scribner, an imprint of Simon & Schuster Adult Publishing Group. Copyright ©1940 by the Bobbs-Merrill Company; copyright renewed ©1968 by the Bobbs-Merrill Company.

LIBRARY OF CONGRESS CATALOGUING-IN-PUBLICATION DATA

Max, Gerry, 1945–
    Horizon chasers : the lives and adventures of Richard Halliburton and Paul Mooney / Gerry Max.
        p.   cm.
    Includes bibliographical references and index.

    ISBN-13: 978-0-7864-2671-3
    softcover : 50# alkaline paper ∞

    1. Halliburton, Richard, 1900–1939.   2. Mooney, Paul, 1904–1939.   3. Travelers—United States—Biography.   4. Voyages and travels.   I. Title.
    G226.H3M39   2007
    910.4092'273—dc22   2007000082
    [B]

British Library cataloguing data are available

On the cover: Compass ©2006 PhotoSpin; Elephants ©2006 PhotoSpin; Matterhorn Mountain ©2006 Corbis Images

Reprinted with corrections

Manufactured in the United States of America

McFarland & Company, Inc., Publishers
Box 611, Jefferson, North Carolina 28640
www.mcfarlandpub.com

To my beloved wife, Carole

Acknowledgments

I wish to thank William Alexander for sharing his many memories. A man of immense pep and curiosity, he seemed, in his eighties, still a young man, and when he died, I cried bitter tears. We had spent countless hours piecing together the fabric of his life, and that of his best friend, Paul Mooney, whom he traveled great distances "to find"; in the end, he had been more places than Richard Halliburton himself. He continued to design other houses (besides the house he designed in 1937 for Halliburton), helped develop the Hollywood Hills, opened an important art boutique on Santa Monica Boulevard, and even appeared in movies, *The McMasters* and *The Shootist* among them. Besides making available and permitting me to use his collection of Halliburton and Mooney memorabilia, Bill introduced me to some of the principal players in the Halliburton-Mooney story who were still living. I also wish to thank Bill's niece Elaine Hofberg, whose keen intelligence and marvelous wit sustained me through some of the more trying parts of my research. I wish then to thank Charles Wolfsohn, Bill's lifelong friend, who knew both Paul and Richard. To Adam and Elinore Hofberg I extend special thanks for their continuing encouragement.

I am especially grateful for help and steady encouragement received from John Murphy Scott, a former copy editor for the *Washington Post*, who shared his recollections of his "Uncle Paul" and other members of the Mooney family. Anton Levandowsky also shared memories of his Uncle Paul, his mother Evelyn, and her family, which enriched my understanding. I am lastly grateful for information given to me about his Uncle Paul by the late Mark Stevens, Eire Mooney's son. All the nephews were of the opinion that James Mooney was a genius and that Paul inherited more than a spark of that genius.

I wish to thank the late Professor John Phillipson of the Thomas Wolfe Society for his initial encouragement. Besides an easy ability to offer from memory lines from authors Thomas Wolfe and Willa Cather, among countless others, John could recite the opening lines of *The Royal Road to Romance*. I also wish to thank Aldo Magi of the Thomas Wolfe Society for his queries as to the book's progress. I wish to thank the librarians at Princeton University, the Bancroft Library at the University of California-Berkeley, Rhodes College in Memphis, the Lilly Library at the University of Indiana, Dartmouth College and the Nebraska State Historical Society for permitting me to use materials germane to this study. Special thanks is given to Simon & Schuster, Inc., for permission to quote from Halliburton's works.

Discussion has enriched understanding. Halliburton enthusiasts Edward Howell, William Short of Rhodes College, William Taylor, the late Dr. William White of the Julia and David White Artists' Colony in Costa Rica and author Errol Lincoln Uys have lent important insights as well as provided documents. I also wish to thank Laguna Beach historian Jane Janz. I finally wish to thank Art Linkletter, who was available with both help and encouragement. Any sins of commission or omission in this glorious adventure are solely my responsibility.

A study of Richard Halliburton and Paul Mooney occasions many trips to many different places. Countless fellow travelers have shown keen interest in their story, and to them I offer thanks for listening to my friendly outpourings. I would especially like to thank my mother, Ruby Max, who, when I was very young, took me through the two *Books of Marvels*. Lastly I wish to thank my wife, Carole, for all her support and love, as well as thank our Himalayan cats, Skylar and Kokoro, who acted as armrests and willing ears during the writing of this essay, and to Djuna, who remained vigilant. I would like to think that they are descended from Paul's cats at Laguna Beach. Perhaps all cats with a nose for travel, sense of the open road and love of comfortable places have an exiguous trickle of the Mooney cats coursing through their veins.

Contents

"I bless God that I was free to wander,
free to hope, and free to love."

Travels with a Donkey in the Cevennes
Robert Louis Stevenson

"Travel broadens the mind. It also quickens the
sympathies and bestows on one a ready fund
of knowledge. And it is useful to talk about
when you get back home."

"I'm a Stranger Here Myself"
Sinclair Lewis

"Sometimes I've believed as many as six
impossible things before breakfast."

Through the Looking Glass
Lewis Carroll

"I am fevered with the sunset,
I am fretful with the bay,
For the wander-thirst is in me
And my soul is in Cathay."

From "The Sea Gypsy"
Bliss Carman
More Songs from Vagabondia

"Be Ye lift up, O gates of sea and land,
Before the host that comes...."

From "Ode on the Opening of the
Panama-Pacific International Exposition
(in) San Francisco—February 1915"
George Sterling

Preface

From Richard Halliburton's address on Montgomery Street in San Francisco, it was an easy walk to the top of Coit Tower. Looking out, one could get an Olympian view of Treasure Island, and dream of the great fair that once took place there. Often, as I watched the ships come and go, I imagined a gorgeously painted Chinese junk, the *Sea Dragon* itself, moving with quiet determination towards the fair's fabled palaces—the Temple of the Sun or the Court of the Moon—or its exhibits—the Streets of the World, Hollywood, and the Court of the Hemispheres. And, nearly the size of the Statue of Liberty, towered the beaconing statue of *Pacifica*. Several times I roamed about the actual fairgrounds. By the late 1970s they resembled more an abandoned industrial park than the grand courtyards of a wondrous world event. Little remained. Still, I could hear the sounds of the fair and see its marvels. I could see crowds gathering at the dock to greet Richard Halliburton and the brave crew that had accompanied him across the Pacific from Hong Kong in that heroic junk.

Halliburton intended to write a book about the *Sea Dragon Expedition*. Only a series of newspaper articles and subscription letters survive, plus the letters inevitably referring to it which he wrote home to his parents. If not by some dim recollection of this and other adventures, the two *Books of Marvels*, tempered to a young adult age group, generally have introduced modern readers to Halliburton. A hodgepodge, they were formed from his earlier books: *The Royal Road to Romance* (1925), *The Glorious Adventure* (1927), *New Worlds to Conquer* (1929), *The Flying Carpet* (1932), and *Seven League Boots* (1935). By the 1960s, only *The Royal Road to Romance* was in print.

The media of his day called him the "Prince of Pilgrims." He called himself a *horizon chaser*, but the horizon seemed a darker rather than lighter blue. Once the bomb, the Cold War and rock 'n' roll became issues, Halliburton seemed at best a curiosity. World War II, which had separated my generation from the one preceding it, made him seem even more remote, even as it lifted into legend Charles Lindbergh and Amelia Earhart, whose celebrity his own once rivaled.

The message of travel writing had remained essentially the same: *let me take you to new and exciting places*. After thirty years perhaps only its mode of expres-

1

sion had changed. Maybe the social visions of the 1930s had only been suspended. Raw and vociferous where Halliburton's books are innocent and polite, Jack Kerouac's *On the Road* piped tunes similar to Halliburton's. If Halliburton is nowhere as deep as Joseph Conrad or as riveting as Jack London, his idea that one should see the world before committing oneself to a collegiate routine seemed timeless to me. So did his insistence that one's destiny may very well lie abroad and not at home. Predictably these messages made my being in school in the 1960s a slightly uncomfortable experience.

Halliburton was a fluent, exuberant writer. He had, however, the defects of his qualities. He tended to overwrite, to give way to gratuitous amateurish philosophizing, and, in moments of high drama, to be trite. Purple patches colored his often drab, matter-of-fact prose, and windy tirades blemished an otherwise well-crafted story. He admitted as much, and sought help from various editors. A style resulted that became, if not the man, the Halliburton image. Most gifted of these editors was Paul Mooney, called after his death "a writer in his own right," as no other line of work could be attached to him.

John Aubrey, in his *Brief Lives*, said of the Elizabethan collaborators Francis Beaumont and John Fletcher that between them was "a wonderful consimility of phansey" and that "Mr. Beaumont's maine Businesse was to lop the overflowings of Mr. Fletcher's luxuriant Fancy and flowing Witt." As fairly modern instances of sharing a "consimility of phansey," the co-authors of the *Bounty Trilogy*, Charles Nordhoff and James Hall could finish one another's sentences. Mooney's job differed from that of Nordhoff or Hall only in the sense that he, an unknown, had to complete the unfinished drafts of a known author.

Earlier biographies of Richard Halliburton have not gone into Mooney's life at any great length, or gone into detail about their collaborations; he is a figure in passing. As if he emerged from nowhere, nothing is said of his family background, and of its prominence in the American Irish community of its day. His mother, Ione Gaut Lee Mooney, was a direct descendant of English royalty and the regent of the Daughters of the American Revolution. His father was American Indian authority James Mooney, an expert on the Ghost Dance religion. Largely self-taught, James Mooney learned a number of Native American languages and, while an ethnologist for the Smithsonian Institution, photographed the Native American way of life and wrote engagingly lucid monographs on Amerindian culture.

Athletic, Paul was also intellectual. He was prickly, and, as he said himself, "temperamental as hell," but he was never tedious or insipid. He sulked, but never whined. While Richard saw money as something to be amassed, Paul seemed embarrassed to have it in his pocket for too long. He read a good deal. He listened to stories. He liked speedy cars. Aviation fascinated him. He once hopped a freighter bound for Constantinople. He loafed around Paris. He smoked, and he drank—towards the end, a bit too much.

He wrote poems. Privately printed in 1927, these poems offer some testimony that he was a devoted fan of Richard Halliburton long before he met him, which may very well have been at one of Halliburton's much publicized lectures. Once they met, Paul became everything, or nearly everything, to Richard. To the extent that Paul chauffeured him to and from the airport, dragged him down to the beach for his "celebrity" tan, and nursed him back to health when he was sick, Paul always remained, in a sense, Richard's man-servant, and confidant. He also remained Richard's principal friend and love interest, though neither Richard nor Paul maintained any more fidelity to monogamy than they did to single authorship of one of Richard Halliburton's books.

Writing the life of a journalist and rover such as Paul is no easy task, especially since the records have, for the most part, vanished. Certain facts co-exist with probable or possible ones. Often one has to paint the scene around him to create his image, and then it is still only dimly seen. This book benefits from the recollections of people who knew both Paul and Richard. It also benefits from the points of view of the many articles and books which have been written about Richard Halliburton since 1965. Omitted portions of the letters, edited versions of which were published in 1940, are used to show, as best they will permit, Richard and Paul at work and at play. Also there are Paul's own letters, about twenty in number, which range in length from a page to several pages. These are vital especially in understanding his role in assisting Ludecke in the *I Knew Hitler* project, which is explored in some detail here; generally, Ludecke's own authorship of this remarkable book is assumed, hands down. Also there are the fragments of an autobiography called "Meanderings," which Paul's friend William Alexander, the designer and builder of Halliburton's House in Laguna Beach, put together. My conversations with Mr. Alexander and members of Paul Mooney's family enriched the portrait. Paul was at once a journalist and photojournalist. He left notebooks, which, deplorably, are lost, as are the many letters exchanged between him and Richard Halliburton. Besides writing letters and keeping notebooks, Paul sent cards and used the telephone. John Murphy Scott remembers one card sent to his family during Thanksgiving that simply read, "Gobble, gobble, gobble and a thousand times gobble." Such information, though fugitive, reveals a good deal more about Paul than mere speculation as to his thoughts on an important American holiday. There are then the many photographs never before published, many of which have been offered for this book by Paul's heirs and by his friend William Alexander.

While the present treatment does not dwell on Halliburton's sexuality, or the sexual relationship which he had with Paul Mooney, some space, as it pertains to the nature of their collaboration and developing friendship, is devoted to it. Earlier biographies, one by Jonathan Root and another by James Cortese, imply rather than assume Halliburton was homosexual. Jonathan Root begins his life of Halliburton with this remarkable statement: "The intensity with which Richard Halliburton lived his life was rooted, someone once suggested, in the distinction that as a boy of six he was the only male student in a school otherwise attended by 350 girls." Root later mentions that Halliburton, at Devil's Island, was "acutely aware of the homosexual courtships of the young and new prisoners by certain convicts" and that is all. He does make it clear that Halliburton sought companionship, specifically male companionship; the reason seems to have been, one could conclude, that marriage was simply too confining, and that his preference for same-sex relationships was rather an avoidance of wedlock. From Cortese, who was a good friend of Richard's father, Wesley, one learns on this issue that Wesley had little regard for Richard's friends, who, incidentally, happened to be homosexual. Though I use the word "gay," I do so hesitatingly. The term does not seem grammatical when contrasted with lesbian, which I am also not sure about. I would prefer "cultured naturalism" or "homo-erotic naturalism" to describe Richard's, and Paul's, sexual outlooks; both insisted, in all events, that one's contact with reality be sensuous, immediate, not indirect or "virtual." Richard seldom used the word "gay," even in its regular sense of being merry— he preferred the word "lively" to describe an essentially virtuous and ardent person. The blurb to one of his books called him "the gayest nomad of them all," but this description merely emphasized the friendly worldliness of this man. In downtown Memphis, Halliburton's home, is the Hotel Gayoso, but no one supposed it a guest house solely open to "gays." A main thoroughfare at the San Francisco Exposition was the Gayway. Similarly, the word "fairy" strikes no note of derision. Halliburton's father wrote a "Fairyland of Geography," but this was meant for children. Neither Paul nor Richard thought themselves damned by their sexuality, or miserably confined to it; they enjoyed it.

Just a word about the relative value of things. I have kept the dollar figures as they appear in the original sources. Readers today might multiply these by at least ten. I have been told that this is a low multiple, a variable one, or one that is just right. The 1930s were lean years, and a man earning $75 a week could support a wife and a couple of kids, and look forward to buying a car and owning a home. Halliburton's house in 1937 cost about $31,000 to build; a sum half that amount would have given him a worthy house even in Hollywood. In one place his net worth is given as $58,000, and is adjudged by Halliburton as substantial, leading me to believe that, while not at his ultimate financial goal, he was halfway there. For the *Flying Carpet Expedition*, which lasted a year and a half, and required an airplane, gas and someone to pilot it, he needed upwards of $25,000. For the *Sea Dragon Expedition* of a few years later, which required a captain, engineer, crew, and ship (cost-effectively put together by low-paid Chinese laborers), he had to scrimp beyond the $25,000 up-front money given to him. These figures today would be far in excess of $250,000, probably closer to $500,000. At the height of his popularity, he commanded $2,000 for a feature-length article. He got $160 each for the 50 newspaper stories he wrote for the Bell Syndicate in 1934–1935. If he received $750 for a lecture—sometimes $900 for a week of lecturing—that was a princely sum and, in today's money, represented $10,000, even more. It was of course nice work if you could get it; his contractor at Hangover House, William Alexander, asked for $1,500 to design and build the house; the contractors received $1.75 an hour, the workers received somewhat less.

Halliburton is himself timeless. He is the timeless marketer of himself. Though unsuccessful in the movies, he did well enough in radio and on the lecture circuit. Television would have offered him a career, perhaps as an emcee. Halliburton never got to writing the truthful book he always wanted to write; he had written an article about the most wicked places on earth, but the article was rejected as not genteel enough for his fans. At first a naive idealist, Halliburton quickly learned that it took money to be one. He wearied then of travel, then of writing about travel; he never wearied about the prospects of making money. The *Sea Dragon Expedition*, rather than a capitulation to folly, will forever offer one shining lesson on mismanagement: that a fear of want coupled with extraordinary self-delusion can lead to failure.

Halliburton's belief that the child is father to the man greatly appealed to the reading public. Throughout America, young men, and some young ladies, once they read Halliburton's books, hit the open road, thinking it a royal one leading to enchantment. Most returned wiser, if not richer, better prepared to face the issues of the day, if not defeated. Some writers, such as F. Scott Fitzgerald and Ernest Hemingway, finding Halliburton's style too gullibly exuberant, ridiculed it. Other writers, such as Thomas Wolfe or, more recently, Susan Sontag, have been attracted to Halliburton, and the spirit of travel he invoked. Paul Theroux heads the list of modern travel writers who have paid tribute to him. Evan S. Connell has so much as called him "the last great traveler." Certainly he wrote great travel books in the beginning of his career. With Paul Mooney, he wrote some of the last great travel books.

Halliburton customarily ended his lectures with the wish that he had taken his audience away from their present world to worlds faraway, at least for an hour. According to John Rust "Brue" Potter, who was with him on his first attempt to sail across the Pacific, he had the habit of beginning his sentences with a present participle: "walking down the street today" or "speaking about the boat." There were many streets, the boat, and that seemingly odd relationship that he had with Paul.

By the way, "Speaking about a marvelous pairing of kindred spirits...."

Introduction:
A Modern Ulysses

As a boy, in the 1950s, I spent long hours paging through Richard Halliburton's *The Book of Marvels*. The pictures of New York City and Niagara Falls from the air thrilled me as much as they made me shudder at the fearful immensity of the world beyond my own backyard. Everyone I knew had their own favorite picture. Mine was of a dirigible touching the "beacon light" of the Empire State Building, an event which struck me as an impossibility. Another was of two young men on a mountain precipice in a place called Yosemite; I always feared the one seated on the edge would lean over too far and fall. Through it all the author seemed a friendly enough guide, going from place to place with an easy step and gently holding my hand. I asked my mother who this "Richard Halliburton" was and where I could find him. I presumed that he was the author, and *no one else*. "He disappeared at sea," she said. "Long ago."

In his lifetime Richard Halliburton was a synonym for romantic travel. His books offered readers relaxed tours to scenic locales, and introduced them in a charming style to strange people and quaint customs throughout the world. He was also a live action figure whose daring was heroic: he climbed the Matterhorn, scaled Mt. Fujiyama in winter, descended into the Mayan Well of Death (not once but twice), slept on top of the Great Pyramid of Cheops, and swam the length of the Panama Canal, even paying the 36-cent toll for his weight. In addition, he led readers into history, retracing Ulysses' wanderings from Troy to his home in Ithaca, emulating Hannibal's march over the Alps aboard an elephant, swimming the Hellespont to rival Lord Byron, and subjecting himself to imprisonment with the inmates on Devil's Island.

The world seemed one grand exposition with all the cultures of the world happily mingled amid new prospects for science and industry and new adventures for the humanities and art. Political upheavals were mere inconveniences to the traveler. Differing ideologies ignorantly co-existed. These were the days of the great ocean liners and streamlined trains, when daredevil fliers spiraled

about the sky and race cars broke land speed records. These were the days of
identifiable Main Streets, before shopping malls and signage took their place.
These were the days before the products of a consumer culture marred the landscape, and before atomic bombs offered a new dimension to fear. These were
the days before television brought the world into every home, and before the
Internet created the global village.

Halliburton himself seemed to have vanished into the chaos of World War
II. He seemed a last gasp of Old World poetry in a world gone mad. Books and
articles about his life, when they began to appear in the 1960s, had first to explain
to readers Halliburton's impact before they explored the details of his life.[1]

Once in a while his name emerged only in connection with new names in
the headlines. In 1995, a news agency, for instance, informed collectors of rock
memorabilia that they could "expect to spend $10,000 to secure a school library
card signed by young Elvis in 1939 to check out Richard Halliburton's *Second
Book of Marvels*." Among writers, the two *Books of Marvels* have had heirs, notably
Lowell Thomas' *Seven Wonders of the World*, "a thrilling and colorful up-to-the-
minute magic carpet journey to the wonders of the world today—not merely
seven, but sevenfold." Seasoned to taste, Halliburton's romantic spin on travel
writing, itself drawing wind from popular novelist Elinor Glyn and travel writer
Harry Franck, held its focus. Among modern travel writers, Paul Theroux is
foremost in acknowledging his debt to
Halliburton.[2]

If today Richard Halliburton's writings have, as Guy Townsend noted, about
"as little relevance to the present-day world
as an operator's manual for a Stanley
Steamer," in 1930 his celebrity equaled
that of Charles Lindbergh, Will Rogers,
Howard Hughes and Amelia Earhart. *Time*
hailed him as "romantic, poetic, enthusiastic, bubbling, impetuous, adventurous,
dramatic, enthralling" and knighted him
"Playboy Richard Halliburton." *The Illustrated Love Magazine*, for women, introduced him as "the Prince of Lovers," a
"dashing, modern Don Quixote, whose
gay vagabondage has led him in search of
romance and adventure to the far corners
of the earth." On the lecture circuit, Halliburton generated health and happiness,
rebellion and wanderlust. He represented
Youth, at least the day's commercial notions of it, and his books were, if nothing

Richard Halliburton, publicity photograph, about 1935 (courtesy
Princeton University).

else, drafts from the Fountain of Youth in capsule, easy-to-swallow form.[3]

Newspapers dubbed him "Romantic Richard," "Richard-The-Literary-Lionhearted" or "Daring Dick." "Charlatan" was a term skeptics unkindly applied to him. Quick to make a buck in the hero racket, to many in the press booth he came off as a poseur—a song-and-dance globetrotter of high-gloss plasticity and sheen. His first biographer Jonathan Root called him a "magnificent myth," implying that he was sort of a Baron Munchausen tailor-made for the audiences of his day. One could rebut, as has an apologist for the Baron, that "the most popular works of travel (or indeed of the imagination) from the *Odyssey* onwards, have been *Voyages Imaginaires*" and that Halliburton, like *Robinson Crusoe* author Daniel Defoe, had with "artful shading" molded "the products of the imagination into the understood terms of ordinary life." Still, Halliburton wasn't quite the prevaricating Baron Munchausen nor the skilled Defoe, but page headers in *Royal Road* such as "The Girl Pirate," "All but the Trousers," "A Free Love Debate," "The Sirens of Seville," and "Once More in Srinagar" evoked the fantastic as much as they did the mundane.[4]

Fans called him "an originator, a trail-blazer," an example to "countless young people," particularly to red-blooded, fun-loving American boys. Hailed a "Prince of Pilgrims" and "headline hunter," through his books, columns, headlines, and lectures, he evoked distant lands and peoples, earning him a loyal following among millions to whom he represented the simple action verbs of he *climbed*, he *scaled*, he *swam*, he *ran*, he *celebrated*. With bold strokes, he played off his image, stylishly insinuating himself into the established celebrity status of laid-to-rest heroes from Alexander the Great and King Richard the Lion-Hearted to Hernando Cortez and Henry Morton Stanley, and of living ones from Lawrence of Arabia and Burton Holmes to Rudolph Valentino and Douglas Fairbanks, Sr. His bestsellers *The Royal Road to Romance* (1925), *The Glorious Adventure* (1927), and *New Worlds to Conquer* (1929) sealed his image as the most traveled person who had ever lived and a man whose home was the world.[5]

Halliburton's adventures abroad recall the Grand Tour begun in eighteenth century England when time abroad was thought to complete a young man's education and prepare him for the rigors of life at home. Closer to Halliburton's time and place, the Nautical Preparatory School in Boston readied cadets over a four-year period for college or business while they toured the world. Enrollees traveled on the steamship *Young America*, "afloat on the blue ocean and visiting every clime." Not everyone could afford this introduction to the world, however, as easily as they could afford a book.[6]

Though Halliburton, in his time, loomed larger than any book he ever wrote, each one filled the bill. He is best known today for the two *Books of Marvels* (besides the tragic grandeur of his disappearance), and his books hold up as well-told adventure sagas in a once-was world. And where they must now fail as guidebooks, they succeed as nostalgic revisitations. A masterpiece of the genre, *The Royal Road to Romance*, at the forefront of his books, is a gospel of the open road, youthful initiative and the hazards of procrastination; it is a true "road" narrative akin to Thomas Nashe's *The Unfortunate Traveler*, Robert Louis Stevenson's *Travels with a Donkey*, Aristide Bruant's *Sur La Route*, Jack London's *The Road*, William H. Davies' *Autobiography of a Super-Tramp*, Stephen Graham's (and Vachel Lindsay's) *Tramping with a Poet in the Rockies*, Jack Kerouac's *On the Road* and Jan Cremer's *I, Jan Cremer*. Sea narratives such as Richard Henry Dana Jr.'s *Two Years Before the Mast* and Herman Melville's *Redburn* also belong in the genre.[7]

With the publication of *The Royal Road to Romance* in 1925, Halliburton, as had Lord Byron after the publication of *Childe Harold's Pilgrimage* in 1812, literally woke to find himself famous. Its lofty imperatives gently declared youth's independence from the stodgy dictates of old age. The book heralded that the moment for another youthful outburst had again come. Live the life of a novel. Better to live poetry than to write it. Move with the flame before the flame dies. Let no one, in whom the flame at last only flickers, tell you who are young that youth is wasted on you. See the world now, while you can walk, climb, and, with self-possession, think. Don't become the old man telling the young man you are now how things might have been, or how much fun you might have had acting out all those dreams of youth—with those arms and legs of youth. "Horizon Chaser," Halliburton wanted to title his book; another time, seeing himself a born-again version of the wandering Greek hero Ulysses, he wanted it titled "Ulysses, Jr." "Reckless Daring," he might have otherwise titled it. With the average life span in America in 1925 just a little over fifty-five years, Halliburton saw the need for someone aged twenty to see the world as far more urgent than today.[8]

Halliburton's message came at a propitious time in American life. As England's *Grand Tour* recommenced after the Napoleonic Wars in 1815, bringing such people as Byron, Shelley and Keats to the continent, so too the opportunity for safe travel abroad recommenced for Americans after the Great War in 1918. All but destroyed were the values of the "ancient regime"—and of those social organizations controlled by old men for which young men had sacrificed their lives. Vitality now was king—at least for optimists like Halliburton. Born in 1900 (the year often cited, as if to keynote a new age dawning), he could reiterate the statement of Erik Satie, born in 1866, that he had "come into the world very young in a very old era." The old era now broken down, new illusions rose from the debris. New cults of youth sprang up; new markets sold youth products. "During the half-century between 1880 and 1930," writes historian Steven Mintz, "parent-child relations underwent a profound transformation. Middle-class family life grew more democratic, affectionate, and child-centered, and the school

Opposite, top: "On the trail of Richard Halliburton." The author (in beret) with friends at the ruins of the Pergamum Library in Bergama, Turkey, 1999. *Bottom*: "On the trail of Paul Mooney's roots." The author near the Ring of Kerry in Ireland, 2000.

and peer group became more significant in young people's lives." To some, this change was not necessarily for the better. Klaus Mann took a dim view of America's youth: he believed them motivated by material success alone; Europe's youth, he believed, was motivated by a higher spiritual calling. Educators like Henry Adams would have agreed.[9]

See more and read less, Halliburton urged; *do rather than wait to do*. The idea that a young man might round out each part of his education by intelligently-directed travel and thereby equip himself with the broadest culture sounded reasonable and most appealing. To pre-collegians who had no clue what they wanted to be when they grew up or to collegians who had no idea once they got to college what they wanted to major in, Halliburton's message was a less than gentle nudge to hit the road.

Fueled by mystic yearnings garbed in idealized notions of history and geography, the message owed much of its inspiration to the poet Rupert Brooke (1887–1915). Brooke was beautiful, British, and bisexual. He had walked the streets of Chicago and traveled to the South Seas. He died in a foreign land, young and full of promise; his life was the stuff from which beautiful dreams are made. Another inspiration was George Leigh Mallory (1886–1924), who, with younger companion Andrew "Sandy" Irvine, had disappeared attempting to reach the summit of Mt. Everest. Halliburton never lost touch with the story, its theatric beauty, and the ghost of Mallory. T.E. Lawrence (1888–1935)—"Lawrence of Arabia"—was yet another source of inspiration, to the passionate degree that Homer's Odysseus (Ulysses) inspired both. Lawrence, as would Halliburton, enjoyed wearing colorful Arab costume—"going native," as it were. Halliburton, like Lawrence, saw himself as sufferer; the severe lashing he received from the sun god when he swam the Sea of Galilee compared, in effect, to the flogging Lawrence, when imprisoned, received from the Turkish bey at Deraa. Like Lawrence, Halliburton subscribed to the Greek idealization of the male body, sought male companionship and love, honored cleanliness, and esteemed youthful enterprise.[10]

Youthful enterprise as a theme for literature was itself nothing new. Mark Twain made it memorable through his immortal Tom Sawyer and Huck Finn. Others merely remodeled it. Guiding lights in the tradition are many and can be traced to antiquity. Notable is the account of St. Willibald's pilgrimage to the Middle East in the 8th century preserved in the oldest extant English travel narrative. In it are themes which have persisted in much travel literature to this day: indeed, Willibald "was irked by foreign officialdom, did not get on with foreign food, often fell ill, indulged in reckless exploits such as peering into volcanoes and successfully smuggling goods through customs" and, rightly or wrongly, was arrested on charges of espionage. Halliburton is Willibald reborn and retailored. Halliburton's charges were secular pilgrims, not runaways, or hobo drifters following the path of juvenile delinquency or a workless world of fantasy. Rather, they were pre-collegians and career-uncertain collegians who, after a leave of absence, would return to school or home enriched by the taste of the world they had received. They were the sons, really, of C.A. Stephens' 1880s' "knockabout club," itself composed of young lads who "in place of the present stationary college" had chosen "a steamship, fitted up and appointed as a college in all respects...." These rivaled Hezekiah Butterworth's young-boys-with-adult-male-chaperon series, the *Zig-Zag Journeys*, subtitled "Vacation Rambles Through Historic Lands." Earlier knockabout models were Oliver Optic's "Young America Abroad" series, which recounted "the varied experiences of the juvenile tourists of the Academy Squadron." Similarly, Thomas W. Knox's "Boy Travellers" series (after 1880) showed young Americans discovering foreign places, as the novels of Henry James, in a sort of Columbian reversion, showed adults discovering Europe. Also appearing in the 1880s was "The Half Hour Library of Travel, Nature and Science for Young People." Later shining models included Elbert Fisher's "Boy Globe Trotters" series (1915). Here, two boys "make a trip around the world working their way as they go"; they "meet various peoples having strange customs," and their own "adventures form a medium for the introduction of much instructive matter regarding the cities and countries through which they pass." Lizzie W. Champney's *Three Vassar Girls Abroad* (1887), subtitled "for Amusement and Instruction," showed the tradition belonged to young women as well as to young men.[11]

As for family travel books, many descend from those produced by Priscilla Wakefield (1751–1832), such as her best-selling *The Juvenile Travelers—Containing Remarks of a Family During a Tour Through the Principal States and Kingdoms of Europe with an Account of Their Inhabitants, Natural Productions, and Curiosities* (1801). Tales about young people in foreign lands were as old as the "Children's Crusade." Jane Andrews' *Seven Little Sisters Who Live on the Round Ball That Floats in the Air* (1861) was "possibly the first American children's fiction with exotic settings ... [with featured heroines] Gemila of the Arabian desert, Jeanette in Switzerland, Pen-se in China, Louise on the Rhine, Manenko in Africa...." In all, writes Gillian Avery, her stories "combine a sense of distant places and strange customs with reassuring details about family life and parents' love, which the young reader learns are the same the world over." As Halliburton's, they aimed at "imparting geography, history and natural history in the guise of fiction, but with a commanding light touch."[12]

Aware of the traditions of travel writing, Halliburton, aided by his publishers, revised them. In becoming a brand name for travel, he also became its piper. Of course his books not only reached young people. They reached grown-ups tired of humdrum tinkering in the backyard, basement or garage, the dead-end job, or the seemingly purposeless life. They reached armchair tourists who wanted a private guide, at little cost, to take them far away while they enjoyed all the comforts of home. They reached travelers who wanted special meaning added to their trips.

Though he always stood in the thick of each chapter he wrote, Halliburton remained to his many readers a one-dimensional figure. He, in fact, led several lives, or was, in a sense, a cake of several layers, frosting foremost. The wildly international rover parading before an admiring public remained best known. The son ever achieving greater success in the eyes of doting parents was certainly behind the scenes. Thoroughly unknown to his public or parents was the gay male most emotionally comfortable in the company of freethinkers, artists and ingenuous young men. The ideal life, the one towards which he secretly aimed, was a quiet one, as beyond the reach of the adoring crowd as any acropolis he had ever visited. Enough money, one or two faithful friends, a shelf of good books, and a pleasant view of the distant sea were all he needed to be carefree. The image went against type.

Linked to his life privately was Paul Mooney. Several years younger than Halliburton, Mooney was a freelance news reporter, travel editor and photojournalist; he also wrote poetry and told amusing stories. Like Halliburton, he had left school for a time and had hopped a freighter to Europe. If Richard, making a name for himself, had swum the span of the Panama Canal, Paul, emulating Douglas Fairbanks, Sr., had leapt from the rooftop of his house to that of a neighbor's next-door and back again. Halliburton hailed from Brownsville, Tennessee, near Memphis. Like Halliburton, Paul was southern, granting that Washington, D.C., in the 1900s, was an overgrown sleepy southern town. Halliburton attended Princeton—finally graduating—while Mooney attended Catholic University, lasting a semester, quitting school about the time the The Royal Road to Romance hit the book stands. As Richard's father, Wesley, of Scottish descent, and harboring a strong work ethic, was a proper southern gentleman with a civil engineering degree from Vanderbilt University, Paul's father James Mooney, of Irish descent, was an American Indian authority, of controversial opinion, employed by the Smithsonian Institution. Wesley, very much alive, partly supervised the direction of his son's career; James Mooney, dead when Paul may have needed him most, kept only a ghostlike vigilance over his son. By comparison, Paul's mother, Ione, like Halliburton's own mother, Nelle Nance (and surrogate mother Mary Hutchison ["Ammudder"], head of the girl's day school Richard attended as a boy), worshipped her son. If Richard feared that a rapid-heart condition would bring him to an early grave, Paul, it is reasonable to suppose, believed the heart condition that killed his father would soon kill him too. Short as each calculated the measure of his life to be, Richard wrung from it rich financial rewards, over a million dollars in his career. Paul, no matter the work thrown him, made ends meet, almost, and the plunge the country took into hard times only worsened matters for him. In 1930, when he met Richard, the die of his professional life was cast.[13]

Fair to say, Paul Mooney *merged* rather than *entered into* Richard Halliburton's life. Halliburton's life had been at full speed. Even at thirty, he had begun to weary of travel; even more so, he had begun wearying of writing up into bestselling copy the extensive notes he had taken of his travels. When still unknown, he had labored for months on the manuscript of *The Royal Road to Romance*, mainly to prune its rapturous, poetic excesses. His style—natural, pellucid, personable—came easily; the format it took did not come as easily. In forthcoming works, editors at Bobbs-Merrill—names such as David Laurance Chambers (also a noted Shakespeare scholar) and Hewitt Hanson Howland, as well as his father, Wesley, Sr.—had assisted him.[14]

Soon after Richard met Paul Mooney, and the two became lovers, Paul became Richard's principal editor. Paul had inherited outstanding writing skills from his father, whose many technical papers clarified ethnographic topics that other scholars obscured in pedantic gobbledygook. Paul, like his father, wrote easily in a style that matched Halliburton's own—simple, direct, enthusiastic, interesting. In the course of his ten year relationship with Richard Halliburton, Paul advanced from editor to co-writer of works bearing the Halliburton name. He ghostwrote *The Flying Carpet* (1932). He also contributed heavily to the content and shape of *Seven League Boots* (1935) as well as the magazine articles and newspaper columns. As Paul's father had been an expert on the Native American "Ghost Dance" ritual, so Paul himself, in a kind of irony, had become an adept ghostwriter, working with the best expression and arrangement of words and ideas without judging too much their meaning. In 1935 he undertook the book *I Knew Hitler*, published by Scribner's, an early study of the dictator then nearing the height of his power in Germany. The book's author was former Nazi diplomat and avowed homosexual Kurt Ludecke, who through rallies in many major American cities and through meetings with prominent American leaders, including Henry Ford, had tried to drum up support for the Nazi cause.[15]

Paul, meanwhile, advanced from Richard Halliburton's partner to business associate. In short order, they contracted with Paul's friend William Alexander to design and build a house for them in Laguna Beach, California. Though intended as Richard's principal home, and Paul's, it remained in Paul's name. Other changes followed. In the past, Halliburton had traveled mostly by himself. Now he and Paul traveled together, chiefly in America, gathering materials for an "American" book. These materials, added to materials from Halliburton's earlier publications, resulted in the two *Books of Marvels*, the *Occident* (1937) and *The Orient* (1938), arguably the single most popular world geography books ever published, and the ones that sat on my grandmother's bookshelves.

If at first Richard Halliburton was for me a picture or two in a book, Paul Mooney was at best only dimly seen. After his son's death, Wesley did the best he could to remove any references to Paul (among others) in Richard's soon-to-be-published letters. Though it was prudent to omit such references, no trace of intimacy between Paul and Richard is even implied—their own letters to one another are lost. Still, from what remains, Richard seemed the sophisticate, Paul the intellectual.

Paul's nephew, John Scott, a Princeton graduate and copy editor for the *Washington Post*, thought Paul "a Byronic hero." The image might need to be updated. As a member of that first generation of youth which embraced Herman

Hesse, Paul most resembles Harry Haller, the journalist in Hesse's *Steppenwolf*, a homeless wanderer troubled by life's mysteries, who seeks meaning and belonging. There is then in Hesse's *Demian*, Emil Sinclair, the outcast questing for identification. The novel's references to parental release and sibling relationships (especially to sisters), its notices of its protagonist Sinclair's wish to live in "the forbidden realm" rather than "the realm of light," and his "readmittance (as the Prodigal Son) to the fold" also mirror Paul's own region of existence.[16]

When he first left home, Paul, like Richard, was a happy thrill-seeker. Like the poet Rupert Brooke, he had an "itching heel," preferred the outdoors, "showed a reluctance to conform," and had a "gypsy-like idleness." By the end of the 1930s, the Depression had sapped much of his zest for life. He had begun to see the sham, as some of his letters make clear, and found it hard to pretend he didn't. He grew cynical, he began to mope, overindulging his love of drinking and smoking. In 1938, two years after the idea for the project commenced, Richard requested that Paul join him in attempting to sail a Chinese junk from Hong Kong to the Golden Gate International Exposition—otherwise known as the San Francisco World's Fair, at Treasure Island. The first overseas trip they would make together, it was also the last.[17]

Satisfactory extended biographies and a number of shorter ones have appeared about Richard Halliburton adding to the "story of his life's adventure" he himself provided. In these, as in the "story," Paul Mooney appears as that "other man," a technical assistant working offstage, an enthusiast of the romantic vision who had devoutly followed the "royal road" and whom Halliburton, the chief priest of the Temple of Romance, had taken under his wing as Pindar's boy. I no longer wondered why Richard Halliburton had disappeared, but rather where Paul Mooney had come from.

Halliburton loomed larger than his books. An invincible, delightfully dumbstruck, warmly informative author, he always gave himself equal billing with the wonders he described. Bleached of the homo-eroticism one finds in Charles Warren Stoddard's *South-Sea Idyls*, the style of Halliburton's best writing, nevertheless, suggests the "pronounced flesh-tint" Stoddard discerned was missing in Robert Louis Stevenson's travel works. Its raw wonderment and picturesque vocabulary even echo Stoddard himself at his best. Halliburton's "zest for living intensely" and "enthusiasm for history and archaeology" often soar from the page. The Halliburton style played lightly; few heavy-handed chords were struck. Satirist Corey Ford found it foolishly funny and superficial. Writers F. Scott Fitzgerald, Ernest Hemingway and Thomas Wolfe, equally amused, thought to emulate it. Paul, with a genius for parody and perhaps incapable of developing a style of his own, easily duplicated it.[18]

1

"Don Peyote"

The early life of Paul Mooney is of many strings, most of which remain unattached, some of which have worn off from a main thread. Pals remembered him as a steady friend, informed and quick-witted, a master of put-down, who always went straight for the jugular, and a showman, daring to the point of recklessness. "Peck's Bad Boy," they called him, a backwoods barbarian with a sense of delicacy and a charming gentleman with no trace of the sod, as comfortable in baggy trousers as in a suit, but plainly up to mischief of one kind or another. He was a loner whose company others sought. Of a quiet animal magnetism, this, along with his clever speech, soft roguish looks and a give-a-damn attitude, made him an exciting friend.[1]

Team sports didn't interest him. Nor did any regimented exercise. Still, he was athletic. A photograph shows him, with friend Eddy Lunt, performing some aerial gymnastics while holding onto a rope. He was evidently agile, even acrobatic in a rough-and-tumble manner. Not overly muscular, he had a trim, well-defined, altogether appealing physique, and little minded being photographed in the nude. He was a capable swimmer. He liked the comforts of home, but often wanted to sever, or at least loosen, the tether by which he was bound to the responsibilities family life entailed. Added in 1990 to the yearbook for the graduating class of 1922-1923 at Washington, D.C.'s Central High School is this entry, which wonderfully encapsulates Paul: "While at Central this cheerful cynic has acquired a shockingly big education with surprisingly little study, but he says his greatest achievement is having skipped fourteen times in one advisory. If the fates are friendly he will take a European cruise, and then return to develop the splendid literary talent he showed at Central."[2]

He never forgot his Irish roots. The family hailed from Ardee (the town of Ferdia's Ford), some sixty miles northwest of Dublin, in Louth, near County Meath, and the river Boyne, where Protestant William III defeated the forces of Catholic James II in 1690. Paul's fiercely anti–British grandfather, James (c. 1821–1861), an unregenerate Irish patriot, boldly taught Irish history, mythology and Gaelic when the British authorities strictly forbade arousing nationalist sentiments. Eventually the promise of setting up an Irish community away from home drove him, as it did many of his countrymen, to America with Ellen Devlin Mooney. They married in New York City and for a time lived in Manhattan's Lower East Side before they ventured west to the valley community of Richmond, Indiana. Here James formally swore off all allegiance to Great Britain. Crummy jobs kept him and his family out of poverty, and from his true calling. Months before his untimely death (of pneumonia), wife Ellen bore him a son. This son, who would become government ethnologist James Mooney (1861–1921), the celebrated "Indian Man," was Paul's father.[3]

This second James on American soil never lost touch with the things of his childhood. Mother Ellen Devlin doted on him and read him the stories of Ireland both she and her husband had cherished. Nearly everyone Irish-born could recite lines from Thomas Moore's *Irish Melodies*, or recall deeds of valor from Ireland's Rebellion of 1798 against Great Britain. James heard yarns from locals about the people and legends of their newfound home. Like other boys in the neighborhood, he attended grammar school. At sixteen, in 1877, not long after General Custer's defeat at the Little Big Horn, he gave an address to his high school class on the righteous motivation of the government's Indian policies, heralding his future career.

His two siblings answered callings which suggest the religious and academic climate that surrounded him as a child. Oldest sister Mary Anne, who became a nun, later started Mount St. Clare Convent; second oldest sister Margaret remained a grammar-school teacher for over fifty years. James taught high school but, after a year of it, he decided he did not want to "surrender his life to endless drill, chalk dust, and farmers' children." He continued to widen his studies on the American Indian, doing his research at nearby Earlham College, and, to give himself a look of stature, the five-foot-five autodidact soon grew a moustache, later a beard. In 1879 he turned his professional attention to newspaper work, first as a printer, then in the editorial division as a reporter for the *Richmond Palladium*. Later, as a secretary of the Richmond chapter of the National Land League of Ireland, he met the "uncrowned King of Ireland," Charles Parnell, a deity among Irish patriots and expatriates alike. Though devoted to Irish independence, Mooney's true interests lay elsewhere.[4]

James Mooney, at age 35. Mooney's signature is below (courtesy John Murphy Scott).

As the result of his years of independent research, he had collected and recorded, in minutest detail, information about the customs of various Native American Indian tribes. All this might have remained just a hobby had not the Bureau of American Ethnology (BAE), established in 1885, stepped in to open a career opportunity to him. After countless written enquiries to department heads and a personal visit to Washington, he finally won an audience with John Wesley Powell, the chief of the Bureau (and former director of the American Geological and Geographic Survey).

Major Powell, who had lost an arm in the Civil War, had achieved fame as an explorer of the Colorado River and Grand Canyon. He had, moreover, provided vivid and stirring accounts of the scenery and the Indian tribes he had encountered there. Powell quickly recognized in the inveterate list-maker Mooney a kinsman of the blood. Like himself, he had "a self-trained intelligence" and demonstrated a sympathy toward "the ethnically marginalized," those outside the "Protestant hegemony." For his part, Mooney shared Powell's belief, first iterated by American Darwinist Lewis Henry Morgan, that human societies had evolved from savagery, to barbarism, then civilization. Powell was determined to advance "ethnological science, so susceptible to the winds of politics and racial conflict," to the highest scientific level. He believed, as did Mooney, that Indian religious beliefs hardly threatened the advocates of Christianity (as some feared), and merited study for their own sake. By the time he hired Mooney, Powell had made the Bureau of Ethnology, "the most important institution in anthropology America had ever seen, and indeed it would remain among the most important such institutions America ever would see."[5]

By the end of the 1880s, the young ethnologist, now a member of the Bureau, had spent significant time with the Cherokee and Kiowa. His participation in their peyote (or mescal) rituals, in short order, drew sharp reprimand from his Smithsonian sponsors in Washington, D.C., and, despite his efforts in establishing the Native American Church, a culture war was launched which kept him embroiled throughout the remainder of his life. Besides his helping to create methodological identity in a field still groping for one, Mooney developed an expertise on the Ghost Dance religion and Indian heraldry. The times were favorable to such a gifted amateur; at first government-sponsored, such activities as he engaged in would become, by the 1930s, the eminent domain of academic departments. Even so, Mooney was touted as a key figure in the Indianist Movement, which would flourish from the early years of the century until, again, about 1930, when interest faded.

Despite the institutional restrictions placed upon him, Mooney was, academically speaking, a cultural revitalist; his research into comparative Indian practices (notably between the Paiutes and Navajos) led him to believe, according to his biographer, L.G. Moses, that "certain groups adopted nativism and revived old ways of life as a consequence of poverty and oppression." Generally reticent, he boasted that "he had made the only picture of Wovoka (the Messiah), Paiute initiator of the Ghost Dance cult." In 1890, after Wounded Knee ended any hope of Indian revival, Mooney journeyed to the Oklahoma Territory to document the Sun Dance ceremony of the Cheyenne and Arapaho.

To some observers, the part of the ceremony in which "young men had to prove their courage" appeared "meaningless self-torture." Tempers flared when "the acting Indian agent accused Mooney and another BAE ethnologist of staging the ceremony and paying the participants for their photographs." While these charges were dismissed, those Mooney flung back had a deeper philosophic foundation. To his sponsors in Washington he was a troublemaker, and maybe somewhat of a crackpot. As two recent Smithsonian observers of the controversy have stated: "It was difficult for the government to accept one of their own men's encouraging ancient beliefs and ceremonies during a time of a national policy of assimilation," and so "it took a great deal of courage for Mooney to champion religious freedom for all." Towards the end of 1892 Mooney, returning to the Southwest to research the ceremonies of the Hopi, Zuni and Navaho, continued to collect artifacts showcasing the distinctive features of their culture for the upcoming Columbian Exposition in Chicago.[6]

Mooney's writings on the Ghost Dance ritual and these other ceremonies, it is safe to say, would stand as launch sites for all forthcoming studies of revitalization movements. Demonstrating a keen interest in all Native American cultural phenomena and the cultural perspectives they informed, they bear the stamp of a brave, courageous man well above his time. Written in a clear, orderly style (which also would distinguish his son's prose), unusual among scientist-scholars of the day, his writings welcome rather than turn the layman away. Their titles convey their range. In 1900 he published *The Myths of the Cherokee*. Other works included the classic *The Ghost Dance Religion and the Sioux Outbreak of 1890* (a lengthy and extraordinary history of the Native Americans of the Plains and the West as well as a detailed ethnography), *The Swimmer Manuscript: Cherokee Sacred Formulas and Medicinal Prescriptions*, "The Aboriginal Population of America North of Mexico," "The Mescal Plant and Ceremony," "Folklore of the Carolina Mountains," and "Notes on Roumanian Gypsies (unfinished)," and research articles on the Powhatan Confederacy. Another of his important contributions was *The Calendar History of the Kiowa Indians* (1898). With others, including Otis T. Mason, he contributed to the famous "Bulletin 30," *The Handbook of American Indians North of Mexico*, a "synonymity" or dictionary of tribal names edited by Frederick Walter Hodge.[7]

Mooney first met his bride-to-be in 1885 when visiting her father, Thomas Gaut. James was twenty-four, Ione Lee Gaut, born "on the feast day of the patron of Ireland," was just seven. "What she thought of the intense young man with the bright blue eyes, arrayed in his customary somber black garb, can only be imagined, " writes biographer L.G. Moses about their first meeting. A dozen years of association with the family reduced any stigma attached to the age difference. His Catholic background versus her Methodist upbringing seemed to make little difference either. On September 28, 1897, at St. Patrick's Church in Washington, D.C., the two wed.

Mooney could believe he had married into American royalty. Noted state officials in her family included grandfather Jesse, a Chief Justice of the Tennessee Supreme Court, and uncle John McReynolds Gaut, a high ranking member of the judiciary. Irish-Scotch in ancestry, Ione descended from English nobility through the Gauts and could account for several eminent jurists in her line. She also could prove direct descent from Lord Edmund Howard, impoverished father of Catherine Howard, the adulterous fifth wife of Henry VIII. Through the Howards a connection can be traced to Henry Howard the Earl of Surrey, famed poet and adventurer. In the 17th century, the Howards immigrated to Maryland. Through the marriage of one Benjamin Howard (son of Discretion Howard and Thomas Isbell), a private secretary in the 1st Maryland Regiment, the family forged a genealogical link with the Lees of Virginia. James and Ione lived all of their married life in Washington, D.C., where Ione became a leading member of the Daughters of the American Revolution.[8]

On November 26, 1904, young James Mooney (later called Paul, his confirmation name, after the shipwrecked St. Paul), was born. For James, returning from a successful tour of duty among the Kiowas—and bitter disappointment over the misrepresentation of exhibited Indian life he was asked to participate in at the St. Louis World's Fair—it was welcome news. Soon after he bought an old Victorian house at 2550 University Place for an expanding family, which ultimately included four daughters, each beautifully named: Ione (II) Lee (1902), Eire (1909), Evelyn or Eivlin ("Lynn") Isbell (1911), who most resembled Paul, and Alicia Howard (1916). A brother, Brian Gaut, named after Celtic hero Brian Boru, was born in 1907.[9]

The known circumstances of the births of several of the children are of incidental interest. Born prematurely in a Kiowa Indian camp, Ione was given the name "Kobetlma" or "Big Mountain Woman." Kiowa women, in the absence of a doctor, had assisted in her birth, and the mother's health was momentarily in jeopardy. Present at the christening of Eire (and earlier the godfather of Brian) was lifelong James Mooney friend Bishop Thomas J. Shahan who, with Mooney, had founded the Gaelic Society. Ione (Gaut) Mooney had by this time converted from Methodism to Catholicism, being received into the church by Bishop Shahan. Alicia was born at home (as was Evelyn, apparently) on the eve of Palm Sunday.[10]

The three-story brick house, with basement and backyard, if one squinted the eyes, appeared a mighty frigate built on land; or it was a giant *Doll's House* whose walls, were they so able, might resound with Ibsenian nuance the whisperings, even loud poutings, of feminine dreams, and outrage. The ground floor had a parlor, dining room, kitchen, butler's pantry, kitchen closet, and a back hall used for storage. The dining room doubled as a library, with the walls covered with bookcases. On top of tables and bookcases were Indian objects; such were not allowed in the parlor, furnished with the family's best ordinary pieces,

Paul Mooney and older sister Ione in the backyard of their home in Washington, D.C., 1907 (courtesy John Murphy Scott).

which later would include a pedestal table once belonging to Robert Edmond Jones, Eugene O'Neill's set designer, and placed there by Paul. On the second floor were three bedrooms and a bath; and on the third floor, two bedrooms and a bath. One of the upstairs bedrooms served as James' study which, besides books and monographs, included stereographs and photographs.

Ione had hired a black maid from southern Virginia to assist her and her daughters in the house's upkeep and in caring for the wide assortment of guests. When James was not visiting an Indian village, Indians from the village visited him, and curious eyes peered from neighboring windows to see march up the steps to the front porch the delegations of Kiowa, Cherokee, and Sioux, in full tribal attire and bearing strange gifts. Ione fretted as the house slowly turned into a depository of beaded necklaces, feathered war bonnets, baskets of intricate lace, blankets, decorated apparel and ceremonial weapons, including a fifteen foot spear which hung in one of the hallways. Likely, one or more of the fifteen two-foot-high Apache and Apache-Kiowa tepees James had made in the 1890s for the Smithsonian stood on a mantle or table. Depicted on these (by Indian artists asked to duplicate the symbolic art found on actual tepees) were porcupines, bears or eagles, who presumably imparted some magical power to certain favored individuals of the tribe. Also depicted were battle scenes between Indians and troopers.[11]

In addition to the Native Americans there was the Irish contingent. This consisted of members of the Gaelic Society, a group that had formed in the district amid the anti–Irish feeling prevailing in America at this time. All thought the Mooney house a neutral, friendly gathering spot, and the head of the household a strong advocate of their ideals. Among the illustrious visitors was the first president of the Irish Free State, Douglas Hyde (1860–1949), who, in late 1905 or 1906, on a visit to President Theodore Roosevelt, dropped by to pay his respects. Every Irishman who visited the home felt the bond yoking them in brotherhood to a patriotic past: all knew with a wink of the eye or clank of the glass the Great Rebellion of 1798 (the "Year of Liberty") when their noble countrymen rose up mightily against their British overlords only to go back in defeat to their plows; all knew of the Great Hunger of 1845 which for decades would bring large numbers of family and friends to America; all knew of the great heroes Wolf Tone, Daniel O'Connell, and Charles Stewart Parnell; all knew of the Land League, Fenianism, and parliamentary reform; all knew of the place names—County Sligo, Cork, Derry and Kerry, Galway, Glengariff, Killarney, Meath and Mayo; all knew some Gaelic; all knew of the storied parish churches and chimneyed cottages and Celtic lore; all knew that better times through worse would fall upon their homeland.[12]

Passed on to Paul were the fanciful stories James Mooney's mother had told him—of "ghosts, giants, leprechauns, and banshees, fairies, witches " and "other marvels of the emerald isles." Epic tales of King Ailill and Queen Maeve of Connacht and the great hero Cuchulainn accompanied tales of Casey and

O'Sullivan, Lundy Foot and Phinnegin, Pat and Mike, Tara, St. Brendan and St. Patrick. Affecting the Irish brogue, Paul could in time recall these or similar stories. Paul never became a duplicate of either of his parents, but from them he inherited some acquired characteristics—notably attentiveness to good manners, listening ability, and intellectual self-assuredness. Of his relation to a beheaded Queen of England, and an adventurer poet who also lost his head, his imagination undoubtedly made much; of his relation to poets and plowmen, his sense of purpose truly made much, and throughout life he would see himself as at once prince and pauper.[13]

The failure of the Irish uprising of 1916 mortified the Mooneys for whom patriotic sentiment towards Ireland always remained strong. Towards America, their patriotic sentiment was as strong. Theirs was always the "first [flag] raised on the block on days of national celebration." Also they made the birthday of every family member a special occasion, and now with six children this was frequent. Though Ione was of Methodist stock, she and James, not a practicing Catholic himself, had vowed, nevertheless, to raise their children Catholic. Married at St. Patrick's Church, their children evidently attended St. Paul's Church (though by this time the increasingly frail and skeptical James had himself steered away from active attendance).[14]

The Mooney family (left to right): Brian, Paul, Ione Gaut Mooney, Evelyn (in lap), Ione, and Eire, 1914 (courtesy John Murphy Scott).

It was James Mooney's habit to go to work only after his children had gone off to school. "All were required to kiss their father goodbye before bounding out of the house," writes L.G. Moses. "If one failed the assignment, he or she was called back from the door." Mooney seemed particularly to like children and subscribed to the higher truths revealed in their bewilderment about life. "An answer to even a child's idle question," continues Moses, "he treated as a new discovery. If the question were asked in his third-floor study, he would direct the inquisitor to his bookshelves, where an appropriate volume could be found. He addressed his sons as 'boy,' and his daughters as 'baby.' He would say: 'Baby, you've asked a question and now you'll find an answer.' Taking a book, he would trace the lines with his fingers and read the explanation." In a household, seemingly genteel and unpretentious, where the father was as often absent as present, where a degree of *mutter-recht* prevailed, where daughters appeared dutiful, pillars of Victorian etiquette, where people in strange costume and of unknown origin dropped by, where there could be suddenly a flood of activity and as suddenly deadly quiet, the evolution of Paul's identity remains unclear. Instilled in him, though, was self-confidence and a sense of his own worth, focused though each of these assets might be by the remarkable achievements of a loving father, and overwhelmed though it was by the favoritism shown him by a doting mother.[15]

Integrating the lives of the children into the activities of adults, as a part of a plan to condition them socially, was a regular feature in the home. Indeed, notes Moses, "whenever the Mooneys entertained guests, they always included the children. It was the same whether some distinguished scientist, author, Bishop Shahan, or members of Indian delegations came to dinner. Oil-rich [visiting Indians] would park their limousines along University Place when they came to visit. After the evening meal, the Indians would assemble in the third-floor study, where Mooney would take down a drum from the wall, and sing with his friends to its beat well into the night." While the few surviving pictures of Mooney would lead one to believe him a clergyman or grammar school teacher, some neighbors, basing their deduction on his "black suits, serious demeanor, and curling hair worn longer than the prevailing fashion," and hearing "the muted strains of Deutsche Lieder" pour forth from the house, thought him a "German musician."[16]

Reportedly these black suits were "always tailored and always the same"— wife Ione said "she never could tell when he was wearing a new one." As seemed practical, "their most prominent feature were the oversized pockets" into which he placed notepaper and pencil. Also he "carried a tin cup, which, in proper season, he would fill with berries he and the children found on their country walks." The children customarily kissed him goodnight before he read to them some story or before all turned in. When Paul was just a boy, his father often was away on field trips. As he moved into his teens, Paul more often saw his father tirelessly at work translating and organizing for publication material he had collected on the Cherokees. As his father worked, he would "alternately sip [from] ... one cup of coffee and [from] ... one ounce of whiskey before he retired."[17]

While one would like to know more about his relationship with his siblings as well as with his mother, Paul's relationship with his father (to whom, except for the high forehead, Paul bore little resemblance) is the most beguiling, and vague. No report of any ill-will between the father and son is known, yet, as Paul's nephew John Scott has wondered, did Paul "feel overwhelmed by his father's persona?"[18]

In January 1911, when Clarence Paine of the Nebraska Historical Society invited him to speak in Lincoln on his researches, the life of the Plains Indians, and the role of women in Indian society, James took Paul on what would be his first excursion west. Father and son stayed at the Lincoln Hotel rather than with the Paines, as Mrs. Paine was seriously ill. While his father gave his talks, Paul was shown around the community by Minnie P. Knotts, the society librarian, who, it seems, later sent postcards of the region back to him.[19]

The trip was an apparent success, but James' failing health assured that another would not happen soon. He wrote to Paine expressing how "two years at a desk" was "killing" him. He noted himself to be in "weak condition" and reported "demoralized home conditions." He added, "We have had almost constant sickness in the house, with the children, all of this year—diphtheria, measles, diphtheria again, and now two quarantined with scarlet fever." Paine was himself to be examined for appendicitis and meanwhile had to tend to his wife's own illness. Job's comforter to himself and to Mooney, he called it a "siege" of sickness and depression that affected the two families.[20]

Paul, just as he was about to enter school (fall, 1911), had himself contracted a case of the "grippe." Even so, he could not have missed his father's struggles for breath and his visible fatigue. Later, in the summer of 1914, an even more weakened Mooney Sr. took both his boys Paul and Brian to a Cherokee settlement in North Carolina (this not too long after returning to Richmond, Indiana and seeing to his ailing mother Ellen Devlin Mooney, who soon would be dead). "While their father worked over his translations," recounts Moses, "young James and Brian spent most of the time chasing the Indians' horses around the countryside, and splashing in the creek that ran behind the store in [the town of] Swaney." One must credit the father's attempt to sanctify with higher symbolic meaning his sons' instincts for play. Long exposure to the laxness the Plains tribes showed in the raising of their children might have influenced Mooney's own permissive ways in the raising of Paul and Brian.[21]

The peyote controversy had, meanwhile, reached a peak with anti-peyote campaigns by Christian groups becoming especially heated. Indian groups, for their part, gently insisted that use of the powerful hallucinogen was a sacrament, not a sacrilege, that put them into direct contact with the spirit world. While James Sr. thought it absurd to eliminate peyote from the ceremony, Paul, from the sidelines, saw the tyranny of a dominant culture condemning as evil the creative expression of a religious people—just as an overbearing authority figure might condemn as misbehavior the harmless free-play of a richly imaginative child. He also saw the righteous indignation of a father, with limited clout in the agency he served, against the ignorance of that tyranny. Paul, in all events, never expressed racist views. Younger brother Brian, exposed as Paul to assorted early multicultural experiences, subscribed to the belligerent racism common in the segregated Washington of his youth, a racism that in many Washington (or American) families would have passed unnoticed, but in the Mooney family was exceptional.[22]

Paul, like his father, and not so much like his brother, enjoyed group activities. "When he was 13 or 14," recalled sister Alicia, "he and all the boys in the neighborhood—about 20 of them—swarmed over our backyard for about a week cutting down and chopping up a tree that had come down." By this time he had a menagerie, which consisted of cats, dogs, a turtle and a ten-inch alligator. A relationship to nature, which his father instilled, remained strong in him, though his own later attempts at a Thoreauesque detachment from society failed through boredom. "I chased the most magnificent red woodchuck, which escaped into a cranny," he enthused about an adventure occurring later in his life. "The day before, I saw a brown weasel, a lovely slinky animal. The day before that, the largest snapping turtle I ever found outside an aquarium crossed the road very sedately...." He mentioned a place "full of impudent chipmunks that disappear like a wink when I try to be friendly, and of squirrels in several varieties." He mentioned his attempts at feeding a nest of baby robins, but balked at the thought of having to "hold the worm in [his] mouth when presenting it." From time to time he wrote up little stories about some little creature or creatures in his midst and offered them to a friend.[23]

Eleven years his junior, sister Alicia later remembered Paul as "a tall-seeming boy in the knee-pants that boys wore then." At fifteen—about 1920 while his father still lived (though challenged in health and about to be confined to his work area)—he discovered some secluded woods not far from their house. Later, with another boy (possibly Eddy Lunt), he went back, pitched tents and camped there a couple nights. When Paul and his friend told Alicia about the wonderful place, she asked if she could see it, and they took her there. Alicia's remembering the incident was probably based more on her amazement that older brother Paul should share a secret with her. Paul's own seeking of a place of refuge, "a secret garden," as it were, seems unremarkable in itself except to note that he sought it all his life. At this early time in his life, one may say that he saw the trees; as he grew older, he more often saw the spaces between them, a secret he kept mostly to himself.

If the woods experience "astonished" Alicia, the rooftop experience, which happened about the same time, "horrified" her. She stood on the ground while Paul and little brother Brian stood on the third-story roof of their house. She

Paul Mooney (bottom) and friend (possibly Eddy Lunt), about 1925 (courtesy William Alexander).

was told by Paul only to watch as he suddenly made the leap to the rooftop next door. The distance was nine feet or more, but the incline was steep and offered little running or landing room with which to work. Alicia wilted in relief. Then Paul, seizing the dramatic moment, coaxed his brother Brian to make the leap. Alicia was by then a nervous wreck. Brian succeeded in making the leap.

One may only wonder why Paul did so dangerous a thing in the first place. He may have gotten the idea from the legendary Sam Patch (1799–1829), a natural born jumper, who to an amazed public had leapt into Hoboken Harbor, Niagara Falls and Genesee Falls in Rochester, New York. One story has it that he intended to leap from the Capitol in Washington. Another suggestion for Paul's heroics was the much-circulated stereograph by noted photographer of Indian life H.H. Bennett (1843–1908) of a man leaping the six-foot chasm separating a main cliff from Standing Rock in Wisconsin Dells. Most likely, though, Paul got the idea from the better-publicized leaps of Douglas Fairbanks, Sr., himself an accomplished acrobat. From his debut film *The Lamb* (1915), set in hostile Yaqui Indian territory, to his blockbusters *The Mark of Zorro* (1920), *The Three Musketeers* (1921) and *Robin Hood* (1922), death-defying leaps, imitated by movie stuntmen with far less panache, were the calling card of the dashing motion picture star. Paul liked to think he could do anything, even imitate Douglas Fairbanks.[24]

2

A Growing Boy

James Mooney spent his last months confined to a favorite wicker chair, this to relieve the miseries of a "mitral insufficiency that had first appeared in 1890" and now caused him "discomfort in his chest and shortness of breath." His fragile heart daily continued to weaken. He was unable to climb stairs and was forced to sit, most of the time, upright. As a result, he very seldom left his bedroom or study. Held captive within this most despondent physical shell, his mind remained active, pestered constantly by a sense of mission and work undone. Unashamed of his diminished condition, he continued to receive visitors, and greeted his children warmly, enjoying with them, as ever, every holiday. Death loomed ever more ominously as Christmas and a New Year approached. In the afternoon of December 21, 1921, with friends in attendance, he offered his confession to Bishop Shahan who "administered Extreme Unction." The next day his heart failed. "His face turned to the east, he died in full possession of his faculties, quietly, with dignity, surrounded by those who loved him." In a poem entitled "Field-Burial," Paul wrote, "No pious prayer would stay the work.... Birth, Disillusion, Death—such is our span; Eternally, man ends where he began."[1]

Thirty-six years he had worked for the Bureau of American Ethnology with little professional or financial reward to show for it. Despite his growing disillusionment over government policies towards the Indians he had grown to love, "he ended his career," writes Moses, "as he had begun it, convinced of the incapacity of one race to rule over another," devoting his attention "to make smaller the chasm in understanding between the dominant culture and those who had once challenged that dominance." He had lived during the so-called "Great Century of Christian Expansion," through times when "Christian identity" was itself "under siege" and through times when people paid heed to automobile magnate Henry Ford's diatribes against non–Christians. If only to preserve the Indian religious ritual in a hostile Christian environment, he had attempted to present it as a stage towards Christianity. And, "If at the end he saw himself as a victim of ignorance and injustice, others saw him as a victim of his own resoluteness." At a memorial held by the Bureau in his honor, Mooney was hailed as "a patriotic citizen tolerant of all spiritual faiths, a fine example of Christian gentleness,... who possessed a marked independence of character and a charming personality as a man and a friend." His funeral was held at St. Paul's Church, December 24, the day before the one holiday of the year with his children he would have preferred not to miss.[2]

Francis Parkman, in a style as palpable as Mooney's own, once noted how the upbringing of an Indian anneals him ultimately against pain; yet, "when he feels himself attacked by a mysterious evil, before whose insidious assaults his manhood is wasted, and his strength drained away, when he can see no enemy to resist and defy, the boldest warrior falls prostrate at once." Years before, to an audience of ethnologists and historians, James had said, "One of these days our children and their children will want to know about their forefathers." He believed that it was "still possible to fill in the record." Paul, hearing these sentiments, wanted to know about his forefathers; how well he would fill in the record, ignore or trivialize it, remains another question.[3]

James' death left Ione Lee the task of raising, nearly alone, four daughters and two sons. Yet, as the Victorian manner had it, the eldest son now became, in theory, the head of the household and the one chosen to provide. At the time Paul was sixteen.

From a family of readers, Paul was himself a most avid reader, and saw literature, especially great literature, as essential to emotional and intellectual development. What stops Paul made as a boy journeying through Bookland can only be guessed. Countless children's books filled the house: the "Oz" books of Frank Baum, the "Tarzan" books of Edgar Rice Burroughs, the animal tales of Ernest Seton Thompson, and stories such as those found in *Peter and His Goose; The Folly of Discontent.* Available too was the *Tip Top Weekly*—"An Ideal Publication for American Youth"—featuring the mostly sports adventures of Dick and Frank Merriwell. German novelist Karl May's stories "about the Indians, Old Shatterhand and Winnetou" perhaps sat next to works by Daniel Defoe, James Fenimore Cooper, and Jules Verne. Major Walter Campbell's *The Old Forest Ranger, In the Jungles,* and *On the Plains* perhaps sat next to Gertrude Atherton's *Los Cerritos* and *Before the Gringo Came,* with its realistic depictions of everyday Mexican-American life. Frontier novels such as *Valley of Silent Men, The Country Beyond,* or road narrative *The Ancient Highway* by James Oliver Curwood, some of whose books were made into successful films, were on the shelves.

Forgotten works from the nineteenth century, hardly unexceptional in a library of, say, 1915, might have included the Reverend James Spong's *Jack the Cabin Boy* or the Reverend Egerton R. Young's *By Canoe and Dog Train Among the Cree and Salteaux* (1890). Old copies of *Harper's New Monthly Magazine,* with their stories of western expansion, Indian life, war and foreign intrigue, perhaps lay on one shelf or another, and copies of *The Wide World Magazine—True Stories of Adventure* about bear hunts, treks across the Sahara, sea monsters, travelers in disguise, around-the-world bike hikes, wild Indians, girl stowaways, the Kazak

Nomads, and the spells of the Red Witch of Modjaji. There were *Call of the Wild* and *Martin Eden*, among other books by Jack London, a writer for whom "romance and adventure" meant "wherever life ran free and great" and for whom it was misery to "go back to my free-library books and read of the deeds of other men and do no deeds of my own save slave for ten cents an hour at a machine in a cannery."[4]

As Paul grew older, he read high-end prose and poetry, travel and history. Available to him was Rupert Brooke's *Letters from America*. Significantly, the book contains a chapter "The Indians" and uses as a resource, in part, the experiences, including photographs, of "a man who had spent many years of his life living among the Indians." He may also have read Brooke's *1914 and Other Poems*. Melville's *Typee* he owned. Almost certainly he had a nodding acquaintance with Cervantes' *Don Quixote* and Goethe's *Faust*. Later, he read books on art and artists (including Picasso and Rockwell Kent) and books about foreign lands. Pierre Loti's colorful narrative of a trip to Egypt, *The Death of Philae* (1909), sat in the bookshelves; then, everyone with an interest in foreign amusements read Loti. His finely bound copy of Petronius' *Satyricon* had beautiful nude photos of adolescent boys and girls, which, according to his nephew John Scott, were "artistic" rather than "erotic." Likely he read James Branch Cabell's *Jurgen* (1919). Filled with strange creatures, fabulous lands, remote times, and the most lubricious sexual innuendo, its story of a hen-pecked middle-aged pawnbroker-poet who rides off on the back of a centaur to discover Youth and Romance enthralled readers.[5]

As a young man Paul read some poets. Notable among these were Ezra Pound, Edwin Markham and Edwin Arlington Robinson; of these, he most liked Pound. The home library at University Place included works by Irish poets James Clarence Mangan, Samuel Ferguson, Oscar Wilde, W.B. Yeats, Padraic Colum and Francis Ledwidge. Of British poets, Byron, Shelley, Wordsworth and Keats held a special place. Paul himself owned a student's annotated Chaucer and a copy of Shakespeare's works. Of American poets, he read Edgar Allan Poe, Henry Wadsworth Longfellow, and William Vaughn Moody. Another poet he read was the black poet Lawrence Dunbar (1872–1906). Gifted, tragically romantic, and alcoholic, Dunbar had once sent to James Mooney an inscribed copy of *Poems of Cabin and Field* (1899), which Paul treasured.[6]

Most esoteric of Paul's books, and one of the few he signed, was *Blue Beard— Being the History of Gilles de Retz of Brittany France Who Was Executed at Nantes in 1440 A.D. and Who Was the Original of Blue Beard in the Tales of Mother Goose* (1928). Antecedent books that dealt with sex and society and filled the home library, items such as Richard von Krafft-Ebing's *Psychopathia Sexualis* or Edward Westermarck's *The Origin and Development of Moral Ideas* (1906), might have primed Paul's interest in what may have seemed to him not deviation, but normal abnormality. Child molester, sadist, and serial killer repulsively obsessed with blood, buggery and butchery, the nobly-born Gilles de Retz (or de Rais) remains the classic pre-modern example of the homosexual criminal. A soldier and marshal of France, Gilles had known "Saint" Joan of Arc, who, as a servant of the cross, road victorious in her black armor and fleur-de-lis into the pages of French history as the "Maid of Orleans." At a time when misery and religious faith peaked among common folk, his castle became a child processing plant where no less than one hundred and fifty boys, abducted from their home or promised the honor of paging, were tortured, murdered by decapitation or bloodletting, and, dead or alive, were sodomized by their grotesquely inhumane lord and temporary master.[7]

Older sister Ione, to whom Paul felt very close, always described her brother as "brilliant." She said that his personality and talent had a "sparkling quality." Youngest sister Alicia noted that he was "good-humored and generous." She thought him coolly detached, and independent-minded, as well as restless and driven. She noted how he walked from their house down the street with a sort of passionate fixity of purpose. "He always looks as tho [sic] he's interested in where he is going," she later remarked. Everyone who got to know Paul knew he was both a careful reader and observer; he pointed out embarrassing typos in the newspaper, Alicia recalled, and he called attention to the absurd. Quick to smile, he was also quick to anger, becoming, she said, "testy and intolerant about anyone who did not suit his own standards." He also disliked people who made false claims about themselves. He kept a low profile, but, like that boy of boys Tom Sawyer, he enjoyed getting himself into these little fixes just to see how he would work his way out of them.[8]

Younger brother Brian, in contrast, had a "mean streak." Few facts explain it. One learns that his father had forbidden him to cut his hair, notable for its curly locks, until he was twelve; that Paul was better liked; and that Paul and he didn't stay in touch once they each left home. In the mid–1930s, while the family still resided at 2550 University Place, Brian, now an adult, picked up his five-year-old nephew Anton's collection of Big Little Books and hurled them down the hall, "pages askew and torn." When little Anton gathered them up again, and said, "You won't do that again," Brian at once grabbed the collection and hurled it again down the hall. About the same time, when Evelyn was "monitoring [the] potty-sitting" of Anton's two-year-old younger brother, Brian "barged into the room, causing great consternation" to Evelyn, who scolded him for the disturbance; Brian responded by slapping her. In his fifties, Brian related to the family that, while walking down a sidewalk in the 14th Street neighborhood of Washington, two young blacks "made some remark he didn't like, so he crossed over and knocked them both down in the street, causing them to run off, mouthing death threats." Likely Brian only fantasized telling off these youths, Anton later suggested.[9]

Paul's first claim to fame, at any rate, took place with his brother at his side. In the winter of 1922, at Washington's Knickerbocker Theatre, as the comedy hit "Get Rich Quick Wallingford" unreeled on the screen, plaster started crumbling off the ceiling. In moments the whole roof of the building, weighted down by heavy snow, collapsed on the panic-stricken audience. A fire quickly broke out and, though some people made it to safety, ninety-eight were killed and a hundred and forty were injured. Rubble needed to be cleared, bodies extracted, and survivors tended to. Paul with Brian and other rescue workers assisted firemen in doing so.[10]

A real-life spectacle had occurred in the make-believe theater. Probably it was some play or movie Paul always walked to so determinedly. The silent screen personalities around to amuse him were many and ranged from Tom Mix to Roscoe "Fatty" Arbuckle to Charlie Chaplin to Rudolph Valentino and of course Douglas Fairbanks. Matinee idol Wallace Reid (1893–1923), ultimately a victim of the real-life drama attending his own addiction to morphine, thrilled audiences in the road car hits *Watch My Speed*, *Excuse My Dust*, *Roaring Road*, and *Too Much Speed*. *Always Audacious* had Reid hopping an ocean liner to South America. These film adventures shaped the dream images of many young Americans, including Paul.[11]

Escape was a common feature in movies and plays, especially if one looked for confirming voices to an already-present impulse. Rising young playwright Eugene O'Neill, himself a drop-out from Princeton who had gone off to sea but, by war's end, a fixture in theatre throughout the country, encouraged young men to seek broader destinies. His first big hit *Beyond the Horizon* (1920) had appeared in theaters in Washington as well as New York. "Supposing," its chief character Robert tells his brother Andrew, as the play commences, "that it's just Beauty that's calling me, the beauty of the far off and unknown, the mystery and spell of the East which lures me in the books I've read, the need of the freedom of great wide spaces, the joy of wandering on and on—in quest of the secret which is hidden over there, beyond the horizon?" Of course the play was a tragedy, but, as Paul would learn, one could always rewrite endings.[12]

Paul had by this time chosen writing as a career. Through his father he inherited and developed the skill; others glorified it. Dying within years of Paul's father were traveler-adventurer Richard Harding Davis and war correspondent John Reed. Of the two, the Harvard-educated Reed served as a role model for many aspiring journalists. His *Ten Days That Shook the World*, about the Bolshevik Revolution in Russia, became a classic while his poem *A Day in Bohemia*, about the degenerate joys he had experienced in Greenwich Village, was a work even casual fans read. High-profile, Reed glowed in the news world for a decade. Wrote Floyd Dell of his friend: "Both in terms of cash and in terms of glory, John Reed stood at the very top of the profession of journalism in America ... [and] was commonly acknowledged to be the greatest war-correspondent in the United States when the war of the world began in Europe." Reed died, at the age of thirty-three, in 1920.[13]

About 1922 or 1923, after he graduated from Central High School, Paul sailed as a cabin boy on a freighter bound from New York to Constantinople and Salonika. How this went over with his mother is not known. He was by temperament impulsive, easily bored, and hateful of restriction, as she well knew. He was not about to fall into a bottomless pit of horror and confront huge sea monsters; he was in the company of many young men who rode the rails or bestrode the ocean waves. For early 1923 Thomas Cook & Sons, to celebrate its first circumnavigation tour in 1872–1873, advertised a four-month "de Luxe Cruise" around the world, making the furthest reaches of the globe seem friendly and merely an extension of home.[14]

Paul's adventure abroad lasted two months. In Constantinople, as in Salonika, he adventurously explored on foot the Moslem quarter, experienced "the prismatic Labyrinth of the Bazaar where one could peer, and pry, and dream the hours away," as did Lady Dorothy Mills, another visitor here at this time, and viewed "the blue and gold glory of the Bosphorus under a brilliant sunshine...." Then, as most curious visitors, he visited the famous mosques, roamed the winding cobbled streets, beheld the shattered monuments, and drew—in the European shops, offices, and warehouses—all sights that would one-day feed his later romantically-hued writings of these foreign places. While it is tempting to suppose Paul visited other cities in Greece besides Salonika, such as Preveza, where Lord Byron first landed in 1809, or Missolonghi, where the poet died in 1824, he does not appear to have done so.[15]

Whatever the discomforts Paul experienced on his long trip, he learned that operating on the move was better suited for him than being settled down. "Why grind away at a correspondent's desk at forty dollars a month?" writes the author of I Knew Hitler, whose views, if not Paul's own, were ones familiar to him: "The worldly experience I gained certainly brought me no nearer to heaven, but it has helped me over many a hurdle here below. I learn to weigh values, to discriminate between the real and the unreal. My life was one of contrasts and climaxes. I developed a genius, good or bad, for attracting curious people. Sometimes I would be plagued by a second self who stood aloof from a spurious show and asked: Are these your people, are these the climaxes you started out to seek? But these moments of self-reproach were far between...."[16]

Shortly after his first major trip anywhere, Paul returned to Washington.

3

New York Confidential

The Paul of about 1925, age 20, was well-groomed for the world outside Washington, D.C. When he brought himself before the mirror, he liked what he saw. Luminous and inquisitive, his eyes captivated, his smile engaged. His hair was full and wavy above a high forehead that asserted keen intelligence and bold enterprise. Of average height, well-formed, and firm-muscled, he modestly prided his physical beauty. He was a respected older brother and a friend looked up to by his peers. He had difficulty coping with routine; in the face of it, he might sulk or run off. His threshold for boredom was low, and he tended to judge any proposal by its exciting possibilities. Boyish, at times disingenuous, he had that rare gift of making someone else a part of his life instantly. For any-one who loved him and wished from him a long-standing commitment, his was an emotionally dangerous appeal; he could slip into as easily as slip out of one's life.

Largely self-taught, he never harbored suspicion, secret contempt or unduly patronized those better educated than he. What he knew he carried lightly, yet knew that without courage intelligence is weak. He was ever surprised about life, a freethinker among the many oddballs in his life to whom open-mindedness and trustworthiness counted. Basically he got a kick out of himself and fully enjoyed the workings of his own mind and just had fun being smart; most of the people around him were not that self-assured, and he could always sense this.

He was closer to the presence of his mother than to the memory of his father. While he had his father's writing skills, his father's influence seems to have been slight. While it is easy to suppose then that the nature of his father's knowledge of Indian lore was bequeathed to Paul, it emerges in him only as an archetype faintly restamped on new bodies of fact. He did not want to repeat his father's life, but, rather, extend it, chiefly by traveling to places his father had only read about.[1]

In 1925, Paul entered Catholic University of America in Washington, D.C. Records indicate that he was a candidate for a B.A. in the school of letters. They do not indicate the courses in which he enrolled.[2]

By the mid–1920s, urban sprawl had brought the farmland campus, once three miles north of Washington's downtown, within the confines of the city limits; however, even by the 1920s, it was "out there." Memory lingered of the school's rural beginnings and of Professor of English Charles Warren Stoddard, who left the area in 1901 to resettle in Monterey, California, where he would be surrounded by some of the greatest writers of his generation, from Bret Harte to Jack London. An unregenerate Catholic, hedonist, and rake, Stoddard wrote the flesh-toned travel classic *Summer Cruising in the South Seas* (1905), whose lush descriptions of island life suggest the sensuous canvases of Gauguin, only with male substituting for female subjects. Also an accomplished versifier, he was dubbed "the Poet of the South Seas."[3]

Stoddard lived at 300 M Street, not far from the Mooneys. His house-mate was a fifteen-year-old altar boy named Kenneth O'Connor, who was affectionately nicknamed the "Waif" or the "Kid." Apparently no one objected to the "unnatural relation." It is equally hard to determine whether anyone thought he "lived in sin." Guests steadily knocked at the door of what became known as "the Bungalow" or "Saint Anthony's Rest." Writers Hamlin Garland and Henry Adams visited, as did "reporters, actors and artists, former students, deposed Hawaiian royalty, famous Catholics, aspiring young writers, friends of friends with notes of introduction." The broad, though differently constituted, open-door policy of the Bungalow resembles the Mooney household of about the same time. In all events, the example of Kenneth, who "sometimes dated girls," but "also had sex with other boys," must stand as testimony that bi-sexual adventurism was alive and well in post–Civil War and pre–World War I Washington, as was ethnic open-mindedness. Paul himself represented a new generation of Kenneth O'Connors, the neighborhood "waif," potentially the new "Kid."[4]

Paul lasted one semester, if that, at Catholic University. He was twenty years old. The year was 1926, late winter or early spring.

Coincidentally, Richard Halliburton's *The Royal Road to Romance* had just risen to the best-seller list. The book may very well have inspired Paul's move. Echoing C.A. Stephens' message of a generation or so before, of "self-education" and avoidance of "the tedious, vegetable life of a college," the book's author urged "hitting the road." Oscar Wilde's message in *Dorian Gray* of capturing the moment before it vanishes is also heralded. Better the short, glorious life than the long, drudging one. Flee from the classroom, its young author urged; see more and read less—and confront the world. Dabs of Gothic horror and touches of Dickens' foundling schools colored Halliburton's picture of students as "bent over their desks dutifully grubbing their lives away" in a "penitentiary room" soon to "degenerate into hideous puppets, haunted by the memory of the passions of which [they] were once too much afraid, and the exquisite temptations that [they] had not the courage to yield to." Cramming the mind with "profitless facts and figures," he thought pointless, "when the vital and the beautiful things of life—the moonlight, the apple orchards, the out-of-door sirens—were calling

In Athens, Greece, in 1925, Richard Halliburton, as the implied fourth of three Parthenon columns, and as he heroically appeared, in a painted version, on the dust jacket of *The Glorious Adventure* (1927) (courtesy Rhodes College, Barret Library Acquisitions).

and pleading for recognition." He called for a "rebellion against the prosaic mold." If classrooms now imprison you, next it will be "apartment walls"; there, you will find yourself "surrounded by self-satisfied people, caught in the ruts of convention and responsibility." Before it is too late, avoid "sinking into a slough of banality," and "taste the drug of romantic travel." Escape to "Adventure!" Or, as it meant to Paul, another intensity, one that didn't confine and restrict.[5] Willa Cather's story "Paul's Case," published in 1905, of a writer attempting to make a go of it in the big city eerily suggests Paul. Subtitled "A Study in Temperament," its subject, a high school student guilty of "various misdemeanors," is accused by his teachers of "disorder and impertinence"; his "hysterically defiant manner" houses a "contempt" for them; and his eyes "remarkable for a certain hysterical brilliancy," which he used "in a conscious, theatrical sort of way," offended those in authority. Only "at the theatre and at Carnegie Hall" did Cather's "Paul really live." Ultimately he runs off to New York where, as Rupert Brooke once said, "Business has developed insensibly into a Religion." In the end it seems he must come home, but jumps from reality into his imagination— in fact, in front of a speeding train as "the blue of Adriatic water, the yellow of Algerian sands" "flashed through his brain."[6]

Thankfully, Paul Mooney was not to be the tragic figure of Cather's story, at least not yet. In New York, he landed a job writing ads, designing layouts, and editing features for a Save-To-Travel association—likely the National Travel Club, run by several banking authorities and steamship lines (including Cunard). Creating and promoting an interest in travel as well as furnishing clients with discount travel information were probably its main missions. Readability was the keynote of the travel ad writing world. Words at once fresh and with a subdued glitter had to reach the traveler's imagination without resistance. Here one may suppose that Paul developed a writing style which was vivid, and which combined clarity with fullness of expression. Besides being in a position to meet important people, attractive discount packages came his way that kept aflame his own passion for travel. The job was presumably menial too. Paul's later job aboard the *Sea Dragon* cranking out thousands of mailers on a mimeograph machine suggests, besides a willingness, earlier training in dealing with boring and repetitive work operations. One could say Paul regularly got ink on his fingers, though in a potentially exciting work environment with career promise.[7]

Truly a New York in transition greeted Paul. New building projects and subway extensions had reshaped the city. Ruins appeared over long stretches of Lower Manhattan and the quainter hideaway spots of Greenwich Village became memories. Said Rupert Brooke, "Cities, like cats, will reveal themselves at night." At night parts of the city suggested the trench warfare of World War I.[8]

It is not clear when Paul decided he was homosexual or even if he made such a decision; he may rather have wondered only where and how to express or fulfill the cravings he naturally felt. Known only is that his sexual orientation drew no reproof from his family once it was manifest. According to Freud, a remote father and over-protective mother might tilt a boy towards sexual "imbalance"; one may be sure only that Paul had heard of such a theory.

Where Paul lived exactly when he first arrived in New York is unknown. A friend's or relative's place has been suggested, implying he had an immediate connection in the city. The YMCA on West 57th, where Richard Halliburton was himself known to stay, is as likely. Because he was an aspiring writer and liked art, one thinks "Greenwich Village," but, by the time Paul arrived, rents had risen in Greenwich Village, forcing many artists to find living quarters elsewhere, and Paul had little money. By 1920 an interregional harmony had been reached between the denizens of uptown and downtown New York, so no psychological barriers existed between those who came and went. Paul certainly knew Greenwich Village.[9]

Famous structures and historical landmarks always appealed to him. Old Potter's Field, where once stood the "old gallows" and where Washington Arch now stood, was one of these. MacDougal Street was famous, as was Bleeker, for its shops and painters with set-up easels. Artistic mecca of the country, Washington Square vividly echoed the names of the leading pioneers in American literature who had lived there—Edgar Allan Poe, Washington Irving, Mark Twain, and Thomas Paine. From 1913 the Village attracted people as diverse as John Reed, Floyd Dell, Edna St. Vincent Millay, Mabel Dodge, Margaret Anderson, Mina Loy and Eugene O'Neill. Paul breathed the same air at least of its Lost Generation and such people as Hart Crane, Thomas Wolfe, Edmund Wilson, John Dos Passos, and Elinor Wylie. Here Paul apparently met raconteur of gypsy life and a gypsy himself Konrad Bercovici, who had written a "romantic biography" of Alexander the Great (1928) and later would write *Savage Prodigal* (1948) about the poet Arthur Rimbaud and his relationship with fellow poet Paul Verlaine. A world traveler, he exalted the special charms of New York where, in the 1920s, one might run into Theodore Dreiser or Sherwood Anderson strolling through Union Square, or see Edna St. Vincent Millay leave her little home not far from Cherry Lane. The Provincetown Playhouse lured theatergoers, and, walking down Bank, Barrow or Christopher Street, one might run into its leading light, Eugene O'Neill who, despite success, "remained the same unaffected, quiet soul."[10]

Paul Mooney as a young journalist in New York, about 1929 (courtesy William Alexander).

Paul understood that reality is layered, and that one layer is no less real than the layer below or above it. French visitors as well as residents

Photograph of New York, believed taken by Paul Mooney about 1929 (courtesy William Alexander).

thought the village a sort of Montmartre West, wild and with a delightful richness of the wonderful and the weird. Sleaze-bags and creative people alike roamed the streets; they danced, they boozed and they partied; some found fame, some burned out. A frolicsome Heaven or Hell it might be depending on how one perceived it. "Improper Bohemians," Allen Churchill called its denizens. Everywhere the liquor was good, from ale to gin, rye to Scotch. Paul preferred gin mixes. And like the proverbial fly in the nudist camp he knew what to do but didn't know where to begin. In "Love in Greenwich Village," Floyd Dell had

called the Village a "place of jocund merrymaking," of brief love encounters
and experiments in love, a "refuge from Mother's morality," and where "one
hoped to find out what one was like."[11]

A fixture on Washington Square for decades, writer Maxwell Bodenheim,
less cheerily, called Greenwich Village "Gonorrhea Mansion," by which he meant
a "universe, a microcosm embodying the bohemia which is merely a distorted
reflection of the Moabite disease called civilization." Careful study of the key
scientific tracts had identified for him the Moabites as "inverted and perverted."
Most were "sex hunters." Among their number were "homosexuals ... egocentric,
depolarized persons." These people "engage in mutual masturbation because
the love-instinct has died within them and they can only assume a master-slave
relationship to each other, which often ends in sadistic, homicidal cruelty as in
the famous case of Loeb and Leopold, heirs of Gilles de Rais [sic], the notorious
Bluebeard of the Middle Ages." Some Villagers would have preferred to be called
"sexual modernists" rather than the degenerates Bodenheim's stormy rhetoric
more than implies.[12]

Gay beatings and police shakedowns were, in all events, common in those
days, and represented the darker side of "Marvel-land"; under this tent of fear,
Paul, brazen in his approaches, had to be careful of his solicitations. Writes
George Chauncey: "Gay men developed a gay map of the city and nicknamed
its landmarks: the Fruited Plain, Vaseline Alley, Bitches' Walk. Even outsiders
were familiar with sections of that map.... But even more of that map was
unknown to the dominant culture. Gay men met throughout the city, their
meetings invisible to all but the initiated and carefully orchestrated to remain
so...." Paul had that map, and acquired a similar one for every city he visited.[13]

Besides reputed gay hangouts, Paul liked going to art galleries, movie
houses, and new theater performances. Close friend William Alexander noted
how Paul had "supplemented [his own] art education" and through his contacts
high-up routinely got them both invited to many exhibits and parties. By the
time he met Alexander in the late 1920s, Paul well "knew the haunts of the Big
City." And, "with his ability to mix with longshoremen, or the elite of New
York" (and, later, San Francisco) he helped Alexander "fulfill an education [oth-
erwise]? not possible." He had a keen interest in black culture. Likely he had at
least a nodding acquaintance with cabarets such as the Club Ebony or speakeasies such as the Lenox Avenue Club. He liked entertainment clubs. The River-
side comes to mind. Here Carl Van Vechten came to see the "wonderful" female
impersonator Barbette. Paul got off on such shows.[14]

Paul met other writers, not necessarily famous ones but, like him, the plod-
ders, and hung around those districts where he might run into literary celebrities. "West Eighth Street," noted Maxwell Bodenheim, "was the Wall Street of
the poetry district" where one could enter "culture taverns" and hear or give a
poetry recitation. "Buddhists, nudists and feudists" all pontificated, some in
verse, some stabbed with exclamation points. Bodenheim saw that "many Vil-

lagers made big money as vanity publishers of poems that had the definite stamp of imbecility." Some of these vanity publications showed up at Albert and Charles Boni's Washington Square Bookshop on MacDougal near Bleeker. Besides work by Ezra Pound, the bookstore published works by William Carlos Williams and, Paul's current literary idol, James Joyce—notably portions of *Ulysses* through the *Little Review* which resulted in criminal action being taken against the store's proprietor, Margaret Anderson. The bookstore also lent space to the famous Theatre Guild and Provincetown Players.[15]

Through a mutual friend, the writer, artist and pianist Eugene MacCown, who knew everyone, Paul may have met Hart Crane, who resided at 45 Grove Street in the West Village. Crane attended parties; he also entertained guests at his apartment. Poet, playwright and folklorist Federico Garcia Lorca, while a student at Columbia, attended one. Perhaps Paul, joining kindred spirits, did so as well. Crane's interests certainly matched Paul's. Trained as an ad man (at Case Western Reserve University), the future author of *The Bridge* found suitable work with the J. Walter Thompson Agency, and later other ad agencies, about the time Paul settled in New York and himself became an ad man.[16]

One searches in vain for specific mention of Paul Mooney in the books by and about the better known figures of the day. Even among kindred spirits, those who shared the same space or frequented the same or similar havens at the same or roughly the same time, his name is absent. A case in point is Carl Van Vechten, both a host and fixture at many parties attended by higher-ups and the up-and-coming. Gay, well-bred, well-read, charming and liberal, Van Vechten held allure for someone such as Paul. Van Vechten, moreover, knew just about everyone, including Eugene MacCown who, again, also knew just about everyone including Paul. Van Vechten knew Konrad Bercovici, but who didn't? At least educated people knew of him through his many books or knew his name from one literary review or another. Van Vechten in his daybooks mentions Bercovici only once, and Eugene MacCown, with some degree of aspersion, only twice, two names that just happened to be lifted into a boat, as it were, already filled with almost every name of the period. Richard Halliburton's name does not appear, though it is independently known that Halliburton lunched with Van Vechten and that Halliburton was also a friend of Eugene MacCown. There is one frigidly terse reference to a meeting with Thomas Wolfe. So it goes. One wishes only that Paul's notebooks, which may date from this time, had survived, to provide such details as Van Vechten offers in his daybooks, or Crane offers in his letters. One must conclude that Paul, in 1926 and 1927, remained at best two steps removed from the mainstream of New York literary life, or that achieving a mark in literature was for him a secondary concern. It may also be that, at twenty-two and twenty-three, he was slightly too young to matter deeply in the lives of the prominent. Known only, from his few poems, is that he wanted a patron and was open-minded in his search for one.[17]

Crane's *White Buildings* appeared in 1926, a year many famous people died: Harry Houdini, Luther Burbank, Rudolph Valentino, and George Sterling. The next year, when the New York Yankees won the World Series, and Babe Ruth hit his famous sixty home runs, Paul quietly, ever so quietly published his *Seven Poems*.

That Paul wrote poems at all intrigues; that he published them intrigues somewhat more. Privately printed in 1927 by the Ramapo River Printers of New York on Christ Head Paper, *Seven Poems* represents the definitive poetic output of Paul Mooney. The edition, a beautiful example of the printer's art, consisted of forty-eight copies; of these, eighteen were personally signed. The volume is slim, the poems themselves short. Apparently it is all the poetry Paul ever wrote.

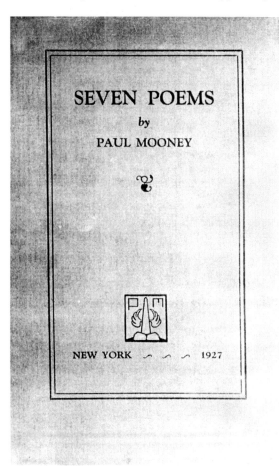

Seven Poems, 1927. Forty-eight copies were printed, and 18 were signed and numbered. Original dust jacket, believed to be exceedingly rare.

Perhaps like his contemporary Mercedes de Acosta, who had several volumes to her credit, he felt "that there were already enough minor poets in the world." Of course, with de Acosta, as with Paul, the self image each had of being a poet never vanished.[18]

Altogether the poems are Paul's identification or calling card; they are his *apologia pro sua vita sexualis*. The book was itself wrapped in a dark navy blue slip case, to suggest the sea, and sailors. Conventional and straightforward, they require for their understanding no virtuoso reader. While they offer glimpses of the outlook, at a certain time, of their creator, they have their limitations as summaries of that life. Carefully-crafted examples of "homosexual self-articulation," to apply critic Thomas Yingling's phrase, they are also confessional, and Hadrianic. Poems from the *Greek Anthology*, written

Richard Halliburton aboard the ship that carried him to Tobago in the West Indies, 1928, where for four weeks he played Robinson Crusoe, as recounted in *New Worlds to Conquer* (1929), which chronicled this and other adventures (courtesy Rhodes College, Barret Library Acquisitions).

two thousand years before, offer a smooth transition to Paul's own poems. As a single poetic utterance, the seven poems are seven days, a week with Monday beginning and with Sunday ending the week; they are secular, and pagan. "Youth," Monday, urges seizing the moment. "Initiate," Sunday, pledges that the poet will no longer stand a "lonely worshiper" before the pagan altar of Venus and Priapus, without a "young sweet idolater" at his side. The other poems speak of adventure, unrequited love, triumphant love, carnal love, death, and burial.[19]

In 1927, for several months, Paul rented an apartment for $80 a month at the new Tudor City, a Tudor-style revival apartment complex, between First and Second Avenue and East 44th and 40th Streets with (then) an unobstructed

view of the East River. Near Welfare Isle and the Queensboro Bridge, Tudor
City, begun in 1925, and not completed until 1928, was still under construction
when Paul moved in. During this time he apparently met and befriended
painters Don Forbes and Leslie Powell, both of whom had set up their easels
at night "under the street lights along the East River and among the black prisms
of the skyscrapers of lower Manhattan." The area was congenial to all types, and
by the late 1920s the "Times Square area had long been comfortable to homosexuals," as one historian has noted. The bar at the Astor Hotel and, about a
block east of 42nd Street, Bryant Park were known trysting spots for gays. From
time to time he returned home to Washington. He still lived at Tudor City
when he published his *Seven Poems*, reneging on his rent, or so it seems, to do
so.[20]

Years later, management, whom Paul called "just a bunch of uncircumcised
Shylocks," still hounded him for the money. "Because the building—and my
apartment—remained unfinished," he later explained, "I moved out after two
or three months, and they got a judgement for the balance of the half-year:
some $250 or so. It covers the time when I was not occupying the apartment,
until they got a new tenant. I sent them a new tenant the week I vacated, but
they refused to take him. Hence they think I owe them something, and I don't.
And they are a nuisance in my financial affairs." Not all the poet's words, or
concerns, are profound or rhapsodic.[21]

That same year, in May 1927, "Lone Eagle" Charles Lindbergh crossed the
Atlantic in a single engine airplane, often flying so close to the waves he could
reach down from his cockpit and touch them. It was *the* news story to cover.
Slinging to his shoulder his camera and notepad, as a medieval archer might
his bow and quiver, Paul boarded a ship bound for France. Whether his work
was freelance or for an independent news agency remains unclear.[22]

He left behind "a hateful crowd of enemies and friends, who rudely thrust
their lives into my life." "Foul lovers" he forsook: "work your will upon my body;
crawl / Along these limbs, foul lovers, like disease; / And you, obscene dissectors,
never cease / To probe within my soul till each part's known; / I am at last a
stranger to you all / And in the grave I lie with Death alone."[23]

4

Streets of Paris

Paul was in his early twenties when he went to Paris; Paris was hundreds of years old. Still, in the 1920s, the bohemian capital of France seemed enchanted, and naively young. Whirl was king, at least for some, as the Third Republic reached its exultant apogee. "Liberty, equality and fraternity" meant triumph over restraint as well as victory over tyranny. Wrote Tennessee Williams, vacationing with his grandfather in Europe about the time Paul arrived there, "when you're in Paris, you might as well leave all dispensable conventions behind." People still talked about the late Loie Fuller doing her famed "Serpentine Dance" or "Danse du Feu" or the late Isadora Duncan, another instant legend of "haute érotique." Replacing the Moulin Rouge in risqué glamour was the Folies Bergère. Here Josephine Baker did her offbeat striptease amid a pageantry of color and swirling movement to capture the delightful decadence of the moment.[1] Paul circulated from arrondissement to arrondissement, to the Marais, to the 6th and 7th—where the publishing houses were—to St. Germain-des-Pres where cabarets abounded, to the 18th, 19th and 20th. Everywhere he heard jazz, saw the great markets of Paris, and listened to Americans. While he is not known to have been among the 100,000 people who greeted Lucky Lindy when he landed there, Paul, an aviation enthusiast by now, likely hung around Le Bourget Field and other airstrips. He saw up close modern marvels such as the Eiffel Tower. A lover of art, he visited the Louvre and glimpsed, nearby, the house of Rodin. As unmistakable was the Trocadero palais, "an enormous building left standing after the exposition of 1878 ... loom(ing) up just across the Seine." Among the "avant-garde marvels" were Le Corbusier's Pavilion of the New Spirit—new reinforced concrete and glass structures forming a main feature of the 1925 Paris Exposition that fired Paul's imagination.[2]

Americans were everywhere. On the Right Bank were the "American Colony" and an American Library. In the Latin Quarter were the *Bal de la Montagne* and the *Sainte-Geneviève*, lesbian and gay roosts. Among the favorite expatriate watering holes was *Le Canard Amoureux* ("The Loving Duck") located "near the city marketplace," where Harry and Caresse Crosby and their international retinue of artists hung out. On the Left Bank at Montparnasse and along the

Champs-Élysées were "specialized gay bars." Montmartre provided theater, dance, and the feeling that, even if one were miserable, one was somewhere special. Beyond Montmartre was "the dark and squalid Rue de Lappe," a seedy thorough-fare for gays—near the Place de la Bastille. For a glimpse of sexual freedom in Paris, add the notorious *Mardi Gras*, and the masked balls which featured *les mat-tachines*, male dancers in masks who poked fun at social conventions.[3]

Paul's activities in Paris are little known. One looks at pictures from the period, of audiences and street cafes, hoping Paul, like Woody Allen's ubiquitous "Zelig," will pop up. Context is required, some coloring of the space around him if only to create his form. He was Irish, so his visiting Paris' expatriate Irish community, the very one made famous a half century ago by writer-painter George Moore, seems likely, if only, as was a hobby of some Americans, to catch a glimpse of James Joyce. Paul owned and admired Ezra Pound's *Personae*, and it is very likely he tracked down the famed poet to tell him so. Safe to say Paul experienced the Paris made famous by writers Ernest Hemingway and Elliot Paul or artists Man Ray and Stuart Davis—the streets and boulevards, the shops and thoroughfares, cafes and arrondissements, many now gone or unrecogniz-able.[4]

In 1928, Paul arrived in the city as a "newsman of some kind," noted his friend William Alexander. At the time his calling card said little: he had pub-lished a volume of verse, he was "different" in the sense that he was homosexual (which meant very little in Paris), and he was the son of a noted American Indian authority whose importance abroad needed even more elaboration than it needed at home. Still, as Alexander claimed, Paul confidently tracked celebri-ties as though it were a sport with him; little more than a handshake or smile might have followed the initial sighting.[5]

Paul probably stayed at a hotel. Paul's sister Ione, after she retired from the Navy Department in 1959, moved to Paris and resided for over two years at the Hotel Dannou, 6 rue Dannou, near the Paris Opera and across the street from Harry's Bar, 5 rue Dannou. She may have heard of the district and its well-located, inexpensive hotels from Paul, whose opinions (and memory) she highly valued. His friend Richard Halliburton found the Hotel Wagram agreeable, and it may have been equally so to Paul. A tempting alternative residence was the Hotel du Quai Voltaire just across the Seine from the Louvre, and once home to Oscar Wilde and other famous literary figures. For over fifty years, this very hotel was the Paris residence of composer Virgil Thomson; Thomson also lived many years at the Chelsea Hotel in New York City, where Paul briefly resided.[6]

Whether Paul met Thomson is uncertain. In Paris, Thomson was for a time a roommate of Paul's principal Paris connection, Eugene MacCown, whose life can now be elaborated. Adept at French and French argot, the expatriate American from Missouri was a key welcoming party to American artists who traveled abroad. Where he met Paul remains unknown. Both were college drop-outs, both were journalists, and both were gay. MacCown may have been related to the S.M. McCowan, the man in charge of Indian exhibits at the St Louis World's Fair of 1904 who had suffered unpleasant dealings with Paul's father James Mooney. Be that as it may, after MacCown decided to leave the University of Missouri, MacCown went to New York. There he joined the New York Art Students League and, in 1921, left the city to study in Woodstock. About 1922 or 1923, he worked his way on a freighter bound for France where, apart from an occasional extended trip to London or New York, he stayed for the next fourteen years.[7]

For a time, MacCown played jazz piano at the Le Boeuf Sur Le Toit, a famous right bank nightspot near the Moulin Rouge. Virgil Thomson called it "a not unamusing place frequented by English upper-class bohemians, wealthy Americans, French aristocrats, lesbian novelists from Roumania, Spanish princes, fashionable pederasts, modern literary & musical figures, pale and precious young men, and distinguished diplomats towing bright-eyed youths." Maurice Ravel was known to go there, as was Erik Satie; the composers known as "Les Six"—including Darius Milhaud and Francis Poulenc, often concertized there, and, as often, co-founder Jean Cocteau showed up with his "black American lover, a drug-addicted boxer named Al Brown." Most of this happened before Paul arrived in Paris. Still, talk never ceased, and was as much about Cubism, Dadaism, Art Deco, Instantaneism and stylized African culture as it was about what one had for dinner and who wanted to sleep with whom.[8]

Celebrities galore flocked the Latin Quarter. No less common a sight were the down-and-outers, many of whom got to know "the chap whose headquarters [were] at No. 107 Boulevard Raspail," Doc Stimpson. Besides supervising the United States Students' and Artists' Club, Stimpson ran St. Luke's Student Chapel and, in effect, "kept a concerned eye on the alcoholics and drug addicts" as well as helped feed and clothe those "younger members of the American colony" in need.[9]

Eugene MacCown provided a similar shoulder, especially for gays on the move, notably talented ones. He was on a first name basis with practically everyone who was anyone. Richard Halliburton knew MacCown, and thought well enough of him, by the mid–1930s, to recommend him as a worthy travel guide to his cousin "Haff," short for Hafford, whose portrait MacCown later painted. Connections bred connections. Hart Crane said that by 1929 he had himself met nearly every other literary celebrity of the day from Gertrude Stein, Ford Madox Ford, Glenway Wescott, to Richard Aldington, Rene Crevel, and Kay Boyle; he said he also met "a hundred others just as interesting, or more so, who aren't particularly known." An introduction from his friend Gene MacCown probably kindled these connections. Both Alice B. Toklas and Gertrude Stein wondered "why Eugene doesn't write his memoirs which would be so much better than all those books by bright young men about Paris whose authors didn't really know anybody and Eugene knew everybody and had so many stories to tell which were all unbelievable and all perfectly true." One might wish that his semi-autobiographical novel *The Siege of Innocence* (1950) were a scrupulously accurate memoir of his days in Paris and not the effetely Jamesian novel that it is.[10]

Among MacCown's many lovers was Surrealist-Communist writer René Crevel (1900–1935), whose "peculiar preoccupations with both suicide and homosexuality" first found vent in the novel *Detours* (1924), for which MacCown provided an introduction as well as the cover portrait of the writer. Crevel returned the favor by making MacCown the hero of his novel *La Mort difficile*. Given the robust surname "Bruggle," the thinly fictionalized MacCown is identified as "an American member of France's gilded youth who is capitalizing on his magnetism and good looks."[11]

Crevel, who dreamt of the vagabond life, saw MacCown as the "voyageur" he wished to be, and the sexual sophisticate he knew he could never be. Mac-Cown, whom Crevel called "Coconette," thought Crevel fascinating, an artist of "mystic carnality." Writer Matthew Josephson pictured Crevel differently, as a "golden-haired young man with the face of a laughing cupid." And, basing his opinion on the seances he held, where he would bang his head on the table for more intense communication with the spirit world, he thought him "a decidedly neurotic type." Ezra Pound noted Crevel's "speaking perfectly good English" and his being "perfectly real, authenticly [sic] young, authenticly anything he was...." Edouard Roditi mentions Crevel's "playful manner" and "legendary good looks," which, by the 1930s, had begun to wane.[12]

Paul's very resemblance to Crevel—in his carnality, sense of beauty, of fun, even the cupid's grin, may have drawn MacCown to Paul after his three-year relationship with the writer broke up in 1927. That MacCown based his novel, *The Siege of Innocence*, on Paul's life may be coincidentally true—despite its dedication to one Frank Richard Urbansky. As many another wanderer in Paris, including the book's hero, Bruce Andrews, Paul walked down looping streets into darkened corridors, into eerie urban landscapes out of De Chirico amid opium smells, from the rue de la Gaieté to the Boulevard Edgar Quintet. The Parisian backdrop of the novel is of course familiar to any student of the Jazz Age, and was to many expatriate Americans living in Paris at this time. The vision remains pleasantly offbeat, sanitized proto-beatnik.[13]

Connected intellectually to Crevel, as Paul later would be to gay activist Harry Hay, was German novelist (*Mephisto*) and diarist Klaus Mann (1906–1949). Mann, like MacCown, was enamored of Crevel who, besides personal magnetism and perfect English, shared his analytical interests in gender, male bonding and identity. Exposed early to the German Youth Movement, he had also developed an interest in American college youth; he traveled in America, in 1927, and, like his better-known father, Thomas, he settled, after 1936, in Los Angeles. It is uncertain whether Paul knew Mann, but, as an acquaintance of MacCown, and later an acquaintance of Paul's friend William Alexander, it seems likely.[14]

Paul shared the views of many better known people of the time, but, again, is once or twice removed from knowing them directly. One would like to think that he, a travel-ad man, met British heiress Nancy Cunard, daughter of shipping tycoon Sir Bache Cunard and American socialite Emerald Cunard. His friend Eugene MacCown knew her; later, MacCown painted her portrait; he also painted Paul's portrait. A progressive art connoisseur, Cunard published some of the leading avant-garde literature of the period through her expatriate Hours Press, including Eugene MacCown's *Catalogue of Paintings and Gouaches*. Among her friends were George Moore, author of *Confessions of a Young Man* and a leading figure in the Irish community, eccentric novelist Ronald Firbank, and Norman Douglas, whose popular utopian fantasy *South Wind* was Paul's mother's favorite book. Like Carl Van Vechten, a "Negrotarian," Cunard's love of African culture culminated in the landmark anthology *Negro*, whose contributors ranged from Countee Cullen, Arthur A. Schomburg, and Zora Neale Hurston to Theodore Dreiser, George Antheil and Ezra Pound.[15]

As flamboyantly liberal as Cunard was Left Bank *frondeuse* Natalie Clifford Barney (1879–1976), a blue-stocking expatriate from a prominent Washington, D.C., family. Likely Paul heard of the legendary Barney. René Crevel dubbed the promiscuous lesbian huntress and leader of a Sapphic salon "*l'amazone.*" Predictably, Eugene MacCown also knew "*l'amazone.*" Well then, he also knew Josephine Baker, lover for a time of mystery writer George Simenon, one of whose stories he later translated, and he knew F. Scott and Zelda Fitzgerald. The list goes on. Did he introduce Paul to any of these luminaries? No one now knows.[16]

His chief connection is with James Joyce, but it is not a personal one. This connection would be lost except for the survival of a beat-up text signed by Paul and dated "Paris, 1928." In MacCown's *The Siege of Innocence* James Joyce is one of the few truly recognizable characters, almost as if the celebrity author with the still hotly controversial novel was now in the public domain. Paul admired Joyce, and, in 1928, he purchased a 9th printing of the first edition of *Ulysses*, perhaps at its place of birth, 12, rue d'Odeon, where the bookstore Shakespeare and Company had its headquarters. The novel's Irish setting, anti–Catholic invective, and myth of the modern urban wanderer held their appeal as much as the style challenged traditional conventions of storytelling. The book at one point sat among Paul's books next to a *Catholic Hymnal*, as if a shared meaning made it easier for him to retrieve the one or the other.[17]

A year before Paul obtained his copy of *Ulysses*, Richard Halliburton had published his less intricate rendition of *The Odyssey*, and had entitled it *The Glorious Adventure*. Halliburton's *Ulysses* is Homer's *Ulysses* reincarnated in himself; originally, he intended to call his first book *Ulysses, Jr.* Like Ulysses, he is clever with words, and shrewd; he dons disguises—goes native, and, thrilled by the chance discovery, he dares to enter vast unknowns; like Ulysses, he is adrift and homeless. As Ulysses, Jr., he is a glamorous celebrity, actor and acrobat; he is Douglas Fairbanks, whose copy of *The Royal Road to Romance* he inscribed, "To

Ulysses—who was the Douglas Fairbanks of antiquity." He is also Tennyson's Ulysses: "To strive, to seek, to find, and not to yield" is his motto. By comparison, Joyce's *Ulysses* is not so grand. Recast as Leopold Bloom, his *Ulysses* operates, often comedically, in a mundane world where ethnic and religious disputes replace enchantresses and raging seas. Paul's *Ulysses*, with some Joyce added to it, is sexually liberated, though exclusively homosexual. If a Catholic, his Ulysses is a liberal Catholic and unrepentant of his own increasing apostasies as he proceeds into Marvel-land and beyond.[18]

Paul likely wanted to visit Ireland, and Dublin, the setting of Joyce's *Ulysses*, but northern France was as close as he got. Ireland then was no happy haven for intellectual freedom. The Cumann na nGaedhael Government (soon establishing the Irish Censorship Board of 1929) condemned and banned writers such as Joyce, W.B. Yeats, Sean O'Casey, Liam O'Faolin, Kate O'Brien and many others. Surely Paul knew of this repression, and, from a safe distance, he could remark on the new tyranny as his grandfather had remarked on the old tyranny.[19]

Paul did travel away from Paris on one known occasion. For about six months he lived, with an unidentified party, in Brittany. By the 1920s Brittany was a well-developed getaway, where motor-tourists drove on extended pleasure trips, or took riverboat sightseeing journeys. In this romantic country, undisturbed by the din and roar of city life, peasants walked along dirt paths and sold produce behind booths. Here were scarfed lasses and barge watchers. Here was life in all its supernal rawness. Amid lofty chateaux or their ruins, farmhouses and windmills etched the sky. Quaint taverns and hotels, many appearing pre–Industrial Age, were scattered all about; some had their village smithy, others their chandlers, coopers, masons, and sardine fishermen. Abounding in the region were picturesque seaside and rural communities—some well-known artists' refuges, others just plain fairytale hamlets, any of which might have served his needs for a quiet retreat—Vitre, Quimperle, Douarnenez, Vannes, Huelgoat, Pont-Aven (where artist Paul Gauguin lived), Belle Isle (where Sarah Bernhardt had her home), Concarneau, Rochefort-En-Terre. Paul might have lived on "a

Evelyn Mooney, her nose bandaged, at the time of her graduation from Central High School, 1929. Evelyn, whose whole world was art, entered Corcoran Art School the following year. Paul and Evelyn adored each other (courtesy Anton Levandowsky).

farm on the coast near Le Havre," where his friend Richard Halliburton found a quiet place to work.[20]

When Paul settled in Laguna Beach, California, these distant locales echoed. Yet, so worshipfully drawn and pictured in *The Book of Marvels* is Mont St. Michel that one must suppose (if tentatively) that it was in a community near here where Paul resided. Not far from the famed cathedral was the infamous chateau de Machecoul where Gilles de Retz, unfettered to the Catholic faith, had guiltlessly thrown himself into the ecstasies of pure eroticism, sadism, and perversion. Near here, Honoré de Balzac, self-exiled, wrote his first masterpiece *Les Chouans*, where men wearing animal skins soon appear as animals themselves.[21]

Like Balzac, Paul, returned to Paris, but with far less accomplished. By 1928, "Paris had grown suffocating," remarked F. Scott Fitzgerald. "With each new shipment of Americans spewed up by the Boom the quality fell off, until towards the end there was something sinister about the crazy boatloads." That same year, Paul returned to America.[22]

In 1932 Hart Crane jumped off the deck of the S.S. *Orizaba*, an apparent suicide; he was thirty-two. Later, in 1935, Crevel, when the Stalinist-influenced Writers in Defense of Culture restricted freedom of expression in the arts, committed a suicide of protest. Paul noted how Gene MacCown, who by then resided at the Chelsea Hotel, was fighting his own demons: "He is getting his health and spirits back," he said. "The experience there was something to share with you, but it can wait," yet, "a strange visit, oppressive, unhappy." The great admirer of Crevel, Klaus Mann committed suicide in 1949.[23]

"Hard times" by then gripped the country. The Stock Market had crashed in late October of 1929. Earlier, in June, Paul attended the graduation ceremonies of his sister Evelyn who went on to study art at the Corcoran Art School. He returned, then, to New York City, still plying his trade as a freelance journalist and news photographer.

5

"The Farm"

In 1930 Paul, as he waited along the curb for a cab, met William Alexander. It was just outside the famed Algonquin Hotel, where congregated the renowned likes of George S. Kaufman, Robert Benchley, Dorothy Parker, S.J. Perelman and Alexander Woollcott. If for no other reason, Alexander, lured all his life by the special qualities he thought put celebrities above other people, waited to get a glimpse of these famed folk.[1]

As one of the two most important friends in Paul's life, and as a person who through emulation of Paul broke from "the prosaic mold," Alexander deserves some attention. The eleventh of thirteen children, he was born Alexander Levy, in 1909, to a prominent Jewish family of Russian-Polish origin and by the name of Chernlin who had recently immigrated to America, there to settle in Brooklyn. Besides showing some athletic skills, Alexander, as a boy, liked to rearrange the furniture in his parents' house to his better liking, and to draw. Once into his teens, he worked at his father Joseph's Brooklyn insurance office, there mailing out bills to clients, and earning for his efforts the nickname "Billy." Following his older brother Joseph Jr.'s lead, Billy, or Bill, decided upon a career in architecture. In 1926, shortly after NYU's School of Architecture opened its doors, he enrolled. Among his instructors were designer Ely Jacques Kahn, architect Raymond Hood, and clay modeler Concetta Scaravaglione (the only woman with whom Alexander was ever sexually intimate). Another instructor was Thomas Wolfe who, before publication of *Look Homeward, Angel*, taught English composition to the school's law, medical, and architecture students. Occasionally Alexander, who was five foot seven, and Wolfe, who was six foot seven, walked together from class at 37th and Fifth Avenue to the main campus in Greenwich Village. As soon as the novel was off the press, Bill brought a copy of *Look Homeward, Angel* for its author to inscribe. Wolfe called his adoring friend "Billy." Bill called Wolfe his "mentor number one."[2]

Before he met Paul, Alexander's best friend was Charles "Charlie" Wolfsohn. Three years younger than Bill, Charlie was more sophisticated than he. A lawyer's son, born in Harlem, Wolfsohn, drawn early on to the world of theater and art, regularly participated in art skits (including a performance as

Above: William Alexander ("Billy" Levy) at the drafting table, 1930, about the time he met Paul Mooney (courtesy William Alexander).

To
Billy Levy
with friendship and thanks
Thomas Wolfe
Oct 25, 1929

Left: Inscription of *Look Homeward, Angel* by Thomas Wolfe to William Alexander ("Billy" Levy), October 25, 1929. Alexander's birthday was October 21; he was born in 1909 (courtesy Elaine Hofberg).

Rembrandt) at the New York Metropolitan Museum of Art under the keen direction of audio-visual pioneer and author Anna Curtis Chandler. While still in his teens, he became a protégé of art dealer Sidney Osbourne, the "black sheep son of the Duke of Kent." He already had, by seventeen, several romances, and one with Richard Halliburton remains a possibility. In time, Wolfsohn became a landscape gardener for the New York Botanical Gardens and a penthouse garden designer of some note. In the early 1930s, with Alexander, he helped dealer-owners, mostly women, install various art exhibits. Cecilia Beaux was one of the artists exhibited, Bill later recalled, as was Florine Stettheimer.[3]

Many of these galleries were located near the Algonquin. Paul and Bill were fast friends, and with Bill often went Charlie. Bill didn't drive a car, and relied on Paul to drive him places. Paul, fascinated by car culture, was a most capable driver, if at times a reckless one, and a proficient mechanic. When Paul wasn't available, Bill hitchhiked or took the train to wherever it was he wanted to go. Bill liked to learn about things—one of his few A's at NYU was in Ancient Civilizations, which he liked because it took him to other worlds. Remarkably, he had gotten a B from Wolfe, who was not known to dispense high grades. Still, Bill didn't like to read as did Paul. He liked stories, but preferred to hear their highlights told to him. As had Charlie, Paul let Bill know what he was reading; he also shared with him his musical tastes. Especially enjoyable to Paul were the live radio broadcasts that aired from the Metropolitan. He especially liked maestro Arturo Toscanini and Wagnerian soprano Kirsten Flagstad. Sundays, he always made it a point to listen to popular announcer Milton T. Cross lecture on classical music. Bill admired Charlie but soon he idolized Paul, who was so plainly unlike the many people whom he so strongly disliked. These included people who shared their dreams, who did romantic grappling in public places, who called their home some cute name, who hummed along to great music, and who put gnomes, storks, ducks, deer on their lawns. He particularly detested people who kicked the back of his theater seat, which Paul impishly might do just to tease a smile from his often too serious and peevish friend.[4]

During the Depression it was not unusual for families to take in boarders, and for a time Paul lived at Alexander's parents' 672 Eastern Parkway home in Brooklyn's uppercrust Flatbush district. Within walking distance was Prospect Park, where stood Frederick MacMonnies' famed equestrian statue of General Slocum, hero of the Battle of Bull Run; nearby was his equally imposing statue "The Horse Tamer." By this time, Paul had made at least one trip to faraway California and had met famous people about whom more will soon be unfolded. Paul's stories of the rich and famous in far-off California, in whose lives he now insinuated himself, thrilled and amused Alexander's parents and siblings.[5]

From time to time, Paul made trips home to visit his mother who, from the time her husband died, worked at the Treasury Department until her retirement in the 1940s. In the late 1930s, providing some emotional relief to Paul, Alicia, who suffered from ophrenia, left her job in New York City to return to

Washington where, still continuing to work, she lived with her mother. In New York, Paul occasionally showed up at his friend Bill's clay modeling class. From there they sometimes went to the beach; sometimes they cruised the streets. Paul's knowledge of "the haunts of the Big City" seemed to Bill long-established; his easy way with people of every calling was a lesson in proper behavior he emulated. Alexander credited Paul, five years older than he, for inducting him into what he called life's "exciting hazards." Through Paul he "fulfilled an education otherwise not possible."[6]

Bill gratefully declared Paul his "mentor number two." If Paul, for his part, saw himself and Bill as the two sex-propelled rovers in Petronius' *Satyricon*, he was leading man Encolpius and Bill his affable companion Giton. Paul introduced Bill to street people, many of whom were racial emigrés from the South. He also introduced him to filth and congestion, to despondency and "slum shock." Together the two explored New York's chic as well as seedy spots, often poking their noses into speakeasies, strip joints, and music halls. Together they explored the "rebel sexuality" of Harlem, where any day the trauma of the poverty and denial accompanying all cries for release might erupt in rioting. Both watched come to a boil what became known as the "Black Ides of March." However, joining in one of Father Divine's "Monster Rallies to Our Lord" was probably the extent of their protest, as they sought different pleasures. Years later, Alexander, who during World War II emceed Stagedoor Canteens for the entertainment of white servicemen, credited Paul for inspiring him to inaugurate, and emcee, a similar canteen for the entertainment of black servicemen.[7]

When shown pictures of Bill and her brother at the beach, Alicia Mooney remarked that Bill looked like Paul's "younger brother." Bill's younger sister Debbie thought Paul "upbeat" and secretly adored him. Little acquainted with matters of sex and gender, she had no idea Paul was not interested in women. She thought him a glamorous person, and throughout her life she kept images in her head of him driving up to the house in a splendid Ford convertible—an early version of the "Eden on Wheels." In succession, Bill's and Debbie's mother died, then their father, in 1932. Afterward, Paul became especially protective of Debbie, and of older brother Billy, whose favorite sister Beatrice was killed in an auto accident that same year.[8]

The family, however, was not left in financial ruin. In 1927, Joseph Sr. had purchased property peacefully tucked away just west of the Hudson River, in the rolling hills around Coxsackie village, in upstate New York just south of Albany. Scattered about a main house were an outhouse and a number of dilapidated shacks; trails led over small hills into secluded bowers; groups and lines of trees filled a large meadow; a stream ran here and there. Among family members and visitors the place became known simply as "the Farm." Even while his parents were still alive, Bill hitchhiked up or drove up here with Paul and other friends. With the death of Bill's parents, the property passed into his custodial care, and eventual ownership.[9]

Paul Mooney at "The Farm," about 1933 or 1934 (courtesy William Alexander).

What had been a family retreat soon became, under Paul's creative super-
vision, an art colony and fitness spa, with a native twist, à la Bernarr MacFadden
and his school of physical culturists. Or it was a sort of Lesbos for male cory-
bants, or nudist camp for uranists devoted to Eros. One can now only guess at
the specific basis of these homosexual rituals and the doctrines inspiring them.

The *Psychopathia Sexualis* of Richard von Krafft-Ebing (1840–1902), which, according to James Robert Keller, "medicalized homosexuality," first appeared in 1893 and influenced later studies in sexual psychopathy (e.g. Magnus Hirschfeld's "third sex" concept, and Klaus Mann's theoretic orientation).[10]

The core members, all of whom preferred male-to-male sex, included Paul and Charlie, besides of course Bill. Painters Don Forbes, Leslie Powell and lyricist John LaTouche were among those like-minded individuals who, according to Bill, at one time or another visited the Farm. Being called nature worshipers or Neo-Pagans would not have offended any of them. Like the "close Cambridge circle" surrounding poet Rupert Brooke decades before, Paul's 'Neo-Pagans' "loved the outdoors, nude bathing, sleeping under the stars" and simply being together in a common bond. They took walks together to faraway farmers for milk and eggs, rode horses, fed the large fireplaces, slept on the hay, went skinny-dipping—everything *au naturel*. Undressed, they painted pictures of each other in one or another of the rooms in the main house, listened to music or read poetry.[11]

Richard Halliburton himself was never a member of the Coxsackie group. When he visited "the world's most picturesque spot," Taormina, in Sicily, in 1925, he took to its baths, and is seen in one snapshot bathing with a number of young men. Taormina was home to photographer Baron Wilhelm Von Gloeden,

William Alexander, Paul Mooney, and Charles Wolfsohn in outdoor rituals. This photograph was taken around 1933 or 1934 (courtesy William Alexander).

whose subjects, like those of his contemporary in Venice the Baron Corvo, were pubescent male nudes. Halliburton evidently met Von Gloeden, who died in 1931, in his mid-seventies, and may well have bathed with his models. At the time, incidentally, Halliburton's traveling companion was an "English young lady" named "Jimmy." At the idea stage was *The Glorious Adventure*, which, with its implicitly erotic tales of enchantresses and monsters, became his Greek book.[12]

Nude culture and the doffing of sartorial superfluities was of course nothing new in America. The American Gymnosophical Association, launched in 1931, met on a thirty-five-acre estate seven miles north of Peekskill, New York. In northern New Jersey, in a picturesque countryside, the New York Sunshine League met. At the Maryland Health Society, wrote an ardent participant, "Everybody was doing something": over here, "Prospective 'Lincolns' were splitting logs," over there, "Men and women together, joined in games of health-giving exercises, denied them in our modern cities of cement sidewalks and brick walls." Other fresh and daring returns to Eden were the Rochester Outdoor League, the Zoro Nature League and the American Sunbathing League. Homoerotic naturalism was also nothing new. Painters from Caravaggio to Thomas Eakins to photographers George Platt Lynes and Paul Cadmus captured male nudes in the rye. Paul's message to his followers was to embrace life in all its rawness. Were he to have built a church on that premise, Jared French's mural of three shirtless hunks celebrating the fertility of the field might be on one of its stained glass windows. Paul Cadmus's, Margaret French's and Jared French's "Fire Island" photographs of themselves as raw flesh against the nurturing background of nature might be on the frontispiece of the church's catechism.[13]

Besides painting, drawing, and writing, visitors to "the Farm" enjoyed the communion of dance. Photographs taken outdoors show Paul, Bill and Charlie in the raw or in loincloths standing face-to-face and huddled together in what appears subdued revelry—these date to 1933 when activities of the sort were well in place. Were it not known that one of the revelers was the son of "Indian Man" James Mooney, the meaning of the scenes might elude the viewer. What appears in one photograph as a dance of Dionysian ecstasy or an induction into Scouting's Order of the Arrow is probably an informed rendition of a Kiowan or Cherokee mystery ritual, in which the participants, released from Earth, attempt to communicate with Spirit Power, and through painful sacrifice become warriors. Or they sought simply to bind themselves to "creation." "The Indian does not consider himself as created, and therefore external to God, or the creature of God. To the Indian there is no conception of a defined God. Creation is a great flood, forever flowing, in lovely and terrible waves. In everything, the shimmer of creation, and never the finality of the created."[14]

Wovoka (adoptive "secular" name Jack Wilson), the Paiute Indian whom Paul's father had known and had been the first to photograph, died in 1932; he was seventy-four. Paul likely knew he had died. His father's posthumous hold on his son's interpretation of the Ghost Dance ritual, if that it was, must remain uncertain, as must Paul's knowledge of Indian lore in general. If the account of Yosemite Falls in *The Book of Marvels* is Paul's, his noting the inconsideration shown by some "miners and adventurers" toward "the welfare and happiness of the Indians" is the nearest he ever came to echoing, in a published work, the interests of his father.[15]

D.H. Lawrence believed that one had to abandon one's own consciousness to understand another: "To pretend to express one stream [of consciousness] in terms of another, so as to identify the two, is false and sentimental," he wrote (explaining what James Mooney knew only too well). "The only thing you can do is to have a little Ghost inside you which sees both ways, or even many ways." In the bluntest way possible the two *Books of Marvels* achieved this vision of "many ways." In a sense, Paul became the "little Ghost" behind the prose.[16]

The Farm photos, in all events, suggest initiation into an alternative gender role. They also sanctify that role. Their inspiration is Native American as well as Anglo-Saxon and Aryan. The German Youth Movement, called the *Wandervogel* or Wandering Bird, strongly warriorlike and homoerotic, compares. "A product of Pan-German and Naturalist sentiments," writes theater arts historian Mel Gordon, "the Wandervogels proselytized a Romantic back-to-nature doctrine, railing against deleterious urban lifestyles and the consumption of alcohol and meat. Forty-kilometer hikes over mountainous paths, the robust singing of German folk-ballads, country-side overnights and frolicking male camaraderie were the signature activities of the Wandervogel." Another German youth group, the Wild Boys, "established Peter-Pan–like encampments in park sites, warehouses, and abandoned apartments. Led by punkish-dressed chieftains, called 'Bulls,' each Wild-Boy association had its own elaborate blood oaths and ceremonies of ritualized sex." Also of note were the League of Free Body Culture and New Sunland League, sophisticated, though popular, brands of *Nacktkulture* that attracted both heterosexual singles and couples.[17]

The Farm rituals, while they suggest those of Native American tribes, also echo those of the Wild-Boys. Sixty years later, Charles Wolfsohn called what he and the other revelers did "performance art." Nothing more. Like Alexander, he deferred to Paul, and considered him, besides older and wiser, "very handsome, very bright, witty, quick in response and in friendship."[18]

Wolfsohn's recollections of Don Forbes and Leslie Powell are less vivid, but, as friends of Paul and Bill, each helps typify the network to which all belonged. Forbes (1905–1951), son of a religious fanatic mother and drunken father, was brought up in orphanages, including one in Lincoln, Nebraska. At seventeen, he ran off to Los Angeles because "everyone was going there." But there he became ever more distraught, and developed anti-authoritarian attitudes. He started painting, calling the gamut of his work "a constant symbolic protest." He also wrote "romantic Celtic poetry espousing lost causes and present ruin, seasoned with theosophy, and [he] also illustrated these." If damned by the bleakness of his views, Forbes was blessed in his friends, who included the soon renowned dancer José Limon, artist Perkins Harnley, and Paul Mooney. In 1931, about the time the Coxsackie group was in full gear, Forbes designed an edition of Arthur Rimbaud's "Une Saison en Enfer." He had a keen interest in Mexico, particularly Mexican mythology, and lived some time, it seems, in the art colony of Taxco, near Mexico City, a place that, with its fiestas, pink-stone cathedral, cantinas, ready hallucinogens and long-haired expatriate artists, presented a get-away opportunity for Paul.

Strong New England and Mexican associations linked Forbes to artist Leslie Powell, who had ties throughout the world and very likely visited the Farm. Powell, from Lawton, Oklahoma, traveled widely in Western and Eastern Europe and North Africa before establishing himself most fully in America. Besides ties to the art communities in San Miguel, Guanajuato and Mexico City, he had ties to Santa Fe and Taos, New Mexico, both with well-established art scenes and serving as home base to a number of Paris-trained artists who painted intimate portraits of Indians and soft pastorals. Powell was friends with both Oliver LaFarge, author of the Pulitzer-Prize–winning *Laughing Boy*, a novel about Navajo Indian life (1929), and with Dr. Kenneth Foster, Director of the Museum of Navajo Ceremonial Art. During his Santa Fe period, Powell attended "Indian dances at nearby pueblos, the harvest festival at Taos Pueblo, the richly costumed Corn Dance at Santa Domingo, the hunt dances at San Felipe and the Great Shalako at Zuni, an all night affair." That Paul, son of the famed Indian ritual authority, attended these public events remains unknown. He did know Powell, and knew him well, and considered Mexico, particularly Taxco, where he had friends, an important retreat.[19]

6

Romantic Richard

By 1930 Paul's world had become a tale of two cities, Los Angeles and New York. With the emergence of talkies and the collapse of the stock market, nearly everyone in the entertainment business—executives, actors, and stagehands, the famous as well as the not-so-famous, their vassals and retainers—headed West to Hollywood for fresh starts leading to happy endings. In 1928 the Tenth Olympiad had been held in Los Angeles, and that same year the International Civil Aeronautics Conference, to create some of the talk of the moment and center world cultural excitement. Against the darkening specter of hard times, Paul trafficked his skills bicoastally as a writer and photo-journalist. He had been abroad twice. To his slightly younger admirers back east, he had the allure of one who had gone west, succeeded, and returned a conquering hero.

By 1930 Paul had met famous people or at least people he believed were famous. Among them was travel writer Richard Halliburton. The two debut books, *The Royal Road to Romance* and *The Glorious Adventure*, vaulted Halliburton into prominence, both as traveler and travel writer. With the publication of *New Worlds to Conquer*, just days after the stock market crash, Halliburton had become a sort of Hollywood celebrity. Movie contracts seemed around the corner, money poured in, and California nobility, such as Senator James D. Phelan, his nephew the philanthropist Noel Sullivan, and Gertrude Atherton, invited him to the exquisite Villa Montalvo in Saratoga. Along with Lawrence Tibbett, Jeanette MacDonald and Grace Moore, Halliburton had been toasted by the Hollywood Women's Press Club. Also, he had been a guest at illustrious Bohemian Grove just north of San Francisco. Each valorous deed he accomplished in the world beyond was followed by an ever more daring or inspired one, and some form of earthly recognition. With his father, Wesley, reluctantly tagging alongside him, he had trudged in the footsteps of Cortez across Mexico. By himself he had climbed to the summit of Mt. Popocatepetl. He had descended twice—the second time for news cameras, into the forbidding Mayan "Well of Death." As a one-man S.S. *Richard Halliburton*, he had swum the fifty-mile strait of the Panama Canal. Later he lived among the inmates on Devil's Island in French Guiana. Most memorably "Poor Richard Crusoe" reenacted Robinson

As thanks for giving a Borneo headhunter chieftain a joyride in the *Flying Carpet*, Halliburton received from him a bundle of human heads. Closer examination showed that a couple of the heads were those of orangutans. The stench emitted from the entire unwelcome bouquet quickly proved overwhelming, and pilot Moye W. Stephens believed them bad luck, so they were chucked into the Philippine Sea. Photograph taken ca. 1932 (courtesy Rhodes College, Barret Library Acquisitions).

Crusoe's castaway life on the island of Tobago (which he called "Alexander Selkirk's Empire").[1]

Happy with fame, Halliburton was not always so happy with its demands. Fox Films expressed interest in turning his books into movies while publicity ads were helping him to secure movie rights for books he thought "not suitable for the movies" anyway. His parents tried to guide him into enterprises that he thought were unsuitable for him. Marriage was one, and a regular job another, but "romanticism" in his mind favored the single man, and settling down simply meant stagnation. He believed that if he got married and took, say, a university position, he'd "become academic and critical and self-conscious, and write refined essays that nobody would read and anybody else could write as well," that he'd "lose the one thing that [made him] an individual—zest and illusions."[2]

The year he published *New Worlds to Conquer* he had written, for *Ladies Home Journal*, a feature entitled "Poor Richard Crusoe and Toosday," announcing his identification with the famed castaway. Robinson Crusoe was the bond of all travel writers, almost a patron saint recreated anew in each generation. "As children," wrote Floyd Dell in *Intellectual Vagabondage*,

> we found in "Robinson Crusoe" a world of our own. We were growing up in the midst of a complex adult civilization that we resented, we were forced to obey rules we could not understand, we suffered pain and humiliation in conflicts with the established authorities; and it was with relief that we escaped to Robinson's island, where we were monarch of all we surveyed.[3]

Pessimism, nonconformism, and escapism characterize this Robinson Crusoe which, simplified to middlebrow specification, is the Robinson idyll of Richard Halliburton, and the Halliburton, bound to self-reliance, action, and service to nature, whom Paul met.

By 1927, Paul had met Richard Halliburton, at least figuratively. That year, in New York, Paul published his *Seven Poems*. One poem entitled "Who Was Not Forward" is a lament about what a lover must do to replace a lover who has temporarily gone away. In July 1927, Richard was not in New York but traveling in the Hebrides—to him a strange place, where, alongside his companion the playwright John van Druten, he relived Boswell's tour with Samuel Johnson (1773). Another poem, "Blondel to Richard Coeur de Lion," is more tantalizing, especially since one of Halliburton's heroes was Richard the Lion-Hearted. "Look, Richard!" it reads, "It is I, thy singing boy, / Have followed thee and found thee, where thou art / By prison chains compelled, and walled apart / By dungeon stone from freedom's sunlit joy." Plainly the poem addresses "love's bond," that of a crooning lover to a beloved in bondage. Still, it is only a poem, a secular psalm quite like that which David wrote to someone named Jonathan. Paul, who identifies this Richard as "My lord, my prince, my loving comrade thou" may have met Richard Halliburton first through his books, "walled apart" from him by the very covers of the books themselves.[4] Where Paul met Halliburton continues to ba·e, and intrigue, as it involves in itself a trip around the world, and entrance through many doors. In part, it touches upon a topic not openly discussed at the time—homosexuality. In practical terms, being gay meant little more to Paul than being the member of an exclusive club; there was no need to flash what to him was not even news. Travel to foreign parts meant a willing suspension of home morality; cultural tourism and sexual opportunism were locked in tight embrace. While Halliburton traveled the globe, his fame ever increasing, Paul traveled anonymously in Europe and America, operating within an ever-widening circle of gay acquaintances, all of whom, while knowing everyone else, had some vested interest in remaining invisible. Paul, as his friend Bill, had casual first encounters, and, later, reencounters with others. Sexual adventure was after all a gift of the open road. It is not so unlikely that Paul, a fan of Halliburton's, pursued him, placed himself where Halliburton might be, even stalked him, as a hero worshiper might chase a hero. Paul's poems, especially "Blondel to Richard Coeur de Lion," suggest as much. Like Paul, Richard spent considerable time in New York in 1926 and 1927. Paul's friend Bill Alexander, incidentally, was throughout his life a celebrity collector, and quite proud of it.[5]

Charlie Wolfsohn or Eugene MacCown, mutual friends, might have introduced them. Bill Alexander suggested that the two met at a party for writer Glenway Wescott. One might begin with Siasconset on Nantucket Island or the Battle Creek Sanatarium in Michigan, where Halliburton spent time recovering from the odious symptoms of hyperthyroidism which ever haunted him while he wrestled with the final drafts of *The Royal Road*. Or they met at the little cottage he rented in East Orange, New Jersey, to whip into shape *The Glorious Adventure*. Not out of the question is the New York office of Bobbs-Merrill, at 185 Madison Avenue. Or the publishing company's Indianapolis office. Possibly editor Hewitt Hanson Howland or editor-in-chief David Laurance Chambers, who propped up *The Royal Road's* "just too giddy and juvenile" early incarnations, recommended Paul for future assignments. Late in 1927, C.P.J. Mooney, editor of the *Memphis Commercial Appeal*, and the man who first published Halliburton, had died; that Paul should replace a trusted editorial servant who bore his name might have carried meaning to Richard, who had a trust in omens. Another contact was Maxwell Aley, a literary agent who confided in Richard without actually representing him. New York thus is a likely place for a first encounter, but Washington, D.C., which Halliburton first visited when he was sixteen (in 1915), and continued to visit, is no less likely. So is Los Angeles; Asia (Constantinople) and Europe (notably, Paris) cannot be entirely ruled out. Once on the lecture tour he could be expected to show up almost anywhere. On any given month in the States, his letters "read like a conglomeration of all the timetables of all the railroads in the United States." On the train, in a ticket line or travel office (Thomas Cook & Sons), at a book fair, convention, travel office, dinner party or the YMCA—all these are possibilities. As the song "Around the World in 80 Days" has it, *it might have been in County Down, in Gay Paree or even London-*

town. Even Mexico City where they both had friends.[6]

In a letter dated July 3, 1932, Richard mentions Paul to his parents as a "friend ... whom I knew in California"—as early as January 1927, when he said he first fell in love with the state? A secure date (and one unhesitatingly agreed upon by others) is 1930, the year a photograph shows the two together with twenty-nine-year-old aviatrix Florence Lowe "Pancho" Barnes at her San Marino estate in Pasadena—then near the home base for the National Air Races and the Powder Puff Derby, and later the home of the "Happy Bottoms Flying Club." While Richard's presence here is clear enough, Paul's mystifies. Paul may have met Barnes—and through her Halliburton—while she and her then beau Texas oilman Don Rockwell were vacationing in Greenwich Village and reveling with the "artists, thinkers, and dissidents who congregated there." Paul never clarified where he met either Richard (whom he would always call "Dick") or Florence Barnes, of whom he always remained fond. After the event, both Paul and Richard were regulars at Barnes' parties, and could be expected to pop in at her house on a whim.[7]

Paul's copy of Richard Halliburton's *The Glorious Adventure* is inscribed, "For Paul—lest he forget. Dick Halliburton, December, 1930, Hollywood."[8]

Becoming weary of travel, Richard, while he searched for an airplane to take him on his next adventure, rented a little bungalow right off the shore in Laguna Beach, and pondered buying a house. Laguna Beach was the one place of natural beauty, and perfect grandeur, still left on the California coast. Here giant bastion-like cliffs gave the illusion of protection from the outside world, and the maddening, solicitous crowd. Peace ruled here as in no other place Richard had ever visited.

Some sixty miles south of Los Angeles between Long Beach and San Diego, Laguna Beach was a weary rover's dream. Hildegarde Hawthorne, granddaughter of the novelist, described Laguna "as a child of that deathless search, particularly by persons who devote their lives to painting or writing, for some place where beauty and cheapness and a trifle of remoteness hobnob together in a delightful companionship."[9]

Nearby was San Juan Capistrano, Corona del Mar and Emerald Bay. Atop one high ridge or another one could almost see Santa Catalina Island. Looking down, one could see lovely houses and sunken gardens. To writer Margaret R. Burlingame the region seemed heavenly: "The abundance of nature is almost overwhelming in its splendor," she wrote. "The variety of scene from the interesting shoreline of the Pacific to the snow-covered peaks of the Sierra Madres, from the luxuriant groves of fruit trees, eucalyptus trees, and woodlands, to the ever-varying California desert only a few miles distant, makes an absorbing and nearly endless pageant for the artist...."[10]

Laguna Beach was probably more lovely and serene in 1579 when Sir Francis Drake, on his trip around the world, sailed past. Still, in the 1930s, it looked nearly as fresh and as clean, now as ever an ideal bathing cove and

alluring seascape "without the usual tawdry amusements of other beach cities."
Though they offered, as Paul said, "a distorted view," postcards with enticing
pictures and inscriptions suggested how "gorgeous sunsets, beautiful trees, sandy
beach, picturesque rocks—and cliffs crowned with beautiful houses and sunken
gardens, long winding walks, romantic trails and the ever murmuring of a restless
sea [brought] one closer to nature." Here *communitas* reached the nearly
commercial-free perfection, which a poet such as Robinson Jeffers, in a weak
moment, might applaud with irrepressible optimism.[11]

Naturally such a place appealed to artists, a good number of whom were
leisure class or hobbyist artists. Receiving national attention were women artists
like Lillian Whiting, Ann Robinson, Marie Kendall and Virginia Woolley, who
formed the "the Laguna Beach Group." Other artists associated with the
"Laguna Beach Art Colony" included regionalists Karl Yens, William Ritschel,
F.W. Cuprien, Ivan Messenger, and Isobel Keil Wurtele. Most saw themselves
not only "tucked away in the hills and canyons, obscured in the thick growth
of California trees, or hidden under the eaves of a cliff" but removed as well
from "the disturbance of a superficial commercialism."[12]

Halliburton marveled at "the sensational vista" and at "the peaceful valley
on the one side and the full sweep of the ocean on the other." As the waves
gently rolled over rock and white sand, as calm breezes whispered, he breathed
exhilaratedly, stirred by the great prospects the beauty of the place inspired.
Beyond where the sea met the sky were corolla-like petals of drifting clouds;
below, the ocean waters, celadon-glazed, soft-rippling, touched a blue-green,
opaline sky. The burning, suddenly tapering colors of the sun, rising, setting,
splashed into Turneresque brilliance, then waned and finally converged into
mystic swirling shapes, into magical diffusions of golden light. Wrote Christopher Isherwood of the play of light brought here at day's end: "When the sun
sets into a clear sea, with a low bar of cloud down along the horizon, its disk
grows distorted, bulging and flattening into a glowing pyramid of red coal, without a top. Then, within half a minute, it slides away under the edge of the world
and suddenly the ocean seems enormous and cold, teeming with wrinkled waves,
unutterably wet."[13]

A music, raw, sirenic and eerily beautiful, the echo of the sea's deadly
temptresses, hovered over the silence. "Sibylline voices flicker"—an image in
Hart Crane's poem "Atlantis" from *The Bridge*—suggests this strange silence.
Halliburton swam daily, and took in the sun's rays—always to painful excess.

One day, while on horseback, trotting, then stopping along the shore,
below the seashore cliff and with all the local Cezannes and Cassetts under sun-
shading umbrellas seated comfortably behind their easels, Richard, with Paul,
gazed far off to the ocean, then back to the landscape and to a path that led to
the summit of a ridge about a tenth of a mile high and to a vision of the house
he would one day build there.[14]

He directed the horse upward along the path, and, at the end of the path, surveyed the flat, perpendicular cliff top which must have reminded him of the mountaintop in Peru where stood marvelous Machu Picchu, "the place where the sun is tied." Just west was a precipice, steep and overhanging, that looked straight down some four hundred feet into a storybook canyon. He at once fell in love with the place, which was then not part of Laguna Beach proper but part of a development called Coast Royal, and bought it for the glowing price of $1,900. Paul bought a lot adjoining Richard's.[15]

By this time Richard and Paul were an item. Each found the other appealing on a number of grounds. Besides history and geography, both shared a love of poetry and art. Paul resigned from collegiate life more definitively than Richard had, but seeing the world drew each from the confinement of the classroom. Both had southern roots: Richard, from Brownsville, Tennessee, and Paul from Cleveland, Tennessee—on his mother's side. Actually, Paul could explain, his mother's ancestors had come to Westmoreland County, Virginia, in the 17th century; by the 18th century, they had relocated to western North Carolina, and in the 19th to east Tennessee. Both liked animals—perhaps more than they liked people, Paul with his alligator and cats and Richard with his mongrel dog named Teddy (after President Teddy Roosevelt) and pony named Roxy. Each had a younger brother: Richard's brother Wesley, Jr., it might be noted, born in 1903, died in 1917 of rheumatic fever. Richard was, moreover, an accomplished dancer, able golfer, tennis player and fairly adept violinist to match Paul's rooftop jumping and other outdoor acrobatics. Both read, Richard taking up Cicero in the original Latin as he broke into his teens, while Paul, later, snapped up Petronius. Both were the stuff that romances were based upon. Indeed, Scottish blood flowed through Richard's veins; also a connection existed between him and Sir Walter Scott. The blood of English nobles, of whom Scott and Halliburton were admirers, flowed through Paul's veins; also a connection existed between Paul and the Earl of Surrey.[16]

In dress, as in manner, Richard was fastidious, even conceited; Paul was casual, even slovenly. Richard had auburn, Apollonian hair to Paul's brown hair. Both had blue eyes; Paul's, though, were more gem-like. Richard was the taller of the two, five feet eight, and perhaps more pleasing to behold, a toned-down Lord Foppingham to Paul's Penrod. Paul, by comparison, seems an angel with a dirty face, a "this gun for hire" sort of anti-hero with, as Richard noted, the mug of a "broken-nose Irishman." Richard, very slightly bow-legged, casually strolled while Paul, looking both pursued and pursuing, rambled or raced. Richard spoke in a soft-toned tenor croon, what a friend described as "a cultivated voice containing no trace of his southern origin." Paul, meanwhile, had a middle-range, sparkling, enthusiastic, even juvenile voice. In conversation, Richard courteously listened and gently informed, as did Paul, though Paul, according to Bill Alexander, listened at times to contradict or to make the witty comeback, while Richard, as the record shows, refrained from argument and consigned any negative thoughts he had to his notes. Paul, at times melancholic, could erupt into rages of profanity, and often crafted nasty remarks to hurl at friends. Richard was as likeable as he was disagreeable, showing a fastidiousness of manner that appeared at once amusing and conceited. Richard hardly drank and, except socially, never smoked (advertisements of him doing so notwithstanding), while Paul did too much of both.[17]

Hollywood scriptwriter David Greggory, who knew a number of the principal figures in their story, including Bill Alexander, thought the match one of polar opposites joining: Richard and Paul "were an ideal team for several years," he wrote, "functioning as two halves of the same coin," with doomed "romantic" Halliburton "ignorant of his real role as an innocent harbinger of disaster," and Mooney the "power behind the throne, the guide, the planner, the diplomat, the appeaser." The view, though offering splendid contrast and resolution, is far too simple. At least it is true that from 1930 Paul Mooney's story is also Richard's story.[18]

Being invited to parties at Pancho Barnes' was "making it," especially in the realm of aviation gymnastics. She had gravitational pull. The year before, she had competed in the first Women's Air Derby, a cross-country race from her home in Santa Monica to Cleveland, Ohio, but was forced to withdraw when her plane collided on one of its stops with a truck. Undaunted, she competed again the following year, and her average speed of 196-plus miles per hour set a new air speed record. Meanwhile, the parties she threw matched on the ground her fast lane in the sky. Soon they became as legendary as the harrowing skydives she performed in Howard Hughes's 1929 aerial thriller *Hell's Angels*.[19]

Barnes went against type, appearing more a grown-up version of one of the Little Rascals than to the manor born. Though a "society dame," the designation didn't quite fit the cigar-whiffing, middle-finger saluting and four-letter word flinging Florence Barnes. A dumpy, ungainly sort, she still intrigued, with money and background behind her to boot. Her grandfather, Thaddeus Sobieski Constantine Lowe, was a professor of chemistry, Civil War balloonist, real estate investor, founder of the Pacific-Lowe Gas and Electric Company, inventor and showman extraordinaire. He earned millions, but died broke. Through his marriage to Florence Mae Dobbins, her father, Thaddeus Jr., re-instated the family fortune, and the couple, strict Episcopalians, soon became prominent figures in Pasadena society. Daughter Flo, wild and adventurous at home, remained restless and unbridled throughout her several marriages. Romantic, faithless, she was also lonely, tough minded but fragile, courageous yet driven, homely yet exhibitionistic. A thrill-seeker, she rode horses, hopped trains, tramped with a burro in Mexico, and flew airplanes, performing stunts and competing in short-distance races. She cursed, she smoked cigarettes and guzzled alcohol—as was said in those days, "like a man." Posing as a male crew member aboard a commercial fishing vessel bound for South America from San Pedro, she earned the nickname "Pancho" and, maybe to appear one of the boys, developed her trademark frankness and what Bill Alexander called her "routine give-a-shit atti-

Aviation enthusiasts in front of the *Flying Carpet* (from left to right): Richard Halliburton, Ramon Novarro, Pancho Barnes, pilot Nelson Griffith, unidentified stunt pilot, Paul Mooney, and Moye Stephens, in Los Angeles, ca. 1932 (courtesy William Alexander).

tude."[20] Barnes attracted all kinds. "Apollos and Venuses are everywhere," wrote Cecil Beaton. "It's as if the whole race of gods had come to California." And every member of this chosen race came at one time or another to Barnes' San Marino estate—sports figures, flying wonders, movie people, news reporters. In the course of an ordinary afternoon or evening, one might run into the likes of Norma Shearer, William Haines, Ramon Novarro (star of *Ben Hur* and *The Arab*), Erich von Stroheim, Rod LaRoque (*The Shadow*), Will Rogers and Ruth Chatterton (skilled aviatrix and actress, *Unfaithful* and *Female*). The money tossed about in Hollywood often appalled Richard: "People of the commonest, stupidest type get $5,000, $7,000, $10,000 a week," he wrote. "Any actor or director or writer receiving less than $1,000 feels ready to join a revolution." Barnes' parties extended this view of Hollywood. "At the same time," wrote Richard, "other people are starving by the thousands. There's the worst depression in history here." Only the rich and upcoming attended Barnes' parties, though Barnes herself judged not who had money and character and who had not. She "had a heart as big as all out-of-doors," said flight pal Moye Stephens, another experienced movie pilot, and would "take in stray puppies, or anything of that nature." Paul

Richard Halliburton, Moye Stephens, and Ramon Novarro, in front of the *Flying Carpet*, ca. 1932. The times had persuaded Halliburton that an adventure not in the air was by now passé (courtesy William Alexander).

was one of these "stray puppies," whom Richard met then and there, Stephens added. The many free spirits who hung around the San Marino estate saw its mistress as the quintessential fag hag, and her place as a safe haven.[21]

The estate was, in a sense, a stage for those stars on earth and those in the sky. In those days air shows were the rage. New gods of the air revealed a "new visual world" of vast beauty and mystery where one might dream of "some eternal being, dwelling in one of the stars, looking down ... upon the earth, but with acuter sight, observing it like an astronomer...." Earthlings and airmen marveled at the "seas of air," the "cloud empires" and thunderstorms, "the mystery of speed" and "the beasts of the earth." Still young was the wonder of flight.[22]

Air-minded people—the day's jet set—flocked to the West Coast where, "amid the world-famed blue skies and sunshine," airplane activity flourished. Aero Corporation of California offered flying lessons. T.C. Ryan Flying School provided advanced aviation training. The Boeing School of Aeronautics in Oakland competed for top-notch students. The Pacific School of Aviation tutored the stars on how to fly. Schools proliferated, as did aircraft builders, air strips, air paraphernalia, air shows, and air fashions; the sky seemed a limitless frontier for exploration.[23]

Since World War I the nation had gotten "aviation-mad." "The Great Air Race of 1924," in which leading pilots of the U.S. Army Air Corps attempted an aerial circuit of the globe, was major news. Four single engine bi-planes with open cockpits began from Seattle on April 6, 1924; after 175 days, only two planes returned. Paul, a flight enthusiast throughout his life, surely knew of this much-publicized episode in aviation. This episode, and others like it which featured two buddies, alone together, braving the elements in some act of great daring, fired his imagination.[24]

Clearly the new flight technology defined the space Paul occupied as much as it erased the space his father had occupied. Communities once associated with the open range and the buffalo now thrived on aircraft-related industry: Wichita, Kansas, had Ace Aircraft Manufacturing Corporation; Lincoln, Nebraska, had Fleetcraft Airplane Corporation; Richmond, Indiana, had the Davis Aircraft Company. Birds painted on tepees had, in a sense, given way to tepees painted on iron birds. Roll over the 1904 St. Louis World's Fair, come to the International Aircraft Exposition of 1930. Paul took an occasional joyride, maybe with Barnes, just "for the fun of it," a phrase entitling one of Amelia Earhart's books on flying. As Barnes had opened the air route to Mexico, it seems reasonable that Paul accompanied her or another flyer to that destination.[25]

Air talk, from the poetry of flight to the grime collected on a twin engine propeller, was "in" talk. The "Lindbergh effect," writes R.G. Grant in *Flight— 100 Years of Aviation*, "inspired a new wave of transoceanic and transcontinental flights, keeping the press supplied with sensational copy and creating a new generation of pilot celebrities." France had Dieudonne Costes; Italy, Francesco De Pinedo; England, Amy Johnson; Germany, Elly Beinhorn; and America, Wiley Post. In Amelia Earhart, who timed her solo trans–Atlantic flight five years from Lindbergh's, America also had its female Lindbergh. People wondered whether planes could fly 750 miles per hour or whether the cost of a flight from New York to Los Angeles—airline passenger service began July 7, 1928—would ever get below Transcontinental Air's then-high $339. Bettors wagered on flying's triple crown, wondering who would win the Schneider, Bendix or Thompson trophies. Roscoe Turner? What were Jimmy Doolittle's chances? So it went. "In" talk included gossip: whether recently divorced publisher George Palmer Putnam would marry Amelia Earhart and whether she would accept. The commercial possibilities of Zeppelin airships was a popular topic, as were everyday philosophies of flying.[26]

Flying, just as motoring a decade before, was sport, adventure, and educational opportunity. Colonel Lindbergh's earlier 9,500-mile flight from Washington, D.C., to Bogota, "over thirteen Latin-American countries, and his return," showed that flight could unite cultures. Seasoned air travelers abounded to form a sort of derring–do elite; roving heroes could travel farther, and they could reach any spot on the globe faster than, say, a year ago. Safety, however, hardly increased with flying's progress in other areas. A case in point was the crash in Kansas, in March 1931, of a Fokker F10 Trimotor operated by TWA, which claimed the lives of eight people, including the legendary football coach of Notre Dame Knute Rockne. That one could die while flying only increased its thrill.[27]

Associated with flight in those days were high jinx society, spectacle, and deadly thrill. Other not-so-romantic associations were fuels, fuel combustion engines, and fuel efficiency. Sponsors of air events naturally included the often not-so-glamourous oil people or their corporate name. Shell Oil Company, for instance, purchased airplanes, and endorsed events.

Oil companies could make a career literally fly or plummet. Actress Blanche Wilcox Noyes kept her name before the public by flying a Pitcairn autogyro for Standard Oil Company. Union Oil Company underwrote Pancho Barnes to three years of demonstration flights. Gilmore Oil also sponsored her round-trip transcontinental flight for the Women's Air Reserve. Roscoe Turner also flew for the Gilmore Oil Company; its red Gilmore lion insignia painted on the side were a match for the real pet lion cub that sat in the co-pilot's seat. Turner also made a small fortune modeling the latest aviation fashions, including black horsehide leather double-breasted coats, breeches, and gabardine helmets.[28]

Halliburton Oil Well Cementing, like the other oil companies, had considerable clout. While flying held its appeal to both sexes, chief executive Erle (or Earl) Halliburton, Richard's millionaire cousin, thought women aviators incompetent, and the recent crash of Marvel Crosson only underscored the point. "Handling details essential to safe flying is one of the qualifications women have not mastered successfully," he noted. He had a short tête-à-tête on the issue with none other than Amelia Earhart, whose suspect flying skills were grist for his mill. Earhart had recently left her job as aviation editor at *Cosmopolitan*, one of Richard's publishers, for a career in flying and was a founding member and president of the women pilots organization known as the Ninety-Nines. Even before this, "the soaring daughters of Eve" were a force to be reckoned with. Against their heavy number, Erle was bold, and he was bumptious.[29]

From Duncan, Oklahoma, Erle also maintained a ranch-style home in Pasadena, and here cousin Richard occasionally stayed. Erle owned his own plane, and his interests in commercial aviation accompanied his interests in meeting the industry's rising fuel consumption needs. Eventually he achieved his greatest fame as a luggage maker, a distinction often given to Richard because of the connection of carrying bags to travel. More charismatic business people such as Howard Hughes, Juan Terry Trippe, and Eugene Vidal would eclipse Erle Halliburton, but, for a time, he was a conspicuous part of the aviation scene.[30]

Globe-girdling was nothing new; only the means to undertake it remained so. While even the Campfire Girls were "Flying Around the Globe," in a book by that very name, the public's appetite for the stunt had long been whetted. Jules Verne had written *A Trip Around the World in a Flying Machine*, Nellie Bly rival Elizabeth Bisland had written *A Flying Trip Around the World* (in 1890 "flying" meant *moving fast*), and a Major W.T. Blake, returning the word to aviation, had written *Flying Around the World*.[31]

Quick to ride any fast fad (or tailwind) before it got too fast out of fashion, Halliburton developed his own plan to fly around the world, and to do so in an open cockpit bi-plane, and, as was his habit, to hobnob with the natives wherever he landed. Erle was of course on hand as an investor. When he bought for himself a new Ford Tri-Motor, he even offered Richard a Lockheed airplane "free" for his upcoming around-the-world adventure. Together Erle and Richard also explored the use of an autogiro, which manufacturer Pitcairn Airplane Company insisted from the start was unfit for around-the-world flight. Other aircraft, in San Diego, Wichita, Detroit, and Chicago were inspected as well.[32]

While looking for a plane, Richard found a pilot in the person of Moye W. Stephens, a TWA captain, who dismissed Erle's offer of the Lockheed on the grounds that it was too big to handle small airstrips and was far too expensive to run in any event. Tall, handsome, protective, the TWA captain had superlative flight skills, and was known to woo a woman's heart as easily as steer a plane. A contrast to the volatile Richard, he was, as Richard learned, "slow and unconcerned with pressures of time and money." Besides flying airplanes since he was seventeen, the twenty-four-year-old Stanford graduate was an able writer and in 1926 published "Ghosts of the Air" in *Weird Tales*, a story about a "Flying Dutchman" of the air. His co-writer was a certain J.M. Hiatt, a classmate and fellow fraternity member of Stephens' at Stanford. By this time, Stephens was now game for thrilling adventure beyond the usual shifts out of Los Angeles and back again. If Halliburton had, as air show host Martin Cole has noted, "the capacity to see, and make others see, the marvels of forgotten worlds," the popular world traveler would have little difficulty convincing Stephens of the romance of "aerial vagabondage." A simple handshake presumably sealed the deal.[33]

Still, preparation was of the essence. Generally Richard's plans were best laid, and his enquiries into the aircraft he would require for the trip were careful and thorough. The plane would have to go from Burbank to New York, London to Rabat, Timbuktu in West Africa to Cebu in the Philippines; over the Atlantic and Pacific, it would be crated aboard ship and then unpacked. The Lockheed Erle Halliburton had offered was rejected, as was the first Stearman, a gas burner, which Richard had personally gone to Detroit to inspect. Reliability and cost decided that the Stearman twin-engine double-winger Stephens had located from a used plane dealer be chosen for the flight. With a fuel capacity of seventy-seven gallons, the cruising range of the aircraft was about 700 miles, and it had a cruising speed of about 120 mph. Its "engine, the 'J-5' 225 H.P.

[was] the same engine that Lindbergh (had) used to fly the Atlantic." Showbiz and efficiency counted; so did appeasement of the gods and good portent. Thus, Richard had the fuselage painted a deep, *sacred* red, and, in black lettering across a gold stripe, he had inscribed on each side the name *The Flying Carpet*, after the magically woven vehicle that had transported Douglas Fairbanks to his fabled destinies in *The Thief of Baghdad* a few years before.[34]

Halliburton likely approached investors while he looked for a plane. Noel Sullivan may have been one such investor. Earlier, on August 7, 1930, Senator James D. Phelan died. The funeral was reportedly the largest ever held in San Francisco. At the Catholic Memorial Service, Ramon Novarro sang while Noel Sullivan accompanied him on the organ. Halliburton, who had been an honored guest at the Villa Montalvo, was in attendance. At the Senator's bequest, Villa Montalvo became an artists' colony under the trusteeship of the San Francisco Art Association with Sullivan its principal trustee. Despite having visible means, his financial support of the *Flying Carpet Expedition* remains clouded. As clouded is Pancho Barnes's support. Friends of Halliburton's before the project, however, were still friends of his after it.[35]

Richard shook hands and peddled his image as globe-trotter. So did Paul. Moye Stephens thought Halliburton a "dominant sort of person," yet Paul "anything but." A photograph exists that shows Paul as an impresario. Relaxed, Pancho Barnes, in her pilot's outfit, stands in the center. Also in the picture is Moye Stephens. The airplane in the background is not *The Flying Carpet*; it may be a Travel Air, Speedwing or possibly Barnes' Travel Air "Mystery Ship." Below the propeller are actor Ramon Novarro and Richard Halliburton. Novarro has his arm around Halliburton, who leans his head towards him. One male in the picture remains unidentified, though it could be oil magnate Erle Halliburton. Cigarette in hand, Paul, bright and perky, steps out from six other aviation enthusiasts to receive the full attention of the camera.[36]

So it seems then that Erle would assist (somewhat), Stephens would fly, Richard would star—and plan, and, apparently, Paul would write the book.

7

Ghostwriting Ritual

The *Flying Carpet* got underway about the same time final hopes were dashed for a film treatment of *The Royal Road* and as sales of Halliburton's last travel book *New Worlds to Conquer* rose. Delays had of course cost precious time. Every adjustment to the *Flying Carpet* took hours. By December 13, 1930, however, the reconditioned biplane was deemed by its overly-cautious pilot to be mechanically sound. Days earlier, to break from the tedious ordeal, Halliburton and five friends, including Paul, had flown in a plane piloted by Pancho Barnes from Los Angeles 300 miles south into Mexico, traveling along the Baja Coast. One day and overnight they stayed at Ensenada—accessible at best by air—where a new casino had opened. Halliburton wrote to Noel Sullivan, on December 15 from the Roosevelt Hotel, that he had never had a "happier trip." Had it not been for "the fury of the last-minute airplane preparations," he confessed, he would have been "painfully lonely," especially with the departure back to New York of mutual friend "Glenn."

On December 22, despite Halliburton's complaint of the strain the recent excitement was causing him, he and Moye Stephens departed from Burbank, California, in their tiny open-cockpit biplane and headed across America. From the warm west to the chilly midwest, the trip was reassuringly uneventful. The plane's first stop was St. Louis where they met for dinner with a Shell official and signed a fuel contract. After heavy fog forced them to land in Fort Smith, Arkansas, they continued towards Memphis where the two enjoyed Christmas, a day late, with Richard's parents, Wesley and Nelle Nance. Next was Indianapolis where they met with Halliburton's enduring friend, Bobbs-Merrill editor David Laurance Chambers. A stop in Pittsburgh followed, then Philadelphia where they met with another publisher who seemed interested in whatever stories the expedition would produce. In Washington, D.C., they met with officials at the Department of Commerce and the State Department. Throughout this first long leg of the journey, which lasted over a month, Stephens' steady handling of the tiny aircraft through inclement weather and strange landscapes had left Halliburton bubbling with confidence in his pilot. In New York Halliburton dined and went to the theatre with movie star Mary Pickford, who was still married to Douglas Fairbanks, had tea with Kathleen and Charles Norris, lunched with Carl Van Vechten, and met, among numerous other well wishers, humorist Irwin Cobb, as well as best-selling novelists Edna Ferber and Fannie Hurst. At New York harbor on February 5, 1931, with the *Flying Carpet* disassembled and crated up, Halliburton and his pilot boarded the White Star line S.S. *Majestic* bound for London. Cost: $450 for the plane, and $270 each for pilot and passenger. Aboard their ship was editor Max Aley, who would play a part in the final product of the expedition, and an editor from *Collier's*. They reached London on February 5 and spent the better part of two weeks obtaining visas, insurance information and maps—what Halliburton, offering omen of the many futilities he would endure in the months ahead, called the "endless red tape and silly regulations."[1]

After London they flew across the English Channel to Paris where the Exposition Coloniale Internationale was celebrating France's recovery from World War I as, in 1915, the Panama Pacific Exposition had celebrated San Francisco's recovery from the earthquake of a decade before. Also celebrated was the continuing spread of Western ideas and technology throughout the globe. "To colonize does not mean merely to construct wharves, factories, and railroads," noted the Exposition's commissioner general, "it means also to instill a humane gentleness in the wild hearts of the savannah or the desert." European colonialism was heralded as the key in the transformation of primitive cultures from savagery to civilization. The United States, the only non–European country present, offered exhibits that represented Alaska, Hawaii, Puerto Rico, the Virgin Islands, and Samoa. Included in the pavilion was a replica of George Washington's mansion at Mount Vernon; Washington, for the record, had opposed colonialism, but, then again, he also advised his successors to avoid foreign entanglements. Also present was expatriate Josephine Baker, who appeared with her black troupe.[2]

It remains uncertain whether Halliburton attended the Exposition. The plane had malfunctioned, and, during the three irksome weeks that went by before someone was found who could fix it, Halliburton griped, or wrote letters home. More red tape also stretched his patience. The American government had not included Spain among its "flying permit requests," so Halliburton's trip stalled pending approval from Madrid. The American government, moreover, did not recognize the French occupation of Morocco, and that complicated matters further. Ambassador of an "open air policy," Halliburton disdained any and all border disputes and national agendas that threatened to hold him up.[3]

From Paris the *Flying Carpet* flew at last to Geneva, Vienna, Barcelona, Fez, Timbuctoo, Antioch, Tyre, Jerusalem, Sidi-bel-Abbes (Algeria), Bucharest, Damascus, Baalbek, Jerusalem, Palmyra, Cairo, Baghdad (atop the ruins of ancient Babylon), Teheran, Delhi, Singapore, Borneo, Manila, and Honolulu. These were places along a southern route: Wiley Post and Harold Gatty, in their eight-day (June 23 to July 31, 1931) around-the-world trip in the *Winnie Mae*, would go the northern route, landing in six Soviet locations among their fourteen stops. Many of the countries Halliburton would visit were either colonies of one of the great European powers or objects of Western colonial interest. Germany was plainly avoided, as was Italy.[4] The *Flying Carpet Expedition* was a major undertaking, a fact borne out with every take-off and landing of the small aircraft. In all, 40,000 total miles were logged at a cost of $50,000, leaving Halliburton heavily in debt. There would also be a $14,000 gas bill from the Shell Oil Company, whose representatives, in exchange for the publicity of a successful flight, promised to refund that sum. Air time hit 374 hours, with some 168 landings recorded.[5]

A glorious adventure, the *Flying Carpet Expedition* was also a harrowing one. In Singapore, Halliburton was almost killed when he caught an anchor line in the propeller of the now pontoon-fitted plane. In Nepal, he had almost gotten both himself and Stephens killed when he stood up in the cockpit at above 18,000 feet to shoot a picture of Mt. Everest, nearly causing the plane to stall. Earlier a lawsuit in England over a libel issue distracted Halliburton; momentary, it could have lasted months. Near mishaps plagued, as much as they provided thrills. Off Jolo, in the south Philippines, they just missed a typhoon that killed over a hundred people. While living among the French Foreign Legionnaires, stalwart men and proud, they suffered from the worst tortures of thirst and piercing heat. During the expedition there were a couple of forced landings, and a couple of averted crashes. Halliburton noted the plane's "limitations" and "the eternal vigilance" to its proper working and "slavery to the machine" as a crimp in his style. For a time they were without weapons, a serious matter as French officials in Algeria confiscated the two .38 caliber revolvers Richard carried from the United States (though Stephens wisely obtained a .45 automatic to replace these).[6]

While Richard toured the world, Paul returned to the East Coast, at least once, spending some time with his friend Bill Alexander. He also spent time in Mexico, from his home base in California. His younger sister, Evelyn, now twenty, had meanwhile gotten married to one Danilo Levandowsky. A year older than Paul, Levandowsky, an agronomist, worked for the National Park Service in Washington, D.C. One of his jobs was procuring and installing the magnolias that surround the Lincoln Memorial. He also did the landscaping on Skyline Drive in Shenandoah National Park. Danilo's father, Vladimir, who had been a general in the Czar's army, worked alongside him. Paul courteously acknowledged the union, delighted that "a Russian of old Russia" was now a member of the family.[7]

When news of the marriage came, in November 1931, Paul had just returned from Baja, a remote wasteland then famous for its ghost towns, Indian cave art and burial chambers, cactuses, potholed roads, red diamondback rattlers and settlements with names like San Jose de Cabo, Las Cruces, and La Paz. Copper Canyon may have been one of his destinations, maybe Tijuana. He wrote that he was "traipsing thru" Baja, and Mexico where he spent months, it seems, as his comment on the slow mail delivery in Mexico suggests. Possibly he visited the Seri Indians, a "primitive race living on both the mainland of Mexico (Hermosillo) and Tiburon Island in the Gulf of California—surprisingly near to the ultra sophistication of Hollywood." As a token to his father's calling, if not his own, he could have gone to the southern tip of the Baja peninsula. Early Smithsonian explorer John Xantus (1825–1894), who had participated in the tribal councils of California's Tejon and Mohave Indians, had explored Baja in the 1850s. It was as desolate then as when Paul found it eighty years later. The tall spreading panicles of agaves and groves of giant cirio trees, as rootlike as they were rood-like, were still as haunting and mysterious.[8]

On these trips, it is not known whether Paul ever attempted to find Wovoka. The Paiute Messiah of the Ghost Dance religion, whom Paul's father James had first photographed in the late 1880s, had changed with the world. In 1894, he "was appearing as a side show attraction at the Midwinter Fair in San Francisco." And: "By 1926 he was having his picture taken with the famous Hollywood cowboy actor, Tim McCoy, who was Governor of Wyoming at the time." A photograph, taken about 1914, shows Wovoka (Jack Wilson), kneeling on the ground apparently holding a chain or necklace. His head slightly turned, he smiles with peaceful resignation. By then he had become quite used to being photographed and getting paid for it.[9]

A constant companion of Paul's, vicariously speaking, was poet Robinson Jeffers, a volume of whose work Paul was known always to carry with him as a chewer might carry a pouch of tobacco. In Jeffers, Paul found analogies to himself, and a hint of what might have been had his father taken his family west. Of Northern Irish roots, the poet's father John Robinson Jeffers, a Presbyterian minister, taught languages and Old Testament literatures at Western Theological Seminary in Pittsburgh, Pennsylvania. As Robinson Jeffers was growing up, the family traveled extensively, mostly in Switzerland and Germany, where the poet was in part schooled. Home, John Jeffers, plagued by chronic health problems, decided to take his family west, and resettled in Pasadena, California. After Robinson completed his education at Occidental College, he married an Irish woman named Una, who especially enjoyed Irish folk songs. They had twin boys, Garth and Donnan, and the four spent 1929 exploring Great Britain and Ireland, as Robinson had done earlier with his younger brother Hamilton and their parents.[10]

Like Paul, Jeffers worshipped nature and loathed human beings, whom he believed God had forsaken. Corporations were soulless; the government was not benevolent. Land development companies and government land programs were predatory and pernicious; they blew up the environment without biological regard, and, in the name of progress, they destroyed sacred Indian burial grounds. Distrustful of the emoluments of technology and the promises of bureaucracy, Jeffers created a gospel of untainted earth and sky, and took refuge in a sort of chthonian mysticism rife with Greek dramatic elements, convinced the modern world and its encroaching evils should best be left outside. Putting iambs of verse into granite stones, he built at Tor House, near Carmel, the famed "tower beyond tragedy" (after a narrative poem of the same name). Near the entrance of the darkly medieval home sat pet hawks and vultures in place of sculpted gargoyles and griffins; in one of its chambers Una had an organ installed.

Besides "recurrent themes of incest, lust and cursed heredity," Jeffers' poems contain themes of uprootedness, uncertainty, imperfect bonding, misanthropy, and the peace that comes with death. Also they redefine man's relationship to the land with a naturalism that is both disturbing and reassuring: "The soil that I dig up here to plant trees or lay foundation stones is full of Indian leavings, sea shells and flint scrapers.... Not only generations but races too drizzle away so fast, one wonders the more urgently what it is for...."[11]

Of Jeffers' books of poems, Paul read *Cawdor* (1928), the heretical verse play *Dear Judas* (1929) and *Give Your Heart to the Hawks* (1933). But his favorite was *Thurso's Landing* (1932), called Jeffers' "most native American, least Greekish tragedy." Supremely earthy, the title poem is also ruggedly romantic. Passions seethe, rise and smolder. In one scene atop a mountain, organs alone seem to copulate bereft of their human hosts while the senses din and dance: with "hands and eyes ... spent desire" is revived to "longer-lasting delight" and "nerve-cells intermitted their human dream; The happy automatism of life, inhuman as the sucking heart of the whirlwind, usurped the whole person, / Aping pain, crying out and writhing like torture." The frontier setting, reminiscent of the slightly later fiction of John Steinbeck, is as carnal as it is beautifully austere: "In the vast landscape above the ocean in the colored evening ... the naked bodies of the young bathers / Polished with light, against the brown and blue denim core of the rest.... The Spanish-Indian horseman dark bronze above them, under the broad red/Heavens leaning to the lonely mountain."[12]

Paul could easily identify with the characters. Indomitable taskmaster Reave Thurso, "square-shouldered and heavy-jawed, too heavy with strength for so young a man," surely intrigued him; hearty and macho Thurso "who chose [for his work-gang] one of the men with his eyes." Reave carried a burden of the heart. Unable to work the land, Reave's father killed himself, and his father's ghost haunted him. Was it himself, or a friend, whom Paul saw in crew worker Rick Armstrong—the "blond young man / Who stooped over the rock and strolled away smiling / As if he shared a secret joke with the dynamite...." and elsewhere "the blithe young firer / Of dynamite blasts.... / Naked and very beautiful, all his blond body / Gleaming from the sea...."[13]

The plot is the Greek epic poet Homer—"On the Range." The plot winds like a rusty, twisting cable, symbolizing insidious progress, which Reave at last cuts. Helen Thurso (Helen of Troy) runs off with Rick (Paris); Reave (Menelaus) stalks them; Helen, once together with Reave again, and while gripped in feigned passion for him, slits his throat, then poisons herself with contraceptive pills. Left to pick up the pieces of what happened are Reave's grieving mother, and, ironically, the insatiable hawks. In a variation of the Greek myth of blood-guilt, Mark, Reave's brother, goes mad when his father's ghost appears to him, then kills a deer as an offering to disquieted human passions rather than a sacrifice to any god.

A great narrative artist, some would say, wrote "Thurso's Landing"; in Paul, a great reader, certainly, read it.

Hardly an indifferent correspondent, Richard meanwhile regularly sent word about his activities and whereabouts to Paul, whom he considered among his Hollywood friends. Worthy of note are several adventures during the *Flying Carpet Expedition* which featured twenty-five-year-old flying ace Elly Beinhorn, styled "the Amelia Earhart of Germany" and "the German Diana of the Air." Beinhorn would later wed legendary race car driver Bernd Rosemeyer and the two would be billed in the press as the perfect Aryan couple. Halliburton, for his part, thought the young heartthrob "so lovely, so fragrant, so feminine," and said so in the foreword he wrote for her book *Flying Girl*. In it he noted how he had first heard of Miss Beinhorn in Timbuctoo, a remote, dusty place of huts and dingy corridors whose dark, pagan hues had always captivated him. Beinhorn's flight to Timbuctoo had preceded Halliburton's own by three weeks.

"Flying Girl" Elly Beinhorn, 1932.

She had flown there by herself, Halliburton, somewhat incredulous, reported, "in an absurdly small Klemm machine, and via the long, desolate, sea-coast and Niger River route." And, "within sight of the mud minarets of her destination," as fate would have it, "her old duct broke, her engine froze, and down came Elly, aeroplane and all, into a swamp." Luckily, she emerged in one piece from the wreckage. Unperturbed, she straightaway borrowed a donkey, made for the Niger River, got into a canoe and paddled her way down to Timbuctoo, to the stark amazement of everyone who bore witness to the impromptu circus act. Of course, commented Halliburton, some of Timbuctoo's "ten thousand Moslem negroes" and "sprinkling of Arabs" were equally amazed when Halliburton and pilot Stephens, "two men from the moon who had flown upon a miraculous gold and scarlet dragon down here to earth," also landed. Later, in Bushire, on the Persian Gulf, Halliburton and Stephens again crossed "flying paths" with Beinhorn. Comrades now, the three formed the "Timbuctoo club," making Beinhorn president, and they spent six weeks swimming, stunt flying, exchanging phonograph records, and sharing experiences. The lead female romantic interest of Halliburton's grand airplane safari, Elly Beinhorn was "the youngest, gayest, most buoyant personality (he) ever met." Her spirit, and derring-do, perhaps induced Halliburton and Stephens on the Nepalese leg of their journey to fly 18,000 feet towards the summit of Mount Everest where the fool-hardy Halliburton, standing up with his camera in the cockpit and nearly stalling the plane, snapped the closest photograph ever taken of the mountain peak.[14]

By January 1932, the *Flying Carpet*, fading in luster and efficiency, "showed the marks of battle with the elements in a hundred lands." In Singapore, pontoons needed to be fitted on for the next leg of the trip, which included water landings. A long delay amid infernal heat followed. Stephens spent his days learning how to fly a pontoon-equipped plane. There was also a brief visit from his brother, who was on a cruise. As was customary, whenever he experienced a snag or layover (as he had earlier in Fez and in Paris), Halliburton, while holed up with his typewriter in one hotel room or another, worked up his notes into various stories and "new chapters." In short order, he finished "From a Persian Prison" and "The Princesses," sending carbon copies to his father. He had brought the total number of words to 57,000, of which he believed 50,000 might be used. Originals of the seven completed chapters, as well as photographs, he sent to Maxwell Aley, a New York literary agent with connections throughout the publishing world. Aley, in turn, may have given the chapters to Paul or to Paul through Chambers. Richard also prepared materials, including one on Timbuctoo and the Foreign Legion, to send to Loring Schuler, the editor of *Cosmopolitan*, who had worked with him on earlier occasions.[15]

Amid all sorts of other loose ends, which included business correspondence and expenditure tallying, the book continued to nag him: "the state of the book faces me night and day," he wrote in torment, "and until [it] is off my hands, I'll not be able to relax." Later, he said that he had "completed" the "Everest story" and that it "demanded days of careful reading in advance" to make it "fairly good," meaning sufficiently hair-raising and thrilling.[16]

It may have been the perfect distraction: Stephens, whom he called "as fixed in his ways as Mt. Blanc," had begun getting on his nerves. After going more than halfway around the world, Moye, he wrote home in bewildered disappointment, "[had] learned nothing—felt nothing; all he cared about was flying." It affected Richard's writing. By May, when coming home was in sight, he said his "imagination will provide color" to what he writes; "once underway," he said at that time that he could produce "a story a week." He added that, "as always, once I get at it my writing powers quickly respond." Earlier, in February,

Richard Halliburton and Moye Stephens near Timbuctoo in the Sahara Desert. Grateful to have skilled pilot Stephens at the controls of the *Flying Carpet*, Halliburton, as his look here suggests, often complained of the "inflexibly commonplace companionship" he had otherwise to endure.

he had stated the same thing: "once underway the writing flows easily." But in those several months, from February to May, one wonders if "imagination" came forward. Clearly, Stephens did not offer the discussion that fired it: "liberation from Moye will do more than anything else to stimulate my imagination. It's gone almost dead in his *inflexibly commonplace companionship* (italics mine)." Halliburton vowed he never wanted to fly again and, as he had said a few months before, he longed for the land-lubbering, sea-drifting "Glorious Adventure days." By the end of April, he had neared the end of his patience, with Moye and the expedition itself, but, by then, the plane was ready to go, and, "running rough," as seemed usual, sputtered its way towards Manila where it was given a "proper overhaul," disassembled, and crated up.[17]

As weary and battered as the plane, Halliburton and the ever-smiling Stephens boarded the S.S. *McKinley* the first week of May. They passed Hong Kong and Shanghai, and stopped briefly in Tokyo. They saw firsthand the increasingly hostile presence of the Japanese marines, and watched as pirates watched them. They ran into one frightening rainstorm. Calmer waters led them then to Hawaii, where they spent eight days or so in Honolulu before heading for San Francisco. In San Francisco, the *Flying Carpet* was unloaded and reassembled. Halliburton stayed at the plush St. Francis Hotel. He spoke at several luncheons and gave at least one formal talk. Then, on June 4, he and Stephens flew off to Burbank, where friends met them. The heroic little biplane that had soared high into the sky was quickly sold to help pay for the trip; less than two years later, in Honolulu, it crashed at John Rogers Airport with one passenger killed and two others severely injured.[18]

The *Flying Carpet Expedition*, though a *fait accompli*, with its final journey from roughly Hong Kong to San Francisco, prefigures the *Sea Dragon Expedition* of a few years later. As "an airplane journey," the adventure was a "complete mechanical success," yet, Halliburton had to admit, one that seldom went as planned. It was not "a mine," in any event, "for [his] type of stories" and in that regard "left much to be desired." From Halliburton such words were vintage, chivalrous understatement.[19]

While the book that commemorated the magnificent journey might be read in a sitting or two, the actual feat—grueling, exciting, and rich with as many futilities as joys—lasted eighteen months. That very book, named after its main protagonist, though sales at first, despite rave reviews, were slow, also earned Richard Halliburton, in just its first year, nearly double his investment. Despite his father Wesley's objections to the manuscript of *The Flying Carpet*— possibly because of Paul's hand in it, the book almost was not published. Richard, however, told Bobbs-Merrill editor-in-chief David Chambers to go ahead and publish it. Reaching the deadline of November 1, however, became as grueling a task, editorially speaking, as the flight itself.[20]

Long before the completion of the *Flying Carpet Expedition*, Halliburton had found the double role of traveler and writer burdensome. Pride of authorship had begun to matter less to him than the grooming of his public image. According to Jonathan Root, Halliburton thought himself "old and jaded," yet feared becoming a "has-been." The thrill of initial discovery had passed: "How to write about thrills one did not feel, he asked himself, and was terrified there was no answer." He remained exuberant, says Root, and about his future he was "full of enthusiastic promise." He said, however, that he wanted "to write about the world as it is, and as I see it, instead of [write] these adolescent romantic tales spun from a few bare facts." The image Halliburton had created of himself had separated and slipped away from the person he had become. "Why can't I just write the truth?" he wondered. At least once he had written the "truth." The article discussed what he considered the most wicked of the wicked cities of the world (Cairo, where prostitution was everywhere). Publishers refused it. Perhaps he had in mind to write the *Inside* books associated much later with John Gunther. Be that as it may, such a book for Halliburton, against type, would have been a bold stroke, showing what sort of man lay behind the sculpted image. He toyed with the idea of writing an "autobiography," which suggests that he was well aware that his books so far were not in any way autobiographical.[21]

Actually he feared sudden death, and old age more than becoming passé and unwanted. Travel still excited him; writing did not excite him as much. So be it. If Odysseus had his Homer, he would have his Homer too. The formula for the romantic travel book now was in place, and had only to be kept pure.

In recasting, enlarging, omitting and refining, Halliburton had bowed to the wishes of his editors, and persevered. For criticism of work-in-progress he had often asked his father Wesley for help, insisting that he "be absolutely brutal in [his] suggestions and criticism." Harsh criticism didn't bother him so much as criticism that wasn't harsh enough. "Whatever quality I possess as a writer," he explained, "comes from the spirit, and not from the word; and this spirit plunges off on the wildest, and, lately, on over-exotic tangents." About *The Glorious Adventure*, he wrote that he had "taken the brakes off," noting that it "all makes for readability—but also for incredulity." He added: "The book is a *true narrative*, with buckets of bright paint flung over it. But if the public got the idea from my style that it's fiction, I'd be done for. This is where I need help." His father remained a final arbiter. Chambers, and now Maxwell Aley, conferred with him about "approach," meaning tone and format. But a wordsmith, and not "inflexible companion," was desperately needed.[22]

Halliburton probably asked Bobbs-Merrill straight-out for outside editorial assistance. He had the clout. Likely he recommended Paul for the job in terms similar to those he gave his parents when, late in January 1932, he wrote to them from Singapore: "He is one of the most intelligent, and pertinent, critics I know, and very capable in a secretarial way." While still in Singapore, even before, he was thinking of deadlines, and a quiet place to work on the book—namely Memphis: "Considering the brevity of my time there, I will need expert assistance to see me through." Namely Paul: "He is a writer himself, and can work upon his own stories when not occupied with mine. I would pay him a small salary, but [when he visits Memphis] treat him entirely as my friend and guest." One wonders, as an aside, what Paul's own stories were, once it is clear what he would do for Richard.[23]

By May, Halliburton began to cave under the pressures of completing the book in time. He seemed to have everything to do at once. One day he was contacting an advertising agency about radio scripts or a product promotion (Lucky Strike cigarettes), another day having lunch (with Lowell Thomas, Pearl Buck, or Carl Van Vechten), seeing some agent, hearing a fellow lecturer (Burton Holmes), or attending a banquet (for Amelia Earhart, in particular), whom Paul seems to have met earlier, as no interest is indicated of his wishing to meet her again. Trips to and from New York, or Hollywood, the public lectures here and there, punctuated an already hectic schedule. By mid–July, overburdened, he reiterated his need for Paul: "More than ever I'll need Mooney in Memphis," he wrote. "His literary eye and ear are extraordinarily fine and his cooperation invaluable." Based upon the little feedback Richard had received from Moye, and how much Richard needed it to kindle his imagination, Wesley apparently concurred.[24]

Most of the book would be done in Alexandria, Virginia, not Memphis. Richard stayed at the George Mason Hotel, presumably with Paul. In mid–August, they moved into the Crocker House on 323 S. Fairfax and split the $25 a week rent, which included a private bath and meals. Later, Wesley cut the portion of the letter that noted Paul's co-habitation to underscore Richard's lone efforts on the book, and other writings, such as the article for the *Saturday Evening Post*, that engaged them. Richard himself had no qualms about the living arrangement. He thought only that Alexandria was itself not the "best place in the world" but, because of its proximity to other interesting places like Atlantic City and Harpers Ferry, he thought his parents might want to visit. In September, Richard moved on, to New York, staying briefly with Max Aley (who had been with Halliburton aboard the *Majestic*); for him it was suitably "quiet and cheap." Shortly thereafter, he and Paul moved into the Standish Arms Hotel at 169 Columbia Heights in Brooklyn. Here they each paid $12.50 for a "simple but comfortable room," which had a great view of the harbor and of Lower Manhattan. By then Richard had "rewritten everything," though in the next few days the Everest chapter received still another reworking. By then also, they had sent finished materials to Bobbs-Merrill, at any rate, and they were getting galley proofs back for final inspection. "Here, Paul has been of especially great service," Richard told his parents. "His eye never misses a slip. I've corrected and returned 90 galleys," which were then sent to Wesley for his approval. Meanwhile, from the more than 1,000 pictures he had taken during the trip, Richard, with Paul's help, selected 64, and for these Richard wrote captions, a daunting task, one taken to the level of an art form by Burton Holmes, which he seemed to enjoy.[25]

Paul Mooney at the Standish Arms Hotel in Brooklyn, New York, just before publication of *The Flying Carpet*, fall 1932 (courtesy William Alexander).

The book was evolving, as both Paul and Richard moved physically closer to the publishing site itself.

Richard throughout the project was extremely grateful for Paul's help. "I've got Paul Mooney writing his own version of [the French Foreign] Legion [story]," he rejoiced. "He's full of excellent ideas, with a much more literary flow than my own. With his suggestions in mind I'll rewrite Legion in my own way." A week later, Paul was still hard at work on "the Book," when Richard asked him to send Wesley carbon copies. He had already mentioned to his father that "most of the changes and improvements are [Paul's] ideas," and he noted specifically Paul's working on the "Jerusalem" chapter. "I've rewritten Fez, but am not satisfied," he told his father, "[and] have Paul working on it." He often commended Paul. Paul had "put his whole heart into this book"—enough so to induce Richard to compensate him. "He has a small income and living quarters," Richard noted, "but I buy all his meals [this was *before they moved into the Crocker House*]. If the *Post* comes thru, and the radio, I'll engage him as a secretary and collaborator at a salary." Of Paul's help, Richard was emphatic in his praise. He gave "8 hours" a day, every day, to the task, even more. His sister Ione Mooney, once paying a visit to Paul and Richard, was reverently told by Richard, who answered the door, to keep her words to a whisper as Paul, upstairs, was furiously writing away—presumably on *The Flying Carpet* manuscript, and should not be disturbed. It was not all work and no play. Often Paul dragged Richard down to the closest beach for a swim to make sure his patron stayed fit and maintained a celebrity tan.[26]

While Richard heaped praise on Paul, ultimately it fell on deaf ears. The original of the letter Richard sent to his father, dated July 7, 1932, mentioned that he had "rewritten" the introductory chapter as well as the Morocco and the Saharan chapters until they read "smooth." Notably troublesome was the French Foreign Legion chapter, which Richard had worked on several times, at Fez and again in Paris. It seemed reasonable then that he should have Paul try his hand at it. "I've got Paul Mooney writing his own version of the Legion— he's full of excellent ideas, with a much more purely literary flow than my own. With his suggestions in mind I'll rewrite Legion in my own way [and] will finish Timbuctoo today...." Scratched out was mention of Paul's help—as elsewhere where it is stated or implied, so the sentence read: "I'll rewrite Legion and will finish Timbuctoo today...." In the published version, none of the toils of composition is noted, though some implicit credit is given to Maxwell Aley. Elsewhere, "Paul and I are working like fiends" in the published version became "I am working like a fiend." Clearly Wesley Halliburton wanted it known that his son wrote effortlessly and received little or no help in writing his books, at least help from Paul Mooney. Wesley expunged other names from his son's correspondence as well. He also expunged his son's mention of financial matters, as though the pursuit of romance should have no price, and also to fend off the peeping eyes of the tax man and creditor.[27]

Though one wishes the carbons and originals of the book still existed somewhere, Paul's full role in the writing of *The Flying Carpet* remains fairly clear. As drafts of the early pages of *The Royal Road* show, Richard's writing tended to be hammed up and prolix. His father Wesley offered trimmed-down versions. Chambers then checked these against the originals, making the fortunate decision to preserve their childlike wonder and occasional immature wording. Richard now made Paul his Wesley and his Chambers. Paul, however, rewrote as much as he edited. Richard provided him with lengthy cue cards, and Paul, with an especially orderly mind and a gift for narrative, gave them rhyme and romance tempered with reason. Work bearing the Halliburton name had to be stimulating and intelligent; it also had to be pleasantly personal, informative and confiding. As a trainer might keep a top athlete fit, Paul kept alive Richard's faith in romanticism while he moderated the "over-exotic tangents" Richard found it hard to resist. Paul lopped off such excrescences without a tear, and culled the "unjust and unintelligent phrases out of [Richard's] work": windy political asides and philosophic preachments he distilled or deleted. He pruned and polished, shortened and compressed; he also artfully embellished. At heart, Paul's instincts were those of the naturalist—and his affinity in this regard is closer to scientist William Beebe than to romanticist Richard Halliburton. But, rather than become a lab assistant to a discoverer, Paul was the literary make-up artist to an actor. He maintained the Halliburton style, providing the "harsh criticism" Richard himself solicited from those who sifted through his initial drafts. In the end it was "bold, imaginative, irreverent writing that dismisses all rules."[28]

Moye Stephens thought Paul, though "not an impressive person in any way," was "undoubtedly intelligent" because "he helped Dick considerably in his writing." Considerably indeed. "Mooney and I worked like dogs," Richard wrote home, on the *Flying Carpet*, and an "Africa" story written (or reworked) for the *Saturday Evening Post*, besides articles for *Red Book* and *Cosmopolitan*. Another time they "worked like fools" producing some "6000 words" for a magazine feature. "As usual, Paul had a new, fresh viewpoint," Richard boasted to his parents; it was July 14, 1933, and by this time both parents had met Paul.[29]

Alicia Mooney believed that a single sentence, a cipher, appearing on page 115 was decisive proof that Paul had written the entire *Flying Carpet*. The sentence, about the bazaars in Fez, is itself a colorful off-handed regard for trifling things such as Ronald Firbank might have composed for one of his jaded, verbally witty novels: "Paltry and useless little mosaic ornaments, ostentatious nothings enticing yellow darioles, idle delights that held infinite surprise." (Italics mine.) Cryptographically, the first letters form an acrostic, which informs that "paul mooney did this." "This?"[30]

James Cortese noticed in this singular work Halliburton's "own romantic style" but also perceived "a touch or two of red paint to make [the places he describes] glamorous—similar to a beautiful woman adding a touch of lipstick," decorative detailing found in every Halliburton book. One of the "red" touches had to have been the chapter devoted to the sex lives of the head-hunting Dyaks or Wild Men of Borneo, which Moye Stephens thought "went overboard." Indeed, *The Flying Carpet* is pitched a full tone higher than *The Glorious Adventure*, and emanates with those fleshy qualities Charles Warren Stoddard attempted to give his best work. With its essays on the "Wild Men" and "Head-hunters" of Borneo, among other charmed Herodotean asides, *The Flying Carpet*, besides echoing James Mooney, is Halliburton's most ethnographic work. A keen knowledge of and enthusiasm for flight also intoned the book. Aviation observer James Elliott Mooney (1901–1968), author of *Air Travel* (1930) and of *Wings Away* (1937), might be mistaken for Paul himself.[31]

Architect Bill Alexander, noting that a house "once planned" might be "replanned," once said to Halliburton about his books that "once rewritten" they in fact had to be "vastly rewritten." Was it "rewriting" Paul did, and little else? Later Richard told his parents that Paul received a flying adventure that had to be "rewritten"; it would "pay him [Paul] $1000 and keep him busy." Paul himself implied that by 1935, his work for Richard had become routine: "I have P.S. some good news to tell you: *Cosmopolitan* insists that Dick must do an article right away for them; I'll help him (only five thousand words) and lo!—the bank account [will receive] a three-hundred-dollar-bang...." Elsewhere he mentioned the $500 which *Readers Digest* had paid for "*our* Main Street story"; yet, about the same story, Richard told his parents, "Did you see the October (1937) *Readers' Digest?* It's out, and my new story's in it—but half as long and not nearly as good as the original." Richard's "own way" in the end prevailed, at least this time.[32] Still, as with all of Halliburton's remaining books, one may wonder how much is Richard and how much is Paul.

As a writer, Paul had to adjust his style to one the public now recognized as that of Halliburton. If one wrote the words and the other the music, it becomes a matter of who did what first. Halliburton, notes Jonathan Root, had "a flair for lyric and purple phrases," but "his only inspiration came from history books and to them he turned, devoutly, whenever he was in need of an idea." As a traveler, Halliburton "immediately reached out for the common man," wrote *Esquire* feature writer George Weller. "Somehow whether he knew the language or not, he managed to talk to everybody. From the common man he got the feel of the country. Little of his technique of acquaintance, at which he was a master, appeared in his books and all of it was badly written. 'I don't know how to write,' he would say. 'I depend on history for inspiration.'"[34]

According to Jonathan Root, Halliburton felt himself "safe ... within an impregnable armor of popular fame and money." Privately, however, he felt a need for the "approval of the literary arbiters" whose income, he could happily remind himself, was far less than his own. Halliburton himself spoke of the "wall" he had built around himself "for self-protection and self-delusion"; it simply rose higher and grew thicker over time. David Greggory and Charles Wolfsohn assumed Paul was Halliburton's ghostwriter and believed that this secret bound them.[35]

Richard created *Richard Halliburton*, a brand name in travel, one susceptible, like any other commercial product, to changes in market perception. Together Paul and Richard, driven by new market forces, modified and enhanced *Richard Halliburton*. In real life Paul advanced from Richard's secretary and housesitter to his publicist and editor, and from these to his business partner and co-writer. To the extent that Paul chauffeured Richard to and from the airport, dragged him down to the beach, and nursed him back to health when he was sick, Paul always remained, in a sense, Richard's man-servant, and confidante. Paul also remained Richard's principal friend and love interest, though neither Richard nor Paul maintained any more fidelity to monogamy than they did to single authorship of one of Richard Halliburton's books.[36]

These were Paul's happiest days; he was making money doing what he did best.

8

Veiled Salome

A hot commodity, Halliburton said once that he would not turn his mind to a proposed undertaking until he was given the money to think about it. Even though he often turned work down, even when the money was there, finances troubled him constantly. His dozen years in the romance business had produced good income from book deals, radio broadcasts, film deals, and magazine articles, but the patrician appearance he cultivated required plebeian windfalls on a regular basis, which only the lecture or "talking authors" tours well achieved. No less than five speaker bureaus landed him engagements "before schools, colleges, town halls or civic groups," not to mention "women's club teas." Often, then, his immediate economic goals seemed met. In a show of pride, he once told his parents that his net worth was $58,000, a considerable sum during the Depression, and he seemed nearly comfortable with that amount.[1]

Economically self-conscious to obsession, he sent home to his parents scores of letters filled with similar financial disclosures and earnings projections. By comparison Paul considered it splurging when he dug into his pocket for another penny to buy a neater stamp than the so-so one that was sufficient. "Hard times," people called it. One thinks of President Herbert Hoover's view of Youth, one less romantic than either Rupert Brooke's or Halliburton's: "Blessed are the young, for they shall inherit the national debt." Dismal forecasts of America's economic future were hardly novel, but Halliburton worried over his investments; indeed, while he expressed fear that the bond market might collapse, he at the same time pondered the fate of reliable stocks and securities. "The economic situation in America is affecting me as grimly as anybody else," he said, "but, to the best of my ability, I must dismiss it from my thoughts." When off abroad somewhere, his father continued to send him "general national news." Richard, for his part, regularly sent his parents money, mostly to pay for the white brick cottage in Memphis he had bought for them.[2]

The house seemed perfect for the Halliburtons, but not quite so for their son, though it served as his second home. On Court Avenue, not far from Southwestern College and Overton Park, it featured gables and a portico in a quiet, fashionable neighborhood. A brick and iron-wrought fence ran around the property, and huge trees shaded the lawn. From time to time settling down appealed to Richard, and in such a place. Often, "wearied by the company of human beings," he preferred just to read or write in solitary comfort somewhere. "Occasionally I do find a fellow spirit," he said, "and then I'm as social as anybody."[3]

Nelle and Wesley Halliburton first met Paul Mooney late in the summer of 1932, in Memphis, or Alexandria, or so it seems. Richard, who had spent time at the Library of Congress while in the Washington area, already had designs of writing *The Royal Road to Romance in the USA*—slated for publication in 1940, and of receiving from Paul some help in the enterprise. Paul's hand in the writings of their son made Wesley cringe. The sight of Paul, too, his very lack of blatant virility and stature, little impressed the Halliburtons, who would have preferred, in any event, a female friend and guest. Moye Stephens had seemed to them a real man, but Paul seemed to them, as he had seemed to Stephens, unimpressive.[4]

The view was not shared. Many thought Paul photogenic, the perfect subject for art. Halliburton, an artist with a camera, often photographed him, as did painter Leslie Powell, who may have intended to paint his portrait from it. Famous for a school of photography and the epochal *Monsters and Madonnas* (1936), Laguna Beach artist William Mortensen may have photographed him as he had Paul's friend William Alexander. WPA artist Don Forbes both drew and painted his picture. Alexander, who at one time thought about becoming a painter, often photographed him. A number of other photographs of professional quality survive, photographer unknown. Paul of course thought himself photogenic, and didn't believe everyone should be the subject of art. When Bill Alexander told him he intended to ask painter Don Forbes to do portraits of several of his family members, Paul snippishly retorted, "Don't you think that asking Don to paint your fat little nieces & nephews is on par with Dick's idea that Gene [MacCown] ought to paint his [equally fat] Park Avenue aunt?"[5]

Most remarkable of all known attempts to capture Paul was the bust done in 1932 by Charles Farrar from a life mask, and cast by Roman Bronze Works. Here Hellenistic realism is powerfully invoked; call it the "Last Vagabonder" or "Last Hitchhiker." The nose appears once broken, the upper lip appears slurred, even deformed, the result, evidently,

Bronze bust of Paul Mooney by Charles Farrar from life mask, 1932, Roman Bronze Works (courtesy John Murphy Scott).

of a well-heaved uppercut delivered in a sleazy back alley or scuzzy bar. A halo of experience rather than of innocence seems resident upon the steady, forward-looking head. Powerful, somber, with a hint of both debauch and the quixotic, Paul appears, if world-weary, also unflinchingly ready to face the next of life's challenges.[6]

A bizarre interpretation of Paul is painter Eugene MacCown's portrait. In a light-blue stripped turtle neck, Paul holds (presumably) the Farrar bust. Among the artist's portraits of expatriate Americans in Paris the most famous was the one he did of Nancy Cunard. MacCown may have seen Paul as the free-spirited male counterpart of Cunard herself. Yet, while the Cunard portrait luxuriates with sophisticated ladyhood, the Paul portrait lixiviates, if not in lye, with bleached heroism. An eeriness shrouds a subject one would think was cloaked in gaiety. Caravaggio's morally dark, enigmatic double self-portrait, of *David with the Severed Head of Goliath*, in which "a young, redeemed Caravaggio holds up the head of a sinful, middle-aged Caravaggio," compares as an earlier *doppelganger*. Closer to home is René Crevel's *Lady Mannequin Seeks and Finds a New Skin*; here the form of a figure is all there is to suggest the real person who implicitly is always changing. In the *Portrait of Paul Mooney*, Paul carries a likeness of himself, as if it were a helmet to be worn, or a trophy to be displayed. The idea carrying around an extra or spare identity may have seemed the perfect joke to MacCown, once the piano player of the "Ox on the Roof."[7]

Paul's mother Ione, who knew enough about art through Paul and daughter Evelyn, thought the MacCown portrait of her son "not so good." Commented Paul, in a letter to Alexander dated May 25, 1935, "The elongation of my face she finds especially objectionable, having known well all these years that she gave birth to a little roundhead." Paul found the portrait not entirely to his liking and hinted to his friend Bill Alexander, who by the way loved the MacCown painting, that MacCown threatened to do a painting of him. MacCown always remained close to Paul, and to his friend Bill Alexander whose copy of *The Siege of Innocence*, about Montparnasse recaptured, he inscribed to "Bill Alexander—belated, but still with affection, April 6, 1951."[8]

Paul told Alexander (then Levy) about his relationship with Richard Halliburton at least a year before Alexander actually met the famous travel writer. The year was 1932, and the place was the Barbizon-Plaza Hotel, on Lexington Avenue at 63rd Street, dubbed New York's "Most Exclusive Residence for Young Women." Halliburton at the time had every right to think himself lucky and blessed. He had a new book out. He had recently signed a contract with United Artists to shoot a movie entitled *India Speaks* by the same producers who had done *Africa Speaks* and for six weeks' acting he would receive $10,000. "A new house, a new book, a new movie," he could exult, "and ... in good health and good spirits–(I) had lots to be thankful for."[9]

Bill Alexander first met Richard Halliburton Saturday, October 22 or October 29, 1932. Or so he said. Halliburton had just given a lecture on the Taj Mahal to 2000 students at Greensboro, among other fun speaking engagements, and had "agreed [later] to accept $10,000 for six weeks' acting in a United Artist picture." By then, too, the menacing task of meeting the deadline was at last lifted from Halliburton, and The Flying Carpet would soon appear. Though Alexander, years later, recalled these events within the context of their meeting, he more likely met Halliburton the following January (1933) when these events were well past. The occasion was an evening performance of Oscar Wilde's risqué drama Salome, adapted for ballet. Featured were dance innovators Gluck Sandor (born Sammy Gluck) and Felicia Sorel, a husband and wife team, who, the year before, established the first professional American ballet company, The Dance Center. Earlier, Halliburton had delivered a lecture in one of the conference rooms off from the hotel lounge—probably to a group composed mainly of women who, through his features in such savvy magazines as Women's Home Journal, adored the writer. Now the writer himself was to be entertained, or to be provided foreplay. In the packed concert hall, he sat next to Paul in the front row. Directly behind them were Alexander and Charles Wolfsohn, who had secured the tickets from his "Uncle Leo."[10]

Exciting, innovative, and erotic, the dancing disturbed the audience more so than did the Richard Strauss music. Sandor's long black twiney hair snarled, his feet curved as the viperous oboes and flutes coiled and wound. "A visionary and spiritual sage of dance," writes choreographer Jerome Robbins' biographer Greg Lawrence, "Sandor also painted hauntingly vivid, Expressionist works." Dancer Jose Limon, who later joined Sandor's company, and whose vagabond life the writings of Richard Halliburton inspired, later called Salome, "with [its enhancing] Constructivist designs by Vincent Minelli," Sandor's choreographic "masterpiece."[11]

Limon, possibly at this very performance, watched as his protégé moved fearlessly about the stage. Limon called Sorel "an infinitely subtle blend of prurience and innocence." Another Sandor protégé, Jerome Robbins, certainly present at later renditions of the work, saw "Sorel as a cool intense foil to Sandor's wildness." While many found the performance "shocking," its raw ethnicity, pagan sensuality and dazzling mysticism thrilled Alexander. A zealot for weird drama, Charles Wolfsohn thought the drama mirrored his own jaded psyche. Paul, studious, amused, pointed out one stage detail or another to his friend Richard. At the climax, when John the Baptist's head—that is, Sandor's replicated head—was served up to King Herod on a platter, Alexander confessed that his blood curdled and that, in the lingo of the time, he got the "jitters." Necrophiliac, sado-masochistic, it was also a dry form of orgasm.[12]

After the performance Halliburton leapt on stage to congratulate the lead performers. Minutes later, Mooney brought his pals Alexander and Wolfsohn onstage and formally introduced them to Halliburton. These days, Halliburton could expect a party to follow a lecture, a show, or both. After one of his own celebrated lectures—actually an intimate chat about his travels with the better-heeled guests of the Barbizon-Plaza, he was invited as a guest of honor, along with famed singer Lawrence Tibbett, himself fresh off a performance of O'Neill's *The Emperor Jones*, to a "stag party" held by Charles Norris. The day, presumably, when Alexander met him, Halliburton had given a similar informal talk, then, later, had gone to see *Salome*.

The party that followed the *Salome* performance, however, was far less tame than the Norris party had been. After congratulations were exchanged, members of the troupe, and their retainers, along with Halliburton, Mooney, Wolfsohn and Alexander, adjourned upstairs to one of the hotel suites. While neither Alexander nor Wolfsohn offered details to me as to what happened next, both are clear as to the dramatic progression of events that led them from spectators of "depravity" to participants in it. Wolfsohn reported that he had met Halliburton earlier in the afternoon. Halliburton, acting "very conceited, snobbish," introduced himself to him as "Mr. Smith." Evidently, a solicitation followed, and the two decided to go out for dinner. "It was chilly outside," consistent with a time late in the fall, and Wolfsohn wore an "overcoat." "Mr. Smith," noting this, commented oddly that he had "pawned his own overcoat for a meal." When the two of them returned to the hotel and to a get-together thrown in a "Mr. Halliburton's behalf," a woman, seeing this Mr. Smith with Wolfsohn, exclaimed, "Oh, Dick! Dick Halliburton—how are you!?" Instantly, Wolfsohn, looking at him for the fool, muttered, "Smith, my ass!"

Though Halliburton freely circulated in the jet set of the gay world of his day, Charles Wolfsohn noted that "the closet rarely opened then." One did not use one's real name. Even so, Halliburton was to him "a strange guy." Wolfsohn also said he once ran into Halliburton at a bathhouse in Coney Island. "I'm slumming," Halliburton told him once their eyes met. Another time, Halliburton "tried to stop me and a friend from biting (i.e., fighting) one another." Though Halliburton tried breaking up what to him appeared less than clowning, Wolfsohn thought Halliburton "felt himself better than other people."[13]

For his part, Alexander thought the "orgy" that graced that night of nights a defining moment in his life; the *Salome* performance had served only as foreplay.

Present, among others, was body builder Leopold ("Uncle Leo"?) Dacelo or DeSola ("Sun Goddess"), an art consultant, photographer and writer for clean-living advocate Bernarr MacFadden, publisher of *Physical Culture*, *True Story*, and *Liberty*, the last of which published Richard's "French Foreign Legion" and "Death of the Czar" stories. MacFadden also was publisher of the *New York Evening Graphic* which, besides condemning sleaze, "reported on the gay scene using the rhetoric of moral outrage." A fitness guru, MacFadden recommended proper diet and exercise in a regimen that included fasting, abstaining from tobacco and alcohol, sleeping on the floor and frequent sex. Halliburton's "Athlete by Inspiration" was just the sort of feature MacFadden Publications solicited, and perhaps through a discussion of this and other writing projects he met muscle-man DeSola. DeSola became Richard's work-out companion and beach buddy. Later, when Wesley Halliburton met his son's hulking friend, he rested assured that at last his son had begun to chum with "a real man." Appearances concealed that Richard's relation with DeSola was as carnal as his relation with Paul. He was for Richard "the other man," as Bill Alexander was for Paul his "other man." Another he-man introduced into the mix was Tony Trapani—from all accounts, a physical fitness buff, airplane enthusiast, beach loafer and aspiring actor.[14]

Years later, Alexander, who likened himself to a swinger and hippie, recalled the scene at the Barbizon-Plaza with a satyr's grin. Openly promiscuous, he often bragged about his conquests, and their number. About Halliburton, with whom the evening at the hotel was his only intimacy, he remarked only that the author was "a proper Southern gentleman."[15]

Shortly after the *Salome* event, Paul, in Manhattan or Brooklyn, was struck down by a "wild taxi." While details of the accident remain unclear, his injuries were noted as two broken ribs, a cracked jaw and cracked skull, besides numerous bumps and bruises. Ordered to remain in bed till he had fully recovered, he apparently went against doctor's orders and met Richard in Kansas City. Soon the two moved into a "grand little house" on 2029 Pinehurst Road in Hollywood.[16]

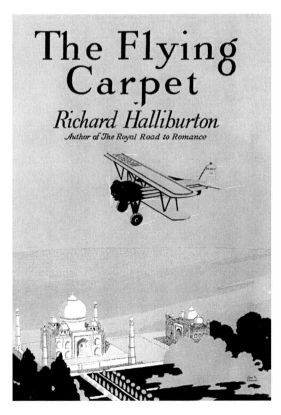

The Flying Carpet appeared late in November 1932. To celebrate its publication, Halliburton had dinner with Moye Stephens, his new wife and their family, all of whom were "overjoyed" by the book. Richard described Moye's wife as "tall and handsome and distinguished and rich—part Jewish, I hear." At the time Richard was shooting scenes at Griffith Park for the movie *India Speaks*, evidently deploring every other minute of it, and its producer, the "the dogmatic and graceless Walter Futter." Oddly, *India Speaks*

The dust jacket of *The Flying Carpet* (1932) was most eye-catching and a major selling point of the book itself (courtesy Lilly Library, University of Indiana, Bloomington, IN).

would be the only feature film Halliburton would ever make.[17]

9
Marvel-land

Richard had recently purchased a secondhand Ford convertible. Usually Paul drove. On Sunday, November 19, 1932, Richard and Paul visited Pancho Barnes at her San Marino estate. The three then proceeded to Ramon Novarro's home. Underway was a boisterous party. "A lot of drunken people were there," Richard said, "so we left early." Before leaving, he learned that Noel Sullivan was "almost sick" having to deal with the administration of the Phelan estate. Actually, Wesley added "sick" after he scratched out "broke," then decided not to publish the letter at all. Evidently he believed that a person's financial condition should not be a matter of public record.[1]

Thanksgiving Day, 1932, Richard and Paul drove some fifty miles down the coast, again with Pancho Barnes, to her summer home. Along the way, they parked by the oceanfront, "shed their clothes," and spent the day pulling clams from the rocks; these in turn were thrown into a pot for a nice Thanksgiving dinner. The mere mention of this incident in Richard's letters home adds charm to their incessant asides about royalties, radio shows, film opportunities and lecture stops. One must wonder then what impact these images had upon Halliburton's straight-laced parents. Richard may have gotten sick that day, as a trip to the doctor shortly after suggests. Happily, his health returned, and the doctors gave him "the grand send off." Paul, meanwhile, "sticking close to the fire," at Richard's Pinehurst Road address, nursed a sore throat. One must wonder, in this matter, what impact these living arrangements had on Richard's parents.[2]

Halliburton continued to watch and promote the sale of his books. In the spring of 1933, on a visit to San Francisco, he called his friend Noel Sullivan to see if he would be available to see him after a "shindig" at the Paul Elder Bookshop on 239 Post Street. At the time Sullivan and his companion Lem Sanderson lived on the corner of Hyde and Lombard in a house having some association with Robert Louis Stevenson. Richard himself found Sullivan, despite his new economic burdens, to be hale and hearty, and apparently not so broke. "The depression doesn't seem to have made either of us any thinner or any older," he told him.[3]

With Halliburton were Paul and Tony Trapani. Both "quite fell in love"

Tony Trapani, 1930. Trapani was a good friend to both William Alexander and Paul Mooney in the early 1930s, then disappeared (courtesy William Alexander).

with Sullivan, according to Richard, and wished him well. A lover of fancy automobiles and driving them fast, Sullivan probably had a good deal in common with Paul. He also had a devotion to Catholic subjects, which held some interest for Paul. The talk of glamorous parties, such as were held at Villa Montalvo, no doubt interested everyone. Sullivan had, at any rate, invited Richard and company to an expensive area restaurant. The bill "horrified" Halliburton: "Had I suspected it was such an expensive place you were inviting us to, I'd not have summoned so many of my motor party to join us. We'd been living on beans, & living in motor camps—& hardly knew how to behave with wine & frog's leg." They proceeded to Palo Alto, where they visited Charles and Kathleen Norris, also good friends of Sullivan's.[4]

Halliburton in 1932–1933 was nearing the apogee of his career. The film *India Speaks*, besides big money, promised him still wider exposure and film opportunities. A triumph at the box office it was not. As inter-cultural communication, the pseudo-documentary could hardly sit alongside Marguerite Harrison's pioneering *Grass: A Nation's Battle for Life* (1925), about the travels of the Bakhtiari tribe of Persia. Produced by Walter Futter, *India Speaks* was, first of all, filmed chiefly in Yosemite Park, not India or Tibet. The kitschy rose garden scene in which Halliburton, a cultured Westerner, woos his teenage co-star Rosie Brown, who plays a Kashmiri maiden, was itself filmed in Griffith Park, not far from Halliburton's Pinehurst address. The so-so film at least inspired the excellent book *India Speaks*, a photographic essay that used stills from the movie to recreate the sensuous rawness of Indian life and worship. The movie itself was again released in 1949, after India gained its independence from Britain, but then, as in 1932, a white man serenading a woman of color offended some. India itself is portrayed in the lobby posters as "Mother of 10,000 sins, where women are treated like cattle and where white girls are sacrificed to Buddha, where 20,000 Moslems thirsted for the blood of a white intruder." *Amen, Paul,* an amused hardcore facer-of-the-facts, might have remarked.[5]

Halliburton of course knew from the start that the film was a stinker. Earlier he had turned down an opportunity to "conduct a movie tropical news tour of South America." It was "too colorless," he said. He should have applied the same wisdom to his making *India Speaks*. His heart wasn't in it, nor was Rosie Brown's. During the tedious shootings they formed a warm off-screen friendship, and he encouraged her to finish her schooling and give up acting. A flash-by in *Gone with the Wind* honorably ended her career in films. *India Speaks,* for its part, suffered from poor timing; the idea of the very Anglo Halliburton courting an Indian woman during the last days of the British Raj struck a discord with viewers, as did Halliburton's shrill voice and arch pacing. Knowing full-well the movie's flaws, Halliburton still promoted the movie. He even introduced showings of it. From the New Roxy Theater in New York, he wrote home, on May 7, 1933, "Am I tired! This five-a-day personal-appearance business is the hardest work I've ever done. Our theater today has been moderately filled, about 2,000 people at each of the five performances. I speak about two and a half minutes and say, among other things, that 'not all the adventures in which I take part on the screen happened to me personally. I am chiefly an actor playing a part.'" Oddly, it never fully occurred to him that he had always been an actor playing a part. Watching the film, Halliburton noted only, "My voice sounds strange to me."[6]

Halliburton was never meant for pictures, and really didn't like how he came off in them anyway. Once Cecil B. de Mille inquired about film rights to *The Royal Road to Romance,* an offer which came to naught when Halliburton, effectively defeating the idea at the outset, asked for $50,000 and a starring role in the movie. Even the books on their own merits seemed not the stuff of popular audience appeal when translated into film. A film version of *The Glorious Adventure* starring Douglas Fairbanks, Sr. never came to fruition, though Fairbanks' *Mr. Robinson Crusoe* (1932) gives some hint, if one overlooks the actor's age, of the famed Defoe castaway as Halliburton had himself gallantly described him in *New Worlds to Conquer*. Halliburton of course liked to insinuate himself into the reputation of Fairbanks, as his Prince of Baghdad lectures, given at the time, suggest.[7]

Halliburton's letters home indicate his active well-being in Los Angeles or New York, among other spots associated with his busy life. He stopped home in Memphis once to see how construction on his parents' new home on Court Street was progressing. Back in Laguna Beach, he was buying fruit at a grocery when the Long Beach earthquake "flung me off my feet, with apples and canned beans and bread on top of me." That was the principal drama in a life of radio rehearsals, talks and book parties.[8]

Paul's work as a writing assistant was now a matter of routine. At home he worked, alongside Richard, as he continued to recover from his injuries slowly but surely. Walter Futter invited Paul and Richard to his home for Christmas dinner, December 1932, but, evidently, the two preferred spending that time in the desert. For $400 he bought a car, a used one, calling it "our new Ford convertible" with which Paul, also a chauffeur for the sake of form, "delivers and fetches me when I need him."[9]

In that car early in March 1933, Richard and Paul both took a motor trip across the country, going first to the Grand Canyon. In those days, white settlements were few. Tourists came in small numbers. Roads were especially rugged and services few and far between. One might still remember Major Powell and even James Mooney. Ellsworth L. Kolb's profusely illustrated *Through the Grand Canyon from Wyoming to Mexico* (1914) and Erna Fergusson's *Our Southwest* (1940) convey the land's untainted allure. Still, commercialism, as shown by the steady trickle of seemingly foreign visitors, had begun to etch the land of the Hopi and Navajo.[10]

On these and other excursions, Halliburton, sounding his ideas to Paul, as he was quite unable to do to Moye Stephens, continued in earnest to gather materials for his book about America, induced in part by "The Century of Progress" Fair that soon would open in Chicago. What he initially entitled "The Royal Road to the USA," then "My Own Country," and what critics would call the "romantic road to royalties," would become in part the first *Book of Marvels*. Halliburton entered the already packed arena of travel books about scenic America. Into this same arena would enter many notable books over the years: Edwin Markham's *The Real America in Romance*, Erskine Caldwell's and Margaret Bourke-White's *Say, Is This the U.S.A.*, to Walt Disney's *Mickey Sees the U.S.A.*, Douglas Brinkley's *The Magic Bus—An American Odyssey*, Charles Kuralt's *America*, and Bill Bryson's *Lost Continent—Travels in Small Town America*, just to name a few. In the 1930s, the Federal Writers Project of the WPA produced the New American Guide Series (notably *Vermont*, 1937). These were dense compared with the later American Mountain Series edited by Roderick Peattie, who, as author of *The Incurable Romantic*, added Halliburton's tonal presence (minus his patriotic dignifications) to the nine volumes that were eventually published.[11]

Against the gloom of hard times, and the engine-grinding cavalcade of the motoring rubber tramps, a new trail began for Paul and Richard, as later it would for Paul and William Alexander, whom Paul encouraged to move west.

Tourist camps, rundown motels and long stretches of drab terrain tainted the romance of it all. Yet as the automobile emancipated women, so too it exclaimed new freedom for everyone, at least theoretically. Excesses on the landscape offered the best in kitsch. Car dealerships and service stations—some octagonal pavilions of terra-cotta, others reminiscent of miniature palaces or gaudy wedding cakes—sprang up throughout the country to exalt the car culture and an America on the move. Savvy when it came to cars, Paul yielded easily to the supremacy of the house on wheels, and kept pace with the best of the automobile guides. Still, even to the most seasoned highwayman, cross-country travel was not without its perils.[12]

America's roads at this time might, with a good squint of the eyes, appear romantic—often enough they wended their way through terrific scenery. One need only look through a 1930s postcard pack of "National Highway U.S. 40," known as the "scenic and historic main street of America." Or read about celebrities who found sport and release from "motoring." While networks of good highways existed throughout the country, the American Automobile Association continued to call for an "intensive development of road construction on a national unified plan." Still, by the late 1920s, the nearly one thousand affiliated motor clubs in America—issuing roadway maps, offering itineraries and targeting highway conditions—could boast about the millions of tourists yearly on the road and the millions pumped into national parks. Responsive to these established facts, Rand McNally distributed an "Auto Road Atlas of the United States," available to the 15,000,000 or so motorists in America."[13]

In those days one still thought of neighbors who spoke to each other from adjoining porches or lawns; one thought of so-called family values and small mom-and-pop cafes. Towns and cities appeared demarcated, identifiable entities. They did not coalesce into one another, and one could get a feeling of where they began and ended. Dirt roads were often main roads. Megaplexes where one industrial compound connected in a complex steel and concrete web to the next seemed austere science fictions beyond the presages, even, of the 1939 New York World Fair's Democracity and Futurama. Gridlock was unknown. Collapsing in suburbia was equally unknown, even if urban congestion was not. As always, being nowhere meant being broke; Nowheresville might mean living in the woods in a log cabin with a brick stove far from modern conveniences and bill collectors.[14]

Gathering material for a book tentatively entitled the "Royal Road to Romance in America" continued. Paul snapped pictures. Both he and Richard took notes. Once finished in Arizona, the two drove through Utah into Colorado, onward into Kansas, then finally through the heartland of America to territory most familiar to them. Eventually they stopped in Memphis, where Richard again may have tried to "sell" Paul to his parents. "It's surprising how well we get along," he again may have assured them. Their journey coincided with the promise of better times in America. A new president, Franklin Delano Roosevelt, offered bold prospects, a new dispensation.[15]

Inklings of a renewed America through a discovery of its past would temper their outlook. The resulting book, however, would "need a lot more definition," but it was clear that Paul was an abler travel companion than Moye Stephens had been. Paul was urbane, spontaneously articulate; with Paul at his side, Richard had someone off whom he could bounce ideas. Later in July 1933, as part of the research tour, he and Paul took motor trips through southwestern Virginia to the Blue Ridge Mountains. There they spent the afternoon at Natural Bridge, in a region once surveyed by George Washington (whose bicentennial Paul and Richard celebrated just by being there) and granted later to Thomas Jefferson. It miffed Paul that he had to pay a dollar admission fee to this natural wonder when the Grand Canyon experience had been free. Grumbling, he paid, and grumbling he saw. From here the two proceeded to Jamestown, then Yorktown, where they toured the famous battlefield. Next, Williamsburg, restored by Rockefeller funding to its splendor as the colonial capital of Virginia, especially delighted Halliburton. They visited Monticello in Charlottesville, White Mountain, Virginia, and the Mountain School Music Festival, then Roanoke. The next-to-last stop was Washington, D.C., Paul's home, and "one of the brightest memories of [Halliburton's] boyhood." Besides the hallowed monuments, Halliburton visited Paul's family, who seemed impressed by his good manners and reputation. That Paul and Richard were homosexuals mattered to them in the least. A last stop was Old Alexandria, Virginia, and the address Richard had given his father, 502 Duke Street.[16]

For extended periods of time, Paul and Richard separated, at some point Paul joining Bill Alexander in New York, Richard joining Leopold DeSola on Long Island. They were never monogamous. In letters home, Richard mentioned going to the beach and to the movies with DeSola ("Leo"). Also at this time, Richard joined the YMCA—wishing he had done so long ago—and spent his afternoons now basking on the rooftop in the hot New York sun.[17]

Sun, and the sunnier side of things—Halliburton was a genteel realist, blissfully unaware of the many vexing events of the day. The more pleasant side of things fed him. From the Scottsboro case of 1932, the Bonus Army marches on Washington, D.C., in 1931, FDR's election in 1932, Upton Sinclair's run for governor of California in 1934, to the Goodyear strike in 1937, one does not hear a peep from him; good prospects must counter dismal forecasts.

Still, what should one make of a book entitled "The Royal Road to Romance in the USA" in 1933? Social and economic outlooks had shifted dramatically from the days of the Coolidge prosperity. "Chronic unemployment," wrote one observer, "meant that hundreds of thousands of young people who normally would have been absorbed into farms, factories, and offices found all doors closed." Hobos were of all ages, and from all walks of life, and they intermingled; they slept in doorways, hopped freight trains, loafed about on the streets, drifted into the Salvation Army, or managed a night or two at the YMCA.[18]

In 1925 the road was an attractive lure to those locked in a dull work or classroom routine, to those unable to loosen themselves from the bonds of a life of drudgery; by 1930, the road had become the dreaded fate of the many who had lost their job or who were unable to afford school, of many who saw dull work or classroom routine as salvation, not release. "Henry Ford, who put 75,000 men out of work and on the road as 'hoboes' in search of work, said of the husbands of the hundreds of thousands of wandering men, women, and children, 'Why, it's the best education in the world for those boys, that traveling around! They get more experience in a few months than they would in years at school.'" In reality, however, royal roads only held romance when they were an option, not a necessity.[19]

Richard's contemporary Louis-Ferdinand Céline had a vision far less royal. The globally cosmopolitan and seamy novels *Journey to the End of Night* and *Death on the Installment Plan* explore the off-the-edge other side of the coin, to which (I suspect) Paul could easily and willingly relate. While Halliburton had a sense of the international political situation, being political was not of interest to him; he in fact thought it a matter of some maturity to have no opinion at all. Given his public image, he would have appeared a loser to his fans for exploring dark themes. Life's joys, not its futilities, were his domain.[20]

10

Vagabondia

Halliburton remained busy throughout 1933; in Toronto a lecture on Rupert Brooke, in New York supper with Lowell Thomas and a preview of his movie *Mussolini Speaks*, supper with satirist Corey Ford, interview with a Russian princess, in Boston a book party at Jordan Marsh's, in Washington, D.C., a chat with President Hoover who was surrounded by six bodyguards, lunch with Huey Long. He was always on the go: "train [from Washington, D.C.] to Cleveland, plane from Cleveland to Memphis, the same plane next day from Memphis to L.A." Back to Laguna Beach again—and the Long Beach earthquake, then another speaking engagement at the Breakfast Club in San Diego where Moye Stephens and his wife were on hand, later a motor trip to Hollywood to do a radio show, two days in Yosemite, two more in San Francisco, a visit to Kathleen and Charles Norris in Palo Alto, a night in Santa Barbara, then New York again, and all points to and from there. His was a life punctuated by maddening rush-rush-rush. A glimpse into any of his letters at this time shows him in the thick of things. He replaced Lowell Thomas as a speaker before an annual Boy Scout dinner in Middletown, New York. In bookstores, noted Wesley, was the "large book, quarto size, of still pictures from *India Speaks*, with the long dramatic captions in which Richard was so adept." A later speaking engagement was at the Baltimore Blind School. "They all knew my stories from braille," Richard commented later. Starting the year had been a poetry banquet, a meeting with Mrs. Nelson Doubleday, and a male-only banquet for famed opera singer and film actor Lawrence Tibbett. In spring, he met with *Cosmopolitan* editor Tom Gavin, sat in at a Pulitzer Prize dinner, and continued to gripe with producer Walter Futter about the poor box office receipts from *India Speaks*. These highs and lows were followed by discussions with Fox Studios about a series of shorts on "royal roads," a beer at the New York Harvard Club with James Eliot Roosevelt after the latter had given a Board of Trade talk ("not a good speaker but a heavyish mind"), and back and forth to Alexandria where Paul stayed when he was not up north himself gallivanting around with his Coxsackie friends. He continued to be a prolific letter writer turning out some seventy-five letters, according to his count, in one day. Plans again were underway, as seemed routine, to send his parents on another trip to Europe. They had just returned from a long trip abroad, and, in all, were nearly as traveled as their son, who zealously arranged their trips.[1]

Towards the end of summer, Richard traveled for the first time to the Chicago "Century of Progress" World's Fair where he met both his mother and his father. His plan was to have Leo DeSola and a friend of his, who would pay for gas and oil, join him and Paul on the trip. By this time the Ford convertible, probably still unpaid for, was sputtering to its death. Eventually he gave it to Paul, conceivably in the belief that it might become a collectible, but, more likely, he thought it high time he buy himself a new car. Alas, he soon had a holy trinity of materialism, "a house and a car ('a swell little second-hand Dodge coupe') and a job (my *child* book)."[2]

Paul liked world fairs and was spiritually connected to them through his father, an adviser of cultural exhibits for the Columbian Exposition in Chicago in 1893 and, again, for the St. Louis Exposition in 1904. Wrote Forrest Wilson of the 1893 Exposition (and it could apply too to the St. Louis Exposition as well): "it was for America a spiritual interlude in the materialism that began its growth after the Civil War—a draft of nectar, incredibly sweet and exhilarating" and though it soon "passed, and its memory faded ... it left in America an adolescent thirst for beauty and hunger for culture that the country has not yet outgrown." Its "courts and colonnades represented to the average visitor nothing less than his vision of heaven." With its theme of science and the blessings of technological progress, the Chicago's 1933–1934 Century of Progress Exposition would be as grand, if not quite as heavenly, as that earlier awakening of the Midwest to the world's many diverse cultures.[3]

The famed Avenue of the Flags stressed its international character. Attractions included the Electrical Building, Horticultural Area, Diorama of the Mesozoic Age (featuring dinosaurs as in the famed Sinclair Exhibit), Oriental Village, the Travel Building, Hall of Religion, the Breathing Dome of the Travel and Transport Building, Streets of Paris, the Private Train of the President of Mexico (and its Dining Salon), Old Fort Dearborn (and Lincoln homes), the Belgium Village, an Electrical Fountain, and innumerable other material paeans to human ingenuity "to celebrate a century of the growth of science, and the dependence of industry on scientific research." Brainchild of world-traveler and millionaire showman Robert Ripley, the Odditorium featured numerous "Believe-It-Or-Not" exhibits most people had only read about in its creator's popular column. Were P.T. Barnum alive he would have figured as the adman with the oddments' only competition.[4]

Altogether the Century of Progress displayed in miniature the past and the present through a maze of wizardry and technology; it was all-time and all-the-world, to many Americans, brought to a convenient doorstep. And, from the Skyride, as from a mechanical bird in flight, one could dream to the vanishing point of modern technology and the limits of human weal.

Before television dulled vision, and the mind's eye, the Century of Progress—called "a riot of color"—must have dazzled. All was sensuous, immediate, festive—the whole world, of the past, the present, and the future, crammed into a tiny space. The enormous audio-visual entertainment center offered an education the dull classroom could hardly suggest, let alone match. "At the end of the Avenue of Flags, that is to say at the main entrance of the fair, was John Storr's *Knowledge Combatting Ignorance*." Indeed, a giant Promethean, boldly nude and well endowed, appeared ready to strike the serpent coiling about his right leg. "The two huge white figures against a brilliant blue background suggested a neo-archaic Heracles and the Hydra," notes Allen Weller. "The repeated vertical panels and the scalloped border were characteristic Art Deco patterns."[5]

Then the exhibits: "The World a Million Years Ago," "Old Heidelberg Inn on Leif Erickson Drive," "The Streets of Paris (and its Café de la Paix and Café de la Rotonde)," "The Atlantic and Pacific Carnival," "The Oriental Village on the Midway," "The Lion Motordrome—on the Midway," "The Old Plantation—on the Midway," "Seminole Indian Village—on the Midway," "Abe Lincoln's Birthplace (Replica)," "The Maya Temple—The Nunnery of Uxmal," "The House of Tomorrow (Steel and Glass)." These just for starters! Halliburton's, Paul's, and Bill's worlds were all enshrined here in what eons hence might be viewed as the La Brea discoveries of 20th century technology—all another phase of the disenchantment of the world through science.[6]

Nudity, peep shows, and exotica everywhere met the eye. Beside the balusters of Science and Technology were the meretrixes of Burlesque and the Risque. One could come and see Little Egypt in "The Streets of Cairo" or Sally Rand as "Lady Godiva astride a white horse" and later as a fan dancer nude behind nothing but two huge ostrich feather fans. And, alas, the "Colonie Nudiste." And what fun might it be if one were unable to "meet the nudists face to face?" Chicago's Mayor Edward J. Kelly, visiting "The Oriental Village" and other exhibits, recommended that they be toned down. "Mistress of Ceremonies" Texas Guinan protested that the stuffed-shirt fair officials were "trying to put fun and pleasure on a business schedule."[7]

Unmistakably "located between the Hall of Science and Soldier's Field" stood the Potola built in the mid–seventeenth century by the Manchu Emperor Ch'ien-lung. A faithful replica of the now-crumbling Golden Pavilion of Jehol with its "Laughing Buddha" and Throne Chair, the temple, completed in Peking, was then transported in 28,000 pieces, and re-erected in Chicago. The Chinese Village on Treasure Island at the San Francisco Exposition of 1939 could boast the Altar of the Green Jade Pagoda, but America's mid section had given Paul, as it would give multitudes, his first glimpse of China and Lamaistic Tibet.[8]

During his visit, Paul stayed with older sister Ione, whose husband, Jack Scott, had unexpectedly died in 1928, and her in-laws. His younger sister Eire, meanwhile, was attending the University of Wisconsin in Madison, and it is possible that they took turns visiting one another. Bill Alexander, chasing after

OFFICIAL

PICTURES

OF A Century of Progress
Exposition

Photographs by Kaufmann & Fabry Co.
Official Photographers

THE REUBEN H. DONNELLEY CORPORATION
CHICAGO

William Alexander pulling a rickshaw with passenger at the Century of Progress World's Fair in Chicago, 1933.

Paul, also stayed with the Scotts or, as he later said, at the fairgrounds themselves behind a bench or on one. While Paul wrote, or roamed, Bill worked either at the Japanese Pavilion or Streets of Paris (possibly at both), the latter of which provided Alexander with his first glimpse of fan dancer Sally Rand "and Her Boys." He also worked for Texas Guinan, at her restaurant, but, he said, he was fired as soon as she discovered he was Jewish. He also posed for pictures in front of this or that exhibit. The title page of the *Official Pictures of the Century of Progress Exposition* shows a young man in shorts and ivy-leaguer pulling a rickshaw with a plumpish, panama-hatted businessman aboard: Bill is pulling the rickshaw. Paul himself sat for one of those "Movie-Of-U" pictures; made to fit snugly in the palm, when tilted, Paul winks, smiles or grins luridly.[9]

Alexander later attached to the whole Chicago experience the special meaning that he had gone there as part of a master plan, not to be near Paul, but to hitchhike up to Taliesin in Spring Green, Wisconsin, and enroll in Frank Lloyd Wright's architecture school. In truth, he never served an apprenticeship there. He had written to the famed architect, and said later that he had spent time with him "as a protege (or worker), not apprentice." His teachers in architectural design at NYU included the stellar name of Ely Jacques Kahn. He also worked briefly for father of the skyscraper Raymond Hood, whose death the next year, at age fifty-one, was a tragic loss to the profession. Whether at Taliesin for two weeks or six months (as he claimed), Alexander was told by Wright himself that

Paul Mooney at Gettysburg, New York, 1934. Photograph taken by William Alexander (courtesy William Alexander).

he should return to NYU and complete his degree, advice Alexander heeded.[10]

Upon graduation in 1934, he received a couple commissions. While employed at the firm of his brother Joseph Levy, Jr., a licensed architect, he assisted in the survey of the WPA–sponsored Slum Clearance Project in Brooklyn. The following year, as a junior engineer working in the Bronx, he designed the conversion of Fort Schuyler into the New York Maritime College as well as did a photographic essay of its buildings. Pictures he took of Fort Schuyler show an embattled structure with cannons, probably from the Civil War, lying on the ground near ripped-open fields or trenches. Also nearby while he engaged in these labors was his friend Paul. From the ruins of Fort Schuyler, Bill, with Paul, went west to tour the battlefield at Gettysburg. Here, as at Fort Schuyler, Bill snapped a number of pictures of his photogenic friend. One shows him leaning against the axle of a breach-loading Civil War cannon. Stoic, thoughtful, as if contemplating human destiny in the face of war, he appears a descendant of Stephen Crane's protagonist in *The Red Badge of Courage*.[11]

11

Mask of Celebrity

By 1935 Halliburton was at the height of his popularity. More than half a million people had by now heard him lecture. Through the Bell Newspaper Syndicate, 40 leading papers throughout America ran full-page spreads every Sunday for a year featuring his latest adventures, one of the largest orders ever given to a correspondent in journalism. He now "traveled for ideas," and had only "to fill a page every week for 52 weeks—about whatever I please." Despite the popularity of these features, the book formed from them, *Seven League Boots*, proved a dud in the marketplace. The book seemed a hodgepodge: life on Devil's Island, the Battle of the *Monitor* and *Merrimac*, the massacre of the Romanoffs, the Sultana of Turkey, Minoan Crete, Haile Selassie, Halliburton (as Hannibal) crossing the Alps on an elephant from a Paris zoo, and so on. Written "with the same contagious zest, the same charm and swing and dash that ... won such unrivaled popularity for his other tales," the book unfolded with the glib ease of Halliburton's (and Mooney's) finest writing. The image of the author as a mahout aboard an elephant he alternately named the "Elephantessa" or "Miss Dalrymple" is an enduring one. Close in spirit to the *Royal Road*, the book itself is a sort of last chapter to the spirit of romantic travel it brilliantly represented.[1]

If *The Flying Carpet* was less than Richard Halliburton's own work in letter and spirit, he determined that his next book would be his own. Nevertheless, Paul remained in the cutting room. After considerable discussion with Halliburton, Paul persuaded him to remove "one little gem out of the chapter on the Romanoffs." He simply "refused to *keep on working on a book* that would contain it [italics mine]." Paul's editorial guidance was everpresent.[2] Paul's veto power, which he used to uphold the Halliburton style of the earlier books, kept the book from becoming a polemic. One example may serve to illustrate:

> I asked a fifteen-year-old schoolboy what they were taught in school about America and western Europe.
>
> "We are taught the history of the Communist revolutionary movement in America and England," he said.
>
> "No other history?" I asked.
>
> "History is just the lives of kings and capitalists. There is nothing in it about the working classes."

This distortion of "education" practiced in Russia, the direction of education by fanatics, struck me as forcefully and unpleasantly as anything I saw. Not a day passed in my travellings about, that I did not talk through my interpreter with children and students. And the moment the fact came out that I was an American citizen, the children looked at me with pitying reproach.

"Why," they ask, "did you torture and execute those two innocent men, Sacco and Vanzetti. Why do you keep Mooney [labor activist Thomas J. Mooney] in prison when he is innocent? Why do you wish to lynch those innocent strikers, and gas innocent veterans who wish to petition your President?"

These questions, and these only, are asked any American who meets and talks with young Russians. They have learned no other information about America, for they are not allowed to learn. No wonder they look upon America as a savage and sadistic land that spends its time thinking up new torments for its enslaved working classes.[3]

Fans of Halliburton must have found these political lessons, though informative, uncharacteristic of him. Despite discouragement from Paul, Richard aimed to reach a next step with his writing, that of educator, just as Will Rogers, in his own cracker barrel style, kept many Americans informed of the key issues of the day. Certainly his story "Communism Comes to America" struck a different chord with readers.[4]

These days Richard and Paul were as much together as they were apart. The letters that Paul wrote to his friend Bill Alexander from 1935 to 1937 bear various addresses, because he was on the road a good deal: his home in Washington, D.C., the Nautilus Club at Atlantic Beach on Long Island, the Vanderbilt Hotel (Park Avenue and Thirty-fourth Street), the Standish Arms Hotel in Brooklyn, and 1823 North Vine Street, Hollywood, California (c/o Cather). The most curious is the Cather address. It suggests an association with novelist Willa Cather, herself Nebraska born.[5]

While Richard traveled, Paul, when not in Alexandria, stayed in New York's famous Chelsea Hotel, a haven for writers and artists. Perhaps here he met writer John Treville LaTouche (1914–1956) and other members who eventually fell into Latouche's widening circle of friends. LaTouche, later the lyricist of "Taking a Chance on Love" and the opera The Ballade of Baby Doe, was quickly admitted into the circle of composer (and Chelsea resident) Virgil Thomson, whom he knew well. A best friend was Jane Bowles; he was also chummy with her husband, Paul Bowles. Bill Alexander, who apparently had a relationship with LaTouche, also knew the Bowleses, both of whom were, then, aspiring writers.[6]

While Paul was in New York, perhaps meeting these and other talents, his mother, meanwhile, had fallen gravely ill and, for a time, was given a series of transfusions to rally her from near death. From her home in Washington, she was moved to a hospital in Cleveland, Tennessee, expressly because she was "bored" and presumably to convalesce. In April, she went to her daughter Evelyn's "cabin in Norris Dam," a rustic area just south of Knoxville, Tennessee, where she arrived "just in time for a local cyclone." Paul, sounding Wolfean, wrote of traveling to the "great bosom of my mother's family" to be at her side.

Slowly she regained her health, but the experience, while it made her stronger, left him dazed and depressed. About this time Paul met Danilo, his brother-in-law, and evidently made a pass at him. Danilo, at the time, worked at a state park which was associated with the TVA, and, almost certainly, spoke with Paul on America's national parks.[7]

During vacant moments in Washington, Paul edited manuscripts or proofs, some of whose very *raison d'être* he questioned: "The world is whirling with bad books," he wrote to Alexander, "and this last-moment struggle with the worst of them leaves me not one second to see you—unless, by some miracle, we get together tonight at dinner time."[8]

In late April or early May 1935, Paul traveled north to Lenox, Massachusetts, an upscale town in the Berkshire mountains known for its wondrous gardens and grand country estates; here, for instance, was novelist Edith Wharton's palatial mansion *The Mount*. Paul, who had first come to Lenox the previous fall, did not adapt as well to his luxurious surroundings as did Henry James when he arrived by chauffeur to the Wharton estate thirty years before, but, like Nathaniel Hawthorne, who had completed *The House of Seven Gables* here, he seemed determined to accomplish some work in progress. The house where he stayed was, in his words "a maze of wires and call-bells—under the rugs, dangling from ceiling, lurking on the walls, hidden beneath pillows." He noted that he could not "so much as slump in the Johnny or turn over in [his] sleep without summoning a delegation of the mere handful of servants, which [he said] is probably just great if you're used to it, but give me the jitters." Clearly too much wealth and convenience oppressed him. However, he said "the countryside is superb—little 'mountains' all colored with autumn, and a quietness. The natives aggregate perhaps a billion in wealth, which they could have saved at the rate of a dollar a year a piece, for they are venerable specimens—the women rattling with jet, the men crawling with verminous spaniels. There is nothing to do except work—moderately; eat, with less moderation; and walk to the Bird Sanctuary and the Nature Museum. Ask me anything you want to know about birds. Next week I'm taking up rocks; the week after, bark."

Lenox each day grew on his nerves, and he missed New York and the Chelsea Hotel. He told his friend Bill Alexander that he had "stolen" from the house what he believed was a volume of the original edition of Audubon's *Mammals of North America*, remarking on its "colored prints that are pretty gay." He lamented that it was one of a three-volume set and that he had searched for the remaining two volumes "from attic to outhouse" without luck. "You'll just have to get along with fewer mammals," he said.[10]

Birds, rocks, bark and mammals kept him from pondering more wearying thoughts. Left-wing politics, the Party line, revolution, art funding and the plight of the working classes were inescapable topics of conversation among writers and thinkers of the time as were banking, capitalism, trade unions, the gold standard and mechanization a generation or so earlier. What Floyd Dell had said characterized the social magazine *The Masses*—"fun, truth, beauty, realism, freedom, peace, feminism, revolution"—characterized the thinking of many intellectuals of the day. Clifford Odets' award-winning play *Waiting for Lefty* (1935), about a New York taxi cab union that moves to strike, contains many of the themes: the inherited miseries of capitalism, the gradual movement towards mass demonstrations, and the will of everyday people to foster their own or new rules. Police and fire squads attempted to suppress *Lefty* where it played to packed houses in Boston, Philadelphia and New York.[11]

Injustices in America had attuned Paul to the political realities of a capitalist democracy still on trial, and to its fragility. Wrote Maxwell Bodenheim: "True villagers" wove "endless carpets of conversation, embroidered with strange designs for living taken from Sappho, Buddha, Plato, Oscar Wilde, T.S. Eliot, Tolstoy, the Marquis de Sade and Spengler. (Villagers discovered Marx in the thirties during the Great Depression)." Add Hermann Broch, whose *The Sleepwalkers* (1932) was a thinly fictionalized look into the growing moral decadence that led to Germany's takeover under Hitler. Each title of the trilogy—*The Romantic* (1888), *The Anarchist* (1903) and *The Realist* (1918)—could, as Freud's three divisions of the psyche, aptly describe the three combined political outlooks of Paul. Paul owned a copy of the book.[12]

Paul's friend Bill Alexander, who chummed with outspoken socialist Mrs. Algernon Polan Banks (wife of the famed writer of the time) and other free-thinkers, later said, "I knew endless people in the C[ommunist] P[arty]. I never went to any of their meetings, but I sympathized with what they had to say." Paul could say as much; he probably attended their meetings as well. Years later, when financial success widened the door of philanthropy to him, Alexander tended to recall fondly his early flings with socialist thinking, and his slightly untrue rags-to-riches roots. Yet his socialism appears to have gone no further than his introducing Harry Hay to Shostakovich's *Fifth Symphony*, a patriotic thriller which the Soviet composer, accused in 1936 of being "politically heterodox," had written "to rehabilitate himself in the eyes" of Stalinist attackers of free speech. Earlier Paul had probably introduced Alexander to both Shostakovich and Stalin.[13]

Among artists and appreciators of art, including Paul and Bill Alexander, the "in thing" at the time was wondering how the government art money was being spent and what freedom in the arts meant. As an active journalist, Paul was himself as concerned, as René Crevel had been, in government laissez-faire regarding free expression in the arts.

Socialist and communist thinking was endemic to the immigrant communities of New York, where the First International of America had taken root. Capitalist democracy by the 1930s had undergone numerous stresses and strains. Responsive to the ubiquitous socialist remedies chanted by radicals and reactionaries alike were some top Roosevelt appointees, advisors, and supporters, besides of course FDR himself. Social democratic broadsides bombarded from every direction in those days. The economic despair that gripped America in the 1930s offered them a ready backdrop. Bread lines, farm forfeitures, and tension-fraught standoffs between management and labor accentuated that despair as did the ambiguous role of the government in the labor movement, libertarian rights and economic policy in general.[14]

A patchwork of liberal socialist ideas framed in the simplest terms formed Alexander's own thought, a good deal of it put there by Paul. This is not to say Alexander was a dummy; this is only to say that he was not as deep as Proudhon, as Luxembourg, as Liebknecht, as Jaures. Few are. He had learned, through his studies at NYU and through discussions with Paul, that advances in production technology were no salve to the miseries of the unemployed. He knew that political equality did not also mean economic equality. He knew that an intrinsic harmony between capitalism and equal rights existed only ideally. He understood why anti–Communist America might be reluctant to ally itself with Communist Russia against anti–Communist Nazi-Germany. Sort of.[15]

Bill uttered catch phrases, Paul could expand them. Bill heard the beat, Paul the timbre. Bill was exclamatory, Paul subtle. Alexander's socialist comments echoed Paul's own; they also kept memory of his best friend alive, at least for him. Alexander was not a ramifier, as his friend and mentor Paul could be, but rather applauded the grandeur of a generality. *Love thy neighbor as thyself* made perfect sense to him, but in no way could he design a program aimed at economic equality. He believed in the impetus behind something called the National Recovery Act; he saw merit, for sure, in the Civilian Conservation Corps and the Works Projects Administration. He believed that these were crisis-intervention programs that might linger but need not last. The national socialism inherent in FDR's domestic economic policies urged all thinking Americans to reexamine their political allegiances. Mainstream magazines, such as *Life*, noted in a friendly manner of address the ability of Hitler, Mussolini, Stalin and FDR to charm and manipulate audiences. Influential public figure Will Rogers, upon returning from Russia, could marvel, in his own decidedly folksy way, how in Russia, despite the fact that people there who go "against the system" were killed, *everyone worked*. People in America took heed.[16]

Some of Paul's ideas, in their original form now nearly irrecoverable, inspired in part the achievement of another friend. Harry Hay (1914–2002), an outspoken Communist Party member and eventual gay rights activist who founded the Mattachine Society, recalled Mooney as a "handsome Lothario, with beautiful young men trekking up and down the hill to the house he [later] shared with his lover [Halliburton] in Laguna." Wanton elderly boy with a touch of satyriasis, rather than Lothario, might have been a better way of putting it. Besides pro-labor and anti–Nazi campaigning, Hay had by this time accumulated a number of curious claims to fame known to Paul. He had sung some of the first songs composed by his friend John Cage (1912–1992), these for the Santa Monica Women's Club (later, the California Composer's Circle). Also he had worked as a "male understudy" for eight actors in George R. Arthur's Playhouse Repertory Theatre. While involved in theater writing and production, he appeared as a stunt rider in B films, sufficient accomplishment, one would think, to recommend him to any Pancho Barnes–hosted party. Years later, in 1941, when Bill Alexander lived on Morton Street in New York, Hay fell in love with him, and left his wife to devote himself fully to the relationship. Talk of "isn't it a small world" followed Hay's spotting on Bill's wall the painting Bill took with him wherever he went, the MacCown portrait of Paul.[17]

Soon each shared his recollections of Paul. If Harry Hay's run-in with Bill was a meeting of the bodies, his run-in with Paul, in 1932, had been a meeting of the minds. He referred to Paul as his "first big gay brother." Often the two of them "talked til dawn many nights." Topics included sexual freedom issues and the creation of rural sanctuaries, the Coxsackie experience offering an instance where gay men from all walks of life might congregate to discover their true selves. The basic ideology of the group later founded by Hay and called the Radical Faeries had its roots in these discussions. Drawn as he was to Paul spiritually, Hay, long after their acquaintanceship, declared that he was not Paul's "physical type"; however, "mentally [they were] well-matched."[18]

Hay's later interest (after 1950) in Native American studies may have been first inspired by his knowing Paul. In 1934 Hay joined the Communist Party; previously, while at Stanford, he majored in drama and read widely the leftist literature available to him. Undoubtedly a main current of his talks with Paul was politics and in particular gay rights, possibly spiced up with comments about this fellow or that. Topic people might have included journalist Dorothy Thompson, author of the anti–Nazi booklet *I Saw Hitler* (1932), and Sinclair Lewis ("one of the foremost American novelists" and one who "exercise(s) considerable influence on American public opinion"), whose *It Can't Happen Here* (1935) fanned liberal Democratic fears. Though appearing in published form later than the time of Hay's talks with Paul, Lewis' questions were ones other political observers shared: "If America gets a dictator will your husband be put in a concentration camp, will you have to stop going to church, will your property be confiscated, and will your daughter lose her job?" "Third Sex" rights were inevitable topics of discussion and, in their context, Paul must be seen as an early disputant, even party-line formulator, of the American gay rights movement of which Hay was a chief architect. Both had to have been noddingly familiar with the theories of Sigmund Freud, Havelock Ellis and (I dare) Floyd Dell's *Love in the Machine Age—A Psychological Study of the Transition from Patriarchal Society* (1930), which appeared about the time they met. Both surely knew of the famous Institute for Sexual Science ("Sexual Wissenschaft") founded shortly after the war in Berlin by Dr. Magnus Hirschfeld; both surely knew of Paragraph 175 of

Opposite: **Paul Mooney in hardhat, 1934, some 220 feet above the water on the Oakland Bay Bridge (courtesy William Alexander).**

the German Criminal Code, which concerned the punishment in store for men who committed homosexual acts.[19]

Knowledge of Paul's political views derives largely from Alexander's recollections of them. Like his contemporary Aldous Huxley, he was (I think) a democratic socialist. Huxley's descriptions in *Brave New World* (1932) of embryo wards producing "designer people," as factories manufactured "designer clothes," would have accorded perfectly with Paul's mordant sense of humor; these embryo wards would, moreover, have fitted in as perfect exhibits in tomorrow's World Fair. Paul was also (I think) a roughed socialist from the Jack London mold—the Depression tilted many in this direction, believing that there were "all sorts of men ... cast adrift by their masters like so many old horses." Like London, he was "content to labor, crowbar in hand, shoulder to shoulder, with intellectuals, idealists, and class-conscious workingmen, getting a solid pry now and again and getting the whole edifice rocking." At least photographs of Paul in hardhat and overalls, as he stands some 220 feet above the water spanned by the newly-built Oakland–San Francisco Bridge, imply some of that idealized proletarian camaraderie.[20]

Though interested in the Russian experiment, Paul, like Huxley, was anti–Communist; a mild case of Russophilia (if only through his probable admiration of American journalist John Reed), he was hardly "Veni, Vidi, Bolsheviki." Perhaps Paul talked about those who had dark visions of the future. Together the two may have watched the May Day Parade down Broadway in 1936. "Fellow WORKERS, join our RANKS!" the marchers chanted. "It was a Communist thing," noted budding young novelist Mary Mc-

Double Portrait of Paul Mooney by Eugene MacCown, 1934 (courtesy William Alexander).

Carthy, who was herself present.[21]

12

"I Knew Hitler"

What would follow for Paul was a Nazi thing, and it put in the forefront all the skills he had acquired as a ghostwriter.

In 1934 or 1935 he agreed to assist a defector from Nazi Germany in the writing of an exposé of the Fuehrer. Breathing a sigh of relief, Paul noted "the fifteen percent of royalties which the job will bring me," adding that the money would provide "useful salvage from the wreck of last winter's work." At the time both he and Richard were "fairly broke." The autobiography *I Knew Hitler*, chronicling Hitler's rise to power, for a moment rescued them from the bread lines.[1]

Literary agent Maxwell Aley, who knew editors at Scribners including Maxwell Perkins, and knew Paul had worked on *The Flying Carpet*, could very well have been the contact person. Because of such a book's financial promise, Halliburton himself could have encouraged his friend to accept the offer. Late in 1934, he had visited Berlin, and watched with a curious eye the changes that had occurred in Germany since his last visit there in 1922. Showing a masterful lack of partisanship, he reported that the "older people seem very cool about Hitler, but the kids are all maniacs on the subject—and they will be in command in a few years."[2]

Besides the money, the subject of the Machiavellian rise of Hitler from obscurity to world leader appealed to Paul. Also, it gave him an opportunity to examine the "hidden Hitler." His name would nowhere appear in the book that was after all the true narrative of a homosexual ex–Nazi who believed in the rumors of Hitler's own gender preferences and their providing a basis for his tyrannical behavior.[3]

Subtitled *The Story of a Nazi Who Escaped the Blood Purge*, the book's ostensive author was one Kurt G.W. Ludecke. Well-traveled, charming, a revolutionary and a man with newspaper credentials, he "had lectured to Germans and German-Americans in Montreal, Toronto, New York and other places." In 1926, he found himself in California, "seeking retreat with the Franciscan monks at the Mission of San Luis Rey," going to San Francisco and then Los Angeles, where he appeared as an extra in Erich von Stroheim's silent *The Wedding March* and where he visited, about the time her paramour Rudolph Valentino died, his "old friend Pola Negri." By these very connections, he may have been a guest at one of Pancho Barnes' parties. An avowed homosexual, this less than perfect specimen of the Nazi male ideal once "revered Adolf Hitler as his hero."[4]

Itinerant ambassador of the National Socialist German Worker's Party, and "well-to-do bon vivant *weltbummler* from Berlin," Ludecke had been ordered by Adolf Hitler to solicit financial support from U.S. anti–Semites. (It should be noted that Hitler also singled out for persecution Catholics and homosexuals, but Ludecke did not solicit their enemies.) The list of potential donors included car magnate Henry Ford ("to Europeans the incarnation of money in its alluring bulk") and the Ku Klux Klan. As early as the 1920s, Ludecke had delivered pro–Nazi speeches at rallies and conferences throughout America with the aim of "building [pro–Nazi] cells" abroad. Detroit was one stop; another was Dearborn, Michigan. Other major stops included Los Angeles, San Francisco, and Washington, D.C.; as an independent journalist, Paul could have heard him speak at any of these cities. In Bowling Green, Ohio, Ludecke met and soon married a certain Mildred, insuring his naturalization, then moved to Brookline, Massachusetts, near Boston. Along the way he met the brilliant World War I German naval commander Count Felix von Luckner, whose remarkable story of survival and escape from a New Zealand prisoner-of-war camp Lowell Thomas had told in a 1928 bestseller. Ludecke also knew Siegfried (and wife Winifred) Wagner, whose father's "vast operatic creations [were] our liturgical music ... Nordic to the last flute-note."[5]

Ludecke, meanwhile, bore witness to the death of countless friends through Hitler's machinations, and was himself imprisoned by Hitler, the very man to whom he had given his soul. Adolf Hitler and the ideology of Aryan supremacy had shown to him their darker side. By the early years of the 1930s, Ludecke, thoroughly disillusioned, was converted from worship to scorn of Hitler and the party he represented. His former leader he now portrayed "as an ice-cold, unscrupulous opportunist whose egomania has distorted him into a Messianic fraud."[6]

For sheer bulk (833 pages), richness of specification and propulsive inner force, *I Knew Hitler* compares with William L. Shirer's *The Rise and Fall of the Third Reich*. Published years after the war, Shirer's book seems a test-tube study, as it puts distance between itself and the threatening weight of its subject; published at the near height of Hitler's power, Ludecke's reads as eye-witness reportage by a patient of the symptoms of a deadly plague about to inflict him. "Kurt G.W. Ludecke," the book jacket announces, "is the first Nazi able to write freely of what he knows and [is] able to say: 'I Knew Hitler.'"[7]

Surely he knew Hitler. On the dust jacket is a photograph of Hitler as relaxed and childlike as one ever sees him. Against an idyllic background of sturdy trees, he is seated up on a blanket laid out on an embankment, legs outstretched languorous as a doll's, hands piously cupped; as a child to a master,

A unique human document of historic value, the amazing inside story of the Nazi movement, a brilliant presentation of the Nazi leaders, living and dead, an absorbing picture of Hitler himself, the first to come from a man who was close to the Fuehrer. This is the autobiography of a Nazi activist who joined the movement as early as 1922, giving to Adolf Hitler his soul. Eventually, he found himself in prison, by Hitler's own order.

SCRIBNERS   **The Story of a Nazi Who Escaped the Blood-Purge**

Now scarce, the jacket for *I Knew Hitler*, published by Scribners in 1937, contains important information on the author and his intentions in writing the book.

he turns his head slightly, with innocent curiosity, to see the column of the newspaper Ludecke, in a beret, is pointing out to him; vanishing into the picture from the book's spine is a swastika, which appears to be prancing forward, into or out from the trees. As if to presume the reader might have doubts, a disabusing note on the jacket informs, "His [Ludecke's] book is not a translation," but written by Ludecke "himself in English, a language he knows well."[8]

Kurt Ludecke's relationship with Paul was from every appearance professional; however, the extent of Paul's participation, or, for that matter, Ludecke's, in the *I Knew Hitler* project, remains uncertain. Ludecke had formed such relationships before. In San Francisco, for instance, he "conceived the idea of giving

Kurt Ludecke, 1935, designated author of *I Knew Hitler*. The photograph was almost certainly taken by Paul Mooney (courtesy William Alexander).

lessons in German and French" and "worked it out" with an English friend who had joined him from Los Angeles "that he [the Englishman] was to present himself as my secretary and I was to be traveller and writer."[9]

One assumes that Ludecke needed to have handled his adopted language well just to have undertaken the rigors of the lecture circuit. He conversed easily with Henry Ford (presumably in English) on abstract political topics and on an "idealistic plane." Munich and Dearborn, he told Ford, shared "the same Weltanshauung," supposedly explaining to him the nature of that "world view" and how the two of them figured in it. He regularly used a typewriter—whether to write in English or German, but this by itself is not proof that he wrote effectively in either language.[10]

Still, how proficient in English was a writer who said he wrote "in a language not my own?" The book's requirements might tax a native speaker's eloquence. Besides explaining America to Hitler, Ludecke had to make his knowledge of his adopted country credible to his American readers. He wanted to meet Henry Ford's publicist, W.J. Cameron (of the *Dearborn Independent*); Cameron had edited Ford's anti–Semitic articles, including "The International Jew: The World's Foremost Problem," and Ludecke called him "the capable journalist who had so successfully phrased Ford's inarticulate racial uneasiness," uneasiness Ludecke found ideologically naive and weak.[11]

Ludecke knew, or might have been told, that his racial attitudes needed some glossing. Certainly he knew that his lectures had fallen on deaf ears. Back to the drawing board, he decided that his pro–Nazi and pro–National Socialist message would resonate best through the use of "native Americans": "What had been my impression after former visits to the United States," he said,

> was now my conviction: the German and German-American element was not the right vehicle for our propaganda. There was only one way to gain American sympathy and support. *We must approach the American-born through native Americans, with an American folkic program.* That would be a hard job for an alien. At the time I was not even an immigrant with his papers; all I had was a visitors visa for a six months' stay which had been once extended.

Excluded as "American-born" were Jews, traditionally (and stereotypically) perceived as homeless wanderers and not, strictly speaking, indigenous. The idea of "reaching the American-born through native Americans" through "an American folkic program" was as ingenious as it was farfetched. But was it original to Ludecke or did he get the idea from someone else? If original to himself, it would stand to reason, theoretically, that he would recruit someone like Paul to refine the idea.[12]

Paul's father, even though it meant disfiguring the truth, had made some efforts to conciliate Indian with Christian religious beliefs. He had made no efforts, however, to evangelize the Native Americans with whom he came in contact. Ludecke's quest was secular: to convert Native Americans to National Socialism.

Ludecke was of course not a Catholic himself; however, he nearly became

Paul Mooney reading a typescript (which may be *I Knew Hitler*) at the Chelsea Hotel, 1935 (courtesy William Alexander).

like one. While he roamed about California in 1926, he took refuge in a monastery near San Luis Rey. There he befriended a kindly, unassuming Franciscan holy man named Father Guardian Albert, who happened to be German by descent. Father Albert straightaway introduced him to the "Good Friday devotions" giving him the opportunity to bear witness, in the darkened candle-lit chapel, to "the Fathers, Brothers, and Novices ... assembled, kneeling before the altar with heads bowed low, fervently murmuring their prayers." The simple splendor of the ritual affected him, "a Nazi pagan," he wrote, as deeply as it affected the "praying monks." The "stillness" of the monks in ecstatic prayer impressed him as did the "stage-craft" in which "a faint light threw on the wall a wavering shadow which steadied into the profile of a humble monk—the spirit of Saint Francis of Assisi."[13]

Shortly after, Father Albert and Ludecke, like Virgil and Dante, set out to "beautiful Pala valley, near an Indian reservation" and "an abandoned mission" to "celebrate Easter Sunday Mass for the Indians and the farmers of the valley." A doctor for the Indians lived in Pala, we are told, as did the proprietor of a general store, "a very pleasant man" who Father Albert knew well. "Most of the Indians are very kind," Father Albert noted, "They are like children, and devoted to the Church."[14]

Catholicism, California, missionaries, ceremonial, and Indians all figure here. Were Noel Sullivan, a devotee of the spread of Carmelite monasteries in California, noted in the book—and he is not, his introducing Ludecke to Paul would be a strong possibility; indeed, Sullivan met Paul, in San Francisco, when Paul was seeking work, shortly after Hitler came to power in 1933. One can be reasonably certain, however, that James Mooney, American Indian authority and expert on the ghost dance, became known to Ludecke, who had studied Indian life during his collaboration with Paul, or that Paul was introduced to him as the son of the American Indian authority.[15]

But collaboration? According to Paul's sisters, Alicia and Eire (Stevens), Paul wrote *I Knew Hitler*, case closed. But if, as Alicia noted, page 115 of *The Flying Carpet* offered a cipher—*Paul Mooney wrote this*—shouldn't a page somewhere in *I Knew Hitler* offer a cipher—a smoking acrostic, as it were? *Obiter dicta*, the casual remarks thrown into the text that seem unnecessary to it, are the closest to such a cipher I have detected. One passage, for instance, intrigues. It concerns Washington, D.C., here not a "city extraordinary" as in the *Book of Marvels*. Ludecke called it a city "I had fallen in love with," then notes with a degree of disparagement the Lincoln Memorial, Pan-American Building, the Capitol, ("freighted with memories of the days when America was Nordic Protestant"), Statuary Hall, the Library of Congress, and, oddly, the Corcoran Gallery, "that pathetic rag-bag." Paul's sister Evelyn briefly attended the Corcoran, and perhaps her dislike for it was communicated to Paul.[16]

These items seem critical potshots, gratuitous in a narrative whose main purpose was not to belittle America, but to explain Germany's changing role in the world. Around this passage, and consistent with this purpose, are Ludecke's claims that "the German people [during World War I] were kept in almost total ignorance of decisive world events" and that Communism's triumph against Germany spelled the "end of the Gentile world." Naturally such views needed coloring. At first it was little more than a "sort of a political manual which [Ludecke] intended to use for [his] activities and to publish, if possible." Paul's reworkings, and additions, fattened it up, but also made possible its publication.[17]

Several letters Paul wrote to Bill Alexander indicate his preoccupation with the book. In one of these Paul mentioned that "Kurt is wiring me to return for a few weeks to do a *final editing* on Hitler (which Scribner has bought)...." Elsewhere he noted that he routinely did "battle with Dick and Kurt to keep unjust and unintelligent phrases out of their books." This implies that in both cases a body of unedited material existed before he looked it over. Paul then just lifted it to a higher impact level.[18]

Consider the description of a certain "Sepp Dietrich," a member of Hitler's staff, and called "the rather evil-looking, short, and burly commander of the bodyguard. He was giving orders to his eight giants, fine, athletic German types. They had zipped automobile overalls over their black-coated uniforms and wore close-fitting aviators' helmets. Armed with revolvers and sjamboks—hippopotamus whips, terrible weapons capable of knocking a man out with one blow—they looked like men from Mars."[19]

Many passages in the book are, moreover, bereft of the rhetorical excesses Ludecke, according to Paul, discharged. The description of the pilgrimage with Father Albert, for instance, is as pellucid and as spare as any with its narrative requirements can become: "On Saturday afternoon Father Albert and I set out through a lovely landscape on our way to Pala. We dined on a ranch with friends of the monk's. Darkness was settling in the folds of the hills when we took the trail again, climbing steadily. A little stream murmured beside us. Soon the night was touching everything with mystery, and boyhood fancies came back to turn the Franciscan into my Indian hero Winnetou, and me into Old Shatterhand, on mustangs surefootedly carrying us uphill." Elsewhere Ludecke writes: "Beside me on the garden park, Father Albert looked almost like a ghost in his monkish garb." To Alicia and Eire, this may have sounded like something Paul might write—if they read the book at all.[20]

To get a sense of Hitler himself, Paul had listened to him speak on the radio: "Today I heard Hitler broadcast from Berlin," he wrote his friend Bill. "He has a strange, compelling voice; a dramatic actor's voice. Kurt almost popped out of his skin drinking up every word. But the speaker who harangued next was such a shrieker that nothing came through ungarbled. He sounded like the Rev. Straton." That Ludecke behaved as he did suggests not only that he needed a cool pen to simmer down boiling passions, but that he was deadlocked between love and hate towards Hitler. Incidentally, on a visit to Washington to see his mother, who, despite a strong constitution, was feeling ill, Paul mentioned tuning "in to Berlin directly by short wave, and [became] furious because an elegant Bach program has been interrupted by a speech the gist of which is that Hitler is as great in politics as Bach was in music, and just as German!" Parenthetically, he added, "it must be midnight in Berlin; an odd hour to play Bach." As best he could, he had gotten into the milieu of Germany.[21]

Paul apparently worked on the manuscript both in Lenox, Massachusetts, and at the Chelsea Hotel on 23rd Street in New York. The preface notes "Sea Spray Inn on the Dunes," East Hampton, Long Island, as the place where the book was written. While in Lenox, friend Richard, bright eyed but travel weary, was on a train somewhere in French Somaliland, Djibouti, then Addis Abbaba. Paul did not like Lenox, which he thought "a citified country spot," and could only think of returning to New York "out of this emptiness and this isolation among people whom I detest." His hosts in what must be judged a comfortable, idyllic setting, were a young woman named Fanny Wellman and her father.[22]

Besides working, Paul, joined by Fanny, drank. They also argued. From the start, theirs was a boisterous, often rowdy relationship. "Ah, Wilderness" it was with picnicking and fun, but it was without the comedic relief the recently-staged O'Neill play offered. Once, when not speaking to Paul, Fanny screamed something into her father's ear, but it might as well have been into Paul's ear because of its noxious impact throughout other quarters of the house. For his part, Paul enjoyed the "very sedate picnics" to which he was invited, picnics "when the chauffeur drives us out to some mild view-spot with hampers full of hot food and camp chairs and rugs." When visitors arrived for "tea or luncheon," he ducked for cover. Unamused by what he called a "jellied Elysium," he complained that "the country was cold, the house gloomy, the radio disappointing, and Fanny and I at daggers' points; I was ready to pack and return to New York."[23]

Fanny Wellman was Paul's companion for about six months; booze was another companion, one less contentious, it seems: "a new typewriter, a sunny day with splendid white clouds, a bottle of gin, a pitched battle with Fanny in which we called each other all the bitches in the world and got *that* over, and your (Alexander's) letter arriving, changed the world." Before long, Fanny refused to drink with Paul. Soon he found someone else to amuse him, lunching one day "with a specimen of the local fauna," an ancient beldame, who assured him that "the country is simply *riddled* with Communists, that there is one behind every tree and in every school, although they refuse to admit their politics and the Government is keeping it very, very quiet because Roosevelt is in favor of Communism." Paul admitted he was "quite rude because [he] got the giggles when she talked." During this period of self-imposed exile, Paul seemed contentedly self-destructive: "regular meals, the minimum ration of strong liquor and country air are doing their deadly work, nor all the hill-climbing in spare hours suffices to walk off the rapidly increasing avoirdupois." He would not allow "health" to get "the upper-hand."[24]

I Knew Hitler appeared in bookstores in the fall of 1937. The book purported to be "a living, breathing portrait ... of the man, not the demigod" and "the story of the progressive disillusionment of a man who once revered Adolf Hitler as his hero" The judge in Detroit who late in 1939 rejected Ludecke's initial application for U.S. citizenship did not think so and called Ludecke "a cheap politician ... dumb as an oyster in the shell ... anti-everything."[25]

The book bearing Ludecke's name, in all events, remains a masterpiece of political self-vindication. Often the writing, with its counterplay of fact and aside, reaches high levels of sociologic contemplation, and, in its studious portraits, of Tacitean eclat: "Artistic and retiring by nature," reads an aside on Hitler, "he had nevertheless thrust himself into the most violent sort of active life. There were times when he gave an impression of unhappiness, of loneliness and inward searching, so poignant that my sympathies were stirred. But in a moment, he would turn again to whatever frenzied task was next on his schedule, with the swift command of a man born for action. Outside the political field his inclinations were all toward art; yet one felt that if he had realized his early dream of becoming an architect, he would have designed great projects, not cottages."[26]

Alternately dry and animated, *I Knew Hitler* makes one think about Hitler rather than about its author struggling to write about him. The book, in the end, sold reasonably well. Though long out of print, copies show up in used book stores from time to time, invariably without the remarkable (and, to some, disturbing) dust jacket which shows a prominent swastika flashing into the front cover design from the spine. If ever reissued, some particle of credit should be given to Paul Mooney who, at least, presided over its creation.

Borrowed eloquence should have its price. The deception, and the small payment he received for it, may have inclined Paul toward heavy—or heavier, drinking. With *I Knew Hitler*, Paul had become, at any rate, anonymously great as a correspondent of contemporary events occurring on a global scale; John Reed or the death-defiant Stephen Crane, himself a war correspondent, hardly would scoff as John Barleycorn sat on the shoulder of such talent. From some hall of drinking immortals, long-gone Jack London prosted him. As with the real-life Jack London, however, moodiness, sullenness, and sudden angry outbursts always lurked about the corner. Money troubles dogged Paul his whole life; his responsibilities to his mother also tore at him.

13
Olympian Detachment

While Paul was putting the finishing touches on the Ludecke book, and the World's Fair was underway in San Diego, Halliburton received a new inspiration. Excited, he told his parents that "there's to be a World's Fair here [in San Francisco] in 1939 to celebrate the bridges"—the Golden Gate and Bay. "The Fair promoters want me to hire a fancy Chinese junk in Shanghai and sail it with Chinese crew and cargo to the Fair." The ship at this point had a name, the *Sea Dragon*, but the name did not have a ship. Through his reading Halliburton had become convinced that the Chinese had conducted trade "with the west coast of Mexico well before Columbus 'discovered' America." He also believed he could profit immensely from a book about his and earlier adventures across the Pacific. Partly behind the idea was physician Dr. Margaret Chung, the first woman of Chinese descent to become a surgeon in the United States, and a vehement promoter of Sino-American relations and of trans–Pacific aviation. At the time she lived at the top of Telegraph Hill, at 1407 Montgomery Street, which offered matchless views of both the Bay Bridge and Treasure Island. Halliburton either lived briefly in the same building or received mail through Dr. Chung.[1]

At a Bohemian Grove performance of *Ivanhoe* held a month later, he saw his alter-ego Richard the Lion-Hearted bless the marriage of Ivanhoe and Rowena, who then entered a magic realm together. The house Halliburton thought appropriate for himself would be, as theirs, "so far away from man and so close to God." And, like so many of the great buildings he had visited, it would be monumental, radiating both "drama and beauty."[2]

Halliburton's visions always had a practical dimension. Property values had begun to soar in Laguna Beach, and Richard thought it first wise to extend his current holdings. "I've been trying to buy the lots adjoining Paul's lot along the ridge," he wrote his parents in November of 1936.

> The owners and I have come to terms—$1100 for 700 feet along the ridge and 150 feet down the slope. I'm giving the plot to Paul in exchange for his lot. He paid $500 for his lot but its present value is $3500. The adjoining property is

larger than the present lot, but has no road—thus the continued low price of
$1100. So as soon as the title is clear on the new purchase I take possession of
the old. There the house—my house—goes up on my lot and the question of
ownership is definitely settled. This was a very happy solution to the complica-
tion. Paul is delighted to have the new property which runs 700 feet along the
cliff. My lot runs 300 feet on the cliff, but is 300 feet down the sea-slope. The
road is in. I've held up work on the house itself till the lot business was
adjusted....[3]

Halliburton had by this time contacted Paul's architect friend Bill Alexander in New York to design and build him a house, a move Paul encouraged.
Besides his studies at NYU with Ely Jacques Kahn and Raymond Hood, Alexander's exaggerated role as a student of Frank Lloyd Wright must have been a selling point for Halliburton. As Lloyd Wright, the son of the famed architect, had
designed an impressive home in Los Feliz for Ramon Novarro, so Richard would
have a student of Frank Lloyd Wright, at far less the cost that Lloyd Wright
charged, design his home.[4]

With Paul at the helm, all would run smoothly. Richard could tour while
Paul supervised the building of what would become known as Hangover House.
The title to the property would be in Paul's name, so that it would not leak out
to Halliburton's fans that their hero had at last settled down. Paul's house management responsibilities included his handling of all the finances, while Richard
worked on the first *Marvels* book and traveled, often in the company of Jack
Hamery who, along with Monica Gray of the Boston Bureau and M.C. Turner
of the Dixie Bureau, booked many of his lectures. He telephoned Paul as well
as wrote letters, but he might be in Laguna Beach only a few hours before taking
off again, maybe to Modesto, up further to San Francisco (where "he motored
across the new Bay Bridge at midnight," then to parts known only a day or two
in advance). And less and less does Paul's name appear in his letters home as a
contributing agent in his books.[5]

Almost the moment plans for the house were known to him, Paul had
briefed Alexander about Laguna Beach. He also sent him a book "about beloved
California ... to whet [his] appetite for the Coast." He even sent him photographs
of the "Laguna lots" and postcards. His report of the community was compre-
hensive: "The town of Laguna," he said, "has become too dressed-up.....

> It is simply swell: not very large yet (and it cannot get too large, ever, account
> the geography); but charming as any resort on the coast. Unlike most places, its
> permanent residents are more sophisticated than the summer visitors, which
> gives it real character; and there must be a community planning body, judging
> by the new building in the village. Scores of new houses have been erected; scores
> more are going up now—residences outside the town center; and not a pink
> Spanish villa among them. The prevailing new style is a modified bastard com-
> promise between Cape Cod and Monterey: bright, attractive, pleasant and perfect
> for the terrain and the purpose of the place. You'll agree that a shore place could
> scarcely be prettier. Also the bars, stores, and so on in the village are far better
> than usual, and better looking are even the gas stations, too, of course![6]

William Alexander, 1936, about the time he was commissioned to design and build Hangover House (courtesy William Alexan-

What serenity now existed, he said, would soon be "shatter[ed] by motor-boats and speed boats." Friend Wes Wall was building on a knoll just below his own. An Englishman (artist Salvador Dali's American sponsor, Edward James?) was presently negotiating with friend Bruce McFarland to buy and build on Bruce's lot, one right next door to him. Too much civilization was there already: "Down [the] hill from me a man is building a concrete slab house; or rather, he is still building the slabs himself, and will set them up in some very modern fashion when he has enough." The "Rancho Aliso," he lamented, was no longer a quiet canyon. "One Rosencranz is going to build cottages [there], boat landings and so on" and create an "artificial bay."[7]

Like other nearby projects, plans to build Richard's house were underway. On the ridge, "the surveyors have finished their work," and "the top of the hill, where the house will go, can be considered as solid rock (unfortunately?) since the gravel is only a few inches deep there." He provided his friend with technical information regarding the intended scale of the house as well as sent him some photographs of the site. As to the house's design, he preferred a "form-poured monolith," a tower beyond noise. He assured him a number of times and in a number of ways that money would be available to carry out the project. Help he did on an article Halliburton was writing for *Cosmopolitan*, for instance, he said would get things rolling: "I'll help [Dick] ... and lo!—the bank account for the house begins with a three-hundred dollar-bang...."[8]

Opportunity and an actual commission, his first major one, beckoned, and Alexander agreed to come out West. At the time he was working in New York for the Joseph Berlinger architecture firm, helping in the design mostly of interiors. He was still modeling too, often, in lieu of pay, accepting artwork from the painters for whom he posed. Importantly, he had failed the state examination for his architect's license and, though he could retake it, he elected not to do so.

Shortly after Memorial Day, 1936, Paul started back East to fetch his friend, "via stopovers in the North," and picked him up in New York in front of the Chase building. His business address at the time was 45 Washington Square. Before coming, he told him that "California has been cold and foggy, but perhaps on our return together, it will smile again." To "relieve the tedium" of the trip back east, Paul picked up a hitchhiker in Oklahoma City. Once in a while he stopped to take photos of the landscape. The Dust Bowl had by then slaugh-

The site of what would become Hangover House, 1936. This photograph was taken by either William Alexander or Paul Mooney (courtesy William Alexan-

tered the Great Plains, just as, one could argue, Manifest Destiny had slaughtered the Indians.[9]

Paul spent a couple months on the East Coast. On a hot, muggy August day, he headed back west from New York for good. With him in his Ford roadster was Bill Alexander, who would make a preliminary survey of the Laguna Beach property. Also with him was a sailor from a Navy yard who had hitched along and just wanted to see the country before returning to base. Alexander, though he hadn't a license, did some of the driving. Later, he would recall how isolated from the eastern seaboard San Francisco and Los Angeles seemed, as if cities on the tip of China. It was less faraway to Paul. He had made the trip across the country several times now, and, at least once with Halliburton, had seen much of the country's natural wonders from glorious mountain ranges to mighty redwoods.[10]

Alexander called the cross-country America of the thirties "a desert," where no farms operated and farmers migrated east and west in search of work. Alongside the road, whole families camped and ramshackle vehicles ground forward. "Hard roads some of the way," Paul had written about an earlier trip from New

Opposite, top: Aerial view of Hangover House, 1938 (courtesy William Alexander). *Bottom:* Ocean view from the living room of Hangover House, 1995. Photograph taken by the author, 1995.

York, "but all fun." Then:

> The desert at last—two hundred and fifty miles of it from Needles, Arizona:
> monotonous, empty, full of mirages and dust-devils, over a hundred in the shade;
> then up through Cajun Pass, and down into the Coast area of So. Calif. The
> whole country changes suddenly—trees, flowers, water, a cold white mist: and
> the road-signs, even. All the rest of the way I had passed the usual warnings
> "Danger—Cattle Crossing" or "Men At Work" and whatnot; but just before I
> got to Pasadena I came to signs which warned motorists (on the main highway,
> mind) that the road was 'Dangerous—Peacocks Crossing.' Home at last, I
> thought![11]

At the Grand Canyon, the three of them parked just short of the edge of
a precipice. Leaping from the car, Paul and Bill ran excitedly to the edge. "Come
on over!" Paul yelled out to the sailor in the rumble seat. "It's beautiful!" "Naw,"
said the sailor, "I saw it before from the other side." Alexander, for his part,
saw the dark red rocks as unpeopled tenements and all the fisher birds as making
a raw living. The pine trees and the sloping rapids drew from him expressions
merely of "Beautiful, so beautiful."[12]

They wanted to put some distance between themselves and the scorching

Paul Mooney at the Ice Caves in Arizona, 1936. The photograph was taken by William Alexander on his trip out West with Paul (courtesy William Alexander).

heat and heavy drought of the Dust Bowl, which had spread across the Great Plains and Midwest, but both found that California was also hit hard. When Alexander first set eyes on the ridge where Halliburton would build his house, he again thought, as if that distant point had been reached, "Beautiful, so beautiful." The Brooklyn boy who knew ghettos better than cloudlands realized, once he breathed the ocean air and heard only silence, that wealth and celebrity lived in places of this world. Secretly he wanted to be well-connected and rich, though, more so than Paul, he was better acquainted with humdrum work. Still, it was Paul who did the work of recruiting men "hungry for work," men who had originally come from the devastated regions of the Dust Bowl, but who, just as likely, were born and bred Californians.[13]

The era of the covered wagon hardly seemed remote. Reasons for going west seemed the same as always—for the "relief of tuberculosis ... and unemployment," Bill Alexander believed. En masse, Okies and Arkies and Texans, the train of workers immortalized in John Steinbeck's *Grapes of Wrath*, migrated to California. Great savers, they scrimped and buried away what they earned with the idea of one day opening up a filling station or grocery store.

The site for the future Hangover House thrilled Alexander the moment he set foot on its glorious summit: "from the crest we could look all the way down into Mexico, all the way up beyond Los Angeles," he wrote months later,

> [and we could] see the snowy peaks which rim the desert, and clearly see the islands eighty miles off-shore. Right below us was a wilderness eight miles broad that begins right behind my land—not a house, or a road, or a man, scarcely a tree—only canyons, peaks, brown slopes, grey cliffs. And below us on the other side was the town of Laguna, miniature but maintaining startling clarity in the peculiar light that came through the clouds. Bill [Alexander] was so thrilled that he wanted to go right down right away and hunt up a real estate dealer who would buy the mountain for him; but since that was impractical for various reasons, we simply stayed there on top of the world and pitied the poor New Yorkers who cannot get higher up than the Empire State Building, at One Dollar A Throw![14]

In time, Alexander saw Laguna Beach as a haven for celebrities, and for gays who were somebodies and gays who were nobodies. He also saw it mainly as an "art colony," where "artists gladly produced oils of guano-covered rocks, seals (alongside these rocks) and waterfront subjects for tourists." Despite the coastal community's reputation as "liberal," Alexander thought it "disallowing" to Jews and black Americans. He found it odd, however, that the Japanese, who farmed the rice fields and managed the orange groves, should hold an exalted position among minority groups. The Laguna Beach "greeter" welcomed one and all, nevertheless. Once it was Old Joe Lucas, who died in 1908; in 1934 it was, as Alexander later noted, Danish wayfarer Eiler Larsen, who had vagabonded his way across the country from New York.[15]

Paul and Bill took up residence just south of the Laguna Hotel on "Hilly Drive" ("Cliff Drive?") in a ten by eleven ocean-front shack with wood-shuttered windows. Paul said simply that it had "a good view." A telephone was installed, number MAIN 4-4288. Nearby, on the three-fourths acre lot, the hired hands set up tents. At dawn, Paul and Bill, rather than drive up the rough approach, hitched rides aboard one or another of the motorcycles the men used to drive to the worksite. Once the shell of the house was completed, the two abandoned the routine, sacking out in the furnitureless living room. Work was not a chief concern. Always on the romantic ready, Bill and Paul hunted for the wild nectar of the field, while each kept a warm pot of honey at home—that is, they had each other or hunk Tony Trapani, whose movie star good looks appealed to both. Paul identified with his four cats—or three (one had run off), as well as the mice they hunted. Ingenious in his appraisal of animals, he knew "when the cat's away, the mice will play," yet less ingenious in his appraisal of men, he knew that the cat who was away might be playing as well.[16]

Now and then Paul, with or without Alexander, drove off to the city. Once (at least) he brought along young Harry Hay (at other times Charles Wolfsohn together with Alexander) to Central Avenue, the "Harlem of Los Angeles." Located here were the city's progressive gay nightspots. He also went to the Trocadero on the Strip and the Club Bali. A favorite pianist and impersonator, Ray Bourbon, appeared at one or the other of these. Wilshire Boulevard also provided gay entertainment. The gay culture had familiar patterns with variations only of those patterns. Toto LeGrand, a roving buddy of Ramon Novarro (like Paul, a Roman Catholic), reported that his friend would "cavort on Main Street and in nearby hotels on most Saturday nights" and "meet for an early Mass at St. Vibiana's Cathedral" on Sunday morning.[17]

Often Richard was away, but little did he mind his friends' passionate embraces with each other or anyone else. He certainly did not like it when they feuded, and once he told Paul, after Paul and Bill had bickered, that he "very bitterly resent[ed] [their] treatment of each other." He knew at any rate that now he had house builders he could trust, while he traveled about, a luncheon engagement here, a promotion there, a lecture just about anywhere and a movie deal maybe—all while he watched sales of the *Book of Marvels—the Occident* and worked on the *Book of Marvels—the Orient*. "Stuck" in New York one day, off to Philadelphia, Kansas City, Pontiac, Michigan, Indianapolis, Atlanta, or Miami the next, he was constantly on the move.[18]

Richard of course was a main focus when he was in Laguna Beach. "Definitely it will be impossible to come into town on the weekend to see you," Paul wrote to Bill, "the more so as I must see Dick late Sunday night, either here or at the Vanderbilt—*positively* his last appearance in these parts for many weeks to come. He is having a tough trip, poor public idol!" Richard always bitterly amused him. And kept him employed. "Busy, busy, busy," Halliburton said, thinking even he might need "two secretaries."[19]

Occasionally, Paul and Bill motored off to Los Angeles, or to San Francisco. Once by himself Paul went up to San Francisco with fellow crew member, "Tim

Paul Mooney looking beyond the Golden Gate Bridge while it is under construction, 1937 (courtesy William Alexander).

Powers, the tattooed man." Sometimes he met up with Richard. One trip with Bill, in February 1937, included two days of going to art galleries and various garden pavilions, walking up and down hills, and visiting the Golden Gate Bridge. Alexander took a number of photographs of Paul, shirtless, gazing out beyond the bridge into the Pacific from (apparently) the Marin County side of the span.[20]

In Laguna, the carnival life of the community drew area crowds. Local arts and crafts ever flourished. The Laguna Art Festival, held in late July and early August, brought quite a crowd. At one festival he and Bill sat on the grass in a eucalyptus grove which faced a curtain supported by two poles. The main event, to Paul and Bill, was a real-life "Discobulus," played by the top laborer of their house-building crew, whose extreme muscular development was said to be the result of the heavy loads of cement he carried up the hill. Of Laguna Beach's artists featured in a Stock Fair exhibit in Pomona, Paul, slightly cynical, had a good deal to say. He had gone there with "Wilson," about whom one hears little else. In a letter to Alexander, who, with Wolfsohn, had set up art exhibits in New York, he revealed the cutting edge of his wit:

> pictures ... A beautiful Karfiol, a Brooke, a Speicher, a Ryder, a Higgens, a fine female by John Carroll, something swirly by Corbino, two good things by someone I never heard of before—Russell Cowles; perhaps the best thing of all was a superb marine by Mattson. Schnakenberg had sent the "Picnic Scene" I was always asking someone to paint: over-dressed ladies and naked men around a

pool in the woods; only he put trunks on the gents and it isn't quite as fetching as I wanted. Still, I'm glad someone painted it at last! There were, of course, the usual clutter of Hopper, Wood, Benton, Poore, Beale, Joe Jones, etc. Altogether a more Stimulating show than I've ever seen before—and at, of all Places, the Stock Fair!

The *only* picture sold from the Laguna Gallery's current show was done by Tom Pillsbury, the local sign painter! And Wesley Wall, impervious to the idea that this partly proved what I said about debased public taste, gleefully sent out publicity to all the papers telling how "a sign painter's daub" (as some critics refer to the works of Laguna painters) set a sales record at the gallery. Well— that put me in my place; but my place is on the sidelines, snickering. I think that if they had sold *no* pictures, it would have been a better record for Laguna.[21]

But the show of shows remained the artists-at-work on the residence on the ridge—the "Halliburton House."

14

House in Flight

The house almost remained forever on the drawing table. For openers, a road (ultimately serpentine) had to be blasted out to get the massive load of concrete and steel up the slope to build it. Even so, from beginning to end, contractors thought the whole idea impractical. Besides work-related problems, floods, washouts, lumber strikes, water-pumping problems—what Paul called "exasperating delays"—slowed completion of the project. To Alexander, the problems, and "how [he] overcame them," seemed "dreamlike." Weeks passed. Work didn't commence full throttle until the end of February.[1]

The ground was hardly broken when rumors circulated of the recurring disagreements between Alexander and Mooney about how to proceed. Halliburton's own wishes may have sparked it all off. "Driven by what he had already accomplished and lured on by what was yet to be accomplished," wrote David Greggory, "Halliburton became at times a sulking child, sometimes an impulsive tyrant, sometimes an exhausted, frightened being, pushed close to the limit of his endurance." He did not suffer advice gladly.[2]

Squabbles galore, it was a wonder anything positive resulted. By now Paul had discovered John Barleycorn in earnest. Under his influence, Paul could become boisterous and stumble about; he could cut up with laughter as well as sink into the doldrums. A teetotaler himself, Alexander welcomed the comparison of Paul to film star James Dean as a start to form some picture of his friend, the James Dean who plays Jett Rink, the drunken oil-rigger romantic in *Giant*.[3]

Heated words often were exchanged between Halliburton and Mooney. Always they reconciled: "Paul drove me in [to the house, from Los Angeles]," Halliburton wrote to his parents.

> He has worked hard all summer and will continue to superintend everything this winter. We left on the best of terms. We clash on almost everything. But it is this very warfare that makes his friendship provocative and stimulating. His companionship provides a daily shock to my own complacency, and a spur to my intellect. Wherever he goes he stirs up the intellectual dust into a storm. For this, I overlook (with some effort) Paul's complete lack of all the negative virtues.[4]

Whatever "negative virtues" might be, the contest of wills over matters big and small produced a grand monument of diminutive proportions. The labor alone compared to building a Pharaoh's tomb, and took nearly as long as building the Empire State Building. Neither causeways nor cranes, however, were used to carry the enormous amounts of concrete and steel this structure required. Manpower alone was harnessed to haul the steel frames and supports up the hill, then place them in exact positions. Sheer manpower was used to lug bucket after bucket of the needed pre-mix cement up the ridge.

"In those days, pre-mix concrete," wrote Alexander, "did not exist; a trestle had to be built to counterbalance the loads of cement carried to the topmost level; mixes were made by collecting the ingredients; a forty-eight-hour pour for one level filled the already-formed and steel-reinforced walls." In the end fifty tons of steel and one hundred tons of concrete had been used to complete the structure.

Often Alexander applauded the work, or singled out the excellent work done by one of the workers. Mr. Sutherland's channel-formed steel-sheet forms used to support the ceiling, he thought, "worked beautifully" and made a "neat patina." Crew members Orville and Pete, who had blasted a roadway and slotted the house's foundation, also earned Alexander's applause. So did one Clarence Burner, a "radical" engineer, who worked out the minimal use of cement and steel to build the sixteen by eighty foot counterbore wall that fronted the house.[5]

As often he was not so happy about the work. One worker, for instance, didn't puddle the cement as thoroughly as he should have, and botched up a foundation wall leaving it pitted with holes. Ruthless in his attention to quality, Alexander fired the man and redid the wall himself. He then changed contractors. Keeping Halliburton regularly informed, he said, "He is honest, but it disturbs me to know that this plebeian appears to be unmindful of our practical and aesthetic objectives." The man said he had built a cement gas station, but was unable to duplicate the work, confessing that he really had no desire to do a house "in concrete." Defections occurred as well. A local contractor, working on the lower garage and vault level, walked from the job after encountering some unexplained difficulties.[6]

Getting workers who could actually do what they boasted they could do was difficult. Desperate need for money forced many to invent skills they clearly didn't have. Most had fled the barren farmlands of the lower Midwest to seek remunerative work of any kind. Many came to the site in rickety old trucks or, like Pete and Orville, on rusty old motorbikes. Years later, when going over photographs he and Paul had taken of the men at work, Alexander threw the majority into the waste paper basket as "architecturally unimportant." A number of these pictures Dorothea Lange would have been proud to exhibit.[7]

Architecture to Alexander was a sort of Tenth Muse, seductive and unforgiving of rejection. He was its servant and a perfectionist whose blood curdled at the thought of cutting any cost or performing any shortcut that compromised

A

B

The photographs shown above through page 144, numbered A–I, show the workers at work building Hangover House, 1937. In two shots (F, G) William Alexander is seen conducting the work activities.

C

D

E

F

G

H

I

Paul Mooney looking over the plans for Hangover House, 1937. Beyond is Laguna Beach. Late in life, Alexander tossed this photograph, and others—mainly of the workers—into the wastebasket. He said they were "architecturally unimportant." Fortunately, he allowed me to retrieve them (courtesy William Alexander). *Bottom:* What Paul probably saw. Photograph taken by the author, 1995.

his vision. If someone installed a doorknob that was different from the one he specified in the original design, he threw a fit. Once when a client gently hinted that he remodel one of his designs, he lambasted, "You have no right to take matters into your own hands without my consultation!" Throughout his life it enraged him when anyone in his family bought, sold or remodeled any dwelling without heeding his advice. This extended to his clients. The costliness of the specifics his designs often required was what clients most dreaded. As one of these clients, and the first, Halliburton was no exception.[8]

Halliburton who had toured nearly every important building, and ruin, in the world was no architectural illiterate. Of course the architect he had chosen to build his great house was not a Gentile like himself but a Jew named Levy—not Imhotep but Solomon. Jews had a reputation in his mind as money grubbers, plain and simple. In the spirit of mentorship, Halliburton, ten years Alexander's senior, insisted that his architect rename himself "William Alexander" to appeal to a Gentile as well as Jewish clientele. On his own copy of *Architectural Record*, which, in October 1938, showcased the Halliburton House, Richard crossed out the Levy portion of "Alexander Levy" as the house's architect, and left the copy in plain sight for Alexander to see.[9]

"Bill Levy," for his part, liked the association with Alexander of Macedon. He did not like the charge, however, that he was trying to milk his client for more money: "Hardly has a penny spent on the lot been wasted," he countered bitterly. Halliburton, for his part, was not amused by the expenditures: "I pleaded, threatened, weaved every danger sign I could weave—tried in every way I knew how, to impress upon you both the fact that you were building more house than there was money to pay for." "You both" meant Paul as well as Bill. "No doubt you and Paul feel resentful over my 'discontinuation of funds,'" Halliburton went on, requesting "an accounting of the sums" he sent to Alexander. These sums amounted to $1,690 dollars including an estimated $450 for food (a figure Alexander had arrived at); then there was "shelter." In 1937 the house cost an estimated $30,000 to build—in today's money, between $300,000 and $500,000, with an additional $2,400 designated as Alexander's "guaranteed fee."[10]

These costs seemed exorbitant to Halliburton—and, at the time, would have seemed so to most people. Irked, Richard at one point asked Alexander to leave, and said he would even pay him to do so. Refusing, Alexander said that he would see the project to its completion. He told his client that, to date, he had received far less than one of the "common laborers" had received in wages. "Your fame means nothing to me," he said. "Your fame as a writer is no incentive for me to work for little or nothing!" Besides, "the people who are capable of taking an intelligent interest in my architecture usually know you only vaguely, if at all." He then made clear his alliance to Paul, money and the house: "Neither your abhorrence of my race, nor your resentment of the sums of 'house money' which Paul says you know he drank down, nor your seemingly total inability to appreciate the house I've built for you, seems to me to release you from your contracted obligation towards me."[11]

Totally exasperated, Alexander made plans himself to walk off the job and hitchhike to Los Angeles or San Francisco. This was in mid–July 1937, and it would have left Halliburton with half a house. Halliburton relented. "This letter, on rereading," he wrote, "sounds brusque and sharp. I didn't mean for it to be like that. I've no charges against *you*, Bill. Perhaps, next year, all these troubles of the moment will be forgotten. Let's hope you'll profit professionally and I'll do all I can to help." Conciliatory by nature, Halliburton practiced, as best he could, Dale Carnegie's peacemaking dictums.[12]

Alexander did his best to keep Halliburton informed of the house's progress. This included news about the always touchy subject of "house finances." Likely at Paul's urging, he even assured his illustrious client once that he didn't have to make the "long trip to California." Booked solid, Halliburton happily conceded that this was "good news." In reality, however, Alexander, and Paul, wished Richard were on hand so he could take charge of operations and see for himself what was costing him so much and why everything was taking so long.[13]

Halliburton often "talked house" with Alexander, who he concluded "justified [his] faith in him" with his "imagination plus common sense." For

Paul Mooney and Richard Halliburton during the building of Hangover House, 1937 (courtesy William Alexander).

starters, Alexander had dismissed the concrete contractor to supervise that job himself, saving his client $15 a day. He purchased materials "at an architect's discount ... works side by side (with the workmen he has hired) so there's no loafing." Alexander, as a result of his ardor, "ran a nail in his foot" and had to go to the hospital to get "tetanus injections."[14]

Paul's activities were less hands on. The boastfully promiscuous Harry Hay saw him as a "handsome Lothario" who had "beautiful young men trekking up and down the hill to the house he [later] shared with his lover [Halliburton] in Laguna." This view makes Paul appear a later-day Gilles de Retz, processing lovers one by one as they scaled the castle on the hill. His pulse, as that of any of a number of characters in *Thurso's Landing*, did quicken from time to time when he watched the men at work: "Work the ass off Jack," he once instructed Alexander, "but on second thought, not that!" Often, he just inspected things, and took lots of photographs (many of which Alexander later discarded as "architecturally irrelevant"). Once in a while, he relaxed on one of the partially completed decks, drew out a book, and, while he read, he smoked cigarettes. Sometimes he chatted with Bill, who liked to wear a little sailor's cap and appear deceptively meek before the camera. They talked about things back east. A trip

Richard Halliburton with William Alexander at Hangover House, 1937 (courtesy William Alexander).

Paul's mother promised to make to Laguna made him nervous simply because he wasn't ready to accommodate her: they talked about "things like that," when they weren't talking about the work and some trip they would like to make. At the end of the work day, he went downtown, for a drink, which was never just *a* drink. Paul weighed his own intake needs at a "minimum ration of strong liquor."[15]

He began to drink ever more heavily, becoming ever more talkative in the process. A favorite hang-out was Mona's bar. Another was the White House Café, gathering spot for the town's "fixtures" including "Pancho" Barnes and, when in town, Bing Crosby. Paul had a couple drinking buddies who landed in jail for drunken driving. Paul too spent a night in jail either for speeding, drunk driving or both; there were probably other close calls. The more he got to know people in the community, the more it became his home; soon he even called himself a "Lagunan."[16]

Whether Paul let it leak that he was writing or co-writing an upcoming Halliburton book is not clear. He was outspoken. He published an editorial in the *Laguna Herald* regarding a current art controversy that got him into a "mess." Perhaps it was about the discus thrower at the Fair who presumably showed too much. Nor was he wishy-washy. Once he shooed away a local artist named Tom Lewis who kept hounding Richard to buy one of his paintings: said Paul, "We can't afford Lewises." There were other importunities.[17]

Often Paul brooded, morbidly, ostentatiously. He griped about the building delays and about some of the people he had to work with. Supervising the work on the house, at least this house, did not agree with him; he wished Richard were there to do it instead of him. Likely in the heat of anger he did call Alexander "incompetent," and Alexander called him "domineering and officious." Orchestrating the vast ritual of work routines and stated daily objectives worked against Alexander's, as well as Paul's, better nature. Getting a crew member named Sparks to show up for work on time was one personnel problem among many. Then there was the matter of the house itself. He called the Arco people a number of times to put "a dumdum on the roof." Without one, one good rain "would ruin the plaster in Dick's room." There was the matter of a pump; yet, "after renewed attention and a new airlock," it seemed to work okay, but Paul insisted that "it may prove necessary to get a meter with a larger capacity." Amid distractions that were ordinary and usual, he had to deal with emergencies. He had to deal with payroll issues too. If Dick's lectures were not paying enough, he knew Bancamerica was always around for a "straight loan on Dick's personal credit." Still, Paul could always afford to buy a painting done by an acquaintance, or find the time to write to a friend. He wrangled with San Diego Electric over another matter, which he said, at last, that he had "emphatically won." Paul could run a ship, and had a high practical intelligence, but preferred using it in other ways.[18]

And each could rest in his own place. The master bedroom, with its replica of a 16th century map of the world over the bed, was of course designed for Halliburton. The second bedroom was for Paul and the third for Alexander— or would this be the dark room? Views mattered as did the play of light into the windows of the house. "You would be touched to see how gradually," Paul wrote to Bill, "he [Richard] realizes the play of sunlight in his room as the sun moves southward. The idea that one can actually *plan* a room to benefit from the orbits of the stars is new to him, and he explains it to everyone who comes here. His latest line, is 'We really have *five* bedrooms, counting the penthouse on the roof!' Naturally we won't but somewhere in his past he gained the fixed impression that a house is rated chiefly by its bedrooms."[19]

Up a couple steps from the patio into the dining room and down a couple steps from the dining room, one entered a living room or rather an arresting view of endless sky and water. There was then a kitchen, or cockpit, which would be equipped with all sorts of gadgetry. Custom-made furniture, designed by Alexander and built by Warren Sparks (the late-comer?) as well as wooden inlays were added. Together Paul and Richard decided it "wittier," Paul wrote to his friend Bill, "to take [the sliding window units'] transparency away entirely" and replace [these] it with "translucent glass bricks," which would still admit light. As an afterthought, Paul suggested that a little pond framed with rocks be built outside in view of the dining room and be made accessible through some sliding doors. Paul, who possibly saw the actor in person and, according to Bill, saw most of his movies, remarked that the shape reminded him of one of "Clark Gable's ears"—according to Alexander, Paul never missed a Clark Gable movie. Later, Paul planted flowers around the pool and added some goldfish to it. In all, he embellished Richard's house as he embellished his books—only this time his name, ironically, appeared beneath the title.[20]

Soon the barren hillside, flattened out to make space for a large garden, would have flowers throughout. Credit for designing it went to Charles Wolf-sohn, who had lent a hand to the project midway, and to local gardener Ernie Bowen with Paul's and the Wilcox Nursery's initial help. "To stand there, with no obstruction in either direction," wrote Paul, "is pleasant." He noted that the road had been "vastly improved on the upper turn," and that soon "the lower run [would] be widened and lowered, and guard-rails set up." Everyone agreed that improvements to the site at least could always be made.[21]

To this end Paul had added his famous litter of cats, long-hairs; and pre-sumably, these multiplied until the cats in the region sixty years later were believed, by his friend Bill Alexander, the descendants of Paul's cats. They roamed about the premises freely. About their destructive tendencies, Paul had no qualms. Alexander liked cats; he just happened to be allergic to them, and watch-ful of their ways. "As for the plants in the boxes," he reported, to Halliburton, "they hold up fairly well in the incessant wind (*maybe not to the cats*), but some do better than others, and we must get more of the hardy ones. Around the fish-pond, the cats refuse to let anything flourish. They pick bouquets of my expensive

The pond Paul created in the rear of Hangover House as an afterthought that he said resembled one of "Clark Gable's ears."

The pond in 1995. Photograph by the author.

herbs, and drag them indoors for play." Far less tolerance was shown Charles Wolfsohn, who, invited by Alexander to do the garden, was a quick pain: "Charlie is beautiful to look at," Paul conceded, "and helpful around the house, but he gets on my nerves in big doses. Bring him out if you wish—he can stay here a while. But stress that 'while.'"[22]

Richard, creative and enterprising, took to spending "small sums" here and there on the house. "The garden grading is about finished, and the Hanging Gardens of Babylon will have nothing on me," he wrote home. "The road, which scared people to death, is smoothing out, and will soon scare nobody. I'm putting in a small forest of two-foot eucalyptus trees on the mountain slopes. They'll be six feet high by next summer."

He then added a "better road, [a] better kitchen, etc" in the belief that these things would make the house "marketable." "The first step in making the house marketable," he would say, "is to make it easily approachable." Laguna had become a boom town, why not become a part of it? "There's no telling what I can get for the house if I ever want to sell it," he enthused.[23]

Onlookers, including architects and teachers of architecture with their students, meanwhile, gathered to watch the builders at work, and soon a booth was built to sell tickets. Some, drifting by, paused to gawk, others to wonder at the slow fulfillment of the impossible dream that contractors assured could

Visitors to Hangover House arrive at the base of the ridge. Tickets were sold at the ticket booth. Note the parking arrangements to the far right (courtesy William Alexander).

never be done. Seeing an opportunity to voice his architectural opinions, Alexander "hire[d], direct[ed], survey[ed] and receiv[ed] college groups for study, design and [he] supervise[d] furniture [design] and landscape[ing]." On one occasion eighty people, including the president of the University of Wisconsin (probably Glenn Frank), were given the guided tour by Halliburton personally. One can imagine him exclaiming how "inexhaustibly dramatic" the views were. Halliburton, nevertheless, discouraged visitors: they bothered him; he also thought they distracted the workers. A couple people begged Alexander, whenever he was around, to build a similar house for them; this alone may have warmed Halliburton to visitors.[24]

Besides onlookers, party line telephones had their eavesdroppers to gather up local news. Everyone wanted to know about the house. Wise to the fact that he was being listened to by the woman with whom he shared a telephone line, Paul manufactured a conversation with friend Eric Linder about the Prince of Wales coming to see the house. The next day the item appeared in the local newspaper.[25]

Even in a community used to the bizarre, people dubbed what they slowly saw emerge as outlandish or, as Alexander later said, "far out." Many observers thought it revolutionary and, even today, many see it as modern. Songwriter Carrie Jacobs Bond ("The End of a Perfect Day," and "God Remembers When the World Forgets") visited the house and "apparently was thrilled." Most were

When built Hangover House was just about the only house on the ridge. View
from knoll on the southeast side, May 1938. Figures in foreground are from left
Paul Mooney (possibly), Ayn Rand (a tempting identification), and William Alexander (almost certainly). Photograph by Carl F. Ziegler (courtesy William Alexander).

impressed by it.[26]

During the nine months of its construction, novelist Ayn Rand, not yet
well known, visited the house, wending her way up the twisting road to the precarious summit. She interviewed Alexander who, from that day forward, would
insist that the many references to rugged individualism in her book *The Fountainhead* were based on things he had told her and that Howard Roark was actually
him; moreover, he insisted that the Enright House mentioned in the book was
actually the Hangover House.[27]

Like the Enright House, Halliburton's house could justifiably appear in a
book that contrasted innovative with traditional modes of architectural design.
In its combination of the poetic and industrial, one sees, if not immediately,
the influence of Frank Lloyd Wright or of his student Rudolph Schindler. Alexander objected angrily to the association with Schindler but enjoyed the one
with Wright, and also with Le Corbusier and Mies van der Rohe. Tennessee
Williams, who lived in Laguna Beach in 1939, called it a "big modernistic residence." For his part, Halliburton hated the term "modernistic" because it
sounded "eccentric and affected"; he preferred "modern." Alexander himself
liked to think of it as the first heavy use of reinforced concrete and steel in the

building of a private residence. In addition to the medieval-like retaining wall or bulwark, the house featured some daring cantilevering, a fire-resistant structure with termite-proof and sound-proof walls, copper doors, custom steel sliding doors, a dumb waiter, and original cabinetry throughout. Light transfused the ultra-modern house. Sun-decks catered specifically to Halliburton's belief that sunning kept his ever-lecturing voice vigorous for speaking engagements. Then there were the gorgeous views and, on a clear, fog-less day, a glimpse, now and then, of Santa Catalina Island, maybe even of "Avalon," home of Zane Grey.[28]

Halliburton's own comments about the house were wildly enthusiastic. "There's a lift and audacity about this house I've never seen elsewhere," he said. "It doesn't sit—it flies." Even as he toiled on the two *Books of Marvels*, he saw the house as equal to any marvel to which he had attached a glowing caption— he had begun to think in captions, actually. "One can sit at one end and look into the heavenly canyon (all brilliant green now after the floods)," he said, "and yet view the blue ocean on the other side through the plate-glass window." He thought it "the most wonderful house in the world." Later, he wrote to his mother: "I agree with [Dad] that once I'm on my mountain-top house I'll be

Hangover House completed, 1938 (courtesy William Alexander).

Paul Mooney's car parked in front of the nearly completed shell of Hangover House, 1938 (courtesy William Alexander).

able to adjust my life onto a calmer plane and grow in spirit rather than in mileage. If I can't get near the Eternal in that house, then it's not in me. I never saw a house so far away from man and so close to God. The peace and serenity of that canyon is enough in itself to make one relax and dream." Still, he felt a need to assure her that, despite its cost, "the lectures have paid for everything."[29]

Paul Mooney and William Alexander in the unfinished dining room area of Hangover House, 1937 (courtesy William Alexander).

Home? One wonders if Halliburton really liked the ultra-modern version of home sweet home. Images of his celibate hero Rupert Brooke dying on foreign shores must have needled him. He was in all events a reluctant homeowner; like Odysseus, he was not meant to be domestic. He liked showing visitors through the house. That he did in a grand manner with his customary style and grace. Like Alexander when he showed people through, he pointed to the garbage disposal, central heating, copper doors, see-through crystal blocks, and the dumb waiter, which serviced the three floors—comforts and conveniences denied him when in foreign parts.

Solitude appealed to Halliburton. Still, he had no intention of becoming a homebody or, as he put it, to "imprison myself on my mountain top in Laguna and turn the dogs on visitors." Mixed feelings about the house continued to vex. One moment, he sounded as though he wanted to sell the house: "a house is good invested capital," he would say. The next moment, he wanted to keep it: it "will always be an anchor," he would say, "tho I'll not be there probably ⅓ of the time." So far, his longest stay at the house had been six weeks—from mid–August 1937 to October 1, 1937, the day Alexander returned from a month-long trip to New York to complete the cabinetry work that still needed to be done. So ⅓ sounded reasonable. Capable of great self-delusion, Halliburton was also great at resolving tensions within himself: "this house is so serene and so beautiful I resent anything that takes me away. I'm torn between two

William Alexander and Paul Mooney on the back patio of Hangover House, 1937 (courtesy William Alexander).

sentiments. Sometimes there is a color in the canyon, or the ocean, that makes me think this the most perfect and most heavenly house in the world—and I'm thrilled that it's mine. But the next minute I find the whole thing a nuisance—remote—a little cold—inaccessible. But as a house—apart from it being my house—it's an *enormous success*."[30]

Actually, I suspect, he did not much care for the house, except for its views: "My last morning there was the loveliest of all. The Pacific was Mediterranean blue and the canyon turning gold. Living there, even in an empty shell, was a daily thrill."

The huge window in the living room drew him, as Captain Nemo from his window in the Nautilus, to watch both the sea and the seas of life. The closest

Top: William Alexander and author in the gallery just outside Richard Halliburton's bedroom, March 1995. It was Alexander's last visit to Hangover House. *Bottom:* The wall map in Halliburton's room, 1995. Photograph taken by the author.

neighbors appeared as little figures miles away, and the distant boats seemed Dufy–like mirages in an endless rainbow of soft colors. Distant emerald isles of ocean waves appeared to him as a silken carpet rolled out from heaven. Mysterious rays of light flickered and streaked through the thick crystaline bricks that formed the wall going along the central corridor past the three bedrooms and the green-patined walkway that faced the canyon below. From the living-room window, the ocean as it converged upon the sky seemed to extend from the mind's eye itself. The little lagoon on the patio offered opportunities to make wishes. One could easily imagine godly homecomings, as well as ghostly visitations.[31]

Still, Halliburton would probably have preferred the "chic enclave" of Whitley Heights with its luxurious in-step "Mediterranean-style houses on hillside lots," each one different, "nestled in hills covered in towering eucalyptus and pine." Not only was it home to such Hollywood legends as Jean Harlow, Carole Lombard, Harold Lloyd, and Charlie Chaplin and, earlier, Rudolph Valentino and Wallace Reid, to name a few, but it was just moments from the film studios

Richard Halliburton in the gallery of Hangover House, 1937, looking out over Aliso Vista Canyon to San Bernardino Mountain (courtesy William Alexander).

and posh Hollywood Boulevard. Burton Holmes' luxuriant bungalow on Whitley Heights, a "little palm-embowered Paradise" Holmes called "Topside," more than rivaled Hangover House as traveler Holmes himself more than rivaled traveler Halliburton. At least it seemed less ponderous. If Hangover House flew, it flew like an anchor. And what a costly anchor! He had only to page through any issue of *The Architectural Forum* to see what kind of fool he had been. Houses in the range of $5,000 to $10,000 were affordable and worthy of showcasing in the magazine. Put down $20,000, and you have the Tuileries Palace. Architect H. Roy Kelly had built a spacious dream home for a Mr. Paul Pulliam in Pasadena for $9,000; for under $6,000 Dominique Berninger had built an equally splendid one for Thorsten Sigstedt, in Brynathyn, Pennsylvania. The house Richard Neutra built for Anna Sten and Dr. Eugene Frenke in California Beach, California, a modern marvel, cost less than $25,000; the Adobe House that Bennett, Parsons and Frost Architects had built near Abiquiu, New Mexico, was only $25,000![32]

From afar, one might mistake Halliburton's home for the bachelor pad of some Olympian (detractors might recommend Vulcan rather than Apollo), or a bastion with ramparts or, yet, a crusader's fortress built high to fend off attack. The protective wall resembled Catalina Island's Desconso, the roof itself a sort of landing summit for the gods. Or something more menacing and mundane. About a year after the house was completed, in 1938, United States Air Force

Atop the retaining wall William Alexander (left) explains Hangover House to client Richard Halliburton, August 1937 (courtesy William Alexander).

A Paul Mooney "art" photograph showing Hangover House reflected in the hubcap
of his car, 1938 (courtesy William Alexander).

pilot Captain Wallace Scott ("Scottie") sent "air photos" of the house to his
boss in Washington, D.C. For years Japanese had farmed the inlands and fished
along the shores of Laguna Beach area. Not having read the local newspapers,
it was the Air Force's belief that the Japanese were charting the coastline and
that the monumental concrete structure was a fortress engaged in espionage.[33]

Be that as it may, Halliburton himself never seemed too impressed with
the house, until it was completed. He didn't call it anything exciting, like "Olym-
pus South" or "Gibraltar West." Hangover House, he christened it because it
overlooked a cliff. The pun proved irresistible to those familiar with the drinking
habits of Paul, who had himself photographed holding the placard that bore
the house's name.[34]

Besides the unfinished house and its mounting costs, the faltering health
of his friend Leo DeSola—not so long ago a pillar of strength and now "only
half alive," his face ravaged by some unnoted disease—troubled him, even as
the "junk idea" made him look calmly ahead. Intimations of his own mortality
nettled him, as they had when a diagnosis of tachycardia took him out of school
as a teenager. The recent *Hindenburg* disaster especially distressed him, even as he

Paul Mooney, 1937, holding up the sign that announced the completion of "Hangover" House. This is the best-known photograph of Paul (courtesy William Alexander).

spoke at length about the "junk idea." As distressing to him was the disappearance of Amelia Earhart. "The ocean of pictures continue to make it horrible," he wrote home. "I'm off flying for good," he decided. "Never really liked it much anyway." This sounded odd coming from a man who had stood up in an open cockpit 18,000 feet in the air to snap pictures of Mt. Everest. He would continue to fly domestically, as he would continue to hedge his bets in another way.[35]

In spring 1937, Richard contacted the Gay Beaman Insurance Agency about inheritance tax, insurance, and Paul's "occupancy of the house," which would summarily end should Richard himself die—indeed, sudden death was always a good possibility with him. The comfort and security of his parents being "most meaningful" to him, he made it clear that the house would be "the joint property" of both his parents. He also made provisions to have Princeton set up a Halliburton library, upon their deaths. Earlier, there was also a "Mooney-DeSola policy" whose provisions are not stated. Immensely practical, Halliburton only took what precautions all seamen from Columbus' day on took, should the worst happen on a dangerous sea mission—make out a will. About this time, he had placed his net worth—including securities, insurance, and the house—at $100,000, a large sum in those days.[36]

With the business of the house now behind them, Paul and Richard spent several days in Morongo Valley, near San Jacinto, and stayed at the Greg Tupper ranch "basking in unmitigated sunshine." Jeffers' "Thurso's Landing" must have sprung to mind. The valley Paul described "as typical desert land," then mentioned Richard and himself driving with Greg and his helper "up a canyon where big trees were growing beside a clear stream." Paul called it "one of the pleasantest days [he'd] ever passed." They "picnicked in the shade in [their] bathing suits, and got moderately plastered on gin mixed with brook water. There were mountain lion tracks leading down to a pool; Indian pottery shards strewn about; an antelope peeked over the brush; all manner of flowers. And of course, no other people." A main topic was Greg's ranch house, which had become ramshackle. Greg himself wished he had asked Alexander to build his house, "not only [admitted to be] far more beautiful and sound [than his], but a hundred times more house for the money."[37]

Paul, meanwhile, had made the rounds in Hollywood looking for a writing job. One wonders if he had to correct potential clients who mistook him for actor Paul Muni. At the time Muni scored big at the box office with *The Life of Louis Pasteur*, *The Good Earth*, and *The Life of Emile Zola*; and, one wonders if, in elucidating, he said, as William Alexander suggested he may have, "No, that's Muni Weisenfreund," Muni's real name.[38]

Unable to find a job in Hollywood, he pined and languished in Laguna. Through insurance agent Gay Beaman, of all unlikely connections, the opportunity to rewrite a "flying adventure" comparable to the *Flying Carpet* project did come his way. The pay was good: $1,000 for a deadline date of four months.

Opposite page through page 168, photographs numbered A–E: Guest bedroom with bed designed by William Alexander (A); second guest room with Japanese grass wallpaper (B); Halliburton's bed and bookshelf with William Mortensen photograph of Alexander and multiple copies of Halliburton's books (C); "Forward Bath" adjoining Halliburton's bedroom (D); living room toward gallery, and canyon, showing rutted finish over reinforced concrete around "Heatilator" and stainless steel rods built-in to support cadmium finish mesh (E). May 1938. Ivy George took photographs A, B and D, and Alexander may have taken C (courtesy William Alexander).

A

B

C

D

E

Whether he took on the job remains unknown. What is known is that he was intending to leave Laguna Beach and journey southward, probably to Taxco, just south of Mexico City. The Tudor Apartments' managers were also hounding him for money he owed from his residency there years back. How they found Paul mystifies, but likely Paul let the whole matter slip by. As there was no urgent need for his services anymore, his friend Bill Alexander had packed up, months before, to return home to New York, in 1938. Paul sent him three books, all signed by Halliburton, to distribute to the "four brats" (unnamed) to whom Alexander would offer them.[39]

Paul was likely packing his bags for Mexico when Richard asked that he join him on the *Sea Dragon Expedition*. By September 1937, the plans to get things underway had gotten "very hot." Reluctant at first, Paul quickly unpacked. The Fair was now the thing, and from that moment Paul's life became fully linked to the fortunes of his famous companion.[40]

Paul, then, had to find responsible tenants who, besides honoring Hangover House, would take care of the lawn and water the eucalyptus trees. Stepping in then were Mary Lou Davis, daughter Dorothy, about nineteen, and son Tommy, about twelve. Fortunately, the Davises adored cats, and gladly would look after the several now belonging to him that prowled about the premises. Mary Lou, according to the report of Juliet Halliburton Davis (presumably no relation to Mary Lou), was to marry Richard. After meeting women from all over the world, he seems to have found American women most to his liking. Yet Mary Lou? Richard's mother thought her a "shirt waist person," or commoner frankly, and

Mary Lou Davis, Dorothy Davis, and Tommy Davis at Hangover House, 1939 or 1940. Paul owned three or four cats (from which, some believe, all of Laguna Beach's cats are descended); two are shown here. Also pictured is one of the junk replicas which Halliburton sent back to the States (courtesy William Alexander).

Mary Lou Davis looking out to the ocean from Hangover House, 1939 or 1940 (courtesy William Alexander).

had expected her son to marry the daughter of a prominent Memphis business-man.[41]

Rumors circulated that Richard was about to marry Mary Lou Davis, a willful and attractive woman in her mid-thirties, and that he would settle down with her at Hangover House. Evidence exists, however, that Halliburton was at least toying with the idea of getting rid of the house. In August 1938, Alexander told him that he had found a "prospective customer." To this Halliburton replied, "The only customer that will ever be willing to take Hangover off my hands will be Orange County, for taxes."[42]

15

"Pacifica"

What Halliburton called the "kid book"—the *Book of Marvels*—was written mostly on the road. The chapters on the Taj Mahal, the Great Wall, and Mt. Fujiyama, for instance, were penned at the Lincoln Hotel in Indianapolis to form, in the end, a hodge-podge of travel spectacle and adventure. Incorporated into the book were materials from previous books as well as from the projected *Royal Road to Romance in America*. At first one large tome was to comprise all his adventures, but it was decided that one volume should be devoted to the Occident and another to the Orient. This would serve the dual purpose of promoting the junk idea and sell more books—at a tentative cost of $7.50 each. Predictably, the newer materials went into the Occident book, and trips to America's shrines, including one to hallowed Fort McHenry where "The Star Spangled Banner" was composed, continued to enrich it. Sequels were touched upon as a further means to educate, and to make money.[1]

Halliburton had big plans for the book. He spoke of trimming the content down 10 percent to reduce "the age level a good year," so that younger readers could read it. Wise to every angle, he thought that if the book were put in the schools, possibly as required reading, then "we'll all retire." A chief feature of the book was its often larger-than-life photographs. Writing up captions for these proved the most onerous task. For the writing of the text itself, Halliburton resorted to his old method of having his father read drafts, to let him know "which are good and which dull." Usually he rewarded him, and his mother, with a trip abroad—this time, tentatively, to "Jerusalem, Egypt, Baalbek." As usual, he rewrote, then rewrote again, towards best effect. Periodically he mentioned the hard work on the book and, as usual, thanked his father for his corrections. As before, he worked with David Chambers on the galley proofs.[2]

Conspicuous by his absence at each and every stage of the writing process was Paul. As supervisor of the Hangover House project he seemed to have his hands full. While Wesley Halliburton wondered what Paul would do for gainful employment once the project ended, it is clear, at least during most of 1937 and much of 1938, that Richard was not going to insinuate Paul's presence into the writing of the *Book of Marvels*. Richard, even though his line of communication

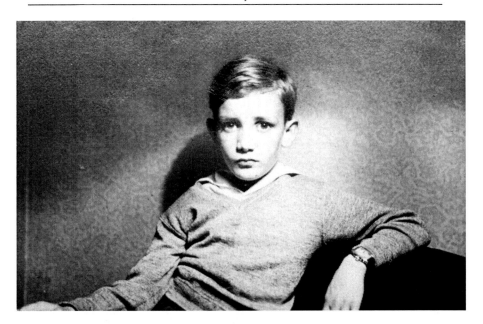

John Murphy Scott, 1935, age 9, about the age level for which *The Book of Marvels* was intended. Photograph taken by Paul Mooney (courtesy John Murphy Scott).

with his parents was remarkably open, wisely applied some principles of selection when he wrote to them; for instance, he didn't specifically mention Paul's embellishments to the house, and he didn't inform his parents that Paul had done work on *I Knew Hitler* (though Paul's very connection with so sinister a subject might not have boded well in a project aimed basically at young people). It stands to reason, however, that Paul, if Richard didn't write home that it was so, offered input into the book and more than glimpsed the carbons that were left at Hangover House.[3]

Busy as much as agitated, Richard these days was truly an action verb, or the complement of one. A confessed loner, still he was not quite the romantic isolate that promotional images of himself might suggest. In the end, he preferred *for his home* not the ostentatious loneliness of a mountaintop, but a trendy city within easy reach of the madding crowd. During his last days, San Francisco was home port to him and became, of all the cities he ever visited, his favorite.[4]

As usual, Halliburton stayed at the Chancellor Hotel, on 433 Powell Street, at the center of downtown, not far from Union Square and the streetcar lines. From here Halliburton, once he had completed the two *Books of Marvels*, carried out his plans for the *Sea Dragon Expedition*. Little less than a mile away was Telegraph Hill. From the top, one could get a commanding view of Treasure Island, where the great Fair soon would open. Further down was the Embarcadero, and the Ferry Building with its daily commuter traffic. In those days few homes dotted the hillside, which, with its wooden ramparts, winding dirt paths, and rocky precipices, seemed an acropolis.[5]

He had opened the first *Book of Marvels* with a celebration of the great city and its two great bridges. As earlier Paul, in hard hat, stood high above the Bay waters of the recently built Oakland Bridge, so now Richard, in hard hat, stood high above the Bay waters of the new Golden Gate Bridge. "High overhead its lights shall gleam," its builder Joseph Strauss waxed lyrically about an undertaking many thought both physically and financially impossible: "Far, far below, life's restless stream / Unceasing shall flow...."[6]

Not everyone was so charmed when the monument was unveiled. Citizens' committees had to buck opposing parties who tagged the bridge a number one target for an enemy bombing mission. Women's groups argued that it would bring a flood of picnickers to Marin County and ruin its serenity. Still, over 200,000 people came out to inspect the bridge when it opened towards the end of May. An array of jet planes from Hamilton Field flew over in a grand salute. At 8:30 a.m., a B-36 bomber of the Strategic Air Control flew low to hail it while the 12th Naval District Band played a medley of rousing marching songs. Commodore Dan London on the yacht *Adventuress*, meanwhile, led the Golden Fleet flotilla, which had come out in full force.[7]

The "junk idea" formed a part of the hoopla. As in 1915 when the Pan-American Exposition announced San Francisco's recovery from the earthquake of 1906, so now the 1939 Exposition heralded the city's emergence as a world-class port. The year 1939 also marked the one hundredth year since the outbreak of the First Opium War between China and Great Britain, and the emergence of Hong Kong as a leading world port. What would be called the "Gold Rush passage," celebrating San Francisco's bridges and linking Asia and America, called for sailing a Chinese junk across the Pacific from one great modern city to another.[8]

The Halliburton name still held magic. The first *Book of Marvels—The Occident* had appeared in 1937, the second *Book of Marvels—The Orient* in September 1938. Both were popular successes. *The Royal Road to Romance in the U.S.A.*, with the junk adventure to be its first chapter, would appear in 1940.

Sponsors knew that Halliburton drew crowds as much as almost any matinee idol of the day. San Francisco publicist Walter Gaines Swanson, journalist Dean Jennings and future radio and televison star Art Linkletter aimed at making Halliburton synonymous with the Exposition itself. Knowing what the hero business was all about, Halliburton gladly obliged. A shareholding corporation was soon formed. "The corporation had to be formed legally," notes Jonathan Root, "a captain and an engineer hired, insurance policies obtained, berthing accommodations at the Fair arranged, promotions planned, and contracts with

Opposite: **Richard Halliburton in a steel hardhat during construction of the Golden Gate Bridge, 1936 (courtesy William Alexander).**

the *News* and the Bell Syndicate negotiated." San Francisco attorney J. Richard Townsend was hired to oversee, and assist Halliburton with financial details and the crew. Nearly a thousand young men and women applied to go along on the trip, but not all were prepared to put up money to do so. Needed money, however, was painstakingly raised, much of it from the families of the young men who would participate in the actual sailing and from Richard's cousin Erle's family. Principal shareholders, putting up $14,000 of the $25,000 required for the voyage, included four young men in their early twenties who would also serve as crew members: the two with sailing experience were Gordon Ellicott Torrey from Bar Harbor, Maine, and John Rust "Brue" Potter from Northeast Harbor; the two with little or no sailing experience were Robert Hill Chase of Milton, Massachusetts, then a senior at Dartmouth College, and George Barstow III of Sharon, Connecticut, a student at the Juilliard School of Music. Fearful that the Japanese would prevent their sailing, the Chinese backers had pulled out completely. Hedging his bets on future gains, Richard added to the $21,000 amount, which seemed to him insufficient, by mortgaging the Laguna property to the tune of $4,000, a quite hefty sum in those days.[9]

For Halliburton, who had failed most of his screen tests, the part was a major one, which the continuing competition among adventurers forced him to accept. Hunter Frank Buck, for instance, was setting up "Jungleland" at the other World's Fair in New York. His book *Bring 'em Back Alive* (1930) and its film version answered the public clamor for real-life adventure more soundly than had *The Flying Carpet* and *India Speaks* combined. The celebrated Robert Ripley ("the modern Marco Polo"), whose "Believe It or Not" amazed a generation and made their creator immensely rich, had his own Chinese junk ready to go wondrous places. New heartthrob Errol Flynn, with both youth and movie box-office success to his credit, threatened to push all three aside. The films *The Sea Hawk*, *Robin Hood* and *Captain Blood* had rocketed him to stardom. He had also published a bestseller, *Beam Ends*, about his yachting adventures in the South Seas.[10]

Money also encouraged Halliburton to accept the part. Not unlike Jules Verne's fictional character Philias Fogg, Halliburton, accustomed to a certain lifestyle, didn't relish the idea of ending up a clerk. Articles the Bell Syndicate and *San Francisco News* commissioned him to write (with, again, Paul's likely help) would pay handsomely, and then there was the profitable lecture circuit, and always another book. Halliburton saw dollar signs galore as he had never seen them before. "Yesterday I went to Treasure Island to examine my anchorage," reads a letter dated August 31, 1938. "It's lovely. Once safe in the Bay, I'm going to have the most exciting concession at the Fair—and make lots of money."[11]

Behind the need for recognition, and money, was the need for change. He had in fact told his cousin John Halliburton that changes in his style were necessary to meet the challenges of advancing age. "The boyish pranks, that were so successful in his early books," he recalled, "would appear rather ridiculous in a middle-age man." Discussions with Paul, who referred to the *First Book of Marvels* (and the *Second* is hardly different) as "the baby book," may have contributed to this realistic assessment. Also, in an America grown cynical, Richard wondered at the very idea of a book on America's greatness.[12]

During the closing days of summer, Halliburton was offered numerous invitations to dine. Publicity events also had him shuttling back and forth. He "even went out to Fleishhacker Zoo," notes biographer Jonathan Root, "and posed astride Marge, their prize elephant, as he told once again of his bizarre Alpine crossing, and he was asked repeatedly if he minded being known as the darling of the women's clubs."[13]

As he had a decade earlier, he made quick trips, some by air, throughout California to women's clubs and other groups to promote his latest project along with the customary message of "right living and achievement." Newspapers covered his activities as a kind of happy diversion from Nazi expansion in Europe.[14]

Details remained. To handle them, he had gotten a "lively agent" named Wilfred Crowell. Still, he had to find a captain to steer the ship, and an engineer to propel it. Besides conferring with Pan-Am officials about radio communication, he had to meet with Fair officials to discuss such things as anchorage, rents and commissions. Insurance needs had to be met. He continued to tour mostly by train to, among other places, Baton Rouge, Louisiana, Cadillac, Michigan, and New York, New York. His trips to Laguna Beach, meanwhile, became less frequent. His last trip to see his house was from June 27 to July 4. He learned then that Paul had been unsuccessful in his job search in Hollywood, and probably then he made his proposal that Paul join the *Sea Dragon Expedition* as his assistant. Disposition of the Laguna property and its management residency certainly were discussed. As "all [his] creative endeavors for the next two years [would] be toward the America book," this too may have been a topic of conversation.[15] Halliburton regularly met with Gertrude Atherton, a founding member of the Writer's League of America, advocate of social reform and leader in promoting a California cultural identity. Now in her eighties, she was still zesty, brassy, proudly tall and nearly blonde. The idea of being a superwoman appealed to her, and in her candid and witty *Can Women Be Gentlemen?* she voiced her opinions about a thinking woman's place in the modern world. She had written an "intimate history" of California; by 1939, she *was* California's history and, like her departed dear friend Senator James Phelan, a strong believer in the cultural progress of the state. From such adventure sagas as *The Doomswoman* and *Before The Gringo Came*, the grande dame of California literature had come of age, in her sixties, with a controversial novel about sexual rejuvenation, *Black Oxen* (1923), which was banned in some communities. She wrote books for young women. She had also written a book for boys entitled *The Valiant Runaways*.[16]

One would like to have recordings of the conversations she had with Halliburton. The lecture platform had made them both spontaneously articulate about every topic in the news at this time, and long ago. Perhaps they chatted about China; she had been everywhere else, but never to any place where Halliburton was now going. Perhaps they chatted about Greece—romantic "ancient Greece." She also held the opinion that Pericles' mistress, the *hetaera* Aspasia, was "a loose and intellectual lady," owning that a woman could be both and not fret about it. She hated ruins, but liked politics and thought Eleanor Roosevelt should be president. Mentioned perhaps was mutual friend Carl Van Vechten, who insisted that she write her life story, *Adventures of a Novelist*, which mentioned Halliburton and which was arguably the last book Halliburton, maybe given a copy from her, ever read. She may have discussed with Halliburton copyright infringement and writers' rights, and Maxwell Aley who, as head of the New York chapter of PEN, the international writers organization, evidently objected to a San Francisco Chapter of PEN and Atherton's heading it. Or she may have shared her memories of the "Emperor Norton, a harmless lunatic in a shabby uniform, driven insane over the execution of Maximilian," who may have passed this way. Or she may have talked about "North Beach—where there [once] were monkeys." Or perhaps they talked about her own first husband, brought back from death at sea in a barrel of rum.[17]

As many as twelve people might be gathered together at one of these weekly get-togethers. The last of these was on Sunday, September 18, 1938, when Richard hosted a farewell cocktail party at the Blue Lagoon in San Francisco's Maiden Lane. Present as a likely guest of honor was Gertrude Atherton. Also present was Dr. Margaret Chung, with whom Halliburton had kept contact. Besides flying credentials, Chung was an advocate for combined American-Chinese resistance against aggression and later a lobbyist for the creation of the WAVES. As importantly, if not more so, she held a key position in flight commerce and communication. Pan Am pilots now landed routinely in Hong Kong. Among their number were members of Dr. Margaret "Mike" Chung's Oakland-based flying club known as "Mom Chung's Fair Haired Bastards." Edwin Muzick piloted the first clipper across the Pacific. Another pilot, Horace Brock, visited Halliburton just before his second junk attempt. Halliburton, the careful planner, and aviation-minded Paul Mooney wanted to rest assured that rescue teams were at hand, should anything happen to them at sea.[18]

Halliburton's mother attended the party and, like Atherton and Dr. Chung, was probably also a guest of honor. Just returned with husband Wesley from a long trip abroad, Mrs. Halliburton told her son that she had especially liked the Azores and Ponta Delgada, which had been his "first glimpse of foreign shores" twenty years before. She had come to San Francisco for the sole purpose of seeing her son off. The papers carried a story and photos of the two together. Likely Paul was present too, as well as one or two of the sponsors of the *Sea Dragon Expedition*. Likely they discussed Somerset Maugham's new book, the autobiographical *The Summing Up*, which Richard had sent her and which she returned to him; besides Gertrude Atherton's autobiography, he intended to read the book during the Pacific crossing. Earlier Richard had applauded the book's "Lucidity—Simplicity—Euphony," virtues which he regarded as his own "literary ideals." What he thought about its deeper messages—that death is not so remote for people after they turn sixty, or the author's own wish to return to a next life, this time with a better brain—is not known.[19]

Nelle Nance had traveled with Wesley far and wide, largely through her son's generosity and attention to the details of scheduling wonderful trips. This was her first trip to San Francisco. She had come without Wesley, and so it was left up to Richard to see that she was well attended. Earlier Paul, or Richard, had met her at the railway station in Los Angeles, and taken her to the Biltmore Hotel, then taken her to see the house in Laguna. Joined by Richard and Paul in Los Angeles again, she dined with in-laws Vida and Zola Halliburton, both investors in the Sea Dragon venture. On September 17, 1938, Richard, Paul, and Nelle Nance proceeded to San Francisco. "Mother and I did the best we could with the fleeting moments we had together," Halliburton later wrote home; "they were very sweet and very happy—and she was patient not to get too restless."[20]

Throughout her stay in San Francisco, Richard informed his mother in great detail about his upcoming trip, assuaging her fears of its possible dangers at every turn. He judged it "less dangerous than [his] flight over the Sahara" and probably less so than his swimming of the full length of the Panama Canal, or of the Hellespont, or his descent into the Mayan "Well of Death." All these too were multiple threat situations, of course with notable differences regarding the nature of the threats themselves.[21]

Though not a duplicate of anything that had gone before it, the venture approximated in scope a number of such ventures from the past. Ocean-navigating junks, as early as the fifth century B.C., had sailed into the Pacific, including one voyage, in 217 B.C., captained by one Hee Li, which supposedly made it to California and left, as clues to its success, words of Chinese origin in the language of an Indian tribe settled there. In 1848 a junk voyaged from Shanghai to London.[22]

In 1893, the replica of a Viking ship, bound for the 1893 Columbian Exposition in Chicago, had sailed across the Atlantic from Bergen, Norway. To the same destination, Columbus' caravels, "full-size replicas of the Nina, the Pinta, and the Santa Maria," had sailed from Spain. Across the Pacific, Los Angeles physician E.A. Petersen, his wife and two Russian sailors, a year before the Sea Dragon, had sailed a 36-foot junk, the Hummel Hummel, from Yokohama to San Francisco; though starting in Shanghai and ending up in San Pedro, it went the same route the Sea Dragon would go.[23]

Earlier, in 1922, a junk had sailed from the port of Amoy to the Aleutian Islands and southward to Vancouver and San Francisco, through the Panama Canal into the Atlantic. Not as fortunate, another vessel had sailed from Yokohama and drifted into Puget Sound, where crew members, starved to death, were found strewn about the deck. Famed Captain Joshua Slocum, in 1886–

1889, had sailed into the open seas, and eventual safety, in a tiny craft, *The Liber-dade* ("half Cape Ann Dory and half sampan"), built from the salvaged wreckage of a ship that had run aground, with his family and a crew of ten. Later, from 1895 to 1898, Slocum sailed around the world in a small sloop the *Spray*, this time alone.[24]

Halliburton drew inspiration from the Chinese warlord who, in 1875, had made the crossing with an armed squadron of junks to protest American exploitation of coolies in the building of the trans–American railroad. He hardly drew as much inspiration from the HMS *Success*, the famed convict ship, a "float-ing museum of old-time penal horrors," which had ominously docked in San Francisco Bay as a feature of the Panama–Pacific International Exposition of 1915.[25]

Halliburton had received some Navy officer training as an undergrad at Princeton University. This included a few classes that amounted to a primer on navigation, if not off-shore sailing experience. Hard now as it is to imagine, he also worked as a waiter in a mess for naval trainees. While he picked up part of the language of navigation—both its salty and technical terms, and a few naval rules and regulations, clearly he was no sailor. "Boats are a new world for me," he admitted, "I've much to learn." Usually he let others do the sailoring.[26]

Paul of course knew even less about boats than Halliburton. By this time Nelle Nance had gotten to know him fairly well. Surely they talked about their trips abroad; both had been to Istanbul and Paris. Still, it is unknown how she reacted when Richard shared with her his "bright idea to make Paul" his "assis-tant." He of course would be paid well for his services. This was a bold move, since by now Wesley was confirmed in his opinion that Paul was a pathetic soli-tary, a freeloader and a drifter. But, insisted Richard: "He'll be splendid with some intense adventurous job, and he will be paid well for his services—the same as I would have to pay anybody else. He's in a rut in Laguna drinking and smoking too much—this violent change will stir him up and give him a new interest in life and work."

Halliburton felt as magnanimous as the Count of Monte Cristo appointing Paul as the captain of his private launch for his devotedness to him, and Paul, as devotedness itself, hardly minded. He may have thought himself doing the noble thing, as Byron had going off to Greece, or John Reed going off to Russia. The appointment, not to mention the build-up, further exposed Halliburton's relationship to Paul: "He has already found occupants for the house—who will care for it properly," Richard said. "He's overjoyed over the prospects of going along—and so am I as I'll have that much more protection."[27]

Halliburton could have chosen to fake the trans–Pacific crossing, but to silence critics who believed he had faked most of what he had written about himself anyway, he had to go through with it. He might have cut some corners, however. Had he and Paul come up from, say, Santa Catalina or even Sausalito, it probably would not have made much difference to the people who attended the World's Fair. The "Chinese Village" would have provided sufficient cultural backdrop. Arrival from any port might have been as glorious as Antony and Cleopatra appearing at harbor in their pleasure barge, with its purple Tyrian-dyed mast fluttering nobly in the wind. The convention delegates and "conventionites" whom he intended to take on sightseeing tours "for $1 a head" around the Bay, once he arrived, would hardly have been disappointed. Halliburton had intended to dock his ship across from the Court of the Seven Seas, as earlier, in 1933, Admiral Byrd, at the Chicago World's Fair, had docked his *City of New York* across from the main Century of Progress exhibits.[28]

Halliburton wanted to make a statement, but he also wanted to retire rich. At the World's Fair he had looked over the anchorage and thought it "lovely," a bank as much as a dock. Already sales from his recent books were impressive. "Once safe in the Bay, I'm going to have the most exciting concession at the Fair—and make lots of money." His logic apparently invincible, he imagined the vast sums that would accrue from the three trips a day tourists would make from the Oakland Bay Bridge to the new Golden Gate Bridge aboard the triumphant junk (now ocean weary and towed by a tug)—each visitor paying $1. The thought of quickly paying off his debts and going well into the black, while it made him tingle with excitement, underscored his faith in his own marketability; "money," he enthused, "from ticket sale[s], souvenirs, radio, stamps, merchandise, letters to school children, and movies." The "Bell letters," saga-like features of the *Sea Dragon Expedition* that were to be sent to subscribers for $5, were another source of revenue.

With a fit, eager crew now assembled—some of whom had earnestly invested in the venture, a successful trans–Pacific voyage seemed assured and without any taint of illusion. Some would make the journey to Hong Kong by ship, others by airplane. Halliburton, his initial work in the plan completed, could smile. Dollar signs and pictures of a comfortable retirement ever formed in his brain. If all went well, for one man at least, the Depression would soon come to an end.

16

The Halliburton
Chinese Junk Expedition

On September 23, Richard boarded the S.S. *President Coolidge* ("going tourist class—$200"). The liner sailed without incident to Honolulu, where Richard and Paul spent some happy moments with friends on Waikiki Beach.[1]

Also on board, besides a diesel engine (in stowage) and diesel engine specialist Henry von Fehren, was Captain John "Jack" Wenlock Welch. A burly Australian of Scottish extraction, the forty-two-year-old seafarer said he could speak Chinese and that he had sailed junks all his life. He had also, so he said, taken cargo ships around the Cape of Good Hope and liners of the United Fruit Company to Central America. Movie producers at both Universal and Fox solicited his expertise on at least two sea adventures.[2]

Though Mrs. Halliburton found Captain Welch charming and good-looking, Richard found him gauche and overbearing, yet did little at the eleventh hour to investigate his credentials. It was not certain, for instance, whether or not the said Captain Welch was a licensed U.S. merchant seaman. When he got the call from Halliburton to skipper his junk, Welch simply told him that he had himself intended to sail a junk on his own to Panama, and from there to Scotland.[3] Conciliatory to a fault, Halliburton referred to Welch as "a veteran seaman" and "master of all manner of sailing ships." Secretly, however, he found the good captain almost too salty both in his language and his off-color stories about his conquests of lady passengers at sea. Paul found him a swaggering boor and, barely out to sea, probably wanted to throw him overboard, but kept to his report writing and mimeographing.[4]

After fifteen days at sea, Halliburton's ship harbored in Yokohama, Japan, on October 7, 1938. Paul had never been to either China or Japan; likely, he never did see Mt. Fujiyama, "The Magic Mountain" of the *Book of Marvels* (the weather was "murky") or "The Great Stone Serpent," the Great Wall. In their next stop, Tokyo, Halliburton and he secured safe conduct documents and other assurances for himself and his crew from the Japanese Foreign Office. These precautions, if perhaps meaningless, were necessary nevertheless. In 1937 Japan had opened up war on China and had launched a major invasion of the Chinese mainland. By 1938, its navy was routinely sinking Chinese junks, and the Japanese stranglehold on Chinese commerce continued to tighten.[5]

Twice before, Halliburton had been in this part of the world, once in 1922 and again in 1932, and knew that danger in the region was always imminent. By turns nervous and coolly resolved, he, together with Paul and Captain Welch, continued towards the China coast. Once there, he boarded a passenger ship headed toward Shanghai where, proceeding southward, he commenced his search for the perfect junk—one whose name *Sea Dragon* had long ago been decided upon. Hundreds of junks he hastily inspected. Most of these were either too old or wholly unseaworthy. In Amoy, a shipwright offered to build him a "first-class Amoy junk in ninety days," but Halliburton refused, saying he wanted one "now."[6]

Letter (top) from "Richard Halliburton's Chinese Junk 'The Sea Dragon' En Route from Hong Kong to Treasure Island." Hundreds, if not thousands, of these so-called "Bell letters" were sent to subscribers who had paid five dollars for progress reports of the *Sea Dragon Expedition*. Uncommon, this envelope, with enclosed multi-page letter signed "Richard Halliburton," and card initialed by Wilfred Crowell, can sell for as much as five hundred dollars today. A smaller souvenir envelope is shown below the full-size one.

Fall had set in and the weather had become chilly when, on October 22, his ship reached Hong Kong, his "last hope" for finding a suitable vessel. There hundreds of junks floating in and out of the harbor met his delighted eyes. The Sino-Japanese War had left the area in a grave state of defense, but, for the moment, he thought the place a safe haven: "Protected by the guns on the tow-ering peaks above the harbor," he wrote, "the junks from this port, thumbing their noses at the Japanese, were fishing merrily along the shore."[7]

Undaunted, Halliburton, within an hour of his arrival, renewed his quest for the perfect junk.

"The war is hardly noticed here," he assured his parents. "Life seems normal in every way." Normal for Halliburton was not necessarily normal for the others who had joined the expedition. The idyllic pictures of China and Japan provided in the last two chapters of the *Books of Marvels* and featuring Mary Lou Davis' son Tommy as a charmed innocent abroad operate on another tier of reality.[8]

Most foreign of the world's great ports, Hong Kong was also the most wildly international. Born of the Opium Wars that had ended nearly a hundred years before, the city was long the principal hub of the British colonial system. Com-prising a great mix of races and nationalities, the population of the colony had grown by 1939 to over a million and a half, and daily continued to swell with Chinese refugees. Expatriates from Great Britain, America, and France lived in its fast-paced Europeanized corridors, while criminals roamed freely about the criss-crossing streets. As security from policing the Colony's borders grew, so did the inability of law enforcement to deal with internal disorder. Halliburton thought Hong Kong "a beautiful and interesting town—in fact I have no troubles of any sort [here]." This is in keeping with historian Ted Ferguson's statement that "the bulk of Hong Kong's white population behaved as though the Japanese menace were a preposterous illusion."[9]

Western ways surely had triumphed, or so it seemed, as many Asians had adopted Western dress, and enjoyed European-style racing, football, dancing, golf and the movies. Westerners, meanwhile, some at least, had developed a curiosity for Chinese culture. For every street named Waterloo or Wellington there was one named Cheung Sha Wan or Pei Ho Street. There were sumptuous municipal buildings with marble porticos and colonnades, plantation-like man-sions, magnificent pagodas and picturesque hovels. Buses honked at clankety Tin Lizzies sputtering down the concrete or rock-laid roads. Horse-drawn car-riages and wooden-wheeled carts rode alongside the cars that honked at the bicyclists and rickshaw pullers. Chinese shadow boxers moved gracefully as sedan chair carriers with their European passengers obliviously passed by.[10]

The rocky peninsula allowed for little in the way of public building or housing. Sidewalks and streets, as a result, were crowded, blocked, noisy, and anarchic. Some led to the harbor where, moored in the slimy green water were the sampans, junks, and jetties of the drab-looking fishing families. Down one major hub or another, babbling coolies and beggars, cigarette vendors, tattoo artists, medicine men, hawkers and fortune tellers let out an ear-numbing cacophony. Floppy-trousered and head-scarfed women in sandals trotted past with some burden on their backs. Prostitutes still beckoned from doorways and sampans; smugglers appeared no different from legitimate traders; spies and pickpockets lurked about, indistinguishably; opium still circulated legally until after 1940.[11]

Richard and Paul took up residence at a boarding house in Kowloon, just opposite Hong Kong Island and a short distance from Dailey's shipyards. The food (if one chose to eat in) was good, the water clean and the rooms clean. A main thoroughfare was then (as now) Nathan Road. Kowloon, from *Kau-lung*, meaning "Nine Dragons" in Chinese, named the nine hills that made up the backbone of the peninsula. From Kowloon one could see the top of Victoria Peak. A short distance away, the Star Ferry regularly took passengers across the harbor to the island. First-class hotels were around. Recommended for its posh European atmosphere was the Peninsula, across from the Kowloon-Canton railway and, familiarly, next to a YMCA; the Luen Shing and Repulse Bay Hotels also bore elegant resemblances to Western a·uence. Also there was the Hong Kong Club. Rundown hotels from the Bund to the Peak abounded.[12]

In the Wanchai district was a popular bar called Nagasaki Joe's, which served beer cheaper than elsewhere. On a far higher scale, in the heart of the colony at Queen's Road and Pedder Street beside Pedder Wharf and near the spot where the famed Lapriak Clock Tower once stood, was the celebrated Hong Kong Hotel, long the mecca for traders, money-lenders, sportsmen, adventurers, cunning rogues, foreign diplomats and British naval officers who came every night for dining and dancing—and also a favorite hang-out of Richard Halliburton. A Japanese man named Joe Yamashita ran the barbershop in the hotel and asked "superfluous questions about the comings and goings of ships." Outside, gentlemen and ladies of fashion boarded or stepped off carriages. Rickshaw pullers were ever on hand. Of course, while it was fun to patronize the upscale hotel, it was cheaper to stay at the less fashionable Kowloon Hotel.[13]

The Hong Kong of 1939 was rawer, more ruggedly sensuous and immediate than it would become years later. The diseases the refugees brought to the island—beriberi, cholera, and malaria—were as dreadful as the smells were odious. Whiffs of salt-sea air came with the odor of souchong, the potent fumes from the soy-sauce factories, and gasoline. Then there was the food which was, in most cases, crummy. Paul had to be grateful he had an indifference towards food. At least in the United States bread lines formed and, when one's turn came, the bread was okay. Here maggots and who knows what other microbes infested it. In the States, the poor person might get only corn flakes and water, but the water was good. Here the water was putrid and encouraged the drinking of alcohol as an alternative. One might still be directed to sample, on a dare, the fresh vegetables or take home one of those huge cooked pigs. One had to wonder what went into the noodle dishes. Cobra soup, for those who weren't used

John "Brue" Potter (left) and Robert Chase (aiming his camera) in Hong Kong among a group of children. Potter bowed out after the trial run of the *Sea Dragon*; Chase boarded the ship on its trial run and on its tragic second run (courtesy William Alexander).

to it, could burn the insides. When boiled, the bean soup, a possible alternative, formed into a kind of building material. The fish of all kinds that dried out on the vendor's mats at least seemed sun bleached. The shrimp was okay, as was the rice, which Richard and Paul ate with chopsticks. Spices, every kind of which stood in barrels for blocks outside the groceries, covered up the taste of most things. Sharkfin products of all sorts made the worldly imagination free-associate as to their uses. Innocent looking fruit and anything that grew above and below the ground could be bought somewhere. There were so-called American diners, and the American Consulate in Hong Kong might tell one where to go. In the long run it was probably best to have a light appetite.[14]

The Star Ferry, which took one across the broad Victoria Harbor, took one away from it all. Once on the island one could catch a bus, then take the Peak Tram, the famous funicular railway, that shot ever upward, as daring as a roller coaster, as gravity defiant, towards the summit of Victoria, some 1,750 feet high. From there one could imagine the Pacific's sixty-three-million square miles and see some of the many islands that were strewn as dice throughout the nine-thousand miles that separated the island from San Francisco. "After night the view is unsurpassed," wrote Nellie Bly fifty years before. "One seems to be suspended between two heavens." From there Richard looked out at what he could see of the sprawling city, the "cultured pearl."[15]

As the *Flying Carpet Expedition* commenced with securing a plane, so the *Sea Dragon Expedition* commenced with securing a junk. Though earnest, Halliburton made his inspections with increasing haste. Most of the junks he looked at were flawed in some way or simply too expensive. One they found in a cove called Gin Drinker's Bay with a "hull ninety feet long" and "built like a battle-ship" could "easily have crossed the broad Pacific in grand style" but cost "three times what we could afford to pay." If by now Halliburton regretted not having taken up the offer of the Amoy shipwright, he at least had become sold on the idea of building a junk and "from [the] keel up." He decided to hire a prominent Kowloon cartwright named Fat Kau to undertake the job. Plump, balding, this astute businessman had four wives, exceptional manners, and a lot of money. Not as regal as he, the shipyard was in the waterfront slums across from a "high-smelling soybean factory between the Peachy Garage and a Gentleman's Parlor for Beauty." It was November 2; Halliburton and Mooney had been in Hong Kong twelve days.[16]

If he thought the monetary costs, labor problems, and delays encountered building his own house in Laguna Beach, California, were exasperating, those he encountered building this house on the sea were insufferable. The looser work ways of the Chinese workers frustrated him from the start. A job that should have taken twenty minutes, using Chinese methods took a week; one that should have been accomplished in seconds, took an hour or more. Hand-cutting tools—in place of machine saws—were part of the problem, the Chinese work ethic another. Showing up to the job site well dressed in his pleated trousers, pressed white shirt and spiffed-up oxfords, he was always on deck to watch the construction, as if his mere presence would speed up operations. It didn't.[17]

Halliburton remained calm. In private, however, he grumbled, mostly to Paul, about the "superlative perversity of the Chinese carpenters" who, thinking work a family affair, brought their wives aboard to watch them toil. At night they

Richard Halliburton supervising the construction of the *Sea Dragon*. Captain Welch is to his immediate right, radioman George Petrich is to his immediate left, and next to Petrich is first mate John "Brue" Potter who bowed out of the *Sea Dragon Expedition* after its trial run (courtesy Edward Howell).

threw parties. Girls arrived. Music began. Vast quantities of rice wine were drunk. At one party Fat Kau directed Wife Number Four, for a fee, to bring "barrels and baskets of Chinese food" (probably rice and fish) to help everyone make the transition from nagging drudgery to ecstatic intoxication. Opium climaxed the event, with smoke curling upward from the carved bowls of these long bamboo-stemmed pipes and from the bowls of gurgling hookahs. Meanwhile, "tailless cats prowled, slant-eyed, among the logs of teak and camphor wood." By midnight all of the workers curled up in their bedrolls, in some cranny near where they had worked, then partied. Next day, they arose, at different moments, not to the sound of any bell, and the cycle merrily repeated itself. So it went: the junk was not constructed so much as it "grew by spurts and whims" with "cabins, storerooms and lockers ... torn out and rearranged three times" according to a hit-and-miss theory of evolution rather than soundly "drawn paper plans." Halliburton could rejoice that the labor costs were low. Using American workers, they would have been prohibitive, as Halliburton learned from building his California home.[18]

Work continued, however slowly. If a crew member lost his way to the junk, the loud pounding, sawing, and hammering of its builders—some fifty of them—led one there. Flames bursting into the wind from a method used on board to bend the twenty foot teak planks that framed the hull of the ship also provided a signal.

Captain Welch was often on hand. Besides ordering the crew around, he bullied them as they practiced their roles. Often he flew into rages over their incompetence. Paul he found particularly incompetent, and he must have chuckled when Halliburton called Paul "an experienced seaman." By now Paul detested him. John Potter thought Welch an "irascible guy" who "seemed to carry around a chronic grudge against the world." Curiously, "he always ate alone at a single table," Richard noted, "while the rest of us were at one large table." Halliburton, though he was moved to label Welch "dictatorial," in his role of mediator had to bite the bullet. Likely Captain Welch and engineer Henry von Fehren didn't hit it off either. Welch after all didn't like an auxiliary engine on board. Von Fehren, for his part, boasted that he had crossed the Pacific many times and that he had "complete control of all the black magic of machinery," including "six years with Diesel engines in motor sailboats." This, however, said little of his merits as a junk navigator, and why a diesel engine should be installed. Paul, for his part, kept busy with the Bell letters, cranking them out on the mimeograph machine until he became an expert at its use.[19]

As had been the case during the final rewriting of The Flying Carpet, Halliburton rejoiced that he had Paul at his side. "He works harder than anybody," he told his parents, "and pulls more than his weight." While he did not come out and say that Paul actually wrote them, he did note that "he has been invaluable with the Letters." As the Expedition's appointed "journalist," it would stand to reason that Paul did more than operate a mimeograph machine.[20]

If Paul grew in Richard's affections, Captain Welch grew in his disfavor.

Richard Halliburton (top) discusses junk issues. Captain Welch is in the white shirt to his left and engineer Henry von Fehren is in foreground in white pilot's cap. The *Sea Dragon* floats in the background (courtesy William Alexander).

He also became a source of worry, unable to offer the leadership the present team needed to insure the expedition's success. "Captain Bligh," Richard dubbed him. He tried his best to avoid Welch, and often disappeared for days, showing up at the junk site only when absolutely needed.[21]

Disappearing wasn't hard. There were the markets. Paul liked the Jade Mar-

The hull interior of *the Sea Dragon* during construction, fall 1938 (courtesy William Alexander).

ket, and purchased several figurines to send home. (About these figurines a few words will appear later.) Richard purchased for his parents or friends a set of black lacquer tables (for mother), China horses, four elephants (for father), a mai jong board (for mother), two ivory heads, and, among other items, a set of five junk models he got in Shanghai (for himself).[22]

Another place to disappear to was the airport. Not just great ships and trains but planes connected Hong Kong to the world at large. Its airport was the Kai Tak (or Tek) Aerodrome, an aviation country club where Pan Am flights and sportier aircraft came and went. With its flights anywhere one wanted to go, it tempted Paul, if not the hard-headed Richard, with the promise of a quick release. There Paul could jaw with technicians, pilots and crew; the hangars provided cleaner haven than those rat boxes called hotels he was forced to stay in. Here he might find "Mom Chung's Fair Haired Bastards" and the Pan Am pilots who landed in Hong Kong, as did pilots from private and corporate air services all over the world. Pilots to whom Dr. Chung had introduced Halliburton kept him and Paul well-informed about weather conditions and routes, and also carried to their destination the all-important Bell letters.[23]

Recounting Halliburton's final days was "The Log of the Sea Dragon," a series of fifteen stories, which the San Francisco *News* and the Bell Syndicate paid him $6000 to write. Restyled versions (by Paul, I suspect) of these Bell *articles* were the "Sea Dragon club" subscription or "Bell" *letters*, called "Letters from the Sea Dragon," of which four from a projected seven letters were written. The now scarce originals, typed and single-spaced, each about 2000 words, ran, in all, to fifteen legal-sized pages. Subscribers who received the letters (for five dollars) were from "every state in the Union, and in several foreign countries." As part of the package, a gold leaflet, or *prospectus*, showing on its cover a coiling dragon protectively encircling a junk at sea, provided a map of the *Sea Dragon*'s route. It also noted that the junk, going by way of the Pan-American Islands used by the China Clippers, would port at Canton, Hong Kong, Manila, Guam, Midway Island, Honolulu, and Treasure Island. Clippers delivered the letters to San Francisco; from there, they were mailed to subscribers.[24]

Sent only were letters from Shanghai (November 20, 1938), Hong Kong (January 18, 1939), Canton (January 27, 1939), and Hong Kong (February 16, 1939). If "storms and currents" or "the war in the East" did not force the crew "to take a different course," letter five would arrive from Midway ("an island now famous as a sea station for the Pan-American clipper planes"), letter six from Honolulu, and letter seven from Treasure Island. Long "souvenir" envelopes (pictured, top, 183), with a sky- or ocean-blue cachet of a junk and its route, bore the return address: "The Halliburton Trans-Pacific Chinese Junk Expedition, Inc., 739 Market Street, San Francisco, California." Sent earlier from San Francisco was a publicity notice about the Expedition and the Bell Letters series. For these a standard envelope, with a reddish version of the cachet, bore the address: "The Richard Halliburton Chinese Junk Expedition—San Francisco—California—P.O. Box 3805."[25]

These letters, besides the articles and those letters Halliburton sent home, answer some questions, notably the key one about the crossing itself. Once underway, Halliburton and company intended to refuel in Manila, Guam, Wake, Midway, and Honolulu, where Pan Am had bases (though at sea they decided to skip Honolulu), and which the Navy assured him was okay. Later, he indicated a route change, noting Formosa (Taiwan) as a final departure point, then straightaway to Midway, next to Honolulu, and, last of all, to San Francisco—in seventy-five days. It was the intention, in any event, of Naval Lieutenant Dale E. Collins of the S.S. *Coolidge*, which had taken Halliburton to Yokohama, "to meet the *Sea Dragon* in Mid-Pacific to give them fresh provisions."[26]

Captain Welch's was a slightly different arc. According to him, the junk would follow a 30 degree course, "about the latitude," noted Halliburton, "of Los Angeles and Charleston, South Carolina." Cold weather, wind and rain wouldn't be a factor, and arrival time in San Francisco would be ninety days. The clippers would take the mail—that was all they would do, though Welch intended to sail directly beneath the aerial course of the planes. While radio contact with the clippers was reasonable to expect, it was unreasonable to expect

Paul Mooney in Hong Kong, 1938 (courtesy William Alexander).

them to make open-ocean rescue missions, should the junk experience grave difficulty.[27]

During his long stay, Paul walked about the docks, and about the city, taking hurried puffs off one cigarette, then a next. If he sampled the opium, then legal and in abundance, no one would have cared. In a film clip taken of him—perhaps on Des Voeux Road or along the Bund, children scamper playfully about him as he walks along. He wears a white shirt, tie and knee-length overcoat. In one hand appears an umbrella, in the other camera equipment—he had been made the expedition's official photographer as well as journalist. He walked, as Alicia once noted he walked, purposefully and, even in so strange a setting, as if he knew where he was going. Halliburton called him "a crack photographer" and, for the first time, he hailed him as a "journalist." Like Jack London, who covered the Russo-Japanese War, or John Reed, who covered the Bolshevik revolution, Paul, witness to history, became a war correspondent, who covered the Japanese invasion.[28]

Halliburton expected Torrey and Barstow (after a fortnight in Japan) to land in Hong Kong on December 1. Chase and Potter were expected to arrive on December 15. All four boys, however, showed up late in November, long before they were actually needed. How he would accommodate them and how they would occupy themselves at first troubled Halliburton. Work tasks on the junk, though, were quickly assigned to them, and, under sharp scrutiny from Captain Welch, they spent some portion of each day, when not sight-seeing, manning their positions on the junk and adjusting to the tackle and gear. Otherwise they were free to roam about the colony. Photographs show Chase and Potter strolling about as if they had been there only a short time and intended to leave soon; from wealthy families, their domiciles could have been the luxurious Peninsula Hotel or Hong Kong Hotel rather than the dingy boarding house or Kowloon Hotel.[29]

Almost from the moment they arrived, crew members bickered among themselves. Torrey thought from early on that the mission was impracticable and the whimsy of one man. Basically, he thought it a poorly managed company of unskilled workers. Chase and Potter evidently disagreed, and this led to "unpleasantries." Torrey eventually "dissociate[d] from the others"; though they both lived another fifty years, he and friend John Potter never spoke to one another again. Halliburton, believing it best that everyone get along, did his best to calm them, but the bickering continued. He paid the $50 fine of cook James Sligh, who had gotten in a heated argument with a local merchant and had been arrested. On earlier adventures Richard had only himself and maybe a companion to concern himself with; now he had an entire crew. To his parents he insisted that Paul "is a great help, and has thrown himself heart and soul into the project."[30]

Paul, however, was not the mediator Halliburton attempted to be. There is "no school like a ship for studying human nature," Herman Melville wrote in *Mardi*. Paul admitted to being "temperamental as hell" and the ship business now made him seethe. "A hundred times a week I determine to return by the first comfortable ship [to California]," he wrote to Laguna Beach friend Lee Hutchings, "instead of spending three months in the human churn we're building here." It was mid–December, and the junk was nearing completion.[31]

"The company isn't entirely compatible," he wrote, naming the source of his misery, then cast aspersions at each and all. We have, he said, "a blustery extrovert for a captain; Dick [Halliburton] for boss; myself, temperamental as

hell; the engineer (whom Richard thought 'a real gentleman'), a very proud
and stupid German ['...born in Germany, naturalized in America' ... who came
along with the diesel auxiliary engine]; one boy [Barstow], a Connecticut Yankee
of the worst [sort]; another longing for his habitual background of zebra stripes
at El Morocco [Potter?]; still another fresh (how!) from Dartmouth and full of
anti–Roosevelt jokes [Torrey?]; and a fourth boy I haven't yet seen [Chase?]." He
went on: "The radioman [Petrich] is tattooed from head to foot, the camera
man is odious in every way. The two Chinese waiters will take the really dirty
work; for the rest of us, work will be merely hard, endless, and at times unfa-
miliar. But the enforced companionship, in crowded quarters, with a collection
of people in whom I haven't the faintest interest physically or mentally, is going
to be a real trial. Not one of us knows anything about sailing. How much I miss
Laguna!"[32]

While Halliburton thought the tattooed radioman's English "dreadful,"
the captain "a tyrant," the engineer "stubborn," and the whole crew "at each
other's throats," he also thought them capable of becoming strong through
hardship and making their way across the Pacific. Such bulldog determination
characterized the man throughout. John "Brue" Potter said he "never saw him
complain or heard him complain." He also said that "he hardly ever smiled and
almost never laughed." In the Bell letter version of this declaration to his parents—naturally far less acrid than Paul's private remarks, the crew members
each have their faults, and are "for the most part amateurs" but "are all quite
prepared ... to be deathly seasick until we get our ship-legs."[33]

One has to applaud Halliburton's calmness amid trying circumstances.
Except for Captain Welch, whom no one liked, and engineer Henry von Fehren,
who was unapproachable, the crew was young and hardly a match for the task
that lay ahead. Radio operator George Petrich and cook Jim Sligh, both Americans, were necessary functionaries (though, as it turned out, radio contact could
have been better and the food served could not have been worse). The veteran
radio operator, Mr. Petrich, had headed the radio department on the Coast
Guard boat that stood watch, in mid–Pacific, to assist Amelia Earhart. That was
perhaps an ill omen. Dartmouth senior Robert Chase, always showing good
attitude, believed the mission could succeed because he believed in Halliburton.
George Barstow III remained cheerful and tragically naive. "He couldn't bring
his piano along," commented Halliburton, "but he did bring an enormous
accordion."[34]

Besides tending to his crew, Halliburton handled public relations as best
he could. He talked a good deal to reporters. He visited the American consulate.
He also met with naval officials who kept a close watch over the building operation. Pirates and Japanese operatives also watched with stone-cold eyes the
tediously slow construction of the dream ship. By the end of November, to save
money, Paul and other members of the crew took their quarters on the *Sea
Dragon*.[35]

17

The Royal Road from Hong Kong

A visitor to Hong Kong a couple years before, Jean Cocteau called the city a "stage set," its shops "dressing-rooms" and its custodians "consummate actors" painted to play some part. If a few crew members vaguely understood what role each would play in the upcoming drama, all saw the Japanese as villainous extras whom they wished would leave the stage.[1]

Hostile fleets of Japanese continued to menace outgoing sea traffic from the British colony, and already hundreds of junks had been sunk. Even with His Majesty's gunners set high up on the cliffs, sailing a ripe plum of a target like the *Sea Dragon* through Formosa Straits into open water seemed high risk. Halliburton attempted humor: "I fear the *Sea Dragon*'s new sails will make a target too alluring for the Japanese to resist—'Let's see if we can hit that red junk at five miles!'" Still, the expedition's mission was taking on the aura of flight rather than high seas adventure; caught in a trap, the ocean seemed the only way out.[2]

Pirates were also to be feared. With its great store of supplies, the *Sea Dragon* would be a most worthy prize. For its safety, rifles and shotguns would have to be brought aboard. Regular watch was kept.[3]

By November 21, the sixty-five-foot masts were completed, and the outside planking had begun. By December 12, the masts were ready for hoisting. Soon the engine and water tanks would be installed. "A lifeboat with sails" also would go on board. Halliburton seemed jubilant. "It's a great thrill watching the ship grow in beauty," he said. By January 1, 1939, the *Sea Dragon* was set to depart. Building it had taken slightly less than the ninety days the Amoy shipwright had said his junk would take. Everyone marveled. Though the building had been "fun," Halliburton said he would not want to build another.[4]

He had instructed Fat Kau to build him a junk that was "big, but not *too* big; colorful, but not garish." The junk that resulted succeeded in the first account, and failed spectacularly in the second. The colors and designs dazzled. The "crescent-shaped hull" was painted "bright vermilion." The twenty-foot

Construction of *the Sea Dragon* is nearly completed, fall 1938 (courtesy William Alexander).

dragon that ran along either side of the poop was painted "blue and green." The bat-wing sails, above which waved an American flag, were dyed rusty orange. The huge (thirty-inch) lobster-like eyes of the creature were painted black. Made of logs cut from a camphor tree, they required four workers to hoist up and fit into place. Painted on the stern, was a huge phoenix fluttering into a rainbow of colors. Above this symbol of good luck, in gold Chinese characters, was the junk's name, *Sea Dragon*, and its port of origin, Hong Kong. Below it, "riding through the clouds on peacocks," were angels from Chinese mythology. Traditionally the dragon represented the male principle in this mythology; the phoenix, rising to immortality from its own ashes, represented the female principle. Halliburton believed, when combined, the two principles meant, simply, strength of purpose.[5]

A "poetry-ship" Halliburton called it. He did not care that it appeared "super-gaudy," but "only hope[d] that some of the paint will stick until we reach San Francisco." Paul was more dead-pan: "The hull is Chinese vermilion, white and black, with orange stripes," he described it to his mother. "The sails were dyed in russet tones. Our stern has huge writhing dragons, the poop is painted with prayers in Chinese, a phoenix, and some mythical figures."[6]

The junk looked not so much like a ship as a floating big top. Yet, with its arching quality and tangerine color, it appropriately suggested the newly completed Golden Gate Bridge, which, like itself, would connect two lands. "If [the junk] sounds like a circus wagon, blame not me," Halliburton enthused, "but [blame] the last hundred generations of Chinese junk-builders—for the most careful research proved that this style, and none other, is proper for the Ningpo style of junk which we have built for our voyage." Showman and millionaire (the "modern Marco Polo") Robert Ripley's junk, the *Mon Lei*, meaning "infinity," was the only glamour ship of its day that compared.[7]

Though based on seaworthy models, the culturally pretentious ocean slicker appeared parade bound, not bound for the headwaters of the world's mightiest ocean. Toy junks—"bedizened, painted galleons from the Orient," chimeric parodies of actual junks that for centuries had sailed the Chinese seas—had inspired its design, as did pictures from books on Chinese maritime life and mythology. Novelty junks of nearly 1,000 feet and metal-plated throughout called "turtle-junks" had existed, as had ones with brothels called "flower-ships," but these had not crossed the Pacific.[8]

Onlookers who gathered at the dock were both stunned and bewildered. The vessel was gorgeous, but could it handle the open sea? "Our ship rides the waves perfectly," Richard wrote to his parents. In the same breath he then told them that, if the ship should sink, the insurance policy that named Paul a beneficiary should be rewritten to make them beneficiaries: "I do not want it to go to his family."[9]

Movie footage in color of the junk was shot at this time by John "Brue" Potter and Gordon Torrey. Among the sequences is one of all the crew members—including Paul—smiling into the camera. Paul sits next to George Barstow and, grinning, makes a comment. Barstow, well dressed and groomed, shows the ease of a young man being photographed for a college commencement. Paul, in civies, puffs hurriedly away on a cigarette; he looks to the right, then to the left, out into the water. The sky in the background is calm and pastel.[10]

Richard Halliburton (far right) with engineer Henry von Fehren (to his right) aboard *the Sea Dragon,* 1938. Captain Welch is the figure on the left (courtesy William Alexander).

In his *Dictionary,* Samuel Johnson defined a ship architecturally as a "large hollow building, made to pass over the sea with sails" and likened "being in a ship" to "being in a jail, with the chance of being drowned." A man of robust common sense, he probably would have dismissed the *Sea Dragon Expedition* as a spit in the eye of Reason.[11]

The prow of the *Sea Dragon* (courtesy William Alexander).

"Dragon" he might have defined as a land creature disadapted to sea travel. The popular Dragon Boat Races, held annually along the coast, and the smuggling skiffs, called "fast crabs" or "scrambling dragons," would hardly have convinced him otherwise. Halliburton was hardly as superstitious as Johnson, and probably would have argued that England's great admiral Sir Francis Drake, who had circled the globe, was nicknamed "the sea dragon."[12]

While a good deal was made about its name, more so was made about the *Sea Dragon*'s seaworthiness. Potter agreed that it was a "Ningpo off-shore deep-water junk," adding "supposedly," but "she lacked a lot of capabilities of the original design." Also, provisions for its safety were hasty, even careless. By comparison to a steamer, it was poorly equipped certainly, and it had, as one crew member noted, "design and handling difficulties." The tiller, "a piece of 8 by 8, ten feet long," was cumbersome, and in a gale might require two strong men to work it. Boards covered the portholes because they took in water when the vessel leaned over. The poop, meant to provide office space for Halliburton, was twelve feet higher than was customary and made the vessel lopsided and tipsy. Much too light, the hull swayed uneasily and bobbed up and down. And when the crew attempted to drive it windward, it alarmingly made as much leeway as headway. Maybe a minor problem—the diesel engine had to be running to charge the radio batteries.[13]

Engineer Henry von Fehren tends to the diesel engine (courtesy Princeton University Library).

A hearty, sea-wise crew might have been able to handle the junk's malfunctions. Experienced seamen, however, put little faith in its chances for success. Lieutenant Dale E. Collins of the S.S. *Coolidge* was fully aware of the "trials and tribulations" that beset Halliburton during the junk's construction and probably offered advice. Plenty of photographs were taken, leading to the belief that the junk was the shill in some sort of espionage game. Captain Charles Jokstad of the S.S. *Pierce*, which had docked alongside the *Sea Dragon*, thought its chances at sea poor at best. After a casual inspection, he noted that its rudder stuck out too far and would break off in a bold wind. The shroud cords, he saw, were held to the hull by screws and not bolts; these too would unfasten in a good wind. He also saw that the auxiliary engine, whose placement in the junk underwent initial debate, was also not as secured to the ribbing as it should have been, and, given a good jolt, could come loose and possibly drive a breach through the vessel.[14]

Halliburton kept faith in the engine, which he thought would assure the ship's forward motion if the winds died. A rival junk, from Wenchow, had sailed for the World's Fair earlier that fall, but it hadn't an engine, so its troubles at sea and running ashore off Formosa seemed to him predictable. Or a good omen. Richard had once had his horoscope done; he may have consulted fortune tellers when he undertook this expedition, though he placed his faith in "Occidental gods," not in "Oriental deities." The Chinese zodiac indicated that the year Richard was born, 1900 (presumably), was the year of the Rat, and that the year Paul was born, 1904, was the year of the Dragon. Who could fathom what it meant? Lloyd's of London, operating in a different realm of possibility, considered the *Sea Dragon*, with or without the diesel engine, potentially unseaworthy—an accident waiting to happen, but, throwing aside all calculation of cost-risk benefits, insured it anyway.[15]

As though all were well or, if not so, could be mended, Halliburton continued to write to his parents. As the year came to a close, he dutifully wished the two of them a merry Christmas and a happy new year. All his presents to family and friends, he assured, had been packaged and sent.[16]

Still, he fretted and paced, more often about the crew than about anything wrong with the junk. "Each member of the crew has some element in his nature that's hard to bear," the letter he wrote home the first day of the new year reads, "the Engineer is stubborn, the captain is a tyrant, the radioman uses dreadful English. But nothing fatal." The six or seven lines which precede this summary comment are scribbled out—not just crossed out, but blacked out with broad strokes. The few intelligible words that follow, and these are crossed out, read,

Opposite, top: Halliburton on the pier (white shirt) watching a performance run of the *Sea Dragon*, 1939 (courtesy William Alexander). *Bottom:* Halliburton on the pier (white shirt) watching a performance run of the *Sea Dragon*, 1939. The shirtless man to his right could be crew member Patrick Kelly, who, after the trial run, decided to stay behind (courtesy William Alexander).

"...and I love [him?] for that...." One can only speculate as to the whole meaning. It may cover up a vicious slander, or a delicate money matter. It may also compliment Paul's shrewd handling of a (covered up) personnel problem.[17]

Further delays, caused by poor weather and the mechanics of the junk's operation, occurred. On January 23, the junk appeared ready to go, as it did on January 1. By this time its cargo had been put on board: a radio, medicine chest, lots of food, some two thousand gallons of oil and another two thousand gallons of water. The crew numbered twelve, "all [of them] American": these included, said Halliburton, "the captain, engineer, radioman, seven seamen including myself, a cook and a cabin-boy." A husband and his pregnant wife who had wanted to come along were told no because of the risks involved in a mid-ocean delivery. Also denied passage was a baby panda because pandas are prone to seasickness. Two white Siamese kittens as well as two Chow puppies were taken aboard instead—that brought the number on board to more than the fearful number thirteen. Halliburton offered the management wisdom that neither women nor pandas could stoke coal or unload cargo. For Halliburton, the strain had been great, and his self-control, aided by Paul, nearly masterful.

The Sea Dragon tests the water for the first time, 1939 (courtesy William Alexander).

Top: The *Sea Dragon* (1939) probably as it appeared when it began its journey out into the open sea (courtesy William Alexander). *Bottom:* A very unusual shot of the *Sea Dragon* docked in the harbor (courtesy Dartmouth College).

"Once at sea," he sighed with apparent relief, "I can relax." The "clashes and quarrels," they too would vanish. Estimated time of arrival was set at the end of April.[18]

Nearly two more weeks passed. Halliburton often disappeared. According to Gordon Torrey, he was "busy with promotional activities." Reported first mate John Potter, Halliburton also "was very interested in and supportive of a Long Island, N.Y. lady who ran a Chinese Orphanage on the Kowloon side," and was photographed with the children. From time to time he was spotted at the Hong Kong Hotel. There, at the hotel bar, next to the popular "Grips" or "Gripps" restaurant, he dawdled with a teenage boy described as "tall and gangly," maybe eighteen years old, "with sleek black hair, an olive complexion and exceptionally slender, tapered hands." This "dark-skinned Latin" and "obviously

While in Hong Kong, Halliburton spent a good deal of his spare time in promotional activities and at a Chinese orphanage in Kowloon run by a lady from New York, fall 1938 (courtesy William Alexander).

part Portuguese" was possibly the "seventeen-year-old youth" named Patrick Kelly, a world-ready lad who had never seen America. Why "the boy gave the impression of enduring rather than enjoying the relationship" is cause for wonder as is why Richard himself seemed preoccupied and bored. World-weariness and self-weariness had merged in Halliburton long ago. What continued to darken his romantic outlook were a sense of the world's intrinsic wickedness and his own pessimism. But it seemed at last his ship would sail.[19]

February 4 opened with great fanfare as the launching of the *Sea Dragon* and the Chinese New Year's celebrations merged. What followed had all the features of a Mexican Day of the Dead celebration, Cecil B. De Mille extravaganza, or Mardi Gras hoopla. The prettiest Chinese girl he could find broke a bottle of rice wine on the *Sea Dragon*'s nose. Mumbling prayers, the Chinese priests ceremoniously awakened the junk's huge protruding eyes while girls and boys, made up in decorous costumes as flames from the bowels of the earth, danced amid loud ear-numbing sounds.

The initial crew of the *Sea Dragon*. Standing, from the viewer's left, are Paul Mooney, engineer Henry Von Fehren, cook James Sligh, crew member Gordon Ellicot Torrey, captain John Wenlock Welch, Richard Halliburton, and first mate John Rust "Brue" Potter. Seated, from viewer's left, are assistant engineer Richard Davis, Robert Hill Chase, radioman George Petrich and crew member George Barstow. Not shown are seaman Ralph Granrud, seaman Ben Flagg, crew member Velman Fitch, the Chinese messboy, and three Chinese sailors (Princeton University Library).

A Chinese priest blesses the mission. The trial run soon commences, February 4, 1939. From the viewer's left are Paul Mooney, George Barstow, Richard Halliburton, John Potter, James Sligh, priest, Richard Davis, Captain Welch and Robert Chase (courtesy Princeton University Library).

> Firecrackers popped, the President Coolidge, moored nearby, sounded great blasts on her horn, and a pair of British Navy planes zoomed overhead. ... indeed, a spectacular departure. The great white-ribbed mainsail was raised, then the scarlet mizzenmast and the *Sea Dragon* gracefully picked her way up the coast of China, past other Chinese junks, past several passenger liners...."

Meanwhile, strolling musicians, gong strikers, bands of entertainers, the puppeteers, lantern bearers, and acrobats in richly colored raiment and painted faces roamed the streets and docks. Odd human creatures sprang into sudden view, and everywhere was the shimmering speed of lively movement and flashing colors. Chants and weird sounds, meant "to drive away the demons of storm and shipwreck," crowded their way into the ears.[20]

The *Sea Dragon* sailed off. The Japanese gunboats had relaxed their vigilance, and the "fishing junks were out again, by the score, by the hundreds, with their bat-winged sails silhouetted against the shining waves." Many gawked at the strange junk passing them. "One entire fleet of fishers," Halliburton reported, "crept close to stare, to exclaim, to shout at us and find out if we were

A close-up of the *Sea Dragon* on its performance run in 1939 (courtesy William Alexander).

real." At some point, Halliburton accidentally dropped a pot of coffee overboard, then let out the only profanity Potter, standing nearby, ever heard him utter.[21]

A radio message sent on February 4 expressed the high spirits of the crew. They were going at a steady clip of over six knots, and in fourteen hours had gotten some one hundred miles from Hong Kong. The "blissful dream voyage" then turned hellish. "At noon on the second day, with incredible suddenness, the sun departed," Richard wrote, "black clouds raced overhead, the wind swept down, the waves rose, we were headed into a storm. Pitching and rolling, our decks awash, we held to our course...." But it pitched and rolled dangerously. Said Potter in his report, the movement caused a "tremendous whip of stays and guys, with some chafing." More severe weather would have made it worse.[22] Vision blurred and bearings all but lost, only steering brought the vessel under control. "One wave pitched us forward so violently that the radio aerial, atop the mission mast, was torn from its lashings, leaving the wire to thrash about in the wind...." Towering some seventy feet from the deck to its tip, the mast, violently ripped and shredded, was nearly stripped off its base. Crew members, some deathly seasick, stumbled about unable to man the tiller, or perform the

Perhaps the most famous image of the *Sea Dragon* as it looked when it was taken out to sea on Halliburton's last adventure (courtesy Lilly Library, University of Indiana, Bloomington, IN).

slightest assigned task. John Potter, "stricken with what was believed a bad appendix," developed a fever that left him cabin-bound. Paul broke his ankle slipping down the hatch that led to the main cabin. Wind and rain made steering by one man hard; "junks do not have steering wheels, but rather clumsy tillers manipulated by block and tackle." Such a tiller is hard enough to handle in calm weather conditions. Every member of the crew, slammed around, felt beaten and exhausted. Pots and pans flew about. Seizing the rail with one hand, crew members fed themselves apples and dry bread with the other. Suffocating fumes, meanwhile, escaped from the tanks and bulkheads into the main cabin. Water leaked through the planking. Radio communication lapsed.[23]

Halliburton and Captain Welch discussed the situation, and decided it best they return to Hong Kong. The first mate's worsening condition left them with no other choice. At the time they were nearly three hundred miles from a safe haven, just fifty miles short of the tip of Formosa, and over four thousand miles from Midway Island. They had thought that, if they could get around Formosa, a northerly current would expedite their speed a couple knots and they would be out of danger.[24]

Once safely docked, Halliburton wrote of the failure as a successful retreat, and merely a trial run: "we swung the tiller with a mighty swing, spun the ship about and set our course back to China." The auxiliary engine throttled and droned full force until, "on the late afternoon of the sixth day, bearded, exhausted and dejected," the crew "caught sight, far in the distance, of the mountains rising behind Hong Kong," now a city heavily under siege by the Japanese.[25]

A few people stepped up for a closer view of the hobbled ship. Not the cheering crowds of the San Francisco Exposition, the well-wishers of a few days before stared frigidly at the men climbing off the junk and the omen of doom their failure represented. John Potter was rushed to the hospital in an ambulance. The doctors suggested he bow out. Gordon Torrey complained of something resembling appendicitis, and he bowed out as well. Impressed by Halliburton's books, he was underwhelmed by their author. He found him a "driven, un-funny, unreasonably stubborn man" who gullibly courted the advice of those who believed the voyage could be done. Even were he fit for the voyage, he probably would not have gone. George Barstow had come down with something, and threatened to bow out. The Siamese cats, quite seasick, would be asked not to return to the junk; the Chow puppies, "excellent sailors," would stay. Seventeen year old Patrick Kelly, who served as a messboy to cook James Sligh, also withdrew; "five days of seasickness," commented Halliburton, who seemed immune to it, "cured the poor fellow of his hunger for adventure." Originally signed on, but not among the final crew, was American engineer Richard L. Davis, whose name it is tempting to link to the Mary Lou Davis who now occupied Hangover House with her two children.[26]

Halliburton called the crew that had been on the first run "sickly amateurs" and wished to replace them with "professionals." Two, maybe three "Scandinavian seamen," he believed, "would do the trick." The new crew, as now gathered, included Captain John Welch; engineer Henry von Fehren; first mate Ben Flagg (a recent Bowdoin College graduate with some cargo ship experience); licensed radio operator George I. Petrich; chief cook James N. Sligh; seaman Richard Halliburton; "able-bodied" seaman Ralph Granrud; journalist and lookout Paul Mooney; Robert H. Chase; George E. Barstow; Velman E. Fitch. Of these, Velman E. Fitch, son of veterinarian E.L. Fitch, merits special note. With a name to inspire sea ballads, the twenty year old, spurred on by *The Royal Road to Romance*, had dropped out of the University of Minnesota to see the world, and now hitched a ride aboard the junk. Also along were three Chinese sailors: Sun Fook, Kiao Chu, Wang Ching-huo, and one Chinese mess boy, Liu Ah-shu.[27]

Paul probably wanted to get into a fast plane or ship. His broken ankle continuing to swell, he was carried off the ship and taken to a hospital, where he was given two weeks to mend. When a repeat voyage was mentioned, he probably wished he had broken his leg. In any forthcoming voyage he saw only "futility and despair."[28]

Halliburton suffered from "a raging eczema the doctor attributed to nerves." He called it a slight "skin itch." His body knew the truth, but his mind rejected it. Fear of debt remained greater for him than fear of death; and he was now forty, self-consciously forty. The money he was sure he would make on radio deals, the lecture tour and the two books continued to fuel his determination. The junk itself would bring $10,000, nearly enough to make him solvent.[29]

Halliburton admitted he was becoming "tired and impatient" but not "downhearted." One failed run only meant that precious time had passed, though it was already two months more than planned. His agent Wilfred Crowell had written to inform him that "a big barge anchored in the small-ships' basin of the Fair" bore the sign, "Reserved anchorage for Halliburton's Sea Dragon"—which meant he must "hurry" and "get there." If he intended to arrive by late May, the dramatic moment was slipping away. On May 27 over a quarter of a million people would walk across the Golden Gate Bridge; the "Golden Gate Bridge Fiesta" that followed would last a week. One could expect that, by the time the *Sea Dragon* cleared the Golden Gate, the loud shouts of enthusiasm those climactic events brought would then lower to quiet awe. The pitched tents of the Great Exposition soon would be drawn. Halliburton imagined the crowds at the Fair gathered to greet him slowly dwindling, and his creditors, now tapping, soon pounding at his door. Fear of want was no less a character trait of the man than it was of the Depression itself.[30]

The ship, meanwhile, was reequipped. More concrete was likely put into the hull to help keep it from rolling. The diesel engine was remounted and secured more firmly. The rigging was adjusted and skylights were added. Leaks were plugged, the hull was tarred and the exterior touched up. To steady the flat-bottomed ship, a 60-foot fin-keel was ordered but reportedly was never installed; to offset the top-heaviness created by the overly high stern, tall masts and large sails, the concrete filler would have to do. Work on the ship took days, as the Chinese carpenters saw no reason to hurry up. The eye screws that secured the guide wires and rudders holding the mast to the decking planks should have been replaced with bolts or even wooden pegs (as were used to hold the planks themselves); whether this was done remains unclear. Ample provisions were again loaded on, including two thousand gallons of fresh water and a three-months' stock of victuals. The auxiliary engine was checked over. To run it a ten-days' supply of fuel was loaded aboard—this numbered dozens of tanks. Missing, if not life jackets, were air tubes and rafts, not to mention electronics equipment, a refrigerator, winches, and a generator.[31]

Paul had written, "You can't imagine the utter resignation and despair we feel in the voyage and nothing to look forward to except the end. G'Bye."[32]

Positive to the end, Halliburton told his parents "now we'll have March, April, May for our crossing—better than January, February, March." Among his last words home were these: "It's been a good—and bad—four months here in Hong Kong—worried and intensely busy building something. I still think I have a swell idea, and that everything is coming out as I dreamed. But, oh, won't I be glad to get home and unload all these burdens and quarreling seamen!" He ended the letter by assuring his parents that he would radio them "every few days," so that they could "follow the voyage" with him. Then he signed off, "You know how much I love you."[33]

18

To Dare or to Be in Debt

On March 4, 1939, at Hong Kong's Kowloon docks, thirty-four-year-old journalist Paul Mooney, his ankle in a plaster cast and with crutches tucked deeply under his arms, hobbled aboard a seventy-five-foot Chinese junk intrepidly named the *Sea Dragon*. A cigarette dangled languidly from his mouth; a well-worn leather camera pack hung over his shoulder. Etched with fear was the enterprising grin that formed throughout his puckishly handsome face, that of a cabin boy gotten older, of a sailor with mutiny in his heart. Fired by impatience and his own hot temper, he boarded the junk probably out of impulse and through some rekindled faith in its harmless mission. Perhaps it mattered that it was a Sunday. A couple crew members steadied him while another crew member guided his steps. Likely he took some pictures from the dock and, again, once he was on board. Years ago, he had jumped rooftops; now he had to cross a vast ocean.[1]

Unknown to a world preparing for war, the *Sea Dragon* and crew, with some new members to replace old, quietly sailed off. A few people were on the dock to wave it good-bye, as they might have done were it any ship. To a few of its crew members, the fanfare that had bade its first departure godspeed echoed eerily. As it passed them in the harbor, fishing boats and other junks indifferently glided by. Slowly, innocently, the ship moved eastward. Halliburton himself, writes James Cortese, was "braced against the mizzenmast, [his] long blond hair bellowed by the breeze, [his] jacket collar open, his eyes on the far horizon, [there to face] one more great challenge."[2] Halliburton once quipped: "You are a fool not to climb Fujiyama once in your lifetime. But you are a worse fool to climb it twice." Despite the repairs and adjustments done to it, inspectors still had to wonder why a second run should fare any better than the first one, which had so dismally failed. Sleek, but still rickety as ever, the wondrous *Sea Dragon*, its American flag proudly waving on the mainsail, promised a triumphant spectacle to the Exposition's visitors as much as it augured burial at sea for its crew. One could only hope that the engine worked and the ship held together, especially through such storms as threatened to overwhelm it during most of its first run. There was no lifeline or trailing ship; headed for Yokohama, the S.S. *Cool-*

idge, about 1,800 miles west of Honolulu, was on a collision course with the junk and had made plans to resupply it, as it would a later junk that attempted the crossing, but the ship remained too far away.[3]

Without incident, the *Sea Dragon* slipped into the South China Sea, beyond the Formosa Straits, Okinawa, pirates and the Japanese navy. Each crew member tended to his assigned task, but for many of them every function of this strange ship had to be new. Days went by.[4]

Messages from the *Sea Dragon*, though terse, were positive:

> March 5, 1939. RADIO JUNK SEA DRAGON VIA SAN FRANCISCO SAILED AGAIN TODAY SOUNDER SHIP BETTER CREW FINE WEATHER RADIO SEA DRAGON SAN FRANCISCO POSTAL TELEGRAPH HURRYING HOME LOVE

> March 13, 1939. RADIO JUNK SEA DRAGON VIA SAN FRANCISCO 1200 MILES AT SEA ALLS WELL

> March 19, 1939. RADIO JUNK SEA DRAGON VIA SAN FRANCISCO HALFWAY MIDWAY ARRIVING APRIL FIFTH SKIPPING HONOLULU WRITE CARE PANAMERICAN MIDWAY AIRMAIL LOVE

Halliburton now had to hurry. With luck, the *Sea Dragon* would reach Midway Island on April 5th, but, if it was to meet its deadline, it would have to skip Honolulu.[5]

All was running reportedly well. At top speed the ship could do "170 miles a day ... 1190 miles a week ... 8000 miles in less than seven weeks." If it kept to this pace, it could reach San Francisco by early May. By comparison, the twin Dollar line passenger vessels S.S. *President Hoover* and S.S. *President Coolidge* could make the trip from Yokohama to San Francisco in ten to fourteen days.[6]

Pirates, if sighted, were not reported; the Japanese, if a presence, made no move on the junk. The smooth sailing lasted two and a half weeks. Wednesday night, March 21, storm clouds gathered. By morning, the winds had reached gale force. Pummeled by violent waves, the *Sea Dragon* pressed on. Unable to use his navigational instruments effectively, Captain Welch now relied upon dead reckoning to figure his position:

> SOUTHERLY GALE HEAVY RAIN SQUALLS HIGH SEA BAROMETER 29.46 RISING TRUE COURSE 100 SPEED 5.5 KNOTS POSITION 1200 GCT 31.10 NORTH 155.00 EAST ALL WELL WHEN CLOSER. MAY WE AVAIL OURSELVES OF YOUR DIRECTION FINDER REGARDS WELCH

The S.S. *Coolidge*, meanwhile, also headed into the storm. The 36,000 ton liner reduced speed. Though a thousand times heavier than the *Sea Dragon*, size didn't allow the ship to rule the huge waves that broke in its path. The ship pitched and rolled dangerously. Water reached over its bow. The number of passengers aboard may have been low, as insurance costs rose and the Japanese threat increased. Over half the passengers became seasick, reported the ship's captain, A.L. Ahlin. A few suffered injuries. Cargo shifted. Objects flew.[7]

Aboard the *Sea Dragon*, things were multiply chaotic. The captain barked orders that were barely heard as the skylights fell to the deck and rigging snapped. Through sheer nervous energy, the crew became hyperactive. Fatigue set in. The men grumbled, then gave out frantic appeals. No one could hear past the noise of the storm. "The seas were estimated to be about 40 to 50 feet high," reported Lieutenant Dale E. Collins, aboard the S.S. *Coolidge*, trailing the junk by several hundred miles; these seas, he said, "would have made things precarious for such a small boat as the *Sea Dragon* and she was undoubtedly having the same weather we were experiencing...."[8]

The last radio contact was received from the fifty-watt Mackay radio on Thursday night, March 23 or Friday morning, March 24.

> CAPTAIN JOHN WELCH OF THE SEA DRAGON TO LINER PRESIDENT COOLIDGE SOUTHERLY GALES RAIN SQUALLS LEE RAIL UNDER WATER WET BUNKS HARDTACK BULLY BEEF HAVING WONDERFUL TIME WISH YOU WERE HERE INSTEAD OF ME[9]

Radio operators in Guam told the Clipper pilots that they had been in contact with the junk, but constant static made it hard for them to make out what was being said.[10]

Aeronautical engineer Amos Wood later noted that the *Sea Dragon* was "on a true course of 100 degrees and at a position of 31 degrees north and 155 degrees east," which location "put the junk at about 150 miles east of a small island named Ganges and about 1,600 miles west of Midway island." Wood considered this a strong indication that the junk was "heading for the Hawaiian Islands rather than directly for San Francisco."[11]

By March 24 radio communication ceased. Though this had happened on the trial run, fears mounted that the *Sea Dragon* had foundered in mid ocean. The last reported whereabouts of the ship was the vicinity of Midway Island, an area that had been pummeled for the past week by severe storms. Midway was south of the ship's intended route, which took advantage of the trade wind, but, as before, confusion set a new course.[12]

By now the *Sea Dragon* was some eight hundred miles southeast of Yokohama. Ocean waves rose ever higher; the ship pitched and rolled, moving leeward and forward, down and up. Lashing waves and howling winds of a violence rarely encountered in that haunting ocean corridor soon began to tear the hapless vessel apart. Furious waves curled around the vessel, wrapping, constricting, and breaking its bones like a monstrous boa, or lashed and threw it about, pulling it apart as a group of playfully mean children might a raggedy doll none wants the other to have. Helplessly the ship, its back broken, its rigging lifeless, see-sawed back and forth in the troughs of the giant sea waves. Among the crew, anarchy reigned as assigned tasks dissipated in the increasing confusion. The distant stars, merging into a blur of faded light, created the illusion of sun bursting through the dark cloud barriers. "Such must have been the darkness before creation," wrote Joseph Conrad in *Typhoon*.[13]

It has been assumed that a typhoon of some force dismantled the ship. In his last message, Captain Welch, however, reported only "southerly gales" and "rain squalls." In the same breath he noted "lee rail under water" and "wet bunks." If during the first run the ride had been bumpy and, after only five days, some of the men weary, perhaps seasick and feverish, the ride now multiplied all those discomforts; the oil from the oilskin wrappings they wore the first time, if they wore the same or similar this time, "washed off" from the drenching rain; all the crew, dejected, found themselves uncertain of their roles amid crisis. At this point, all that was needed for the ship to go down was enough deck water to put her level with the sea; the ten tons of concrete and the inordinately large diesel engine, if it hadn't broken loose and smashed a hole in the hull, would have done the rest, taking the ship some three miles down in minutes. Crew members tossed from the ship would soon die from exposure.[14]

Another Chinese junk, the Tai Ping, reported seeing the Sea Dragon as it slid into the abyss. An American freighter, the Jefferson Davis, which was headed for San Francisco, however, passed within miles of the Sea Dragon oblivious to its distress. Skipper John Anderson, himself completing the 6,000 mile voyage across the Pacific, later told reporters that his vessel had trailed Halliburton "until we were separated by a typhoon"—possibly of the very rare Force Eleven on the Beaufort scale (though Dale E. Collins reported a Force Six), the severest ever reported in that ocean corridor, indeed, a perfect storm or nearly so.[15]

At Force Six, winds move at over 25 mph; larger than moderate waves form. "Whitecaps [are] everywhere; there is more than moderate spray." At Force Eleven, winds move at over sixty-four m.p.h. (though typically the Scale measures wind force rather than wind speed); waves are mountainously high, the "sea [is] covered with white foam patches," and visibility is threateningly reduced. From Force Six to Force Eleven, sailors, using seaman's terms, move from "strong breeze" towards "moderate gale," then to "whole gale" and "active storm"; beyond are "hurricane" conditions. As for the Sea Dragon, winds gusted and lashed and may have exceeded seventy miles an hour. Waves rose to well over thirty feet high.[16]

A more violent storm creates another picture. Towering waves peaked, fifty to seventy-five feet, then crashed with their great weight on the open deck. Bearings soon were lost. The ship, on the crest of a great wave one moment, plunged headlong to the bottom the next, with tons of water falling on its deck. A moment later, another great wave lifted the ship high into the air and threw it back into the sea as an alley cat might fling a helpless rodent into a brick wall for its sport. Another great wave while in a mighty and coiling roll perhaps tucked it under itself until it was upside down, then dropped it deck down on the churning waves. The panic of those still on board, who had managed to grip on to something, a rail or rope, lasted only seconds. A storm of such magnitude, as a Force Six storm could reach, likely pulled the ship apart; in seconds, it was drawn and quartered, splintered and crushed. Halliburton, once dubbed a "make-believe Ulysses," had once threatened (if I recall) to write a novel called *Hell*. This could have been its watery version. The *Sea Dragon*, top heavy with far too much sail and poop for its size, pitched and yawed. By now, as before, even the strongest members of the seasick crew were far too weary to man the rudder. Likely the rudder just blew off. Watertight bulkheads were not in place to offer a last corridor of escape. It hardly mattered. A good-sized headlong wave could tip the ship on its side or roll it over. Earlier Gordon Torrey had noted how "solid water could come right over that low spoon bow, wipe out the sky-light truck and fill the lower deck section with enough water to enable that great heavy Diesel engine to take her to the bottom." The crashing, violent fury of the storm could as easily rip the diesel engine loose, snap the rigging or bring down the masts, leaving the junk a basically limbless, brainless raft with enough ballast on board to carry it three miles down to the ocean floor.[17]

Scenarios of the ship's fate vary. Inevitably details from the trial run are chosen to illuminate it. What wasn't fastened down flew off the ship. Cords snapped. The heavy downpour of rain soon had the crew drenched and chilled to the bone; the oil-skin jackets, if they put them on as they had during the trial run, didn't help. The wind tore equipment loose. Two, three, four members of the crew had to work the tiller while someone did lookout. Comparable ocean outings also illuminate the drama on board. Dr. Petersen's 36-foot junk the *Hummel-Hummel*, half the length of the *Sea Dragon*, had run headlong into a storm in which waves, "roaring and foaming for the kill," as Dr. Petersen put it, "leaped up, gleaming while in the night, to drop their liquid weight upon the decks." On June 14, 1939, a twenty-nine-ton junk under a Russian captain and crewed by two Norwegians began its voyage from Kobe, Japan, to the San Francisco Exposition; on July 12, in the mid–Pacific, it radioed the S.S. *Coolidge* for a re-supply of food and water, which it quickly received; no further mishaps were reported. The S.S. *Coolidge* itself had bucked the very same storm that overthrew the *Sea Dragon*, and may show, besides the difference between a safe and a match box at sea, the difference too between a whale and a turtle without a shell. Adventurer and writer Tim Severin's voyage aboard the *Hsu Fu*, a bamboo raft, fifty years later offers keen glimpses as to the work level a crew can achieve when faced with imminent dangers.[18]

The *Hummel-Hummel* completed its crossing from Shanghai to San Pedro, and Dr. Petersen survived to remark on the high morale of his crew. Morale on the *Sea Dragon* may not have been as high. Years before on the S.S. *President Madison*, Halliburton mentioned the "ten days we remained at sea," and how "each day I loathed the ship more. It was my first experience as a seaman on a passenger-boat and it will certainly be the last." He thought voyages on a freighter different, at least the one in which he had been a seaman. "On a freighter a man's life is his own; the ship belongs to him, its decks, its bridge, its hold. He brooks no repression other than the bo's'n's...." Little did awful conditions matter: "twenty-four seamen were bunked in tiers in one crowded compartment in the depths of the hold, where the odors of fetid food, drifting in from the galley alongside, were always with us. Fortunately, we were so dead tired by night, we did not know or care whether we were breathing air or laughing-gas."[19]

Neither the passenger liner nor the freighter experienced so violent a storm as now gripped the *Sea Dragon*. One can hope, for pity's sake, that those aboard had little idea if they were breathing air or laughing gas.

Click, a sensationalist tabloid of the day, published a photo spread of Halliburton's life, and presumed death. It included an artist's conception of what actually happened. Violently thrown upside down, the ship is cast through vortices of wind and water as through a black hole. Its mast has blown off and appears as a giant bat taking flight. Each member of the crew is flung in a different direction. The caption reads: "Through roily seas that mountained as high as forty feet when they broke over her bobbing bow, the S.S. *President Coolidge* struggled at a slow six knots through a black typhoon in the usually calm eastern Pacific. Somewhere nearby, the same angry sea was tossing about a craft which compared to the Liner *Coolidge* as a match box does to an office safe."[20]

Those who heard about the tragedy formed images of Halliburton's last moments. He had been happy, when in his twenties, he bade farewell in hottest India to the *Gold Shell*—"that clumsy old tanker and her blasphemous crew" and, "as she steamed up the Hooghly" he "exclaimed with Shelley: *Oh wind, if this be spring, shall I ever live through the summer?*" Perhaps images flashed of blizzards, of the Hindenburg exploding, of the two cars stalled on the railroad track the train he once was in hit—"What a mess!" Maybe Paul said, 'Great Amelia's ghost!'[21]

Paul, like Willa Cather's "Paul," "his teeth chattering, his lips drawn away from them in a frightened smile" he "dropped back into the immense design of things." But, before this, unlike Paul, unlike the others, "once or twice he glanced nervously sidewise, as though he were being watched." Perhaps, too, "when the right moment came, he jumped. As he fell, the folly of his haste occurred to him with merciless clearness, the vastness of what he had left undone." For Paul the pitching and heaving of the waves rocking the ship in a ritual dance, one of death, propitiated nature; or it was supreme hubris, to tamper with the delicately balanced universe, to try to upset it, as poet Robinson Jeffers had suggested?[22] One can only imagine.

What was said in the end may have been trite, neither dramatic nor cinematic. Pitiable, eerie cries and groans might have been heard. The crashing winds and waves made it hard for the crew to communicate. Ravaged, tired faces were all they saw.

Halliburton, who had retraced Ulysses' wanderings around the Mediterranean, might have written that, in his last adventure, mighty Poseidon had roared up angrily from the depths of the sea and, in league with Aeolus, headstrong god of winds, had punished him for attempting the impossible.

He had now come full circle. Fifteen years before he had delivered "mail pouches" to American and British consulates in Yokohama. He had arrived there "penniless," and with only one dream, to "get back to the [golf] links in America!"[23]

19

Earth, Air, Fire—and Water

At Treasure Island the sign, "Reserved anchorage for Halliburton's *Sea Dragon*," still beckoned. Management waited.

Time, featuring Ginger Rogers on the cover, reported in "People" that "Rover Boy [Richard] Halliburton set out from Hong Kong in a Chinese junk for San Francisco, intending to make a fashionably late appearance at the Fair. Fortnight ago the junk was reported lost in mid–Pacific, at week's end was still missing." Just above the notice was another news item and a picture of Mr. and Mrs. Harpo Marx. The reader's eye moved on, then turned the page.[1]

Halliburton's agent at the Fair, Wilfred Crowell, had requested that the U.S. Naval Department conduct a search for the missing vessel.[2]

The U.S. Coast Guard in Honolulu, believing that the *Sea Dragon* was simply experiencing bad weather, and hence was not lost, kept its search teams docked. The Japanese navy outright refused to lend a hand. Pan-American Airways, however, informed its fliers to keep a sharp look-out for the junk. Steamers were also informed to be on the look-out. The fullest search was conducted by the U.S.S. *Astoria*. With three planes aboard, the Navy cruiser was ordered by the Secretary of the Navy to conduct a thorough search, setting out from Guam, and, beginning just north of Marcos Island and retracing the probable path of the ship. In all it covered over 162,000 miles, but turned up no sign of the *Sea Dragon*.[3]

On May 17, 1939, the *Washington Star* carried a small news item about native son Paul Mooney and his disappearance: "Navy Planes to Hunt Halliburton, D.C. Aide," read the headline, followed by the subheading: "Search Order Revives Hope for Mother of Crew Member." Paul was said to be thirty years old; he was thirty-four. His last letter was said to have been postmarked February 27; in it Paul had said that the *Sea Dragon* was provisioned for a month, and he wished he were in California again. Another feature (apparently from the *Star*, June 16), indicated that hope for finding the *Sea Dragon* had been abandoned by Paul's grieving mother. Paul was noted as "a bachelor and something of a writer in his own right" who had "set sail with noted adventurer and travelogue writer [Richard Halliburton] last year at the outset of the Chinese expedition."

Ione Gaut Mooney visits Laguna Beach, fall 1954. It is believed that William Alexander, seated next to her, received the teak chest at this time. Mrs. Mooney died shortly after this photograph was taken (courtesy William Alexander).

His letters home while "journeying through war-torn China" were described as "long [and] newsy." While the Navy search had provided her with a ray of hope, Paul's mother told reporters that she had lost hope of recovering her son.[4]

Paul's sister Alicia believed he had cheated dire Fate itself. She told Paul's friend Bill Alexander, "My favorite brother never was destined to die in bed; he got one more thrill when he looked upon a typhoon making toward him; and if fast thinking yet could save him, he's still around." Alexander, stunned and ever-mournful, liked to think Paul, if truly dead, had died serving some obscure poetic cause. Ironically, Paul's poems associate earth images with death, yet he died at sea.[5]

Grief stricken, Paul's mother held to her heart the few letters her son had sent to her from Hong Kong. His last letter, postmarked February 27, just days before the *Sea Dragon* set sail, reported that "with all the interest the trip held for him, he would be glad to see the coast of California again." Daughter Eire meanwhile comforted her with news of her own pregnancy, telling her that she was about to give her a grandson—she had no doubt about the gender—who, she assured, would take Paul's place in her heart. A son, Mark, was born on

Opposite: Artist James M. Garrett's conception of the *Sea Dragon's* final moments. Published in *Click: The National Picture Magazine*, October 1939.

Alicia Mooney in Laguna Beach. She brought her mother Ione Gaut Mooney with her (courtesy William Alexander).

New Year's Day, 1940. Though it was both a financial and mental burden, Ione Mooney held on to the property in Laguna left to her by Paul, thinking he might one day return. At her death in 1955, her children and heirs sold the property for $6,000 through the Bank of Laguna Beach to a Cincinnati couple (though Ione's and Alicia's preference was that Bill Alexander should develop it). Saddled with the miseries of cumulative property taxes from this and a Maryland property over some years, the family, according to Alicia Mooney, "want[ed] to get of the real estate business with all speed." The proceeds from Paul's property were divided equally among Ione's five remaining children.[6]

As to the dispensation of worldly goods, conflicts of interest were bound to occur. Even before Halliburton was declared officially dead, perhaps prematurely, on October 5 (by the Chancery Court in Memphis, who gave as the date March 23 or March 24), his parents had come to Laguna in late August to settle his affairs. Though the house had cost over $31,000 to build and would escalate in value tremendously over the years, they were willing to get it off their hands for $25,000. Real estate agent Alice M. Padgett suggested in a letter that the Halliburtons, besides being perhaps overly motivated, seemed to the denizens of Laguna Beach high-handed. Evidently, "they took every book that was written by Dick and boy are they bitter when any one mentions Paul. And every one did. You know that Paul had some good friends here and really Dick was scarcely known and every one praising and expressing fondness for Paul, and OH BOY."

Wesley had little liking for his son's friends; on his dismissal list were William Alexander and of course Paul. "The thorn in the sore spot is that Dick willed the house and insurance, etc. to Paul except in case they both were lost at sea [and] in such case they went to the Halliburtons. There is several thousands worth of insurance tho that goes to Paul's mother."[7]

Much later, Paul's family learned that possibly three insurance policies existed, but as the insured and beneficiary both died in a common accident, the proceeds went to the estate of Richard Halliburton. Alicia Mooney was herself informed that Halliburton had made out a life insurance policy to Paul with the Jefferson Life Insurance Company of Greensboro, North Carolina. Richard once referred to it as the "Mooney-Desola policy," which indicates that provision had been made to both his friends. Writing to the company she was told that Halliburton had left three such policies to Paul, but, according to the law, when the insured and the beneficiary die in a common accident, the insurer and not the beneficiary is considered the survivor. Therefore, any proceeds were collected by the estate of Richard Halliburton. Halliburton, as any sailor who takes to a dangerous mission at sea, was equally prescient about the Laguna property and how it should be disposed should he die. At the eleventh hour he wrote home: "If Paul and I [sink?] together the insurance policy made to him goes to you." Then he emphasized, "*I do not want it to go to his family* (underscoring his)." He noted that he had written to Gay Beaman about this and had indicated his wishes on a change of policy addendum. On the brighter side, he mentioned his debt situation, but confidently assured that "box office profits" from the *Sea Dragon Expedition* would clear all of them. Halliburton had admitted to a "tough summer," one unmitigated by the "strain" that followed, which featured "clashes and quarrels," some with Paul, over means and ends, and he believed "once at sea" all would pass. It should be noted, too, that by the end of the next decade, property values in Laguna had tripled the value they held in 1939.[8]

Among the "succession of tenants" were Mary Lou Davis and her two children, Dorothy and Tommy, who would occupy Hangover House for about a year. In a number of photographs that were taken of them outside Hangover House, masterpieces of the aesthetic macabre, the three appear as models in a dreamscape, immune as caryatids to aging and death. One shows them posing in front of a miniature model of a Chinese junk; Dorothy and Tommy, looking into the camera, are each holding one of Paul's cats while Mary Lou is looking at the junk. In another, young Tommy appears in front of a giant facade of the Taj Mahal. Individual photo-portraits of Dorothy and Mary Lou make them appear as fashion models for *McCalls* or *Woman's Home Journal*, magazines that published Halliburton's stories.[9]

Ultimately Wallace Scott and wife Zolite would own the house, bought at auction for the fabulously low price, in 1941, of $7,500; it had cost nearly $32,000 to build. Over many decades their love for the house would stay. When skater and film star Sonja Henie (whom Alexander had known through the party circuit as a "friendly person") and, later, actor Van Johnson offered to buy the house for ten times what it had cost to build, the Scotts refused to sell it. Johnson, incidentally, was dating Henie about this time. Still, as late as 1947, it was the belief of "many Laguna people including the Red Cross" that actor Van Johnson, not the Scotts, resided in the house. Mention should be made that Salvador Dalí sponsor Edward James also briefly occupied the house.[10]

"In 1945," wrote Halliburton biographer Jonathan Root, "a section of wooden keel with several ribs attached floated ashore at Pacific Beach, California, a point to which the junk's remains could have drifted, but no authoritative decision was ever made." Earlier, in December 1939, the *Boston Post* noted the British consul's report of "the wreck of a junk sighted in latitude 4-14 north, longitude 104-41 east but [the consul] gave no other details." Later, July 1940, Captain Charles Jokstad of the S.S. *President Pierce*, the very same man who had inspected the *Sea Dragon* a year and a half before, reported having to "slow speed because of damage to his ship's tailshaft when driftwood resembling the rudder of a Chinese junk was sighted" and "covered with barnacles of approximately a year's growth." Commanding Officer Dale E. Collins in a letter wrote the following:

> You have perhaps read in the papers that about one year ago (June or July I believe) several old, water soaked, timbers were washed up on the beach in California.... The papers claimed that the timbers were the exact type, size, and kind, as used in the "*Sea Dragon*," the carvings and workmanship were unmistakably Chinese and experts believed the timbers to be actual pieces from the Wreck of the "*Sea Dragon*." It is indeed possible that these timbers were part of the once proud "*Sea Dragon*" but it is only conjecture and circumstantial evidence, and perhaps a little dramatic wishful thinking. Anyway, it makes a fitting end to the story of Richard Halliburton that sections of his last adventure would come finally to rest near his former home at Laguna Beach.

This possibility seems miraculous.[11]

Amos Wood, however, thinks it not so miraculous. "It is believed," he wrote, "that during the gale and heavy seas the *Sea Dragon* lost her rudder, breached, foundered, and sank.... When the [ship] broke up, the engine and ballast certainly took the main hull to the bottom some three miles below. When it hit, it must have broken off more pieces. Parts would break away and pop up to the surface for some time, thus the floating debris would be strung out for a long distance." Eventually, near Okinawa, "such debris could have caught the northbound Kuroshio Current and then headed east toward western American shores. This drift voyage would take roughly 1,700 days, making its estimated time of arrival no sooner than January 1944." Later, "a portion of a wooden keel with ribs attached, thought by some to be from the *Sea Dragon*, was beach-combed at Pacific Beach, California, in 1945—only 450 miles south of San Francisco, Halliburton's destination." Underwater archaeologists might recover the diesel engine, steel flywheel or coffee pot Halliburton lost over the side of the ship. Using the most sophisticated bathometric scanning devices, these would be remarkable findings. Everything becomes nothing sometime; after forty-five-hundred years, even tin oxidizes—towards that end, it loses its shape and sheen.[12]

What then of the crew of the *Sea Dragon*? Fish feed first on the eyes of the dead. Romantics believe in enchanted isles and lost heroes living there. "Death is at all times solemn," wrote Richard Henry Dana aboard ship, "but never so much so as at sea.... A man dies on shore—you follow his body to the grave, and a stone marks the spot ... but at sea, the man is near you—at your side— you hear his voice, and in an instant he is gone, and nothing but a vacancy shows his loss...."[13]

Friend Gertrude Atherton, who had seen Halliburton "the day before his last farewell," wrote, "Alas, that he should be one ... for whom the magic talisman [of a little Buddha he wore] failed! Nor did an unkind Fate permit him to die in action, an end to his brilliant life that he would have infinitely preferred."[14]

Tennessee Williams, who would live in Laguna Beach, suspected that, like the travel writer's earlier attempt to fake his own death when he swam the Helle-spont, Halliburton's disappearance was "a big publicity stunt." Others shared the opinion. And of course for some his ghost still roams about Hangover House, though, for Bill Alexander, whose attachment to his first great friend remained ardent, it was more likely Paul's ghost that roamed or had set himself up on a desert island somewhere to write, a talented ghost to the end.[15]

Theories of Halliburton and crew tucked away somewhere on a remote desert island persist. Possibly descendants of Paul's cats roam about the ridge at Hangover House, and through the eyes of these presumed psychic watchmen one may see the timeless eyes that once beheld their master of long ago. At the Fair, had one gazed long enough into the pool of water beside the "Court of Reflections," a phantom ship, shimmering in the ripples of turquoise and gold, might appear amid sounds of "the souls of long-drowned sailors crying from the deep." For some Halliburton's ghost stands throughout the world as a colos-sus directing travelers on their way.[16]

Some reviews of Halliburton's life were not so rapturous. "Halliburton was something more than a bad writer," a *Time* magazine article read in part, "a rather-hard-to-take public figure. He was an appealing, confused individual, a U.S. phenomenon, a U.S. symbol. The nice son of a nice U.S. environment, he never entirely outgrew or betrayed it. He was essentially, if mildly, an artist and a rebel, [but] he achieved neither art nor rebellion. He was an innocent, sort of Byron-of-his-time."[17]

Like Lord Byron, he swam the Hellespont. And like Lord Byron, he wrote that he would rather have done so than have written all his poetry. In a materially dazed age, he remained an idealist; not a naive one, for he knew that it took money to be one, and money is as insistent a theme in his letters as adventure; so is drudgery as much as romance. Still, he was a genteel knight, a summer day in winter, unreal but welcome. He was courteous to a fault, and, as the Christmas gifts he shipped home just before the *Sea Dragon*'s final voyage bear witness, he had a sense of the fitness of things.[18]

William Alexander, about 1985, on the deck of the home he designed and built in the Hollywood Hills and called the "House in Space." From there he had a clear view of the Pacific Ocean. He never forgot Paul. He kept a plaster bust of him in his work room, and, when near some of the things of Paul's he owned, mumbled to him as though he were at his side (courtesy William Alexander).

Paul, too, had this sense, and, constant to his thoughts, was his family. He was, importantly, "something of a writer in his own right," who sent home "long, newsy" letters. Besides these, he sent home, in his last days, several jade fig-urines. Among these are one of a ferocious dragon-like dog, guardian of home and hearth, and another of a philosopher, presumably Shoe-hsing, God of Longevity. The dog actually resembles a cat, and the philosopher perhaps reminded him of his father. Along with other items, these reached his mother in a teak chest built (almost certainly) at the Kowloon shipyards by the same cartwrights who built the *Sea Dragon*, and as such the only scrap of wood from the junk expedition to survive. Eventually it became the property of Bill Alexander. For a time it held papers belonging to Halliburton and Mooney—letters maybe, clippings. Besides the name "Paul Mooney," carved on the outside is a saying, in Chinese characters, from Confucius' *Analects*, which, translated, reads:

> Top: This is my treasure chest
>   Which holds all my books and pictures.
> Left Side: When things go wrong
>   I'd rather travel in a junk
>   on the high seas, with the chest.
> Right Side: When things go right
>   If I need my book, I'll take them out.
>   If I don't, let this chest guard them.
> Front: When young, beware of fighting;
>   When strong, beware of sex;
>   When old, beware of possessions.

Paul and Richard died within Confucius's second warning.[19]

Travel writer Burton Holmes reflected on his own life, years later, one that had reached Confucius' third warning, then passed beyond it:

The teak chest Paul Mooney sent home bears an inscription from Confucius' *Analects* as well as Paul's name. The chest may have been made by the same workers who built the *Sea Dragon* and hence is the only "splinter" left from *the Sea Dragon Expedition*. Photograph taken by author.

My wise friends saved and economized, went without things they wanted, denied themselves the costlier pleasures of the table, the bouquet of vintage wines and the, to me, supreme joy of going places, seeing things, and taking possession through travel of the whole wide world.

And now where are we? We, they and I, are all at the same dead-end of life's highway. They are weighted down by all the leaden burdens of their golden hopes gone wrong. They have their memories but these are memories of wise, dull, and frugal days of systematic piling up of hard-earned dollars in safe places where those dollars would increase and multiply and be there to console for all the pleasures that their owners had denied themselves and all the fun that they had missed.

"I, too, have nothing but my memories, but I would not exchange my memories for theirs. I have possession of a secret treasure upon which I can draw at will. I can bring forth on the darkest day, bright diamonds of remembered joys, diamonds whose many facets reflect some happy dream that has come true, a small ambition gratified; a long-sought sensation, caught and savored to the full, a little journey made, an expedition carried to success, a circumnavigation of the globe accomplished.[20]

The Fair closed on October 6, 1939. Coincidentally, this was only a day after Halliburton's official death. Much re-tailored, it reopened on May 25, 1940. Between those dates, on December 15, *Gone with the Wind*, starring Clark Gable and Vivian Leigh, premiered at Loew's Theater in Atlanta: it would be one Clark Gable movie Paul would miss. If not a splinter of the junk survived, the music of the San Francisco Exposition survived in the "fabled [though eerily memorial] 24 September 1940 San Francisco Concerts." Among the featured performers was Judy Garland who, through an orgy of applause, sang "Somewhere Over the Rainbow." In Laguna Beach, completely oblivious to the big Fair held further north, the Festival of Arts, featuring painting, sculpture, music, drama, literature, dancing, photography, and crafts, opened on July 28 and closed on August 6.[21]

Others of note passed with Richard Halliburton and Paul Mooney. Portents seem to have family connections. René Crevel, age thirty-four, same age as Paul, died in 1935; Lawrence of Arabia, age forty-seven, also died that year; film producer Irving Thalberg, age thirty-seven, died in 1936, composer George Gershwin, age thirty-eight, in 1937; Thomas Wolfe's death, two weeks before his thirty-eighth birthday, occurred on September 15, 1938, just days before Paul and Richard left San Francisco. On January 28, 1938, German race car driver, and husband to flying ace Elly Beinhorn, Bernd Rosemeyer, driving one of Auto Union's Silver Arrows, died in a crash on the Frankfurt-Darmstedt autobahn attempting to set a world speed record. Remarkably Elly Beinhorn herself lived well into the 21st century. William Alexander nearly reached it.[22]

Of Paul's siblings, the most traveled was Eire, Eire Stevens. A foreign service officer with the State Department and the United States Information Agency, she toured Germany and Africa. She was also executive officer of the information service in Lagos, Nigeria, in the 1960s and also saw official service in Algiers.

Often in harm's way, she died in 1996, age eighty-six.[23]

The *Sea Dragon Expedition* had its survivors. Gorden Ellicott Torrey died in Rockport, Maine on November 1, 1992, at seventy-eight. For twenty years he was the district manager for Texaco Cina Limited. In Japan, during the occupation, he served on the U.S. Army's Petroleum Advisory Board. Later, he left Texaco to join the States Marine Isthmian Lines and eventually became its vice president. He and his wife, Payson, had four daughters and two sons. John Rust Potter died on December 4, 1996, at 82. He had married Anne Hopkins, daughter of Dartmouth president Ernest Martin Hopkins. During World War II, he served as attaché to the British office of naval intelligence with the United States Navy in Bombay, India. If he did purge himself of the wanderlust, he never lost his interest in sailing and often was seen, later in life, aboard the black-hulled sloop *Antiope* cruising the Long Island Sound. He left four children. The other Dartmouth volunteer, Robert Hill Chase, left behind a $750,000 fortune, a figure that would have financed many *Sea Dragon Expeditions*, willed to him by his grandmother, Edith W. Gallagher.[24]

On December 12, 1939, Douglas Fairbanks, after years on cruise ships exploring the world and recently married to Lady Sylvia Ashley, opted to sit out the war from the safety and luxury of his home overlooking the Pacific in Santa Monica; given to hard drinking, and heavy smoking, the once rough-and-tumble, acrobatic actor, who performed his own stunts, died of a heart attack, in his sleep, age fifty-six, which seems young, for him. Between these two deaths was Halliburton's own disappearance, the timing of which his friend Paul, in the role of poet, would have understood. James Joyce and Virginia Woolf, he might also have noted, still lived, living into a beginning, until 1941, not into an end, as 1939 seemed.[25]

April 1939 saw the publication of *Action Comics* #13; it marked a year since the appearance of Superman, who was really newsman Clark Kent, as *Romantic Adventure* had really been Richard Halliburton. On July 4, 1939, baseball great Lou Gehrig gave his famous farewell speech before 62,000 cheering fans at Yankee Stadium; he died two years later. Sigmund Freud, tired of the pain his throat cancer caused him, died on September 23, 1939, wondering still what women wanted and quite uncertain of the meaning of Hitler. Weeks later, on November 14, the Macy's Thanksgiving Parade was given its first television broadcast. *Television*—it would have been a new medium for Halliburton to conquer.

Halliburton's letters to his mother and father were published in 1940. They end, "The rest is silence." Beneath the line is a picture of waves calming down from a storm towards a stillness. A film take of the calm following the storm might show the water, asleep now, and overhead a softly burning sun lodged in the socket of a light-blue sky. In the background, faintly plays Fred Astaire's spirited rendition of Gershwin's "They All Laughed," maybe from an ocean-liner miles away, then over it plays Josephine Baker's "La petite tonkinese," its phrases as lilting as the cascading waves indifferently toppling over one another towards another storm. On March 16, only a week before the *Sea Dragon's* dis-

Paul's third or fourth cat, supposedly, walking about the "lobe" of "Clark Gable's ear" at Hangover House in 1939 or 1940 (courtesy William Alexander).

appearance, the most renowned movie of make-believe ever produced, *The Wizard of Oz*, finished shooting. On August 17, 1939, the film, starring Judy Garland in the featured role of Dorothy, opened at Loew's Capitol Theatre on Broadway in New York City. The line that ends it, "There is no place like home" also ends *The Royal Road to Romance*.[26]

Southeast Asia and the southwest Pacific remained hotbeds of hostility. On December 23, Guam and Wake would fall to the Japanese; two days later, on Christmas day, 1941, Hong Kong fell.

A month after the premier of *The Wizard of Oz*, Hitler, whom Paul knew, sort of, invaded Poland. Hitler wanted to create a horrible world that was large; Paul wanted to live in a wonderful one that was small.

Appendix A: Seven Poems by Paul Mooney

The Ramapo River Printers
New York, 1927

Youth

The slow light fails
all down the long, long way I go
and fades the way I came;
But where I walk, the flame
of Youth burns evenly, and in its glow
Fear shrinks and pales.

Blondel to Richard Coeur de Lion

Look, Richard! It is I, thy singing boy,
Have followed thee and found thee, where thou art
By prison chains compelled, and walled apart
By dungeon stone from freedom's sunlit joy.
My sharp sword gleams beside my harp; I vow
These sounding cords, this cutting edge, will charm
Or slay the fouls who would thus work thee harm—
My lord, my prince, my loving comrade thou!

Ho! Do thy gaolers think that linked steel
Can tether thy fair limbs while I be free?
Could they not sense how my own heart would feel
The weight of every chain that burdens thee?
Be brave awhile—no prison forge can weld
Bonds strong to hold as our love's bond has held!

Field-Burial

Here, where we sow and reap across old graves
Of unmarked, unremembered men, our fields
Spring greener than their wont. Each furrow yields
Rich elements to this tall corn, that waves
Aloft, their only monument. No staves
Of Latin song are sung for these, nor kneels
One priest with interceding prayer, nor peals
For them one bell through long dim holy naves.

Yet peace, you unknown, unmourned dead—be still!
No pious prayer would stay the worm, and none
Could ever warm your clammy bones; nor will
You need another epitaph than one:
Birth, Disillusion, Death—such is our span;
Eternally, man ends where he began.

Who Was Not Forward

All night I was awake for you
Till dawn. I saw the morning breeze
Gather a mist that strangely grew
Like pale fruit on the twigs of trees.

I slept not, though the hours were long
And dark. I heard the first bird fly
Among the leaves, and heard its song
Prelude the dawn from dim sky.

And still I longed for you, and still
My empty arms held only air,
My lips kissed naught but space, until
I sobbed aloud to have you there.
        . . . .
O last night's love, whose timid feet
Delayed until the sun was high!
O laggard love! And did you greet
The noon as fancy free as I!

Release

I am invaded by a hateful crowd
Of enemies and friends, who rudely thrust
Their lives into my life; who void their lust
Like goats upon my flesh—Poor flesh! Once proud
But now too weary for pride!—Who question loud
Of This and That, and speak of Shall and Must
And ask me, Why? until a great disgust
Enwraps and chokes me, like a poisonous cloud.

But work your will upon my body; crawl
Along these limbs, foul lovers, like disease;
And you, obscene dissectors, never cease
To probe within my soul till each part's known:
I am at last a stranger to you all,
And in the grave I lie with Death alone.

Initiate

No more am I a lonely worshipper
At Venus' and Priapus' shrine,
For thou art there, young sweet idolator,
To make thy prayer with mine.

And on the secret altars all night long
We pour wine pressed from curious fruits;
And all night through we sing Love's ancient song
To a melody of flutes.

For me, you chant Love's litany; for you,
I spill the newly-vintaged wine;
And from one fire, whose flame burns ever new,
My perfume drifts with thine.

These are good shrines, where it is sweet to pray;
So kneel again—entered the Hours
To slow their speed, and day by day delay
The waning of Love's powers.

And when, at length, I pour my wine until
Only the lees are left some night—
Swear, swear, that thou wilt worship with me still,
Beloved acolyte!

Epitaph for a Seer

Be kindly, Earth, to this returning soil
Cast back by heedless Life upon thy breast.
Unbend thy mighty majesty, and dressed
In falling rains, fulfill the gentle toil
Of burying a man. And then, to foil
These tardy fools, when they shall later quest
For him whose vision is their present jest,
Wreath vines about the grave, coil on green coil.

For it was thine—this clod, that breathed an hour,
Labored and loved, grew sleepy in due time
And slept; that, waking, called its dreams sublime
And strove to live them with its little power.
Resume what was thine own, O Earth, and let
It dream no further glories, but forget.

Appendix B: Letters

ITEM 1 Richard Halliburton carefully and conscientiously planned his travels; chance mishaps, such as, in his trip around the world, when he narrowly crashed his plane into the only refueling tank in the desert en route to Timbuctoo, were to be expected. The typed letter to Harold Pitcairn (below, and dated November 4, 1930), indicates his interest in using a Pitcairn gyro for his trip around the world and his eagerness to confer with its owner at his factory. The Pitcairn gyro was one of several airplanes he considered as his "Flying Carpet" before he chose for the trip the single prop Stearman biplane. The letter is signed by Halliburton in the same deliberative, unhurried manner in which he signed his many books.

```
                              Roosevelt Hotel,
                              Hollywood, California

                              November 4th,
                              1 9 3 0 .


Mr. Harold F. Pitcairn,
Pitcairn Airplane Company,
WILLOW GROVE, PENNSYLVANIA.

Dear Mr. Pitcairn,-

          Mr. Earl Halliburton and I are very grateful
to you for your telegram in reply to ours.  I am terribly
disappointed that you feel the autogiro is not yet ready
for a round-the-world trip.  I can fully understand what
difficulties might arise if I were in need of spare parts,
with no service station near.  However, might it not be
possible to ship ahead several sets of giro blades along
with the spare parts for my engine, which I will have to
send anyway?  Also, would it not be possible for my very
expert and experienced pilot to come to your factory along
with me and take a thorough schooling in the servicing and
operation of your new device.  We could then be our own
service station.

          The more I consider the possibilities of a
trip around the world, with the new Pitcairn, the less
interested I am in flying any other plane.  Naturally,
it would not rebound to your profit if anything went wrong
```

with the ship, - especially as there will be a concentrated
searchlight of publicity turned upon my expedition should
I use the giro.   On the other hand, as I am in no hurry
whatsoever, and plan to travel leisurely and cautiously,
there would be ample opportunity to wait for proper weather,
and to give the ship and engine the sharpest attention.

        The pilot who is to accompany me (my own flying
ability is not sufficient for a round-the-world flight) has
had a vast experience and I should hate to substitute any
other pilot for him, but I would be entirely willing, if
you so recommended, to take with me, one of your own Pitcairn
test pilots, provided we could find one who might be interested
in accompanying me.   Safety, both for my plane and for my
neck, is to be my first commandment.   Nor is it my purpose
to take longer hops than the ship is well equipped for.   I
plan to dismantle it several times, and not try to fly any

Mr. Harold F. Pitcairn,   Page No. 2.

long water stretches.

        Tomorrow night - Wednesday, November 5th,
I am accompanying Earl Halliburton to Tulsa, Oklahoma,
in my Lockheed, and would be obliged to you if you would
communicate with me there, c/o Earl, S.A.F.E. Way Air-
lines.   I shall be there three or four days.   If the
conditions I have set forth in this letter have put a
different light on the situation, and have been convincing arguments in favor of my using a Pitcairn giro after
all for my Flying Carpet, and if you would be willing to
confer with me at your own factory, I would gladly fly
from Tulsa on to Philadelphia immediately upon your advice.

        This combination of your ship and my flight
has such dramatic possibilities and such potential profit
for us both that I am exceedingly reluctant to abandon
the idea so long as there is the slightest hope of bringing it to pass.

        Again my homages to you and my sincere
appreciation for your telegram.

                        Cordially,

                        Richard Halliburton

Permanent Address:
Richard Halliburton,
Roosevelt Hotel,
Hollywood, California.

Address from Nov. 6th
        to   Nov. 11th:
c/o Earl Halliburton,
S.A.F.E. WAY AIR LINES,
Tulsa, Okla.

ITEM 2 Halliburton thought highly enough of the house William Alexander designed and built for him to include it as another marvel in his *Book of Marvels.* Reads the inscription: "For Alex Levy (i.e., William Alexander) who built Hangover House—another Marvel from Dick Halliburton who is proud to live in it."

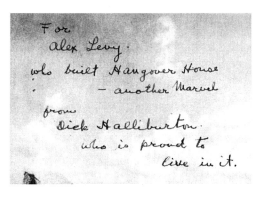

ITEM 3 Paul's letter to Bill (i.e., William Alexander), dated 1935, is a rare sample of Paul Mooney's handwriting. In it Paul quotes Richard, who is concerned about the rift in communication that for some unknown reason had occurred between Paul and Bill. Halliburton had written to him from Cairo. The letter preserves the only known direct communication between Paul and Richard that apparently has survived. Paul's handwriting reflects a cheerful, open disposition. It is remarkably similar to Richard's handwriting, and has led me to believe that Paul Mooney could replicate Richard Halliburton's signature, as well as emulate his writing style. Compare, as strongly similar, letters "a," "r" and "l." Author's collection.

broke for years to come, so work is
not a bad idea. There won't be any
more New York for me until I
come for the Ford — far in the future.
I don't want to wait that long to see
you, but perhaps we can plan for you
to drive back here with me when
the day comes?

A note from Dick says in part: "I

---

am glad you have seen Bill again. I
was beginning to very bitterly resent
your treatment of each other." He is
in Cairo now; will be back in June perhaps.
As for me, I want to take mother to the
coast before then.

Gene remained (MAC COWAN) in Whitinsville to
paint a portrait, so don't try to reach
him — in case you want yours — at
Hotel Chelsea. His address is c/o Philip
Sasell, Whitinsville, Mass. And he is
getting his health & spirits back.

The experience there was something
to share with you, but it can wait. A
strange visit, oppressive, unhappy.

No, the stamp is just to give you
something to look at — worth the
extra penny! I'd give five times
that much to be with you this moment.

as ever

Paul

2550 University Place, Washington D.C.

A Note on Sources

The principal published primary source for Richard Halliburton's life is Richard Halliburton, *The Story of His Life's Adventure As Told in Letters to His Mother and Father* (New York: Bobbs-Merrill Company, 1940): hereafter, *RHL*. Originals of the letters, edited, often severely, for publication by Halliburton's father, Wesley, reside in the Richard Halliburton Collection, Manuscripts Division, Department of Rare Books and Special Collections, Princeton University Library (and are here published with permission of the Princeton University Library); hereafter, *RHL-P*, as they contain omitted portions from the published versions. Five scrapbooks, comprised of newspaper clippings, programs, and features of Richard's public life and put together during his son's lifetime by his father, reside at Rhodes College in Memphis, Tennessee.

A chief biography is Jonathan Root (1923–1967), *Halliburton—The Magnificent Myth* (New York: Coward-McCann, Inc., 1965): hereafter, *JR*. A more recent biography is James Cortese, *Richard Halliburton's Royal Road* (Memphis: White Rose Press, 1989): hereafter, *JC*. Cortese was a friend of Wesley Halliburton.

Among the short biographies is Guy Townsend, "Richard Halliburton: The Forgotten Myth" (August, 1977), reprinted, *Memphis Magazine*, April 2001, memphismagazine.com/backissues/april2001/coverstory2.htm. Other short accounts include Chip Deffaa, "On the Trail of Richard Halliburton '21: A Young Alumnus Searches for the Man Behind the Legend," *Princeton Alumni Weekly*, May 13, 1973; Alan Landsburg, "Richard Halliburton, *In Search of Missing Persons* (New York: Bantam, 1978), pp. 9–29; David M. Schwartz, "On the Royal Road to Adventure with 'Daring Dick,'" *Smithsonian*, March 1989: 159–178; Michael Blankenship, "A Fellow Traveler," *The Advocate: The National Gay and Lesbian Newsmagazine* 18 July 1989, pp. 38–43; Gerry Max, "Richard Halliburton and Thomas Wolfe: When Youth Kept Open House," *North Carolina Literary Review*, no. 5, 1996, pp. 82–93; and Gretchen Kelly, "Richard Halliburton—In Search of Adventure," *Metrosource*, spring, 1998, pp. 38–42.

The fullest short treatment of Halliburton in his lifetime is Dorothy Dayton, "Richard Halliburton, 'Prince of Lovers,' Talks About Women and Love," an interview, *The Illustrated Love Magazine*, March 1930, pp. 36–41. Also of note is Mildred Harrington, "Dick Halliburton Has Followed the Royal Road to Romance," *The American Woman's Magazine*, October, 1926, pp. 26–28; 218, 220, and 224.

A few Paul Mooney letters survive, addressed to William Alexander; hereafter, *PML-WA*. There are also a number of letters from William Alexander to Richard

Halliburton; hereafter, *WA-RH*. In turn, there are letters from Richard Halliburton to William Alexander; hereafter, *RH-WA*. The majority of these, and several originals, were used based on copies given to me by William Alexander (1909–1997) with his permission to use them as seen fit. One letter was lent by Paul's nephew Anton Levandowsky and is used with his permission. Other materials were given to me by John M. Scott, Paul's nephew and Ione's son; named after her mother, Ione, born May 19, 1902, and Paul, born November 26, 1904, were very close. Besides taped interviews, Alexander also left notes for an autobiography entitled "Meanderings." Originals of these, or copies thereof, will be deposited in the Rhodes College Collection in Memphis beside other notable Halliburton materials. Alexander also indicated that Paul kept notebooks, which were lost when Hangover House changed hands in 1940. Materials related to Hangover House, formerly owned by William Alexander, now reside at the University of California–Santa Barbara. The letters Richard Halliburton wrote to Noel Sullivan—hereafter RHL–NS—are housed at the Bancroft Library at the University of California–Berkeley.

The *Sea Dragon Expedition* is sufficiently documented. Besides dozens of still photographs, many taken by the U.S. Navy, there is a 16 mm. home movie, in color, associated here with expedition members Gordon Ellicott Torrey and John Rust "Brue" Potter. The film, shot chiefly by Robert Hill Chase and John Potter, contains key footage of Richard Halliburton and Paul Mooney, other crew members, the building of the *Sea Dragon*, the accompanying celebrations (including frames of Fat Kau), and the ship's tryouts into Victoria Harbour. Crew member Robert Hill Chase, the expedition's photo-documentarist, is credited with shooting the film, or much of it (Potter, Torrey and Chase all appear in it). Unlike Chase, Potter and Torrey both elected to stay behind after the *Sea Dragon's* first run (which Torrey also chose to forego), hence the footage's convenient identity as the *Potter-Torrey film*. Shot chiefly by Robert Hill Chase, and sent home from Hong Kong to his parents in Massachusetts, the color film, located in the 1980s among Chase family memorabilia by Halliburton enthusiast Michael E. Blankenship, might rather be identified as the *Chase film*. The original is now in the Richard Halliburton Archive at Rhodes College's Barret Library and some copies circulate. Of note, the film shows John "Bru" Potter carrying a German twin-lens Rolleflex; this camera, as did Paul Mooney's Kodak, snapped pictures of the *Sea Dragon* and its crew which, with independent news photo releases, complement scenes from the film. In 2009, additional film footage, a five-minute B/W Hearst newsreel outtake, "Richard Halliburton and the *Sea Dragon*," was located by the author at the UCLA Film and Television Archive.

The materials in my collection that are related to this essay will one day be donated to Rhodes College and form the Gerry and Carole Max Collection of Richard Halliburton and Paul Mooney items. The collection also will include William Alexander's "Meanderings" and other papers and the David Greggory letters and Halliburton screenplay.

As noted, most of Halliburton's books were long out of print but, as the runs for these were large, copies—certainly reading copies—are common, especially early reprint copies. Originally published by Bobbs-Merrill, *The Royal Road to Romance* has been republished by Travelers' Tales; The Long Riders' Guild Press has published this title as well as *The Glorious Adventure, New Worlds to Conquer, The Flying Carpet*, and *Seven League Boots*.

Notes

Introduction

1. For a reappraisal of Halliburton see David M. Schwartz, "On the Royal Road to Adventure with 'Daring Dick," *Smithsonian*, March 1989, pp. 159–178.

2. The Elvis Presley item is mentioned in *The Guardian* (September 25, 1995), p. 11 (quoted). Quoted is the dust jacket of Lowell Thomas, *Seven Wonders of the World* (Garden City: Hanover House, 1956). For Elinor Glyn (1864–1948), see, in general, her *Romantic Adventure* (New York: Dutton, 1937); also see *Addicted to Romance: The Life and Adventures of Elinor Glyn* (London: Andre Deutsch Limited, 1994), pp. 1–2. For Halliburton's annoyance at being linked to Glyn, see *JR*, p. 125. Author of the shockingly prurient novel (for its time) *Three Weeks* (1907), Glyn defined "Romance" in her autobiography as "the essence of chivalry ... of fine actions inspired by delicate sentiments ... aroused (not) by thought of personal gain, but rather by the impulse to render homage to another." *Romantic Adventure* (New York: Dutton, 1937), p. 2. For Harry Franck's influence see *JR*, p. 57. Also quoted is Paul Theroux, *Chicago Tribune*, 11 December 1995. For additional perspective on American travel writing, hear Paul Theroux (who omits mention of Richard Halliburton), "Introduction," *The Best American Travel Writing* (Boston: Houghton Mi·in, 2001), 5 compact discs.

3. Quoted is Guy Townsend, op. cit., p. 1. For an assessment of Halliburton's fame in his lifetime see *JR*, pp. 20–21. Cf. *JC*, pp. 2–3. Also see Allen Churchill, *The Literary Decade–A Panorama of the Writers, Publishers, and Litterateurs of the 1920s* (Englewood Cliffs, N.J.: Prentice-Hall, Inc., 1971), pp. 264–269. Quoted is *Time*, 30 May 1927.

4. Quoted is John Carswell, in R(udolph) E(rich) Raspe and Others, *Singular Travels, Campaigns and Adventures of Baron Munchausen*, with an introduction by John Carswell and with illustrations by Gustave Dore (New York: Dover Publication, 1960), p. vii. For Halliburton's attempts to imitate "Daniel Defoe's archaic style" see *JR*, p. 164.

5. The eulogy of Richard Halliburton as "originator," etc., appears on the dust jacket of *RHL*.

Offering epithets, including verbs, of Halliburton in action are the dust jacket blurbs of *The Royal Road to Romance* (New York: Bobbs-Merrill, 1925), *The Glorious Adventure* (New York: Bobbs-Merrill, 1927) and *New Worlds to Conquer* (New York: Bobbs-Merrill, 1929).

6. For "The Nautical Preparatory School," see *Harper's Magazine*, no. 627, August 1902, "Schools & Colleges," unpaginated. "The Cadets of this school," advertisements read, "will study English History and visit Westminister Abbey; they will construe the stately periods of Cicero and visit the Colosseum at Rome; they will trace the history of Greek Art and Arms and inspect the Acropolis and the sites of famous battlefields; they will read of Egypt and explore the Pyramids; they will read the Bible and see the places where dawned the light of Christianity. They will round out each part of their education by travel intelligently directed—an opportunity that a man of broadest culture might well envy." With "the organization and discipline [that] of the U.S. Navy, modified to meet the conditions ... the first year the ship will sail from Newport, R.I., September 1, travel 16,000 miles, touching at upwards of 50 ports in England, Norway, Germany, France, the Mediterranean, the West Indies and return to Newport the following June for a four-months' vacation." For the Grand Tour see Adrian Tinniswood, *The Polite Tourist—Four Centuries of Country House Visiting* (New York and London: The National Trust Harry N. Abrams, 1989), pp. 67–68.

7. *The Royal Road to Romance*, in efforts to link it firmly to its genre, was at first entitled *Horizon Chaser* and also *The Wandering Gentile*. For its final name see *JR*, p. 99. Regarding Richard Henry Dana, Jr., note Wright Morris (1964) who, in his Afterword to *Two Years before the Mast* (1964), wrote: "Dana did a good deal for the life of the common seaman, but we cannot adequately assess what he did for the uncommon writer and dreamer. Richard Halliburton's *Royal Road to Romance* and books that every season contribute countless detours are in the direct line of descent from Dana's *Two Years before the Mast*." Afterword to Dana, *Two Years before the Mast*, op. cit., p. 398. Cf. *JR*, p. 64. Melville's great tales of

the sea—*Typee* (1846), *Omoo* (1847), *Mardi* (1849), *Red-burn* (1849)—owed their stark realism to the earlier work.

8. For publication information about *The Royal Road to Romance*, see *JR*, p. 98 et seq. Also see *RHL*, p. 253.

9. Two Halliburton's passports in the Princeton Collection give as his date of birth, January 9, 1899, not 1900. A letter Halliburton sent to Noel Sullivan notes the same date of birth for the purpose of receiving an accurate and meaningful horoscope reading. Noel Sullivan Papers, Box 34, letter dated February 11, 1928, Bancroft Library, University of California-Berkeley; hereafter, *RHL-NS*. Quoted is Erik Satie (*"Je suis venu au monde tres jeune dans un temps tres vieux."*) from Ornella Volta, *Erik Satie*, translated from the French by Simon Pleasance (Paris: Editions Hazan, 1997), p. 183. Also quoted is Steven Mintz, "Revolt of Modern Youth," *Huck's Raft—A History of American Childhood* (Cambridge, Mass. and London: Belkamp Press of Harvard University Press, 2004), pp. 213–232. For Klaus Mann, see Peter T. Hoffer, *Klaus Mann* (Boston: Twayne Publishers, 1978); the study focuses on Mann's play *Gegenuber von China* (1929) and quotes from his second autobiography, *Der Wendepunkt*, pp. 58–63. On American youth in the twenties, see Paula S. Fass, *The Damned and the Beautiful* (New York: Oxford University Press, 1977), pp. 227–230. For the influence of Halliburton on some younger members of his audiences see Andy Turner, "The Royal Road to Carolina," *North Carolina Literary Review*, no. 5, 1996, pp. 88–89. Also see Errol Stephen Uys, *Riding the Rails—Teenagers on the Move During the Great Depression* (New York: TV Books, 1999), pp. 19–20, 185 and 186. Henry Adams' *The Education of Henry Adams*, published in 1907, was an instant classic and became required reading at many American colleges.

10. For George Leigh Mallory see Peter and Leni Gillman, *The Wildest Dream: Mallory—His Life and Conflicting Passions* (London: Headline Book Publishing, 2001). Also see Richard Halliburton, "The Top of the World," *Second Book of Marvels—The Orient*, pp. 227–241, which recreates Mallory's career and final assault on Mt. Everest. For Halliburton's interest in Rupert Brooke, who knew Mallory, see *JR*, p. 70 et passim. Halliburton gathered notes for a biography about Brooke he intended to write once he retired, but he never got around to doing so. Later, Arthur Stringer wrote *Red Wine of Youth—A Life of Rupert Brooke* (Bobbs-Merrill Company, c1948), and acknowledged Halliburton's seminal research towards writing the life himself. See *JR*, p. 275. Also see *RHL*, pp. 274–278 and 379. For Halliburton's lifelong fascination with Brooke, see *The Glorious Adventure*, pp. 115–127; cf. *JR*, pp. 251–252 and *JC*, pp. 111–114. Also see Paul Delany, *The Neo-Pagans— Rupert Brooke and the Ordeal of Youth* (The Free Press, New York, c1987), pp. xiii–xviii, 4–5, and 77–81. For Halliburton's interest in T.E. Lawrence, see *JR*, p. 190 and 191. Cf. Jeffrey Meyers, *The Wounded Spirit: T.E. Lawrence's "Seven Pillars of Wisdom"* (St. Martin's Press, New York, 1989), pp. 119–126. Cf.

Desmond Stewart, *T.E. Lawrence: A New Biography* (New York: Harper and Row, 1977), pp. 240–244. For Lawrence's notion of cleanliness, see Meyers, p. 123. For his concept of Greek idealizations as a rationale for male love, see Meyers, pp. 122–123. For the incident at Deraa see Thomas O'Donnell, *The Confessions of T.E. Lawrence* (Athens, Ohio: Ohio University Press, 1979), pp. 107–130.

11. For Willibald, see Richard Fletcher, "Faith to Faith—When Worlds Collide," *History Magazine* 4, no. 4, April 2003, pp. 37–39, quoted at p. 39. For the antiquity of travel writing in the West see Tony Perrottet, *Route 66 A.D.—On the Trail of Ancient Roman Tourists* (New York: Random House, 2002) (notably, "books of wonders") pp. 55–56. Traveler and news correspondent (for the *New York Herald*) Thomas Wallace Knox (born in 1835), who twice went around the world, must count as a predecessor to Richard Halliburton, especially with his companion motif. Heavily illustrated, the Thomas W. Knox books appeared in the 1880s and 1890s. For Knox see Appleton's *Cyclopedia of America Biography*, edited by James Grant Wilson and John Fiske (New York: D. Appleton and Company, 1887–1888); edited by Stanley L. Klos, 1999. Oliver Optic was William T. Adams, a contemporary of Knox. For other women travelers see Milbrey Polk & Mary Tiegreen, *Women of Discovery—A Celebration of Intrepid Women Who Explored the World* (New York: Clarkson Potter, 2001). Most of these books, long out of print, are often available on the Internet.

12. Quoted is Gillian Avery, *Behold the Child— American Children and Their Books 1621-1922* (London: The Bodley Head, 1994), pp. 121–122.

13. The main threads of Halliburton's life are now well-known. Information, in particular, about his father appears in *JR*, p. 39 et passim.

14. For former editors, see *JR*, pp. 104–106; also, *RHL*, p. 253.

15. Only a few studies of Hitler appeared before the outbreak of the war. See Giles MacDonogh, Translator's Preface, *The Hitler Book—The Secret Dossier Prepared for Stalin From the Interrogation of Hitler's Personal Aides*, edited by Henrik Eberle and Matthias Uhl (New York: Public Affairs, 2005), pp. xviii–xxiii. Curiously the book does not mention the Ludecke book.

16. For the history of translations of Hesse (1877–1956) see Joseph Mileck, *Herman Hesse—Life and Art* (Berkeley: University of California Press, 1978), pp. 368–369. *Demian* was translated by N.H. Priday for Boni & Liveright in 1923. For the first French translation of *Siddhartha* see *Herman Hesse and Romain Rolland, Correspondence, diary entries, and reflections, 1915 to 1940*, introduction by Pierre Grappin and translated from the French and German by M.G. Hesse (New Jersey: Oswald Wolff Humanities Press, 1978), pp. 98–99. Basil Creighton translated *Steppenwolf* (London, Secker: 1929; New York: Henry Holt, 1929). While German editions were available—and it is unclear how conversant Paul was in German—a French translation of *Siddhartha* (were he conversant in French) appeared in 1926, and an English translation of *Steppenwolf* in 1929. Used here

was *Demian* (Bantam, 1966), with introduction by Thomas Mann and translation from the German by Michael Roloff and Michael Lebeck, pp. 6–7 and p. 37.

17. For traits of restlessness (quoted) shared with Brooke, see Arthur Stringer, *Red Wine of Youth—A Life of Rupert Brooke* (New York: Bobbs-Merrill, 1948), pp. 26–27.

18. For Stoddard's criticism of Robert Louis Stevenson, see Nicholas Rankin, *Dead Man's Chest—Travels after Robert Louis Stevenson* (London: Phoenix Press, 1987), pp. 166–167. For sexuality in Halliburton, see, for instance, *JC*, p. 125. Parodists of Halliburton were many; often they were famous in their own right. Thomas Wolfe had considered doing a "parody or satire" on Halliburton, writes Richard Kennedy. Kennedy identified the forgotten Halliburton (in 1970) as an "intrepid traveler and author of adventure books whose name was synonymous with romantic adventure to Wolfe's generation." See *The Notebooks of Thomas Wolfe*, edited by Richard Kennedy and Paschal Reeves (Chapel Hill: University of North Carolina, 1970), I, p. 312, n. 14. For F. Scott Fitzgerald see *Correspondence of F. Scott Fitzgerald*, edited by Matthew J. Bruccoli and Margaret M. Duggan (New York: Random House, 1980), p. 207. On p. 269 is an odd item, a letter, dated October 1931, sent to Fitzgerald from Hemingway—actually a picture of Hemingway with the inscription, (apparently) in Halliburton's hand, "To Scott from his old bedfellow Richard Halliburton[,] Princeton 1931." Later, in a letter to Edmund Wilson dated September 1951, Hemingway calls Halliburton "the deceased Ladies Home journal adventure writer." See *Ernest Hemingway—Selected Letters—1917–1961*, edited by Carlos Baker (New York: Charles Scribner's Sons, 1981), pp. 732–733. Humorist H.W. Haneman, calling his piece "A Kubla Great Boys," parodied Halliburton as a comic Marco Polo. Haneman also spoofed Mary Roberts Rinehart and Ernest Hemingway, among others. See his *In the Facts of Life—A Book of Brighter Biography Executed in the Manner of Some of Our Best or Best-Known Writers, Scriveners & Scribes* (New York: Farrar and Rinehart, 1930). For Corey Ford's treatment of Halliburton see *JR*, pp. 117 and 157. As many another writer, Halliburton could be ever more simplified and condensed. The thirteen-page feature "The Challenge of Fujiyama" appeared in Mary B. Pennell and Alice M. Cusack, *The Children's Own Reader*, Book Six, illustrated by Rodney Thomson and others (Boston: Ginn and Company, 1929); other writers adapted thus included Henry Wadsworth Longfellow, Nathaniel Hawthorne, and Oscar Wilde.

Chapter 1

1. For these views of Paul's personal qualities, thanks are given to members of Paul's family and to his friends.

2. "Central High Alumni Record" (for James Paul Mooney, for graduating class of 1922–1923),

Volume 96, May 1990, Washington, D.C., submitted by Michael E. Blankenship; copy furnished by Paul's nephew Anton Levandowsky. Information is also in letter from Alicia Mooney to William Alexander, April 14, 1939. When Paul attended Central High School, the District's schools were segregated, and Central and Cardozo were two separate schools, one white, one black. In 1949—before integration—the Washington, D.C., School Board closed Central High and moved Cardozo into Central High's old building. In the 1920s, however, no particular connection between the two schools existed. John M. Scott, letter to author, 8 February 2001. Cf. Cardozo High School: www.exploreedu.org/index.php?id=308.

3. See Lester George Moses, whose *The Indian Man: A Biography of James Mooney* (Lincoln and London: University of Nebraska Press, 1984) proved indispensable. Also see William Colby, *Routes to Rainy Mountain: A Biography of James Mooney, Ethnologist* (Ph. D. dissertation, University of Wisconsin, 1977). Cf. Raymond DeMallie, "Introduction to the Bison Book Edition" of James Mooney's *The Ghost-Dance Religion and the Sioux Outbreak of 1890* (Lincoln and London: University of Nebraska, 1991), pp. xv–xxvi. Also of assistance have been Mark Stevens (1940–2005), Paul's sister Eire's son, John M. Scott (1926–), Paul's sister Ione's son, and Anton Levandowsky (1932–), Paul's sister Evelyn's son. For Ireland's history, see Seamus MacManus, *The Story of the Irish Race* (New York: Devin-Adair Company, 1921), in the belief that Paul himself consulted it. Among later sources is Terry Golway, *Irish Rebel—John Devoy and America's Fight for Ireland's Freedom* (New York: St. Martin's Press, 1998), which glimpses Irish-Americans and radical Irish nationalists in America at the time Paul was growing up. See pp. 182–187 et passim.

4. Cf. Moses, pp. 3–5 (quote from p. 5). On James Mooney's high school address, see Moses, p. 219. Also see Colby on his newspaper work, and other activities at this time, pp. 36–38.

5. For Powell, compare DeMallie, pp. xvii–xviii. See also *The Smithsonian Experience* (Washington, D.C.: The Smithsonian Institution, 1977), pp. 158, 159, 161. Also consulted was Edwin Corle, "Powell," *The Grand Canyon—A Panorama of the Southwest* (New York: Duehl, Sloan, and Pierce, 1945), pp. 113–127. Powell (1834–1902) wrote accounts of his treks down the Colorado and the Grand Canyon, which James Mooney certainly read and son Paul almost certainly knew of. See Eliot Porter, *Down the Colorado, John Wesley Powell Diary of the First Trip Through the Grand Canyon.* (New York: Arrowwood Press, 1988). Wallace Stegner's *Beyond the Hundredth Meridian: John Wesley Powell and the Second Opening of the West* (Boston: Houghton Mi·in, 1954) recounts Powell's life and his role in Western expansion. On Mooney's coming to the Bureau see Moses, p. 18 et seq. and Colby, pp. 44–46. Quoted phrases, about Mooney, and the developing importance of the Bureau of Ethnology, are from Donald Worster's *A River Running West—The Life of John Wesley Powell* (New York and London: Oxford University Press, c2001), pp. 408–409.

6. Quotation from Carl Mautz, *Biographies of Western Photographers—A Reference Guide to Photographers Working in the 19th Century American West* (Nevada City, Calif.: Carl Mautz Publishing, 1997), p. 334. See also Edwin Daniels (text) and JD Challenger (paintings), *Ghost Dancing—Sacred Medicine and the Art of JD Challenger* (New York: Stewart, Tabori & Chang, 1998), pp. 23–24, 39 et passim. For "revitalization" of cultures and Mooney's influence, see L.G. Moses, op. cit., pp. 94–95. The anthropologists quoted are Paula Richardson Fleming and Judith Luskey, *The North American Indians in Early Photographs* (London: Calmann and King Ltd, 1986), p. 144. For another view of Mooney's "blasphemy," see James Conaway, *The Smithsonian—150 Years of Adventure, Discovery, and Wonder* (New York: Alfred A. Knopf, 1995), pp. 184–185. For the peyote controversy see Moses, pp. 179–205 and Colby, pp. 454–506. Cf. Omer C. Stewart, *Peyote Religion—A History* (Norman and London: University of Oklahoma Press, 1987), p. 34–39; Mooney is called a full participant-observer with the Indians he was studying...." For the development of applied anthropology from Washington-based government departments to academic ones see Katherine Spencer Halpern, "Women in Applied Anthropology—The Early Years," *Hidden Scholars—Women Anthropologist and the Native American Southwest*, Nancy J. Parezo, editor (Albuquerque: University of New Mexico Press, 1993), pp. 189–201, at 189–190.

7. For a James Mooney bibliography, see L.G. Moses, supra, pp. 267–280. Also see James Mooney's *History, Myths, and Sacred Formulas of the Cherokees: Containing the Full Texts of Myths of the Cherokee (1900 and the Sacred Formula)* (Fairview, N.C.: Bright Mountain Books, 1992). For his work in collaboration, see *The Smithsonian Experience*, op. cit., pp. 158 and 159. The famous "Bulletin 30" of *The Handbook of American Indians North of Mexico* (U.S. Government Printing Office, Washington, D.C., 1907 and 1912, 2 vols.), was edited by Frederick Walter Hodge. A reprint of Part 2 of the Fourteenth Annual Report of the Bureau of Ethnology to the Secretary of the Smithsonian Institution of James Mooney's *The Ghost Dance* was reissued in 1996 by JB Press, Inc., North Dighton, Massachusetts.

8. Cf., Moses, pp. 113–114 (quoted). On Ione Lee Gaut, see Records Request #106225, D.A.R. (microfiche). Paul considered these connections true. Paul owned a copy of Burton J. Hendrick's *The Lees of Virginia—Biography of a Family* (Boston: Little, Brown and Company, 1935).

9. Anton D. Levandowsky offered information on Paul's name as well as that of Paul's father, noting that James had no middle name and that Paul was never referred to as James Jr. Letter, October 26, 2000. Also, interview, March 13, 2005. "Eivlyn," according to Levandowsky, was "her sister Eire's Irish concoction—she was always Evelyn." Letter to author, July 3, 2003. For the birth and activities of James Mooney at the time of Paul's birth see Moses, supra, pp. 156–157. For photographs of the family see Moses, after p. 96. For information on the births of the children, see Moses, pp. 132–133 (Ione), 157 (Paul), 163 and 168 (Brian), 167–168 (Eire), 173 (Eve-

lyn), and 194 (Alicia). For a 1914 portrait of the Mooney family (sans James) see Moses, after p. 96.

10. For Bishop Thomas J. Shahan, see Moses, pp. 168 and 195.

11. The house still stands, now in a rundown neighborhood, never recovered from the 1968 riots. My thanks to John M. Scott for the description of the house, letter dated 4 December 2001. Alicia Mooney mentioned plans for a weekend drive "to deepest Virginia carrying household things to a colored maid we had 35 years ago—and an 9-by-10 enlargement, mounted, of a picture she posed for in the alley behind our old house." Letter from Alicia Mooney to William Alexander, 24 May 1955. The delegations of Indians may have come to Washington to have their pictures taken at the Smithsonian. See Robert F. Berkhofer, Jr., *The White Man's Indian* (New York: Vintage Books, 1978), illustrations, 9. An exhibit of the tepees at the Renwick Gallery of the National Collection of Art (from December 1977 to November 1978) is mentioned in a letter of Alicia's. Letter from Alicia Mooney to William Alexander, 21 June 1978. Robert Edmond Jones (1887–1954) revolutionized the art of set design and was associated with many of the great theatrical productions of the first half of the 20th century. His lectures awed listeners, and his book *Drawings for the Theatre* (New York Theatre Arts, Inc., 1925) is now considered a masterpiece. The Jones pedestal that Paul owned remained in his mother's possession, then was passed to his sister Alicia, who may have sold it. Letter from John Scott to the author, 21 February 2004; also, 15 May 2004.

12. For Hyde's visit see Moses, p. 163. Also see Dunleavy, Janet Egleson and Gareth W. Dunleavy, *Douglas Hyde—A Maker of Modern Ireland* (Berkeley: University of California Press, 1991), pp. 262–263. Consulted for Irish history in general were Breandan o hEithir's *A Pocket History of Ireland* (Dublin: O'Brien Press, 2000), Thomas Pakenham, *The Year of Liberty—The Great Irish Rebellion of 1798* (London: Weidenfeld & Nicolson, 1997). For Mooney's joining nationalist group see Moses, pp. 6 and 164.

13. See D.R. McAnally, Jr., *Irish Wonders* (New York: Gramercy Books, 1996), illustrated by H.R. Heaton. These "Popular Tales As Told by the People" collected in the 19th century by McAnally (1810–1895) may have been familiar to Paul. See Moses about stories read to the children, which may have included some that had been read to James Mooney when a child, pp. 4, 196.

14. The early family history follows Moses, p. 194 et seq. On James Mooney's Catholicism, see Moses, p. 64.

15. Ibid., Moses, pp. 194–195. Moses cites Eire (Mooney) Stevens as a source. p. 262, n. 66. Other members of the family also reported their "memories" to him, p. 3. In an interview Paul's friend William Alexander said that Paul told him little about his family, though he mentioned his mother, Ione, from time to time. He recalled James Mooney only as a government employee who, according to Paul, "got in trouble with the Smithsonian for his getting high with the Indians he was sent to study."

16. Ibid., p. 195. The "new preface by the author" of the reissued *The Indian Man* (Lincoln and London: University of Nebraska Press, 2002) corrects "oil-rich Kiowas" and "oil-rich Osages": Eire Mooney (Eire Stevens), he notes, "remembered that the automobiles belonging to visiting Indians frequently lined the curb outside her family's home in Washington," p. vi.

17. Ibid., p. 196.

18. Letter to the author from John Scott, 3 February 2004.

19. Cf. Moses, p. 172.

20. For the trips with his father, see Moses, pp. 171–173 and p. 180. Also consulted was the correspondence, now at the Nebraska Historical Society, between Clarence Paine and James Mooney: 22 November 1910, 26 November 1910, 4 December 1910, 5 December 1910, 9 December 1910, 31 December 1910, 4 January 1911, 5 January 1911, 19 January 1911, 28 January 1911, 14 February 1911, 31 March 1911, 25 March 1911, 8 April 1911, 26 November 1911, 28 November 1911, 5 December 1911, and 7 December 1911. For Tavibo and Wovoka see pp. 172–173; cf. DeMallie, p. xxi. For Ellen Devlin's death see Moses, pp. 177–178. For Indian mores, and childhood activities, see Ian Frazier, *Great Plains* (New York: Farrar, Straus & Giroux, 1989), p. 47 et seq.; also see his comments on Wovoka and the Ghost Dance, pp. 41–42.

21. See Moses (quoted), p. 180.

22. For the changed mission of the agency after the departure of Powell see Worster, op. cit., pp. 536 et seq. as adults. Brian and Paul were friendly, but not close as adults. According to John Scott, Brian Mooney (born in 1907) was a "loner." He took some engineering courses at Catholic University, but never graduated. Though he spent most of his life in the Washington, D.C., area working for the government, he did work briefly in the 1930s in the oil business in Houston, Texas, possibly as a surveyor. There he married, divorced, then remarried a woman named Mildred; from an interim marriage, Mildred had a daughter named Jacqueline ("Jackie"), whom John Scott considered his younger cousin. In 1970, Brian died of the same heart ailment that had taken his father. He is buried in National Memorial Park in suburban Virginia near Alicia Mooney, Evelyn Mooney (Levandowsky) and Danilo Levandowsky. Letters to author, 6 June 2004 and 13 June 2003 (Scott) and 18 June 2003 (Levandowsky).

23. Alicia Mooney (quoted) recalled these incidents in a letter to William Alexander, 14 April 1939. John Scott also shared his recollections in a letter to author, dated 20 October 1998. Quoted are two letters of Paul Mooney to William Alexander, PML, dated 25 May 1935 and 3 June 1935. According to Scott, Ione Mooney had, among the many children's books in her library, a copy of Frances Hodgson Burnett's *The Secret Garden* (1910). Letter to author, dated 21 February 2004.

24. For Sam Patch see Paul E. Johnson, *Sam Patch, The Famous Jumper* (New York: Hill and Wang, 2003). In the *Book of Marvels—The Occident*, Paul appears to be the figure before Niagara Falls beholding a "curtain of water—thousands and thousands of tons of it—hurling itself over the precipice." More likely, it is Halliburton himself, pp. 50–51. No mention of Patch is made in the "Niagara" section; mention is made, however, of "a tight-rope walker named Blondin [who] stretched a wire across the boiling chasm from the American to the Canadian side and performed amazing feats upon it," pp. 52–53. For the Bennett stereograph (#1101 in the Bennett catalog) see Betsy Reese, *The Life and World of Henry Hamilton Bennett* (Wisconsin Dells, Wisc.: H.H. Bennett Studio, 1975), p. 4. For the leaps of Douglas Fairbanks, Sr., see. *The Fairbanks Album*, Drawn from the Family Archives by Douglas Fairbanks, Jr., with introduction and narrative by Richard Schickel (New York: New York Graphic Society, 1975), pp. 50–53, p. 74, and pp. 118–119. For his stunts (including use of an occasional double) see Booton Herndon, *Mary Pickford and Douglas Fairbanks: The Most Popular Couple the World Has Known* (New York: W.W. Norton & Co., 1977), pp. 170, 209–210, and 232–233.

Chapter 2

1. Cf. Moses, pp. 218–219. "Field-Burial" is from Paul's *Seven Poems* (New York: Ramapo River Printers, 1927), p. 3.

2. Cf. Moses, pp. 219–220 (and for quoted material). For Indian customs and Christianity see pp. 190–194. For the memorial, in part, given on p. 220, see the epitaph of close Mooney associate John R. Swanton, "James Mooney," which appeared in the *American Anthropologist* 24 (1922), pp. 209–214. For Henry Ford, see Neil Baldwin, "The Christian Century," *Henry Ford and the Jews—The Mass Production of Hate* (New York: Public Affairs, 2001), pp. 27–35.

3. See Moses (quoted), pp. 172–173. See Francis Parkman (quoted), *The Oregon Trail*, edited with an introduction by David Levin (New York: Penguin Books, 1982), p. 300.

4. For the authors as well as subject areas familiar to James Mooney, see Moses, pp. 3–4. John M. Scott recalled the books belonging to his uncle Paul and those shelved in the upstairs study at 2550 University Place in a letter, 21 February 2004 and through interviews. For Karl May (1842–1912), whose novels thrilled Hitler, see Kurt Ludecke, *I Knew Hitler* (New York: Charles Scribner's Sons, 1937), p. 524. *Harper's Magazine*, readily available on newsstands in America, provided stories of fun and adventure that compare with the Karl May light thrillers. Begun about 1900, *The Wide World* today is not so well-known. Consulted in particular were the following issues: November 1923, December 1923 (52, no. 308), September 1924 (which, as was typical, provided a map indicating where each story in the issue took place), April 1924 (52, no. 312), July 1927, December 1927, February 1928, and October 1928 (51, no. 366). For Goethe's *Faust* see p. 18. It

is tempting to suppose that advice given to Kurt Ludecke by his father was also advice given to Paul by his father; in full, he thought young Kurt Ludecke too young to tackle the second part of Goethe's *Faust*: "Wait until you are thirty," he instructed, "and read it again when you are forty-five." Asked by Hitler for the titles of books that aptly described America, Ludecke offered, among others, William Prescott's *Conquest of Mexico*, a likely source for "Popocatepetl" in *The Book of Marvels—The Occident*, pp. 96–107. For classical writers (e.g., Homer, Plato, Cicero, et al.), political philosophy, and biological tracts, which Ludecke (at least) read, see p. 29–30. Quoted is James Branch Cabell, *Jurgen* (New York: Dover Publications, 1977), p. 14. Major Campbell's book on India, copies of which are now scarce, was published in 1853 in London by Arthur Hall, Virtue & Co. For James Oliver Curwood (1878–1927), see website: *www.sdl.lib.mi.us/curwood.htm*, Shiawassee District Library. Quoted is Jack London *John Barleycorn* (New York: Modern Library, 2001), p. 45, also p. 39.

5. See Rupert Brooke, *Letters from America*, with a Preface by Henry James (New York: Charles Scribner's Sons, 1916), pp. 135–146. Brooke's travels took him mostly to America's eastern seaboard and parts of Canada. A number of books belonging to both Richard Halliburton and Paul Mooney were among the books shelved at Hangover House. Photo enlargements indicate one by Kent, another presumably about Picasso, Cervantes' *Don Quixote*, and Melville's *Typee*. For Pierre Loti (1850–1922), whose fame is not as well understood today as Melville's or Dana's, see Lesley Blanch, *Pierre Loti—The Legendary Romantic* (New York: Carroll & Graf Publishers, 1983), p. 105 et seq. Also see "Loti, Pierre," *Who's Who in Gay and Lesbian History—From Antiquity to World War II*, edited by Robert Aldrich and Garry Wotherspoon (London and New York: Routledge, 2001), pp. 276–277. John Scott mentioned Paul's owning the *Satyricon* in a letter to author, April 2001 (quoted).

6. John Scott now owns the Chaucer and the Shakespeare once owned by Paul.

7. For Gilles de Retz (variously spelled), see Colin Wilson, *The Mammoth Book of the History of Murder* (subtitled, *The history of how and why mankind is driven to kill*) (New York: Carroll and Graf Publishers, 1990), pp. 51–58. For a comparison of Joan of Arc (1412–1431) and Gilles de Rais (1408?–1440?) see A.J. Dunning, "The Burning Heart," *Extremes—Reflections on Human Behavior* (New York: Harcourt Brace Jovanovich, 1992), pp. 9–21. "Gilles de Rayes" claimed his sadism resulted from his reading Suetonius' *Lives of the Twelve Caesars*. See Doctor Albert Moll, *Perversions of the Sex Instinct—A Study of Sexual Inversion*, translated by Maurice Popkin, Ph.D. (Newark: Julian Press, 1931), p. 129.

8. Alicia Mooney (quoted), letter to William Alexander, 21 June 1978. John Scott reiterated the impression many had of Paul as "brilliant" in a letter to author, 29 November 1998.

9. Anton Levandowsky (quoted), letter to author, 8 June 2003.

10. John Scott provided some details of the rescue mission. The Knickerbocker (later the Ambassador) Theatre stood at the southwest corner of 18th Street and Columbia Road NW. For a description of the catastrophe see Douglas E. Evelyn and Paul Dickson, *On This Spot—Pinpointing the Past in Washington, D.C.* (Washington, D.C.: National Geographic Society, 1999), pp. 10 and 171.

11. For Wallace Reid see David Carroll, *The Matinee Idols* (New York: Arbor House, 1972), pp. 113–122.

12. On *Beyond the Horizon* see Stephen Black, *Eugene O'Neill—Beyond Mourning and Tragedy* (New Haven: Yale University Press, 1999), pp. 216–217; also, pp. 246–252. *Beyond the Horizon*, in *Four Plays by Eugene O'Neill*, with an introduction by A.R. Gurney (New York: Signet, 1998), act one, scene one, quoted, p. 10. Mention of the Provincetown Players occurs in William Alexander, "Meanderings," unpublished; in conversation, Alexander mentioned both his own and Paul's interest in Eugene O'Neill and the avant-garde theatre of the time.

13. For John Reed (1887–1920) see *Ten Days That Shook the World* (New York: Modern Library, 1934), with an introduction by Granville Hicks. Quoted is Floyd Dell's assessment in John Reed's *Daughter of the Revolution and Other Stories* (New York: Vanguard Press, 1927), p. vii. Allen Churchill devotes considerable space to journalists and avant-gardists John Reed, Mabel Dodge, Margaret Anderson and others who defined the milieu into which Paul was introduced in the early 1920s. See *The Improper Bohemians—A Re-Creation of Greenwich Village in Its Heyday* (New York: E.P. Dutton & Company, 1959).

14. The trip is noted in a letter from Alicia Mooney to William Alexander, April 14, 1939. For possible impressions Paul received of Constantinople see Rolland Jenkins, *The Mediterranean Cruise, An Up-to-date and Concise Handbook for Travelers* (New York and London: G.P. Putnam's Sons, 1923), pp. 135 and 136. For the Thomas Cook & Son around the world deluxe cruise, the brochure booklet *A Golden Jubilee Cruise Around the World* (New York: Thomas Cook & Sons, 1922) was consulted; the cruise was to set off from New York on January 24, 1923 and to return on May 25, 1923.

15. For clues as to Paul's activities in Constantinople, see "The Ghosts of Santa Sophia," *The Flying Carpet* (Indianapolis and New York: Bobbs-Merrill, 1932), pp. 138–148. Despite calling Paul a "Byronic hero," John Scott does not believe Paul visited other places in Greece. Letter to author, 11 January 2003. See also Lady Dorothy Mills, *Beyond the Bosphorus* (Boston: Little Brown and Company, 1926), p. 14 (quoted).

16. See Kurt Ludecke (quoted), *I Knew Hitler*, op. cit., p. 20.

Chapter 3

1. These impressions continue to be those left by family and friends. The photographic record also is ample and suggests Paul's fondness towards being photographed.

2. The *Yearbook* for 1925–1926, at the American Catholic University History and Research Center and University Archives, has Paul and his course of study listed on the freshman roll-call only.

3. Throughout its history Catholic University, founded in 1889, has been located on Michigan Avenue and 4th Street; Caldwell Hall, also known as the Divinity Building, was its first building.

4. For Charles Warren Stoddard see Roger Austen, *Genteel Pagan—The Double Life of Charles Warren Stoddard*, edited by John W. Crowley (Amherst University of Massachusetts Press, 1991). On his years at Catholic University of America, see pp. 121–129, 136–138 et passim; on Kenneth O'Connor and the Bungalow, see pp. 132–146 et passim (Austen, quoted p. 133). Also see Robert L. Gale, *Charles Warren Stoddard*, Western Writers Series No. 30 (Boise: Boise State University, 1977) and An Encyclopedia of Gay, Lesbian, Bisexual, Transgender and Queer Culture (GLBTQ), http://www.glbtq.com/litera ture/stoddard_cw.htlm. When asked about Stoddard's reputation, Paul's nephew John Scott agreed that the name would have been familiar to Paul, as it was familiar to him. Letter to the author, 16 February 2005.

5. In *The Royal Road to Romance*, a major traveling companion to Halliburton is named "Paul McGrath," an architecture student from Chicago who plays the mandolin; usually he is just "Paul," someone Paul might have identified with during any reading of the book. See p. 59 et passim. See Richard Halliburton, *The Royal Road to Romance*, pp. 2–3 (quoted). For the book's debt to Oscar Wilde see p. 3. The "apartment walls" are noted in *The Glorious Adventure* (New York: Bobbs-Merrill, 1927), quoted, pp. 18, 19 and 20. For kindred views see C.A. Stephens, *Off to the Geysers* or, *The Young Yachters in Iceland* (Philadelphia: John C. Winston Co., 1873), p. iv (quoted).

6. See "Paul's Case," Willa Cather *Collected Short Stories—1892-1912*, edited by Virginia Faulkner (Lincoln and London: University of Nebraska Press, 1965), pp. 243–261; quoted pp. 243, 251, and 260. Quoted is Rupert Brooke, *Letters from America*, op. cit., p. 26.

7. William Alexander noted Paul's work for this group in interviews with the author. He said he received this information from Alicia Mooney (though it is not present in any of the letters she wrote to him). Alicia Mooney noted her brother's visits home (from New York) in a letter to Alexander, 14 April 1939. Halliburton biographer Jonathan Root notes that, besides "at least one book to his credit," Paul "had also done some professional ghost writing," but does not specify its nature, p. 172. Cf. Blankenship, "A Fellow Traveler," op. cit., p. 40. Vague as the matter currently stands, a number of magazines might have carried ads Paul wrote; these never bear the name of the writer. *Travel* was rich with ads and had a wide circulation. Another, *The Cunarder*, besides photo-illustrations of distant lands, included transatlantic "notabilities" such as Gloria Swanson and Rudolph Valentino, before, during or after departure. For an idea of the travel

ads from this period see *20s All-American Ads*, edited by Jim Hefmann with an introduction by Steven Heller (Cologna, Germany: Taschen, 2004), pp. 572–635. Paul was an able typist, noted William Alexander (who was not). For Paul as a mimeograph operator, whose use he had to learn, see *RHL-P*, 15 October 1938.

8. For New York see Helen W. Henderson (born in 1874), who wrote a number of *loitering* books, including one on Paris, London, and Washington, D.C.: *A Loiterer in New York—Discoveries Made by a Rambler through Obvious yet Unsought Highways and Byways* (New York: George W. Doran, 1917), p. 191. Quoted (about cats) is Rupert Brooke, *Letters from America*, op. cit., p. 29.

9. For Richard Halliburton and the YMCA location, see *JR*, p. 97.

10. For Greenwich Village at this time, see Malcolm Bradbury (general editor), *The Atlas of Literature* (London: De Agostini Editions, 1996), pp. 186–189. Also consulted were works by Floyd Dell whose novels appealed in general. His nonfiction works—notably *Intellectual Vagabondage* (1926) and *Love in the Machine Age: A Psychological Study of the Transition from Patriarchal Society* (1930), appealed specifically to the intelligentsia. Dell's autobiography, *Homecoming* (New York: Farrar & Rinehart, 1933), is an invaluable record of Greenwich Village life-in-transition after 1913, see p. 283 et seq. Also see Konrad Bercovici, *Around the World in New York*, illustrated by Norman Borchardt (New York: D. Appleton-Century Company, 1938); see especially "The American Quarter: Greenwich Village," pp. 157–181, quoted (on O'Neill), p. 163. Through Paul, Bercovici met William Alexander, who traveled by car across the country with him in 1937; later, in 1946, Alexander designed Bercovici's home in New Canaan, Connecticut. Alexander mentions going to see the Provincetown Players, and notes that it was Paul who introduced him to the theatre. See Alexander's "Meanderings" and interviews with Alexander.

11. For gathering spots, see Churchill, *Improper Bohemians*, op. cit., pp. 162–166 et seq. Also see Stanley Walker, *The Night Club Era* with an introduction by Alva Johnston (Baltimore and London: Johns Hopkins University Press, 1933) for the "Nepenthe Club," and other uptown hangouts, pp. 26–50. Quoted is Dell, *Homecoming*, op. cit., pp. 258, 271–273, and 390–391. (12) Paul's 1927 poem "Blondel to Richard Coeur de Lion" idealizes the "master-slave relationship" of which Bodenheim speaks. For Bodenheim's fame, see Upton Sinclair, *Cup of Fury* (Great Neck, New York: Channel Press, 1956), pp. 85–87. For his descriptions of Greenwich Village see Maxwell Bodenheim (attributed), *My Life and Loves in Greenwich Village* (New York: Bridge Head Books, 1954), p. 29. For the "sex hunt" see Bodenheim, p. 73; pp. 62 and 65; on the "hunter" see pp. 34–35. Besides R. Krafft-Ebing's *Psychopathia Sexualis*, the "key scientific tracts" Bodenheim claims to have read probably included works cited in Vernon A. Rosario, *The Erotic Imagination* (New York and Oxford: Oxford University Press, 1997), especially those cited in "Perversion and Nationalism," pp. 83–89.

Also see "Timeline of Sexual Perversions," pp. 177–179. Another key work is Andre Gide's *Corydon*, a pivotal work on the gay psyche, published in 1923. For another view of the Village, see Lincoln Kirstein, *Paul Cadmus* (New York: Imago Imprint, 1984), pp. 26–27. Kirstein called the Hogarthian panorama of village types in Paul Cadmus' *Greenwich Village Cafeteria*, "a 1930s version of Trimalchio's feast in *Satyricon*." Compare Dell, *Homecoming*, pp. 258, 271–273, and 390–391. Also see Caroline Farrar Ware, *Greenwich Village, 1920–1930*, with a foreword by Deborah Dash Moore (Berkeley: University of California Press, 1994), p. 252 et seq.

13. For gay hang-outs in New York see George Chauncey, *Gay New York—Gender, Urban Culture and the Making of the Gay World 1890–1940* (New York: Basic Books, 1994), p. 204. See also Daniel Hurewitz, *Stepping Out—Nine Walks through New York's Gay and Lesbian Past* (New York: Henry Holt and Company, 1997), p. 255. To learn more about "sexual modernism" and Greenwich Village in the first years of the century, see Christine Stansell, *American Moderns—Bohemian New York and the Creation of a New Century* (New York: Henry Holt and Company, 2000), pp. 225–308.

14. William Alexander, "Meanderings," (quoted). Consulted was Carl van Vechten, *The Splendid Drunken Years—Selections from the Daybooks 1922–1930*, edited by Bruce Keller (Urbana and Chicago: University of Illinois Press, 2003), pp. 178–179. Alexander mentioned visiting various New York cabarets, speakeasies and entertainment places with Paul, whose knowledge of these places seemed to him well-established. Among Paul's effects, in Alexander's collection, was a photo of a 1920s' impersonator doing "Cleopatra."

15. See Maxwell Bodenheim, *My Life and Loves*, op. cit., pp. 21–22 (quoted). For the Washington Square literary scene see Bradbury, op. cit., pp. 86–89.

16. For Crane's training as a copy editor and advertiser, see John Unterecker, *Voyager—A Life of Hart Crane* (New York and London: Liveright, 1969), p. 201, and pp. 289–291. For Crane's activities see letter, 24 January 1924, p. 171. Also see Hart Crane, *The Letters of Hart Crane, 1916–1932*, edited by Brom Weber (New York: Heritage House, 1952), p. 171, 166–167, and 343–344. For the "social, artistic and Bohemian fabric of New York in the twenties" and other celebrity literary parties see Mercedes de Acosta, *Here Lies the Heart* (New York: Reynal & Company, 1960), p. 126 et passim.

17. See Van Vechten, "Index," *The Splendid Drunken Twenties*, p. 314 et seq. For Halliburton's lunch with Van Vechten, *RHL-P*, January 28, 1931.

18. Three of the forty-eight printed copies of the poems are now known to exist, one (with navy blue dust jacket) a gift to sister Ione and her husband, Jack, another a gift to his sister Eivlyn, and another now in the special collections at Stanford University, placed there possibly by Moye Stephens, a graduate of Stanford, or Harry Hay, who attended Stanford. Quoted is Mercedes de Acosta, *Here Lies the Heart*, op. cit., p. 135.

19. See Thomas E. Yingling, *Hart Crane and the Homosexual Text—New Thresholds, New Anatomies* (Chicago and London: University of Chicago Press, 1990) (quoted), p. 26. Also quoted is *Seven Poems*.

20. For comparable residences and prices of New York real estate just before the stock market crash, see *The New Yorker* (which mentions Tudor City), 28 September 1929. The information on Don Forbes and Leslie Powell is from a privately printed exhibit guide (I suspect, by Powell himself) dated about 1967, *Leslie Powell: Paintings from a Life's Journey*. Regarding homosexuals and Times Square (quoted), see James Traub, op. cit., pp. 117–118. Also see Timothy F. Gilfoyle, "Policing of Sexuality," in William R. Taylor (ed.), *Inventing Times Square—Commerce and Culture at the Crossroads of the World* (Baltimore: John Hopkins University Press, 1991).

21. Ten years after Paul had broken his half-year lease, the management at Tudor City attempted to garnish the monthly checks he received from employer Richard Halliburton. Letter from Paul Mooney to William Alexander, 8 September 1937.

22. William Alexander mentioned in an interview with the author that Paul's trip to Paris was related to Lindbergh's solo flight and that he may have worked as a freelance journalist there.

23. Paul Mooney, "Release," *Seven Poems*, op. cit., p. 5.

Chapter 4

1. See Tennessee Williams, letter, 19 July 1928, *The Selected Letters of Tennessee Williams, Volume I—1920–1945*, edited by Albert J. Devlin and Nancy M. Tischler (New York: New Directions, 2000), pp. 16–18, at 17. For Halliburton (if not Paul) at the *Folies-Bergere*, see *The Royal Road to Romance*, op. cit., pp. 27–30; conceivably, Paul used the book as a road map of places to go. In interviews, William Alexander noted that Paul enjoyed theatre, notably jubilantly decadent shows with a dance component. For Josephine Baker, see Tony Allan, *The Glamour Years—Paris 1919–1940* (New York: Gallery Books, 1977), pp. 45–61 et passim. See also Carole Marks and Diana Edkins, *The Power of Pride—Stylemakers and Rulebreakers of the Harlem Renaissance* (New York: Crown Publishers, 1999). For Loie Fuller (1868–1928) see Sisley Huddleston, *Paris Salons, Cafes, Studios* (Philadelphia and London: J.B. Lippincott and Company, 1928), pp. 257–264. For Lindbergh's impact on landing in Paris, May 21, 1927, see Richard Nelson Current and Marcia Ewing Current, *Loie Fuller—Goddess of Light* (Boston: Northeastern University Press, 1997), p. 326. Also see Kurt Ludecke, *I Knew Hitler*, op. cit., pp. 310–313; and, Caresse Crosby, *The Passionate Years*, op. cit., pp. 141–142.

2. For Paris's different arrondissements see Philippe Meyer, *A Parisian's Paris* (Paris: Flammarion, 1999), pp. 204–206. For Halliburton in Paris, before 1925, see *The Royal Road to Romance*, pp. 27–33

("Mademoiselle Piety"), quoted at p. 31. For the pop-ularity of walking tours and other leisure activities of the "lost generation," see Tony Allan, *The Glamour Years*, op. cit., p. 92 and, in general, pp. 85–109. For Le Corbusier and his ambitious plans for the "City of Light," see Colin Jones, *Paris—The Biography of a City* (New York: Viking, 2005), pp. 397–402. For Le Bourget in Halliburton's books, see *RHL*, p. 320.

3. For gay Paris see Michael D. Sibalis, "Paris," *Queer Sites*, edited by David Higgs (London and New York: Routledge, 1999), pp. 10–37, at 29. On Mardi Gras in Paris see pp. 27–28. For the "Quatre Arts Ball," see Caresse Crosby, *The Passionate Years* (New York: Dial Press, 1953), op. cit., pp. 132–133; for "The Loving Duck," see pp. 118–119.

4. For views of Paris at this time, consulted were Elliot Paul, *The Last Time I Saw Paris* (New York: Random House, 1942), pp. 5–7, et passim; Robert E. Gajdusek, *Hemingway's Paris* (New York, Charles Scribner's Sons, 1978); and John Leland *A Guide to Hemingway's Paris with Walking Tours* (Chapel Hill: Algonquin Books, 1989). Also see Elizabeth Hutton Turner, *Americans in Paris (1921–1931)* (Washington, D.C.: Counterpoint, 1996), and the special notice given to artist Stuart Davis, who arrived in Paris in 1928 and sketched sites, many now gone, that surely provided Paul a recognizable context, pp. 31–37. For eye witness reportage see Joseph Roth, "America Over Paris (1925)," *Report From a Parisian in Para-dise—Essays from France 1925-1939*, pp. 27–31. For the bar and café scene, see Tony Allan, op. cit., pp. 85–98 (notable for text and period photographs). For the night club and bar scene, text and period photographs, see Billy Kluver and Julie Martin, *Kiki's Paris—Artists and Lovers 1900-1930* (New York: Harry N. Abrams, 1989; 1994), pp. 166–170 et pas-sim. John Scott suggested Paul's meeting Pound to me in a letter dated 11 January 2003. Scott, who wrote a feature on Pound for the *Washington Post* on the occasion of the poet's death, owns Paul's copy of Pound's *Personae* (New York: Boni and Liveright, 1926).

5. Quoted is William Alexander, interview, 1997.

6. For information on Ione's stay at the Hotel Daunow, I am indebted to John Scott, who stayed at the same hotel several times in the 1960s. Letter to author, 29 May 2004. For tips on hotels in Paris, see De Acosta, *Here Lies the Heart*, op. cit., p. 170. Also see René Crevel, *Lettres de desir et souffrance*, op. cit. For the Wagram Hotel see *JR*, p. 71. For Harry's Bar see p. 188. For residences associated with Virgil Thomson and Eugene MacCown, see Anthony Tommasini, *Virgil Thomson—Composer on the Aisle* (New York and London: W.W. Norton, 1997), pp. 42 and 100.

7. For Eugene MacCown (1891?–1966), and his social milieu, see Robert Byington, "Interviews with Virgil Thomson, Eugene MacCown, Quentin Bell and Hugh Ross Williamson," *A Sacred Quest: The Life and Writings of Mary Butts*, edited by Christo-pher Wagstaff (Kingston, N.Y.: McPherson & Com-pany, 1995), pp. 25–52. MacCown, says Byington, "was fairly prominent in the artistic-social swim of

Paris," p. 34. Also see *Selected Letters of Virgil Thom-son*, edited by Tim Page and Vanessa Weeks Page (New York: Summit Books, 1988), pp. 50 and 54 (under "McCown"); also see Virgil Thomson, *Virgil Thomson* (New York: Alfred A. Knopf, 1966), pp. 55, 57, 61 and 89. Also consulted was the dust jacket of MacCown's novel *The Siege of Innocence* (New York: Doubleday & Company, 1950). Also see Kay Boyle and Robert McAlmon, *Being Geniuses Together—1920-1930* (Garden City, New York: Doubleday and Company, 1968), p. 111. For S.M. McCowan, see Moses, p. 156 and Colby, p. 403. For a vivid account of Paris at the time (despite a mistaken idea when René Crevel died, and how), see Janet Flanner, *Paris Was Yesterday, 1925-1939*, edited by Irving Drutman (New York: Harcourt Brace Jovanovich, 1988), pp. vii–xxiv (Crevel, p. xiv).

8. For the "Boeuf sur la Toit," from a ballet by Darius Milhaud, see Brenda Wineapple, *Genet—A Biography of Janet Flanner* (New York: Tichnor and Fields, 1989), p. 66. See also Sisley Huddleston, *Paris Salons, Cafes, Studios* (Philadelphia and London: J.B. Lippincott and Company, 1928), pp. 230–231; Dar-ius Milhaud, *My Happy Life—An Autobiography*, translated from the French by Donald Evans, George Hall and Christopher Palmer, with an in-troductory essay by Christopher Palmer (London and New York: Marion Boyars, 1995), pp. 104–105; and Roger Nichols, *The Harlequin Years—Music in Paris 1917-1929* (Berkeley: University of California Press, 2002), p. 117. In Kathleen Hoover's and John Cage's *Virgil Thomson—My Life and Music* (New York: Sagamore Press, Inc., 1959), MacCown is referred to as "an American painter-pianist who replaced Wiener" as pianist at the Boeuf, p. 43. In general see Douglas and Madeleine Johnson, *The Age of Illusion: Art and Politics in France—1918-1940* (New York: Riz-zoli International Publications, 1987), pp. 122–123; and Lisa Appignanesi, *The Cabaret* (New Haven and London: Yale University Press, 2004), p. 124 et seq.

9. For the many celebrities in Paris at the time see, for instance, Huddleston, supra, pp. 252–253. Also see Milhaud, supra, pp. 82–88; cf. Patrick O'Connor, *Josephine Baker*, compilation by Brian Hammond (Boston: Bulfinch Press Book, 1988), p. 40 et seq. For Killian "Doc" Stimpson see reporter Paul Shinkman, *So Little Disillusion—An American Correspondent in Paris and London 1924-1931*, edited by Elizabeth Benn Shinkman (McLean, Va.: EPM Publications, Inc., 1983), pp. 87–88.

10. The origin of Halliburton's friendship with MacCown is mysterious, especially as letters from the 1920s are the least in number among the many he wrote. MacCown seems to have been known to the Halliburton family: "Glad Eugene recital was such a success," Richard writes home (evidently his parents had gone to a concert featuring MacCown). *RHL-P*, January 23, 1932. Later letters mentioning him are dated 15 May 1937, 23 June 1937 and 2 July 1937, and are omitted from the published versions. For the named and unnamed participants at par-ties Crane attended see Hart Crane, *Letters*, op. cit., 1 May 1929, at p. 341. Cf. René Crevel, *Lettres de desir et de souffrance*, avec Preface de Julien Green

(Paris: Libraire Artheme Fayard, 1996), p. 226. For
MacCown's involvement in Crane's life, see Unterecker, op. cit., pp. 587–588, 595–597. Crane's
relation with MacCown begins certainly by 1924.
See Unterecker, p. 343, and Index for other references. Toklas' comment about MacCown appears
on the dust jacket of his *The Siege of Innocence*.

11. Crevel's *Detours, avec un portrait de l'auteur par
Eugene MacCown grave sur bois par G. Aubart*, appeared in 1924 in a limited edition of 1000 copies
(Paris: Editions de la Nouvelle Revue Francaise).
See David Rattray, Introduction, *Difficult Death* (San
Francisco: North Point Press, 1989), p. xvii. Crevel
was an original member of the Surrealist group,
which included Andre Breton (whose *Manifeste du
surrealisme* also appeared in 1924). For a biographical abstract of Crevel see Gerard Durozoi, *History of
the Surrealist Movement*, translated by Alison Anderson (Chicago: University of Chicago Press, 2002),
p. 662. Also see Francois Buot, *Crevel* (Paris: Bernard
Grasset, 1991), p. 79; and, "Crevel, Rene," *Who's
Who in Gay & Lesbian History*, op. cit. pp. 110–111. For
a fuller account see Eddy Batache, *La mysticite charnelle de René Crevel* (Paris, 1976). On Crevel's "peculiar preoccupations" and their "origins" (in the suicide of his father following a "homosexual scandal")
see Edouard Roditi's invaluable Introduction to
Rene Crevel, *Putting My Foot in It*, translation by
Thomas Buckley (n.p.: Dalkey Archive Press, 1992),
p. xx. For Roditi's description of Crevel's relation
with MacCown, see pp. xviii–xix; for Crevel's other
friends in the American expatriate community of
Paris see pp. xviii–xx. On Caresse Crosby's keen eye
for literary talent see Anne Conover, *Caresse
Crosby—From Black Sun to Roccasinibalda* (Santa Barbara: Capra Press, 1989), p. 16. Also see p. 18 on the
stable of writers the Black Sun Press courted. In *The
Passionate Years*, Caresse Crosby writes at length
about her relationship with Crevel. As Black Sun's
editor, she said she was "proudest of [Crevel's "Mr.
Knife and Miss Fork," from his novel *Babylon*], for
into it went not only our separate skills [Max Ernst's
illustrations, Crevel's text, and her own layouts], but
our inseparable friendship as well," pp. 302–306.

12. Quoted is Matthew Josephson in his *Life
among the Surrealists* (New York: Holt, Rinehart, and
Winston, 1962), pp. 217–218 et passim. For Crevel's
view of MacCown, compare Buot, *Crevel*, supra, pp.
72, 73. Quoted is Ezra Pound, Foreword, René
Crevel, *Putting My Foot in It*, translation by Thomas
Buckley (n.p.: Dalkey Archive Press, 1992), p. ix.
Also quoted is Edouard Roditi, Introduction, to
same book, p. xxiii. Also see Josephson, op. cit., p.
217.

13. For a review of *The Siege of Innocence* (New
York: Doubleday, 1950) see Pamela Taylor, *The Saturday Review of Literature*, May 4, 1950, p. 30. For
Paul's resemblance to Crevel see the photograph by
Jean Rouvier on the cover of *Correspondence de Rene
Crevel à Gertrude Stein*, traducion, presentation et
annotation par Jean-Michel Devesa (Paris: L'Harmattan, 2000); or, as remarkable, the photograph
by Man Ray of Crevel with Tristan Tzara, circa 1928,
in Durozoi, *History of the Surrealist Movement*, op.

cit., p. 5. Also see Timothy Baum, "Rene Crevel,"
#36, *Man Ray's Paris Portraits: 1921–39* (Washington,
D.C.: Middendorf Gallery, 1989). In *The Siege of Innocence*, Joyce appears cameo-like with "his wife, his
son, and a formidable lady in an astrakhan toque
and rattling silver chains," p. 109. "Eugene [himself]
and Rene" are acknowledged, as Joyce, and others
(though not Paul Mooney), by their real names, p.
137.

14. For Klaus Mann, see Crevel, *Lettres de desir
et de souffrance*, op. cit., 258–259. For the sorts of issues of political and sexual identity that Mann addressed see James Robert Keller, *The Roles of Political
and Sexual Identity in the Works of Klaus Mann*, Studies
on Theses and Motifs in Literature, Horst S.
Daemmrich, general editor, vol. 56 (New York: Peter
Lang Publishing, 2001), pp. 1–5 et passim. Also see
Eddy Batache, *La mysticite charnelle de Rene Crevel*
(Paris, 1976). A first-rate critical-analytical study of
the novelist and critic in English is Peter T. Hoffer,
Klaus Mann (Boston: Twayne Publishers, 1978). Also
see Josephson, op. cit., pp. 258–259.

15. For Nancy Cunard (1896–1965) and Eugene
MacCown, see Anne Chisholm, *Nancy Cunard—A
Biography* (New York: Alfred A. Knopf, 1979), p. 90
et passim. Also see *Negro* (London: Wishart and
Company, 1934). On Cunard's Hours Press see her
*These Were the Hours—Memories of My Hours Press Re-
anville and Paris 1928–1931*, edited with a Foreword
by Hugh Ford (Carbondale and Edwardsville:
Southern Illinois University Press, 1969). For the
MacCown book, see pp. 87–91 (a black and white
view of MacCown's portrait of Cunard is opposite
p. 88) and p. 210. For Virgil Thomson's connections, including MacCown and Cunard, see pp. 67–
70; for Cunard, see pp. 91 and 125. For "Black
Montmartre" and the "Harlem Renaissance Overseas" see Tyler Stovall, *Paris Noir–African Americans
in the City of Light* (Boston and New York: Houghton
Mi·in Company, 1996). For "white American expatriates" and "Left Bank habitues" in the 1920s,
among whom Paul must be counted, see p. 78 et
seq. For Cunard, as rebel, Circe, poet, bon vivant,
and, as inspiration for Hemingway's Brett Ashley,
see Mina Loy, *The Last Lunar Baedeker* (New York:
Farrar, Straus, Giroux, 1996) edited by Roger L.
Conover, p. 205. Also see Ruth Brandon, *Surreal
Lives—The Surrealists 1917–1945* (New York: Grove
Press, 1999), pp. 240–242. For the Cecil Beaton
photo-portrait of Cunard see *Cecil Beaton—Photo-
graphs 1920–1970*, Philippe Garner and David Alan
Mellor (editors), (New York: Stewart, Tabori &
Chang, 1995), opposite p. 110. For Rene Crevel's
first meeting with Cunard see *Correspondence de René
Crevel à Gertrude Stein*, op. cit., p. 237. For mention
of Norman Douglas' *South Wind*, I note Alicia
Mooney's letter to Bill Alexander, 22 February 1955.
For the term "Negrotarian," see Carole Marks and
Diana Edkins, op. cit., p. 204.

16. For Natalie Barney see George Wickes, *The
Amazon of Letters—The Life and Loves of Natalie
Barney* (London: W.H. Allen, 1977), pp. 21–24. Also
see, op. cit., Crevel, *Lettres de desir et de souffrance*, p.
180, and Buot, *Crevel*, p. 254. For Barney's reputed

promiscuity see Alistair Horne, *Seven Ages of Paris* (New York: Alfred Knopf, 2002), p. 336, and pp. 334–335. See in general Mary Louise Roberts, *Disruptive Acts—The New Women in Fin de Siecle France* (Chicago: University of Chicago Press, 2002). Cf. Shari Benstock, *Women of the Left Bank* (Austin: University of Texas Press, 1986). MacCown translated, among other works, George Simenon's *Inquest on Bouvet* (London: Hamish Hamilton, 1958). Gerald and Sara Murphy introduced F. Scott Fitzgerald to MacCown. Cf. Amanda Vaill, *Everybody Was So Young* (Boston and New York: Houghton Mi-in Company, 1998), p. 183. Fitzgerald reportedly asked MacCown if he was a "homosexual," then, more memorably, asked him to describe the homosexual sex-act.

17. Paul's copy of Joyce's *Ulysses* is presently in the author's private collection.

18. See *RHL-NS*, 11 February 1928. Also see Mark Cocker, *Loneliness and Time—The Story of British Travel Writing* (New York: Pantheon Books, 1993), p. 4. Lines from Tennyson's "Ulysses" open *The Glorious Adventure*, p. 17. For "Ulysses, Jr." see Evan S. Connell, "The Last Great Traveler," *Oxford American: The Travel Issue*, March/April 2001, pp. 124–129, at 126.

19. See, for instance, Breandan o hEithir's *A Pocket History of Ireland* (Dublin: O'Brien Press, 2000), pp. 68–71.

20. For Brittany, see Mortimer Menpes with text by Dorothy Menpes, *Brittany* (London: Adam and Charles Black, 1912). For Pont-Aven see pp. 137–161, and for its artists' fads see pp. 138–139. Also see Francoise Cachin, *Gauguin—The Quest for Paradise* (New York: Harry N. Abrams Inc., Publishers, 1992), pp. 25–31. Also consulted was Russell Richardson, *Europe from a Motor Car* (New York: Randy McNally & Company, 1914). Richardson notes how France "had become a land of motor tourists" and notes too the pastime of "chateauing," p. 221. Also see Caresse Crosby, *The Passionate Years, op. cit.,* pp. 136–139. Quoted phrase is from *RHL,* p. 320.

21. For Mount St. Michael see *The Book of Marvels—The Occident, op. cit.,* pp. 187–198.

22. Fitzgerald's summation, originally appearing in *Scribner's Magazine,* can be found in Richard Holmes, "Scott and Zelda: One Last Trip," *Sidetracks, op. cit.,* p. 323.

23. On Crevel's death see Anna Balakian, Preface, to René Crevel, *Babylon,* translated and with an afterword by Kay Boyle (San Francisco: North Point Press, 1985), v–vi. Also see Ruth Brandon, *Surreal Lives—The Surrealists 1917–1945* (New York: Macmillan, 1999), pp. 373–375. Quotes is PML-WA ("you"); see Appendix B, Item 3, p. 242 for text.

Chapter 5

1. In numerous interviews Alexander expanded and clarified his recollections of Thomas Wolfe and Paul Mooney. His "Meanderings" also contains key information.

2. Thomas Wolfe taught at NYU from 1924 to 1930. Alexander bought, for his twentieth birthday, October 21, 1929, the first copy of *Look Homeward, Angel* Wolfe (claimed Alexander) signed for a student—"To Billy Levy, with friendship and thanks Thomas Wolfe. October 25, 1929." Concetta Scaravaglione (1900–1975) is best remembered for her monumental *Woman with Mountain Sheep* for the Federal Building at the 1939 New York World's Fair. In 1947 she received the Prix de Rome for her work. Alexander spoke often of Scaravaglione in conversation, and mentions her in "Meanderings."

3. Charles Wolfsohn (born 1912) believed that he, first of all, and secondly Paul, educated Alexander in "art matters." Probably so. His mentor Anna Curtis Chandler was the author of such books for teachers as *Pan the Piper and Other Marvelous Tales, Famous Mothers and Their Children,* and *Story Lives of Master Artists.* Wolfsohn's other mentor, the dapper and urbane Sidney Osbourne, a collector and traveler, held a high management position at the Hooker Chemical Company. Interview with Wolfsohn, 1 June 1996. The back of an envelope among the Halliburton letters at Princeton and dated 19 October 1928, bears a note in pencil from "Charlie," no last name. In interviews Alexander noted the exhibits and a couple artists whose shows he helped set up.

4. Alexander noted Paul's musical interests during interviews. Halliburton seems to have gone with Paul to a concert at Carnegie Hall, *RHL-P,* April 12, 1933, and to the "smaller of the two Rockefeller Center theaters," *RHL-P,* May 1, 1933. Richard's own favorite singer was tenor Richard Crooks, *RHL-P,* October 21, 1937. He also seems to have liked Lily Pons, a reigning diva in opera circles at the time, *RHL-P,* December 6, 1936. Alexander's list of "Pet Peeves" appears in "Meanderings."

5. Several photographs survive of Paul's cars. For Brooklyn and MacMonnies' statues in Prospect Park see Helen W. Henderson, *A Loiterer in New York,* p. 422 et passim.

6. For information on Paul's family, John Scott, letter to author, May 29, 2004. Thanks is extended to Alexander's niece Elaine Hofberg and (through telephone interviews) his sister Deborah Frey (1915–2003) for information about Paul's stay at the Levy house. Letter from Elaine Hofberg, et al., dated October 18, 2002.

7. For gay spots in New York at this time see Chauncey, op. cit., pp. 349–351. Cf. Daniel Hurewitz, op. cit., p. 253. For Harlem as a "gay enclave," see Chauncey, pp. 15, 136, 244–245. For Harlem's gay clubs, see pp. 246–249. Also see John Loughery, *The Other Side of Silence: Men's Lives and Gay Identities: A Twentieth-Century History* (New York: Henry Holt and Company, 1998), pp. 45–46. For Harlem at this time see Stephen Graham, "Harlem," in *New York Nights* (New York: George H. Doran Company, 1927), pp. 242–251. Also see Nancy Cunard, *Negro—An Anthology,* collected and edited by Nancy Cunard, edited and abridged, with an introduction, by Hugh Ford (New York: Frederick Ungar Publishing Co., 1970). Also see Roi Ottley, *New World a Coming—Inside Black America* (Boston: Houghton-Mifflin, 1943); for racial unrest see pp.

153, 154, and 155; for the "Black Ides of March," see pp. 151–152. For Father Divine (aka George Baker, 1879–1965), whose church was headquartered at 455 Lenox Avenue, see *The Black New Yorkers*, written by Howard Dodson, Christopher Moore, and Roberta Yancy (John Wiley and Sons, New York, 2000). Also see *The Encyclopedia of New York City* edited by Kenneth T. Jackson (New Haven: Yale University, 1995), p. 393.

8. Alicia's recollections of Bill and Paul appear in a letter to William Alexander (quoted), dated May 24, 1955. Deborah Frey (Levy) shared her recollections of Paul during a telephone interview.

9. Interviews with Alexander, and his niece Elaine, who several times visited "the Farm," enriched the account given in "Meanderings."

10. For Bernarr MacFadden's debt to Indian culture and the "benefits the Indians derived by going around naked," see Mary MacFadden & Emile Gauvreau, *Dumbbells and Carrot Strips—The Story of Bernarr MacFadden* (New York: Henry Holt and Company, 1953), pp. 9–11 and p. 70 (quoted in note). For the *Psychopathia Sexualis* see first complete translation into English by Franklin S. Klaf, M.D., M.P.H. (New York: Stein and Day, 1965). Krafft-Ebing's ideas resonate throughout Doctor Albert Moll's *Perversions of the Sex Instinct—A Study of Sexual Inversion*. Translated from the German in 1931, it was in its day the most readable and accessible book to cover the varieties of sexual experience, including the activities of "Uranists" or those devoted to the "Eros of Urania," pp. 15–16. Also see Philip Hoare, *Oscar Wilde's Last Stand—Decadence, Conspiracy, and the Most Outrageous Trial of the Century* (New York: Arcade Publishing, 1998). Described by David Bergman as "the most positive and influential essays on homosexuality in the early twentieth century," another landmark essay was Finnish sociologist and philosopher Edward Westermarck's "Homosexual Love" from his *The Origin and Development of Moral Ideas* (1906). The book flatly assumed "that homophobia, rather than homosexuality, is what needs explanation." An ethical relativist, Westermarck challenged the objectivity of moral values. "He asks," Bergman notes regarding the present topic, "how did the prohibitions against 'sodomy' arise? His answer, after a look at ethnography, is that homophobia arose from the disgust many humans feel toward sexuality in general and from the need to control 'unbelief, idolatry or heresy.' He contends that as 'people emancipated themselves from theological doctrines,' they regard homosexuality with 'somewhat greater leniency.' Such tolerance is the proper response to 'a powerful nonvolitional desire exercise[d] upon an agent's will.'" David Bergman, "Ethnography," glbtq (An Encyclopedia of Gay, Lesbian, Bisexual, Transgender & Queer Culture) http://www.glbtq.com/literature/ethnography.html. A copious writer on marriage practices, Westermarck 's best known work on the subject is *The Future of Marriage in Western Civilization* (1936). Also of interest is Paul Robinson, *Gay Lives—Homosexual Autobiography from John Addington Symonds to Paul Monette* (Chicago: University of Chicago Press,

1999). For information on German sexologist Magnus Hirshfeld (1868–1935), who, in 1925, opened the first institute for the study of sexual behavior, which, in 1933, was closed by the Nazis, see Aldrich and Wotherspoon, op. cit., pp. 210–212. While a wave of sexual freedom spread across the United States after World War I, in some areas at least, abortion and homosexual acts were still considered criminal. The following offers one look at how homosexuality was viewed in the 1930s. At a meeting of the APA, September 9, 1935, a Dr. Louis W. Max (no relation to the author), under the belief that homosexuality was a psychological or social pathology, spoke on "Breaking up a Homosexual Fixation by Conditioned Reaction Technique," the first dramatic use of aversion therapy (through electric shock) in treating homoneuroses in young men. See *Gay American History: Lesbians and Gay Men in the U.S.A.*, documents compiled by Jonathan Katz (New York: Thomas Crowell and Company, 1976), pp. 164–165. These therapies were of course recommended before UCLA psychologist Evelyn Hooker's researches in the 1950s, which resulted in the removal from the American Psychological Association's *Diagnostic and Statistical Manual* of homosexuality as a psychological disorder. Also see John Loughery, op. cit., "Days of the Code," pp. 57–81, after p. 67. Also see James Robert Keller, op. cit., pp. 12–14. Biographer Jonathan Root chose to ignore these issues. He mentions "America's moral revolution" in the 1920, and "the emergence of literature such as *Well of Loneliness*, by Radclyffe Hall, a bold and sensitive novel about the tortures of lesbianism." He also notes that the "book, oddly, was suppressed in England, a country which had been among the strongest critics of American puritanism, provincialism and pruriency." See *JR*, pp. 149–150. For the word "gay" and gay social cliques at the time, compare William J. Mann, *Wisecracker—The Life and Times of William Haines, Hollywood's First Openly Gay Star* (New York: Viking, 1998), p. xvi. For the word "homosexuality" see Byrne Fone, *Homophobia—A History* (New York: Metropolitan Books, Henry Holt and Company, 2000), p. 383. In general see "Modern Ethics" for developing views on the topic in Paul's time, pp. 288–315; also see psychiatrist Alfred Adler and his views, published in "The Homosexual Problem" (1917), that homosexuality is a stigma requiring concealment or a defect requiring a cure, p. 373. Also see David F. Greenberg, "Repression and the Emergence of Subcultures," *The Construction of Homosexuality* (Chicago: University of Chicago Press, 1988), pp. 301–346. In *Naughty Marietta* (1935) starring Nelson Eddy and Jeannette MacDonald, Captain Richard Warrington (Eddy) says, "People are rather gay in this quarter of town," meaning they are merry as "gay" implies throughout this and other movies of the day.

11. For the Neo-Pagans, see David Breashears and Audrey Salkeld, *Last Climb: The Legendary Everest Expeditions of George Mallory* (National Geographic, 1999), p. 32 (quoted in text).

12. Princeton University owns the snapshot. See *RHL-P*, November 26, and December 6, 1925; cf.

RHL, pp. 256–258 (quoted at p. 258). Letter, July 11, 2005. For Baron Wilhelm Von Gloeden (1856–1931) see Bruce Weber, *Homo-Erotic Fashions*, Part 1—Male Bodies on Internet. For Halliburton's companion "Jimmy," see *The Glorious Adventure* (Indianapolis: Bobbs-Merrill, 1927), p. 243 et seq.

13. Consulted for information about the nudist culture of the day was *The Nudist*, Official Publication (of the) International Nudist Conference (Outdoor Publishing Company, 45 West 45th Street, New York); specifically, "Nudist Life," November 1933, pp. 23–27. For Jared French's mural see Justin Spring, *Paul Cadmus—The Male Nude* (Chesterfield, Mass.: Chameleon Books, 2002), p. 16, fig. 15. Also see Leddick, op. cit., p. 41 et seq. French's mural was done for the New York State Vocational Institution in West Coxsackie. The "Fire Island" photographs appear in *Collaborations—The Photographs of Paul Cadmus, Margaret French, and Jared French* (Santa Fe: Twelvetrees, Press, 1992). For Paul Cadmus (1904–1999) and the work he was doing at this time see David Leddick, *Intimate Companions–A Triography of George Platt Lynes, Paul Cadmus, Lincoln Kirstein, and Their Circle* (New York: St. Martin's Press: Stonewall Inn Edition, 2001), p. 50. John M. Scott recalled that "Paul had a book of his [Cadmus'] drawings" and wondered if Paul "knew Cadmus when he lived in New York." Letter to author, February 8, 2003. The book in question may have been an exhibit catalogue: possibly, New York City, American Artists Group, Inc., *Original Etchings, Lithographs and Woodcuts by American Artists*, Catalogue No. 1., August, 1936. For another view of alternative life-style weekending at this time see, in general, Helen A. Harrison & Constance Ayers Denne, *Hamptons Bohemia—Two Centuries of Artists and Writers on the Beach* (San Francisco: Chronicle Books, 2002).

14. The photographs, one a photo-postcard, are in the author's collection. A letter Paul sent to Alexander mentions the photographs, and is dated September 23, 1935. The photographs could be much earlier than 1935. Elaine Hofberg remembers going to "the Farm," from the time she was three or four years old, which would be from 1929. For Indian ritual literature about this time see Mary Austin, "Aboriginal" Literature, *Non-English Writings II, The Cambridge History of American Literature* (New York: MacMillan, 1931), III, pp. 609–634. Also see Omer C. Stewart, *Peyote Religion*, op. cit., 36–40. In these dances, peyote ingestion is key, and in the Coxsackies rituals no vision-altering drug was apparently present. Forms of dance ceremonial abound. See, for instance, Tom Bahti, *Southwestern Indian Ceremonials* (Las Vegas, Nevada: KC Publications, 1970). Also see A. Hyatt Verrill, "Dances and Ceremonials," *The American Indian—North, South and Central America* (The New Home Library, 1927), pp. 135–155. For Wovoka and the Ghost Dance ritual, see Stephen Jay Gould, *Questioning the Millennium: A Rationalist's Guide to a Precisely Arbitrary Countdown* (New York: Harmony Books, 1995), p. 56. Quoted is D.H. Lawrence, "Indians and Entertainment," *Mornings in Mexico* (New York: Alfred A. Knopf, 1927), pp. 99–122, at p. 116.

15. For mention in the *Book of Marvels* of the poor treatment of Indians see "The Highest Waterfall" (Yosemite Falls), Richard Halliburton, *The Book of Marvels—The Occident*, op. cit., pp. 18–27, at 18 (for quoted material). The concluding, almost casual remark, is noteworthy in this context: the Sierra Valley is certainly a "hidden paradise of peak and waterfall" (and, seeing it today) "we can understand why the Indians, driven from this happy hunting ground out into the barren plains, died of homesickness for Yosemite," p. 27.

16. Lawrence, supra (quoted), p. 105.

17. For *Nackkultur* in Germany (specifically in Berlin) see Mel Gordon, *Voluptuous Panic—The Erotic World of Weimar Berlin* (Feral House); for the "Wandervogel" see pp. 94–95, quoted at p. 95; for the "Wild Boys" see pp. 96–101; for the "League for Free Body Culture" and "New Sunland League" see p. 144 et seq.

18. Charles Wolfsohn, taped interview, June 1, 1996.

19. In 1946, Forbes painted a portrait of Alexander's niece Elaine Hofberg, who offered her recollections of the painter. He died in 1951 of a lung ailment, brought on by his long exposure to toxic paint substances. Quoted is the review of William H. Littlefield for the *Falmouth Enterprise*, Falmouth, Massachusetts, August 12, 1966, where Forbes' pictures were exhibited. Also consulted was Bess Adams Garner, *Mexico—Notes in the Margin* (Boston: Houghton Mi-in Company, 1937), p. 55 et passim. Consulted for information on Leslie Powell (1905–1970) was Leslie Powell, "Painting from a Life's Journey (1967), pp. 7–9 (quoted). Cf. D.H. Lawrence, The Dance of the Sprouting Corn," *Mornings in Mexico*, supra, pp. 125–138. Also see Simone Ellis, "The Taos Society and Early Taos Art," in *Santa Fe Art* (World Publishing Group, 2004), p. 20 et passim. In a letter Halliburton mentions Paul "leaving Laguna and probably go[ing] to Mexico where he has friends" *RHL-P*, July 6, 1937. The friends included Leslie Powell and Don Forbes.

Chapter 6

1. For Halliburton at the Villa Montalvo early in 1930, see *RHL*, p. 304. Also unpublished letter from Richard Halliburton to Gertrude Atherton, Bancroft Library, MSS C-H 45, Box 5), date illegible May 17 or November 17, 1928. For Halliburton at Women's Press Club and Bohemian Grove see *JR*, p. 172. Halliburton as a traveler as well as a traveling salesman, the product he sold being himself. An important contact was philanthropist and patron of the arts Noel Sullivan (1890–1956), an Irish Catholic and world peace advocate. A key figure in the social and cultural life of San Francisco and Carmel, he was a member of the Bohemian Grove Club, and heir to the fortune of his uncle Senator James Duval Phelan, three-time mayor of San Francisco, banker extraordinaire, and builder of

the 175-acre Mediterranean-style estate known as Villa Montalvo in the Saratoga foothills just south of San Jose. During WW I Sullivan bought a fleet of ambulances and volunteered their use at the Western Front; it is believed Hemingway based the ambulance driver in *A Farewell to Arms* on Sullivan. Active in a number of social fronts, he advocated the abolition of the death penalty and supported Carmelite monasteries in California. He championed the "Negroe cause"—including among his friends Countee Cullen and Langston Hughes. On his Hollow Hills farm in Carmel Valley, he sheltered animals and practiced organic farming. See, in general, James P. Walsh and Timothy O'Keefe, *Legacy of a Native Son—James Duval Phelan & Villa Montalvo* (Los Gatos, Calif.: Forbes Mill Press, 1993). For the ambulance service and Hemingway see Jerry White, "Cryonics Quintessence," *edgar@spectrx. Saigon.Com* (Edgar W. Swank). Halliburton's letters to Noel Sullivan are at the Bancroft Library, University of California–Berkeley.

2. For marriage and commitment see *RHL*, p. 273 (quoted). For Fox Company, see p. 305 (quoted). See also *JR*, p. 169 et seq. Also see *RHL-P*, March 7 and 14, 1936 (omitted from published version, *RHL*, p. 377). For a published view, see "The Prince of Lovers Talks About Women," *The Illustrated Love Magazine*, op. cit., quoted on p. 41.

3. Halliburton's feature "Poor Richard Crusoe and Toosday" appeared in the December 1929 issue of *The Ladies Home Journal*. Quoted is Floyd Dell, "Robinson Crusoe"—subtitled "The Desert-Island Fantasy–The Failure of Columbus–The Utopia of the Bourgeoisie–Rousseau on the Pioneer," *Intellectual Vagabondage* (New York: George H. Doran Company, 1926), pp. 26–34, at 26–27. For a recent view see Bruce Selcraig, "The Real Robinson Crusoe," *National Geographic*, July 2003, 26, no. 4, pp. 83–90.

4. For the Van Druten trek see *RHL*, p. 271 et seq. See "Who Was Not Forward," *Seven Poems*, p 4. Quoted is "Blondel to Richard Coeur de Lion," p. 2.

5. For the sexual side of travel see Ian Littlewood, *Sultry Climates—Travel & Sex* (Da Capo Press edition, Cambridge, Massachusetts, 2002). According to Littlewood, the 19th century produced three notable types of traveler—the Connoisseur, Pilgrim, and Rebel, all of whom saw travel as linked to sexual passion, among other things. While Richard Halliburton is not mentioned, Rupert Brooke is at some length, pp. 171–177 et passim, as is Lord Byron at somewhat greater length, pp. 105–118 et passim. For Paul's pursuit of Halliburton, see "Blondel to Richard Coeur de Lion," *Seven Poems*, op. cit. For Halliburton in New York, see *RHL*, pp. 260–267. For Alexander's autograph hunting, there is the evidence of the extraordinary signature collection he owned as well as suggestions in "Meanderings." Several times in 1929 he walked with his teacher Thomas Wolfe from their uptown classroom location to NYU's main campus at Washington Square. Fellow students told him he was "shadowing Wolfe." Marilyn Monroe was his last fixation, and he owned one of the last certifiably genuine signatures of the star who shopped at his Hollywood art boutique, The Mart.

6. For earlier editors see *JR*, pp. 99–100, 103, 104–106. Richard's letters are filled with references to Chambers, a main supporting actor in his literary life. For Siasconset, *JR*, see p. 103; for East Orange, see p. 122. For the Wescott party, December 1927, see *RHL*, p. 279, though no mention is made of Paul. For Mexico City see *JC*, pp. 116–120.

7. See *RHL-P*, July 3, 1932. For Halliburton's 1927 trip to the West coast see *RHL*, pp. 266–267. Biographer Root believes Halliburton met Mooney at one of Barnes' parties. *JR*, p. 172. For Barnes' background, parties and possible connections with Richard, see *JR*, pp. 172–174. Cf. Allan R. Ellenberger, *Ramon Novarro—A Biography of the Silent Film Idol, 1899–1968; with a Filmography* (Jefferson, North Carolina: McFarland), pp. 86–88. For Barnes in Greenwich Village see Lauren Kessler, *The Life and Times of Pancho Barnes* (New York: Random House, 2000), p. 40. For later encounters between Barnes and Richard as well as with Paul, see *RHL-P*, November 20 and November 30, 1932. The photographs in back are dated 1932, and may very well date to this year. It should be noted that William Alexander identified them as belonging to this year decades later when he began organizing his papers.

8. The book is in author's collection, a gift from John M. Scott.

9. Hildegarde Hawthorne, *Romantic Cities of California*, illustrated by E.H. Suydam (New York: Appleton-Century Crofts, Inc., 1940), (quoted) at p. 42.

10. Margaret R. Burlingame, "The Laguna 6 Group," *The American Magazine of Art* (Washington, American Federation of Arts), 24, no. 4, pp. 259–266, at p. 259.

11. Post Cards—"R. M. Married, Laguna Beach, California," include several "made only by Curt Teach & Company, Inc., Chicago, U.S. A." Paul sent similar cards to friends and family. Paul sent postcards, "ancient" ones, he said, to his friend William Alexander. The photographs he took (and may not have sent) he thought poor because the weather that day had been "gloomy." Quoted is Paul Mooney, *PM-WA*, February 27, 1935.

12. See Burlingame, "The Laguna 6 Group," supra, p. 266. Also see J.S. Thurston, *Laguna Beach of Early Days* (Culver City, California: Murray & Gee, 1947), pp. 190–192.

13. Halliburton's first encounters with Laguna Beach are recollected in a letter dated October 15, 1936. See *RHL*, pp. 383–384, quoted at p. 384. For full text of letter, see *JC*, pp. 151–153. Quote from Christopher Isherwood is from his *Diaries*, I, 1939–1960 (New York: Harper Collins Publishers, 1997), pp. 241–242. For another description of such a sunset see Monica Highland, *Greetings from Southern California—A Look At the Past through Postcards* (Portland, Oregon: Graphic Arts Center Publishing Company, 1988), p. 30. Also see p. 31 et passim.

14. See *RHL*, p. 383; *JC*, pp. 151–153. Also see *JR*, p. 213. In an interview William Alexander noted that Paul accompanied Richard on this climb up the

ridge. Cf. Blankenship, "A Fellow Traveler," op. cit., p. 42. The date given is 1937, surely he means 1930.

15. Cf. *JR*, p. 213 and pp. 254–256. Also see "Halliburton: Adventurer's Legend, Mansion Are All But (Forgotten)," *Los Angeles Times*, Orange County, Part II, September 3, 1989; see also "The House That Richard Halliburton Built ... And Never Lived In," *Look Magazine*, December 19, 1939, pp. 64–65. On the cost of the ridge see *JR*, p. 213, and *RHL*, October 15, 1936, pp. 383–384. For Paul's lot, see *RHL-P*, November 3, 1936. For a description of the house, see "House for Writer Affords Privacy and Spectacular View," Alexander Levy, B. Arch. Designer, *Architectural Record, Building News*, October 1938, pp. 47–51. Also see *JC*, pp. 152–153 (which adds text omitted from the October 15, 1936 letter in *RHL*). For a general description of the house see *JR*, p. 255, and, again, *RHL*, pp. 383–385 (which also features pictures, opposite p. 369 and 370). For "Machu Picchu" see *The Book of Marvels—The Occident*, op. cit., pp. 142–143. The cliff-top is pictured in *Letters*, opposite p. 369. Also noted is Halliburton's "The place where the sun is tied," with four photos of Machu Picchu, *Ladies Home Journal Magazine*, September 1929.

16. For Richard's childhood activities and interests see *JR*, pp. 39–42; p. 42 (quoted). For his Scottish roots, see *RHL*, p. 1.

17. See *JC*, p. 181 (quoted). For Halliburton's voice, see Cole, (quoted), p. 47. In the one recording of him this author has heard his voice is shrill, and dulcet. Impressions of Paul's voice have come from William Alexander and John Scott. For Richard's description of Paul, see *RHL-P*, July 16, 1932.

18. Quotations are from David Greggory's screenplay (unpublished) "The Adventures of Richard Halliburton of Hangover House." "The spin of the story," Greggory writes in the preface, "concerns the volatile friendship of Dick Halliburton and Paul Mooney, who were thrown suddenly together by history in that extraordinary period." Greggory (1909–1991) discussed with Bill Alexander, his companion after 1949, both parties. Though historical in some, it is whimsical in other regards. Too many speeches dull the drama, and added characters sully the truth. In one episode, for instance, a female news photographer, given the name Toni Britton, unites in "real love" with Paul to "protect Dick" (and his public image) from the bad press the exposure of his gay relationship with Paul might incite. For the Tennessee Williams connection see Lyle Leverich, *Tom—The Unknown Tennessee Williams* (New York: New Directions, 1995), p. 498.

19. For Barnes' flight exploits see Gene Nora Jessen, *The Powder Puff Derby of 1929—The True Story of the First Women's Cross-Country Air Race* (Naperville, Illinois: Sourcebooks, Inc., 2002), pp. 37–43. On the cross-country race in which Barnes competed see Jessen, pp. 206–209. Also see Tom D. Crouch, *Wings—A History of Aviation from Kites to the Space Age* (Smithsonian National Air and Space Museum, Washington, D.C., 2003), pp. 280–282.

20. For Pancho Barnes' life, and that of her remarkable grandfather Thaddeus Sr., see Lauren Kessler, *The Life and Times of Pancho Barnes* (New York: Random House, 2000). Concerning Hell's Angels and other film stints, see pp. 80–83. On "habitués" at Barnes' parties see Kessler, pp. 62–64. Barnes' own telling of a "life story," much of it in her own distinctive argot with photos, appears in Grover Ted Tate, *The Lady Who Tamed Pegasus—The Story of Pancho Barnes* (Bend, Ore.: Maverick, 1986). See also Barbara Hunter Schultz, *Pancho: The Biography of Florence Lowe Barnes* (Lancaster, Calif.: Little Buttes Publishing Company, 1996). Also see General Chuck Yeager and Leo Janos, "Pancho's Place," *Yeager—An Autobiography* (New York: Bantam Books, 1985), pp. 172–185. And Robert A. Hoover, *Forever Flying* (New York: Pocket Books, 1996), pp. 113–115. For additional information on Thaddeus Sobieski Constantine Lowe, see Charles M. Evans, *War of the Aeronauts—A History of Ballooning in the Civil War* (Mechanicsburg, Pa.: Stackpole Books, 2002), pp. 36–39 et passim.

21. Quoted is Cecil Beaton, *The Wandering Years: Diaries 1922-1939* (Boston: Little, Brown and Company, 1961), p. 189. Also quoted is Richard Halliburton, *RHL*, p. 306. For Novarro and other guests see, besides Kessler, William J. Mann, *Wisecracker—The Life and Times of William Haines, Hollywood's First Openly Gay Star*, op. cit., pp. 80–83. Also see David Carroll, *The Matinee Idols*, op. cit., pp. 132–138. Quoted are Moye Stephens' impressions of Barnes from an interview between the pilot and Michael Blankenship, September 20, 1986, in *JC*, p. 128. For Moye Stephens, see Ronald Gilliam, "Moye Stephens Piloted More Than 100 Types of Aircraft and Flew Around the World in the Flying Carpet," *Aviation History*, vol. 9, issue 6. July 1999. The remarkably sharp black and white photograph that appeared with this article shows a certain Jim Angel, Richard Halliburton, Florence "Pancho" Barnes and Moye Stephens posed in front of the *Flying Carpet*.

22. For similar views on celebrity in the 1930s see *Amelia Earhart*, Nancy Porter Productions film for *The American Experience*, PBS, written, produced and directed by Nancy Porter, 1993. For views presented here, compare the comments of author Gore Vidal, whose father Eugene Vidal was an important figure in early aviation. Quoted is Peter Supf, *Airman's World—A Book About Flying*, translated (from the German) by Cyrus Brooks (London: George Routledge & Sons, Limited, 1933), p. 13 and titles. Supf flew planes for the Fuehrer.

23. Consulted for information on flying lessons, schools, shows, etc., was *Aero Digest*, November 1929, notably pp. 188–193; for sites of aircraft-related industry, see pp. 169, 213, 192; for the International Aircraft Exposition of 1930, p. 99. Premier aviation periodicals of the period also included *Popular Aviation and Aeronautics*, *National Glider and Airplane News*, and *Western Flying*. Air travel, like the automobile, fascinated Paul, yet of his contributions to any of the paying flight periodicals—*Universal Model Airplane News*, *Aeronautics*, or *Flying Aces*, no articles by him have been identified.

24. See *The Great Air Race of 1924* (VHS), PBS: The American Experience, narrated by David Mc-

Cullough, produced by David Grubin, 1989, AMEX-201-DAE4 (60 minutes).

25. For the air route to Mexico see Jessen, supra, (quoted) p. 251.

26. Consulted in general was Paul O'Neil, *Barnstormers and Speed Kings* (Alexandria, Virginia: Time-Life Books, 1981). Quoted is R.G. Grant, *Flight—100 Years of Aviation* (DK Publishing, Inc., New York, 2002), p. 120. Also see Tom D. Crouch, *Wings—A History of Aviation from Kites to the Space Age*, op. cit., especially "Big Business 1927–1935," pp. 239–276 and "The Roar of the Crowd 1927–1939," pp. 277–315. For cross-country flight costs see, for instance, *Time*, November 17, 1930, p. 28: September 23, 1929, pp. 62–63; in those days "Aeronautics" was a regular section of the national news weekly.

27. For Lindbergh's flight, see his "To Bogota and Back By Air—The Narrative of a 9,500-Mile Flight from Washington, Over Thirteen Latin-American Countries and Return, in the Single-Seater Airplane 'Spirit of St. Louis,'" *National Geographic* 53, no. 3, May 1928, pp. 529–602. For the Rockne disaster see R.G. Grant, *Flight*, supra, p. 138.

28. For oil company and other sponsors of flyers see Jessen, supra (Noyes), p. 235; (Turner), pp. 185, 25; (Barnes-Hughes, p. 207; Barnes-Gilmore, p. 251). For Turner also see Grant, op. cit., pp. 129–130, and Crouch, op. cit., pp. 288–289.

29. For Marvel Crosson see Jessen, supra, pp. 129, 172 and 186; for Amelia Earhart (1897–1937) and Erle Halliburton (1891–1957), see pp. 167–168. Also consulted was "Rotogravure Section" (on women pilots, including Barnes, Crosson, and Earhart), *Air Travel News*, December 1929 3, no. 12, pp. 33–56, quoted at p. 33.

30. For Erle Halliburton and Richard, see *JR*, p. 123. Also see *RHL*, p. 309. For Juan Terry Trippe (1899–1981) see Crouch, *Wings*, op. cit., pp. 344–355. For Howard Hughes (1906–1975), at this time, see T.A. Heppenheimer, "Howard Hughes, The Innovator, The Method Before the Madness," *Invention & Technology* 14, no. 3, Winter 1999, pp. 36–46.

31. Reference is made to Julianne DeVries,' *Campfire Girls Flying around the Globe* (Harper and Brothers, New York, 1933), Jules Verne's *A Trip around the World in a Flying Machine* (Chicago: Donahue and Company, 1887), Elizabeth Bisland's *A Flying Trip around the World* (New York: Harper and Brothers, 1891), and Major W.T. Blake's *Flying around the World* (London: Heath Cranton Limited, 1923). For the origins of the *Flying Carpet Expedition* see *JR*, pp. 174–178; also see *RHL*, p. 307.

32. In the author's collection is a letter, dated November 4, 1930, from Richard Halliburton to Harold Pitcairn in Willow Grove, Pennsylvania. See Appendix B. Halliburton gives, as his permanent address, the Roosevelt Hotel, Hollywood, California. He also gives as his address from November 6 to November 11, "S.A.F.E. WAY AIR LINES, Tulsa, Oklahoma, c/o Earl Halliburton." Also see *RHL*, p. 309. For Richard's efforts to find the right plane, see *RHL*, pp. 307–310; cf. *JR*, pp. 175–177. Also see Richard Halliburton, *The Flying Carpet* (New York: Bobbs-Merrill, 1932), p. 15. For Erle's help, see *JR*, p. 177.

33. For Richard's search for a plane and pilot, see pp. 172–175. For the career of Moye Stephens and a summary of the Flying Carpet adventure itself, see Ronald Gilliam, op. cit., "Moye Stephens Flew More than 100 Types of Aircraft and Flew Around the World in the *Flying Carpet*, Aviation History, July 1999. Also see Gilliam, "Around the World in a Flying Carpet," *Aviation History*, vol. 14, issue (May 2004). For an earlier treatment see *Tarpa Topics, the Retired Trans World Airline Pilot's Magazine* (April, 1996). Also see Martin Cole, "The Flight to Never-Never Lands," *Their Eyes on the Skies* (Glendale, California: Aviation Book Company, 1979), pp. 42–70, quoted at p. 45. For Stephens' temperament, see *RHL-P*, March 23, 1932; also as "a combination of masterful pilot and personal shackle" for not taking "any part in servicing the plane" see May 10, 1932. Stephens' and Hiatt's "Ghosts of the Air," about "skeleton aviators piloting their broken planes far up in the silent heights"—"*Flying Dutchman of the Air*," appeared first in *Weird Tales*, June 1926; in 1993 Barnes & Noble reissued it in *100 Ghastly Little Ghost Stories*, ed. by Stefan R. Dziemianowicz, Robert Weinberg, and Martin H. Greenberg, pp. 176–182.

34. Regarding Richard's care in planning, John Halliburton noted that "All his [cousin Richard's] trips except the first, 'The Royal Road to Romance,' were carefully planned beforehand." To this end "he would purchase numerous books on the area that he planned to visit." *The Royal Road* and "parts of his other books" he wrote "in longhand" seated at a desk he [John] now owned. Letter, John H. Halliburton to Michael Blankenship, July 8, 1986; copy used by permission of William Alexander. Also see Moye Stephens, in *JC*, p. 127. For the Stearman acquired by Stephens and its specifications, see Cole, supra, pp. 48–49. See *RHL*, p. 311 et seq. For the meaning of "red" here compare D.H. Lawrence, *Etruscan Places* (New York: The Viking Press, 1932), pp. 77–78. For another description of the plane including a test run flight to Ensenada, and the Casino there, see *RHL-NS*, December 15, 1930.

35. For the Phelan funeral services, *RHL-NS*, December 15, 1930.

36. For Halliburton peddling his celebrity see, for instance, Schwartz, op. cit., pp. 170–172. For Stephens' opinion of Halliburton and Mooney, see *JC*, p. 128 (quoted). The photograph of Halliburton with Novarro and Mooney, etc., is in the author's collection; copies circulate. Other photographs show Halliburton and Novarro aboard and in front of the *Flying Carpet*. See, for instance, Blankenship, "A Fellow Traveler," p. 41. Ramon Novarro biographer Allan R. Ellenberger notes that, in 1933, Mary Pickford introduced the explorer (Halliburton) to Novarro at a party at Pickfair. The photographs taken with Pancho Barnes of Halliburton and Novarro together indicate that by 1930 the two knew one another.

Chapter 7

1. Cf. *JR*, pp. 177–178, 169–170, and 180; also see Cole, p. 49 et seq. and *RHL*, 311 et seq., p. 313

(quoted). For time spent in New York, see *RHL*, p. 312; also see *RHL-P*, June 28, 1931. Also see Ronald Gilliam, Around the World in a Flying Carpet," *Aviation History*, op. cit. Quoted is a letter from Richard Halliburton to Noel Sullivan, dated December 15, 1930, and used by permission of Bancroft Library, University of California-Berkeley.

2. For the *Exposition Coloniale Internationale* see Arthur Chandler, "Empire of the Republic: The Exposition Coloniale Internationale De Paris, 1931," *World's Fair Magazine*, 8, no. 4, World's Fair, Inc.; also *Contemporary French Civilization*, Winter/Spring 1990; expanded and revised version, 2000: http:/charon.sfsu.edu/PARIS EXPOSITIONS/1931EXPO.html. For Josephine Baker there see Tony Allan, op. cit., p. 48.

3. See *RHL*, p. 314 (quoted). For the itinerary see *RHL*, pp. 313–339. Also see *JR*, pp. 177–180; cf. *JC*, pp. 123–125.

4. Rand McNally published Wiley Post's and Harold Gatty's *Around the World in Eight Days—The Flight of the Winnie Mae*, with introduction by Will Rogers, in the fall of 1931, about the same time *The Flying Carpet* appeared. The Soviet itinerary included Moscow, Omsk, Novosibirsk, Irkutsh, Blagovesh chensk, and Khabarovsk.

5. For Shell see *RHL*, p. 313; also *RHL-P*, January 23, 1932, p. 7; November 5, 1932. Also see *JR*, p. 177. For the figures and expenditures, consulted was John Halliburton, letter to Michael Blankenship, and Cole, op. cit., p. 69. For the debts incurred see *RHL-P*, July 3, 1932, which reports $12,000 and $20,000. Cf. *JR*, p. 203.

6. For the dangers see Guy Townsend, op. cit., p. 3. Cf. *JR*, p. 201 (pontoon incident) et seq. Also see *RHL*, p. 324 (in Sea of Galilee), p. 334 (over Bangkok), p. 338 (Jolo) et passim; and *RHL-P*, January 23, 1932. For the Mt. Everest experience see *JR*, pp. 199–200. For the gun matter see *JR*, p. 189.

7. My thanks to Paul's nephew Anton D. Levandovsky for permitting me to use Paul's letter, dated November 19, 1931, and for information about his family background in interviews and in a letter, July 3, 2003.

8. For Baja see Erle Stanley Gardner, *The Hidden Heart of Baja* (New York: William Morrow and Company, 1962). In a letter dated July 6, 1937, Halliburton mentions Paul "leaving Laguna and probably go[ing] to Mexico where he has friends." For the Seri Indians, see *JC*, (quoted) p. 138. Also see *RHL*, pp. 351–352 (July 13, 1934). For Halliburton's whereabouts at this time see *Letters*, pp. 324–331. See also John Xantus, *Travels in Southern California*, translated and edited by Theodore Schoenman and Helen Benedek Schoenman (Detroit: Wayne State University Press, 1976), pp. 89–91 and p. 225. Later, William Alexander, following in Paul's footsteps, visited most of the places noted here to procure native goods for his antique shop, The Mart, in Los Angeles. The Hotel Rancho de la Palmilla in Los Cruces he designed in the 1950s for former Mexican President Abelardo Rodriguez's son was done, in part, as a cenotaph for Paul.

9. For Wovoka see Fleming and Luskey, *North*

American Indians in Early Photographs, op cit. (quoted), p. 144. For the photographs see pp. 165 and 166.

10. Jeffers' verse had long appeared in leading journals (notably Harriet Monroe's *Poetry, A Magazine of Verse*, June 1926, 28, no. 3); by 1930 he was *au courant*. According to John M. Scott, Paul carried around copies of two long poems by Jeffers. Letter (undated) to author, about May, 2001. Alicia Mooney noted three Jeffers' books her brother carried with him, *Thurso's Landing, Give Your Heart to the Hawks*, and a third one she was unable to recall, but which John Scott believes was *Dear Judas*. Letter from Alicia to William Alexander, April 14, 1939(?). Poet George Sterling (1869–1926) wrote the first biography of Jeffers: *Robinson Jeffers—The Man and the Artist* (New York: Boni & Liveright, 1926), the account of the poet's life available to Paul. Also see see James Karman, *Robinson Jeffers—Poet of California*, rev. ed. (Story Line Press, Ashland Oregon, 2001). Besides a review of *Thurso's Landing*, a capsule biography of Jeffers appeared in *Time*, which featured Jeffers himself on the cover, April 4, 1932, pp. 63–64. For a favorable view of Jeffers, seen as in the vanguard of so-called "eco-poets," see Michael Schmidt, *Lives of the Poets* (New York: Alfred A. Knopf, 1999), p. 703 et passim. For Jeffers' themes see Schmidt *Lives of the Poets* (New York: Alfred A. Knopf, 1999), p. 703. On "Hawk Tower," see James Karman, op. cit., pp. 50–51. For Jack London and ideas he shared with Jeffers, not in the area of practical agronomy, see Alex Kershaw, *Jack London—A Life* (New York: St. Martin's Press, 1997), p. 302. Whether Paul ever met Jeffers is uncertain. In a letter dated July 28, 1936, Halliburton himself mentions visiting Carmel, which was "full of interesting poets and artists," *RHL*, pp. 381–382. Paul was introduced to, and dined with, philanthropist Noel Sullivan, a good friend of both Robinson and Una Jeffers, but no mention is made here of either the poet or his wife. Letter from Richard Halliburton to Noel Sullivan, March 24, 1933, Noel Sullivan Papers, Bancroft Library, University of California—Berkeley.

11. *Time*, supra, quote at p. 64. Compare Floyd Dell, "Shell-Shock and the Poetry of Robinson Jeffers," *Modern Quarterly III* (September-December 1926), pp. 268–273. Cf. Douglas Clayton, *Floyd Dell: The Life and Times of an American Rebel* (Chicago: Ivan R. Dee, 1994), pp. 228–229. Worse hatchet jobs on the poet followed the decline of his reputation from the mid–1930s. See, for instance, Kenneth Rexroth's essay in *Saturday Review* (1957), summarized in James Karman, op. cit., p. 143. Compare Martin Seymour-Smith, *Who's Who in Twentieth Century Literature* (New York: McGraw-Hill, 1976), pp. 180–181. For a skeptic's view regarding "the romanticization of Nature," and over-glorification of the "savages in America," see Keith Sagar, *The Life of D.H. Lawrence* (Albuquerque: University of New Mexico Press, 1980), pp. 144–146, with Lawrence liberally quoted throughout.

12. *Time* (quote), supra, quote at p. 64. Quoted lines of verse are from Robinson Jeffers, *Thurso's Landing, The Selected Poetry of Robinson Jeffers*, 13th

printing (Random House, New York, 1959), pp. 266–357: p. 276, III, lls. 17–33, p. 277, lls. 1–9. The frontier, p. 268, lls. 17–23; also see "The Place For No Story" (p. 358) which is an eco-poetical evocation of "the coast hills of Sovranes Creek" noted in the poem.

13. Ibid., *Thurso's Landing*, p. 267, II, Ils. 13–15 (Reave); p. 266, I, lls. 5–6, p. 268, II, lls. 5–8 (Rick).

14. Quoted is Richard Halliburton, "Foreword" to Elly Beinhorn, *Flying Girl* (Geoffrey Bles at Two Manchester Square, London, 1935), pp. 3–7. For the "preface" see *RHL*, p. 357. Copies of the book are rare. For the Beinhorn episode see"The Flying Fraulein," *The Flying Carpet*, pp. 254–258; pictured, opposite p. 254. Compare *RHL-P*, February 4 and March 23, 1932. Elly Beinhorn-Rosemeyer was born in 1907 and has continued to live into the 21st century. See *The Pioneers and Aeromodelling—Independent Evolutions & Histories*: Elly-Beinhorn-Rosemeyer (1907–), www.ctie.monash.edu.au/hargrave/bein horn.htm/ The German (Leipzig) edition of *The Flying Carpet* entitled *Der Fliegende Teppich* (*Der Welt aus der Vogelschau*) appeared in 1934 or thereabouts. For the "Foreword" see *JR*, p. 236. Halliburton, introduced as "Richard Halliburton, World Traveler, Author and Epicure," wrote a one-page note, and not strictly speaking a foreword, for *One Hundred Years of Delightful Indigestion: Memphis' Priceless and Treasured Receipts* (Memphis: James Lee Memorial Academy of Art—Memphis, 1935). Neither Halliburton nor Beinhorn were first in reaching and reporting about Timbuctoo: in 1924 Lady Dorothy Mills wrote an account called *The Road to Timbuktu*.

15. For new chapters and carbons, besides delays, see *RHL-P*, February 18, March 8 and March 23, 1932. Compare *RHL*, p. 336. For completed chapters and materials sent to Aley, *RHL-P*, March 23, 1932; for Aley and Chambers, see *RHL-P*, February 4. For Aley's relation to Halliburton see *JR*, p. 187. For Loring Schuler see *RHL-P*, March 8, 1932. See also *JR*, pp. 132, 186, 187 and 188. For plane performance see *The Flying Carpet*, (quoted) p. 352; also, *RHL*, p. 335. For hotels, including the Ra·es, which proved insufficiently quiet, *RHL-P*, February 4, 1932, p. 3.

16. For Halliburton's need to finish the book, see *RHL-P*. March 8, 1932 (quoted). For disassembling of the plane, *RHL-P*, May 10, 1932. For Everest story, *RHL-P*, March 23, 1932; May 10, p. 11 (quoted).

17. For Halliburton's remarks on Stephens, *RHL-P* (Mt. Blanc), March 23, 1932; May 10, 1932 ("Liberation ..."). For Halliburton's writing habits, *RHL-P*, February 4, 1932; May 10, 1932 (quoted). For "Glorious Adventure days," *RHL-P*, February 8, 1932.

18. See *RHL*, p. 337–339; condenses *RHL-P*, May 10, 30 and 31, 1932. Cf. *JR*, p. 203. For the fate of *the Flying Carpet*, see *JC*, p. 129.

19. For the trip's inability to inspire stories, *RHL-P*, January 23, 1932.

20. For Wesley's dislike for Paul see *JC*, p. 128. For Chambers and his role in the book project, see *JR*, p. 209. For the respect Richard showed Cham-

bers see pp. 104–105. Chambers' name appears repeated in Halliburton's correspondence home for the years 1931 and 1932. Chambers reported that sales of the book were "painfully slow," but, added Richard, "books [were] not selling anywhere." See *RHL-P*, December 8, 1932, which also mentions the reviews. For the deadline, and mounting awareness thereof, *RHL-P*, March 23, 1932. For mounting profits, see *RHL-P*, May 23, 1933.

21. For Halliburton as a "has-been" see *JR*, p. 187; p. 204 (quoting Halliburton in context of Sea Dragon Expedition). A high-brow version of Halliburton was Vincent Sheean, who, like Halliburton, had left a good school (University of Chicago) to see the world, and who, unlike Halliburton, reported without frill the so-called "truth" about foreign places. See his *Personal History* (Garden City, New York: Doubleday, Doran & Company, Inc., 1936). Halliburton admitted that Eugene Wright was a "real rival," whose *Great Horn Spoon* (1927) "is dangerously like my books, but after all it's *like* and the edge has gone." That "edge" may have counted to Halliburton more than the "truth," *RHL*, p. 279. Halliburton thought Peter Fleming's *Brazilian Adventure* (1934) "extremely well written, but of no importance as exploration or story-telling." For him, the "truth had to have a story-line; an accumulation of bald, unadorned facts was insufficient. "See *RHL-P*, November 27, 1936. For mention of the "autobiography," see *RHL-P*, January 28, 1931. The "wickedest cities" or "Cairo—The Capital of Sin" is among the Halliburton materials in the Princeton University Library.

22. See *RHL*, p. 263 (quoted). For advice from Maxwell Aley, and Chambers, see *RHL-P*, July 3, 1932. For Aley's help, *RHL-P*, September 5 and September 12, 1932.

23. *RHL-P*, January 23, 1932 (quoted, p. 6).

24. *RHL-P*, July 16, 1932 (quoted). For the banquet for Earhart, see *RHL-P*, July 3, 1932.

25. For hole-ups during the writing of the book see *RHL-P* (quoted), Monday, August 22, 1932 (Alexandria and Crocker House); (quoted) August 15, 1932 (Standish Arms Hotel); September 5, 1932 (Max Aley's); September 5, 1932 and September 15, 1932 (galleys). For Burton Holmes see *Time*, August 4, 1958, "Milestones." See also *Life*, August 11, 1958, pp. 8–9. In general see Burton Holmes: *The Man Who Photographed The World—Travelogues 1892-1938*, with introduction by Irving Wallace and selected and edited by Genoa Caldwell (New York: Abrams, 1977), 318–319. For his friendship with Halliburton, see *JR*, pp. 118–119, 273. Also see *RHL-P*, April 12, 1933. For Aley aboard the *Majestic* (to London), see *RHL-P*, January 28, 1931.

26. *RHL-P*, July 7 (quoted) and July 16, 1932. See *JC*, p. 125 (quoted); p. 128 (Stephens quoted). John Scott noted the visit of Paul's mother, Ione, to Paul in Alexandria in a letter to author, June 6, 2004. Wesley notes Richard working (on the book) with a friend, *RHL*, p. 340. Photographs survive of Paul Mooney at the Standish Arms Hotel at this time. Literary agent Maxwell Aley evidently offered some advice on how to proceed, p. 340. Michael

Blankenship notes that Halliburton asked Bobbs-Merrill for an "assistant" and Bobbs-Merrill put Mooney "on their payroll." See "A Fellow Traveler," op. cit., p. 40. For Paul's collaboration in the eventual book see *JR*, pp. 204–205. For Halliburton's own serious attention to the book, see p. 209. For financial topics, see, for instance, *RHL-P*, August 27 or September 15, 1932.

27. *RHL-P*, July 7, 1932 (quoted); also August 22 (Monday), 1932. Compare *RHL* (which generalizes these few months with a few choice quotations from the letters), p. 340. For earlier work on the French Foreign Legion chapter, see *JR*, pp. 185–186.

28. For manuscript versions see Halliburton Collection at Princeton University and at Lilly Library at the University of Indiana. *PML-WA*, September 23, 1935. Beebe, author of *The Edge of the Jungle* among other notable works, was one-time director of Tropical Research Station of the New York Zoological Society, and a known underwater explorer, or "sea vagabond." To learn more about him see the Official William Beebe Website. For the "bold" writing see Bobbs-Merrill dust jacket of *The Flying Carpet*.

29. See *JC*, p. 125 (Stephens quoted). *RHL-P*, July 16 (quoted) and July 14, 1933 (quoted).

30. A postcard (in author's collection) from Alicia Mooney to William Alexander (dated 1977) replicates the line, and underscores the beginning letters, Halliburton Collection: Rhodes College, Memphis. Cf. *JC*, p. 128. Also see *JR*, p. 209.

31. See *JC*, p. 125 (quoted). Evidently Stephens was referring to the courting rituals. See *The Flying Carpet*, p. 331–332. For James Elliot Mooney see *Who Was Who in America, 1968–1973* (Marquis Publishing), p. 507.

32. Alexander's exact words may be quoted in full: "As your books, once written, have to be vastly re-written, so this house (once planned) had to be replanned—chiefly through Paul's intercession. He (Paul) enlarged it far beyond the original plans which I had drawn for a $9000 house; and I always supposed that he was acting as your agent. That his intercession improved the house, there can be no doubt. But naturally it raised costs. So did that abominable weather of the winter of construction, and the temporary building boom, and the strikes." The eight-page sternly-worded letter, dated March 30, 1938, may never have been sent. For the "flying adventure" see *RHL-P*, July 6, 1938. Paul mentioned the *Readers Digest* article in a letter to Alexander dated September 8, 1937. About this same article Richard told his parents that he would see the editor of *Readers Digest* later "about more stories," adding, "I could probably write lots of them *if I had the time*." (Italics mine). *RHL-P*, September 20, 1937. The feature for *Cosmopolitan* (January 1936) was apparently "I've Eaten Christmas Dinner All around the World," which related Halliburton's run-in with Soviet police, his battle with pneumonia, and his being served boiled octopus at a monastery. For the earlier *Cosmopolitan* article see *RHL-P*, July 14 and July 26, 1933.

Other snippets of work attributed to Halliburton

are distilled versions of earlier published work. "Up The Matterhorn," for instance, appeared in New York's *Hotel Montclair Musings*, in November 1934. Its lead, "The man who has traveled the world takes us on a thrilling climb up one of its most glorious mountains," suggests an independent hand. Issue 2, no. 3, November 1934 pp. 12–13. Official Publication of the Hotel Montclair, Lexington Avenue Between 49th and 50th Streets, New York, Arthur See, editor. The Hotel is mentioned in *RHL-P*, March 23, 1932. Truer to Paul's talents was the feature "Half a Mile of History" which appeared in *Readers Digest* in October 1937.

33. See Aubrey's *Brief Lives*, edited from the original manuscripts and with a "Life of John Aubrey" by Oliver Lawson Dick (Ann Arbor: University of Michigan Press, 1957), pp. 21–22. Of incidental note, Charles Hall's sensational *Pro Patria* excursion to Pitcairn Island, and the shipwreck that followed was news both Richard and Paul might have noticed. See *Time*, September 24, 1932, p. 67.

34. Also see *JR*, p. 107 (quoted); and George Weller, "The Passing of the Last Playboy," *Esquire*, April, 1940, after p. 58 (quoted).

35. See *JR*, p. 114 (quoted). Also see *RHL*, p. 270 (quoted). Consulted was David Greggory's screenplay (unpublished) "The Adventures of Richard Halliburton of Hangover House." Evidently Paul was Wolfsohn's source for his opinion; Alexander, and, possibly, Tennessee Williams, whom Greggory knew as early as 1941, was Greggory's source. For the "wall" he had built around himself see *RHL-P*, January 23, 1932 In a letter from Laguna Beach dated May 10, 1939, Tennessee Williams writes, "People around here say that Paul Mooney, mentioned as his collaborator, actually did most of his writing for him." *The Selected Letters of Tennessee Williams*, Vol I, 1920–1945, edited by Albert J. Devlin and Nancy M. Tischler (New York: New Directions, 2000), pp. 172–174. For Halliburton's opinion on "modernistic," *RHL-P*, October 9, 1937.

36. Cf. *JR*, p. 205.

Chapter 8

1. Letters referring to financial matters (omitted in published version) include *RHL-P*, January 23, 1932, November 20, 1932, June 22, 1933 and June 26, 1933. For a dramatization of Paul and Richard discussing the topic of money, see *JR*, pp. 32–33. For a measurement of Halliburton's success against the values of the time, as well as the opportunities that came his way, see *JC*, p. 137. For the lecture circuit see *JR*, pp. 98–99 and 215–216. The house is pictured in *RHL*, opposite p. 338, and *JC*, after p. 95 (noted on p. 133). For Halliburton's turning down work see, for instance, *RHL*, p. 341.

2. For social and economic conditions in general see Watkins, *The Great Depression*, op. cit. Also see *RHL-P*, January 23, 1932 (quoted).

3. The house is pictured in *RHL*, opposite p.

338, and in *JC*, after p. 95 (noted on p. 133). For Halliburton's admission of an unsociable nature see *RHL*, pp. 385–386. Dated November 27, 1936, the letter omits his opinions of women and men.

4. For the "Royal Road to Romance in America," see *RHL*, pp. 397–398. Also see p. 390, on "our America book." For the circumstances of "The Royal Road to Romance in the USA" see *JR*, pp. 246–247; cf. *JC*, p. 157. For the titles of books Halliburton researched for the book, see *JC*, pp. 157–158. For research conducted on the book, *RHL-P*, June 25, 1938.

5. Paul long admired Powell's work, notably "Exit From Brooklyn" which he had seen, in the spring of 1935, in an exhibit of the artist's work at the Corcoran Gallery in Washington. For William Mortensen (1897–1965), whose photograph of Alexander stood beside editions of books by Halliburton in Hangover House's master bedroom, see *Pacific Dreams— Currents of Surrealism and Fantasy in California Art, 1934-1957* (UCLA at Armand Hammer Museum of Art and Cultural Center, 1995), pp. 150–153. Edmund Teske, another friend of Alexander's, is also featured, pp. 172–175. The exhibit of Powell's work at the Corcoran is mentioned in a letter to William Alexander, dated April 2, 1935. A letter from Paul to William Alexander, January 13, 1936, mentions a "picture" of him done by "Leslie," whom Alexander identified as Leslie Powell. Paul mentions a picture (possibly a photograph) Leslie Powell did of him in a letter to his friend, Bill, dated January 13, 1936. Prints of pictures shot by Mortensen are mentioned in a letter Paul wrote to his friend Bill, September 8, 1937; also found here is the dig at Alexander's nieces. Here, as in letter on p. 242, "Gene" could refer to Eugene Hoenigsberg, Paul's Brooklyn roommate. See *Brooklyn Eagle*, October 5, 1939.

6. The bust, signed by Farrar, notes "1932" and "Roman Bronze Works." The bronze bust is now in my collection. For a Caravaggio connection see Desmond Seward, *Caravaggio—A Passionate Life* (New York: William Morrow and Company, 1998), quoted opposite page 119.

7. Of MacCown as an artist, poet-critic Robert McAlmon had this to say: "MacCown still paints like whoever may be the chic painter of the moment. Then he was out–Picassoing Picasso, with just what is needed lacking." Kay Boyle and Robert McAlmon, *Being Geniuses Together—1920-1930* (Garden City, New York: Doubleday and Company, 1968), p. 111. Yet see his portrait of Nancy Cunard in *Nancy Cunard: Brave, Poet, Indomitable Rebel 1896-1965*, edited by Hugh Ford (New York: Chilton Book Company, 1968), after p. 170. Cunard remained close to Mac-Cown, who is mentioned frequently in her writings. For example, see *Grand Man–Memories of Norman Douglas* (Secker and Warburg, 1954), pp. 67–69. The quote is from *Grand Man*, p. 140. For further comment see Hugh Ford's introduction to *Negro*, xii, op. cit., n. 21 above. On the mannequin idea see Nicole Parrot, *Mannequins* (Calona, Paris, 1982).

8. Paul's mother, Ione, thought the MacCown portrait of him "not so good." Letter from Paul Mooney to William Alexander, May 25, 1935. Used by permission of Mr. Alexander. Editor and publisher Edouard Roditi (1910–1992), who knew René Crevel and apparently MacCown, thought Mac-Cown "deservedly forgotten even in his native Kansas City." See "Introduction," Rene Crevel, *Putting My Foot in It*, translation by Thomas Buckley with Foreword by Ezra Pound (Dalkey Archive Press, 1992), p. xx. Gay activist Harry Hay, who became romantically involved with Bill Alexander, recalled Eugene MacCown's painting of Paul in his Morton Street apartment in 1941. About this time Alexander had developed an acquaintanceship with Jane and Paul Bowles, friends also of John LaTouche. I made efforts to correspond with Paul Bowles about this part of his life in 1994 and 1995 without result. For the Hay connection see Stuart Timmons, *The Trouble with Harry—Founder of the Modern Gay Movement* (Alyson Publications, Boston, 1990), p. 111. The Mooney bust is in my collection. Regarding the MacCown portrait of Paul, John Scott has insisted that there were several versions.

9. Alexander insisted it was the Barbizon-Plaza, which, incidentally, was near the Dance Center at 105 West 56th Street. Cf. Greg Lawrence, *Dance with Demons: The Life of Jerome Robbins* (New York: G.P. Putnam's Sons, 2001), pp. 16–17. The Barbizon aimed its ads at the "Young Woman," exhorting, "Follow in the footsteps of hundreds of successful career women in New York ... Live at the Barbizon where you're surrounded by cultural and recreational activities that provoke outstanding accomplishment." *Mademoiselle: The Magazine for Smart Young Women*, October 1938, p. 3. The Barbizon Plaza featured a library, art gallery, mezzanine concert hall and "topical talks by eminent contemporaries."

Another hotel, the Plaza, on 59th and Fifth, with its famous Oak Room, might seem a better choice for what occurred that evening. With its appeal to wealth and celebrity, it figures as a setting for stories by F. Scott Fitzgerald and is mentioned in *The Great Gatsby*. Also it "was a familiar trysting place for gays." See George Chauncey, *Gay New York: Gender, Urban Culture, and the Making of the Gay Male World 1890-1940* (New York: BasicBooks, 1994), p. 350. Cf. Eva Brown, *The Plaza—1907-1967: Its Life and Times* (New York: Van Rees Press, 1967), pp. 146–147; pp. 67–68. For the "Oak Room" see p. 138. See also the *Encyclopedia of New York City*, pp. 907–908. Halliburton mentions the Plaza in a letter (cut from published letters), February 4, 1933; I suspect he meant the luxury hotel on 59th off Central Park. See Chauncy, p. 182. For Halliburton's joy in a new house, etc., see *RHL*, p. 342 (quoted).

10. For the lecture on the Taj, other lectures and the movie deal see *RHL*, p. 341. For Salome performance see Amanda Vaill, *Somewhere—The Life of Jerome Robbins* (New York: Broadway Books, 2006), p. 34. Stage productions of *Salome* were many, and were often adapted to taste. Cf. Lawrence, p. 18. Its insistent sensualism was always easier to heat than to cool. The 1906 Met premier in New York of Richard Strauss' *Salome* had "horrified the more conventional who witnessed it by the sensuality of its theme and its presentation," *New York Times*, November 6, 1932, p. 6. A "condensed" version of the opera with

Maria Jeritza and Nelson Eddy under the baton of Fritz Reiner played about the time Alexander saw the performance staged at the Barbizon Plaza (also noted in *New York Times*). Halliburton himself noted that he had seen the provocative Strauss opera at the Metropolitan in New York. See *Seven League Boots* (New York: Bobbs-Merrill, 1935), p. 304 et seq. He may have heard about the scandalous London performance of dancer Maud Allan (1873–1956) which, in 1908, had rocked British society and inspired critics to label her fans the "Cult of the Clitoris" and "Cult of Wilde." See Hoare, supra. Several early screen versions existed. The most famous, produced in 1923, starred Alla Nazimova in the title role. Rudolph Valentino's wife, Natacha Rambova, had designed costumes and sets, based on Aubrey Beardsley's drawings, for an "all-gay" cast production. Michael Morris, *The Many Lives of Natacha Rambova* (New York: Abbeville Press Publishers, 1991), pp. 83–93. Also see Gavin Lambert, *Nazimova* (New York: Alfred A. Knopf, 1997), pp. 255–257.

For the career of Gluck Sandor (1899–1978), and his influence, see Greg Lawrence, *Dance with Demons: The Life of Jerome Robbins*, op. cit., pp. 16–21 et passim. Also see Deborah Jowitt, *Jerome Robbins—His Life, His Theatre, His Dance* (New York: Simon and Schuster, 2004), pp. 16–19; and Vaill, *Somewhere* supra, pp. 29–37. Sandor later became a painter of note. See *Floridian: A Closer Look*, City Citizen, p 13D. For the career of Felicia Sorel (1906?–1972) see *Biographical Index* (New York: H.W. Wilson Co., 1974), 9: September 1970–August 1973. For highlights in the career of Gluck Sandor (died March 11, 1978), see *New York Times*, Section 2, p. 2, c. 3. Also see *Washington Post*, Alan M. Kriegsman, "Dancing on the sunny side: Master Choreographer Jerome Robbins," *Washington Post*, March 4, 1979. Also see "Dancing Through Life—Jerome Robbins in a 'Proustian' mood," in *Newsweek*, March 6, 1989, p. 56, where Gluck Sandor is referred to as a dance guru and early influence on Robbins. Like Alexander, a Russian Jew, Jerome Robbins (1918–1998) was originally Jerome Rabinowitz. For Robbins' life story, see Marian Zailian, "Robbins' Band of Merry Musicals—Broadway Legend's work lights up San Francisco," *San Francisco Chronicle*, Sunday Datebook, August 11, 1991, p. 18. For dancer José Limon (1908–1972), born in Culiacan, Sinaloa, Mexico, of French and Spanish descent, and a touch of Yaqui Indian, see Daniel Lewis, *The Illustrated Dance Technique of Jose Limon* (Harper and Row, Publishers: New York, 1984), p. 13. Also see José Limon, *An Unfinished Memoir*, edited by Lynn Garafola (Wesleyan University Press, 1999). For the Sorel-Sandor link to José Limon see "Controlled Recklessness and Frida Kahlo Images," *New York Times*, November 11, 1995, Section C, p. 13, c. 1. Forbes completed a portrait of Limon, by February 1, 1942, the date of *The Art Digest* where it appeared, a copy of which was among William Alexander's papers. For Halliburton's influence on Limon, see Barbara Pollock and Charles Humphrey Woodford, *Dance Is a Moment: A Portrait of Jose Limon in Words and Pictures* (Pennington, New Jersey: Princeton Book

Company, 1993), pp. 10–11. Also see Lewis, op. cit., pp. 13–14.

11. Recommended is Wayne Koestenbaum's *The Queen's Throat—Opera, Homosexuality, and the Mystery of Desire* (Poseidon Press, New York, 1993), p. 228. Cf. Philip Hoare, "Salomania," *Oscar Wilde's Last Stand*, op. cit., pp. 65–88, notably 83–84. Halliburton or Mooney (perhaps recalling the Gluck Sandor/Felicia Sorel performance) narrates without elaboration the horrific tale of Salome in his *Second Book of Marvels—The Orient* (New York: Bobbs-Merrill, 1938), pp. 114–117. For Jerome Robbins' and José Limon's opinions see Jowitt, op. cit., p. 19.

12. These comments are based on interviews with William Alexander, who also notes the "orgy night" in "Meanderings." Interview (taped), June 1, 1996. Also on Coney Island see Chauncey, *Gay New York*, pp. 210–211. Halliburton himself mentions a "bang-up party" at the Plaza (probably another party than the one mentioned here), January 3, 1934: "about 40 to dinner .... gold plates and six wines" and the ensuing parade of "sixteen Packards [hired by the hostess] to take [himself] and a group of fabulously rich people) to the Russian Ballet" and later to the "Casino in the Central Park, the most expensive night club in New York...," *Letters*, p. 349.

In a questionnaire (done about 1988), Alexander indicated that he did not believe Halliburton's parents knew (or were willing to accept) that their son was gay. He also said that Halliburton's publisher, Bobbs-Merrill, may not have been aware of it.

13. Richard Halliburton, letter, January 23, 1932, omitted from published version. For the fame of Lawrence Tibbett at this time, see *Time*, January 16, 1933; for that of Kathleen Norris, see *Time*, January 28, 1935.

14. For the contents of the *Graphic*, and Bernarr MacFadden (1868–1955), see Robert Ernst, *Weakness Is a Crime—The Life of Bernarr MacFadden* (Syracuse: Syracuse University Press, 1991), pp. 93–101. Also see Mary MacFadden and Emile Gauvreau, *Dumbbells and Carrot Strips—The Story of Bernarr MacFadden*, op. cit., and Clement Wood's *Bernarr MacFadden, A Study in Success* (New York: Beekman Publishers, Inc., 1974). For the gay bias in MacFadden's publications, see George Chauncey, *Gay New York*, op. cit., pp. 323–324. For censorship of MacFadden publications, see *Time*, June 20, 1932, p. 25. For *Liberty* publishing Halliburton's stories, see *JR*, pp. 214 and 236. William Alexander offered the anecdote about Wesley Halliburton's meeting with Leopold DeSola. See *RHL-P*, March 10, 1933, p. 8, for "Leopold de Sola" and his affiliation with MacFadden Publications.

15. Alexander offered a description of the "orgy" that compares with Lucienne Frappier-Mazur's definition, as "a presentation of a *collective* act focusing on excess—be it of sex, of food, or of language—and on confusion: mingling of bodies, hybrid foods (such as fish and fowl), blurring of the line between natural and artificial...." See *Writing the Orgy—Power and Parody in Sade*, translated by Gillian C. Gill (Philadelphia: University of Pennsylvania Press, 1996), pp. 1–2. Also see Brenda Love, *Ency-*

clopedia of Unusual Sex Practices (Greenwich Editions, 2000), pp. 46 and 282. Alexander owned books about the Greeks, and, in our conversations, thought them a brilliant culture partly because they deemed homosexual practices "okay." In general see Eva Cantarella, Bisexuality in the Greek World (New Haven: Yale University, 2002).

16. See RHL-P, November 5, 1932 (quoted). For the house, including pictures of it drawn by Halliburton, see RHL-P, November 13, 1932 (quoted).

17. See RHL-P, November 20, 1932 (quoted). For publication date see JR, p. 212.

Chapter 9

1. See RHL-P, November 20, 1932 (quoted). For the clambake see RHL-P, November 30, 1932.

2. See RHL-P, November 30 (quoted); December 8 and December 11, 1932 (quoted).

3. For book sales, RHL-P, February 4, 1933. For Noel Sullivan see RHL-NS, March 24, 1933 (quoted). Consulted for Noel Sullivan's and Lemuel Sanderson's addresses was the San Francisco Exposition and Bay Counties Telephone Directory, May 1939.

4. See RHL-NS, March 24, 1933 (quoted). For Sullivan's interests, and the parties at Montalvo, see Emily Wortis Leider, California's Daughter—Gertrude Atherton and Her Times (Stanford: Stanford University Press, 1991), pp. 312–313.

5. For India Speaks see JR, 209–210 et passim; cf., JC, pp. 131–136. For Grass see Elizabeth Fagg Olds, "Marguerite Harrison," Women of the Four Winds—The Adventures of Four of America's First Women Explorers (Boston: Houghton Mi-in Company, 1985), pp. 155–230, at p. 226 et passim. Quoted is the lobby poster for India Speaks in my own collection.

6. Cf. JR, pp. 209–210. Also see RHL, p. 345 (for his voice, quoted) and p. 346 (for 2000 people," quoted). Also see RHL-P, November 20, 1932. For the "tropical news tour," see RHL, p. 269 (quoted).

7. For Cecil B. De Mille see JR, p. 134. For Douglas Fairbanks, Sr. see JR, p. 137. Also see RHL, p. 280. For the Baghdad lectures, RHL-P, March 13, 1933.

8. For activities see RHL, p. 344. For the earthquake see RHL, p. 345 (quoted).

9. See RHL-P, November 20 (quoted).

10. See RHL, p. 346; cf. RHL-P, March 24, 1933. Noted is Ellsworth L. Kolb, Through the Grand Canyon from Wyoming to Mexico with a foreword by Owen Wister, a new edition with additional illustrations (76 plates) from photographs by the author and his brother (MacMillan: New York, 1936). I saw reprints of the 1915 edition, which likely Halliburton saw. See also Erna Fergusson, Our Southwest with photographs by Ruth Frank and others (Alfred A. Knopf, New York, 1940). For changes to the landscape compare Elizabeth Compton Hegemann, Navajo Trading Days (Albuquerque: University of New Mexico Press, 1963). Hegemann's photographs and narrative are from about the time Paul and Richard traveled through the region.

11. For other views of the inspiration for the "Royal Road to Romance in America," see RHL, pp. 397–398.

12. Cf. Emily Hahn (1905–1997), Times and Places (Thomas Y. Crowell Company: New York, 1970), pp. 72–73. Consulted also was Motor Annual, specifically, November 1935.

13. Quoted is "Organized Motorist," American Motorist, March 1928, pp. 22–23 and continued on p. 33, at 22. Also consulted was Frank E. Brimmer, "Billions for Scenery," same issue, pp. 9–10 and continued on pp. 30–31. In general see Karl Raitz (ed.), The National Road (Baltimore and London: John Hopkins University, 1996). Also see Michael Wallis, Route 66—The Mother Road (New York: St. Martin's Press, 1990). Transcontinental crossings seemed routine after World War I, though Bill Alexander, on his first trip to the West in 1935, noted the dangers he anticipated. Compare Curt McConnell, Coast to Coast by Automobile—The Pioneering Trips, 1899–1908 (Stanford: Stanford University Press, 2000), p. 307. Also consulted was Alden and Marion Stevens, The Stevens America—A Traveler's Guide to the United States (Boston: Little, Brown, and Company, 1950).

14. For concepts of urban planning and fairs, see David Gelernter, 1939—The Lost World of the Fair (New York: The Free Press, 1995).

15. See RHL-P, January 23, 1932.

16. Consulted for National Bridge was a Souvenir Folder of Natural Bridge, Tichnor Quality Views, Boston Views of Sky-Line Drive, Virginia, Shenandoah National Park, Asheville Postcard Company, Asheville, N.C. Also see RHL, p. 346, and p. 347; cf. RHL-P, July 20, 1933. John M. Scott related the story of his "Uncle Paul's" bewilderment about the cost. For the "colonial tour," see RHL-P, July 20, 1933. For the need to define the project, see RHL-P, June 1, 1933 (quoted) and June 22, 1933. Also see Book of Marvels—The Occident, op. cit., p. 73 et seq. For Halliburton and Paul's family, I am dependent upon the recollections of Paul's nephew, John Scott. In a letter to the author, dated June 21, 2002, Scott indicated that Paul's family had no qualms about his homosexuality.

17. For Leopold Dacelo (or DeSola) and Halliburton's joining the YMCA in New York, see RHL-P, May 23, 1933. In areas noted as gay, such YMCA locations as may have appealed to him included Sloane House on W. 34th, and the West Side Y on 63rd at Central Park. Cf. George Chauncey, supra, pp. 155–157.

18. Views in text reflect those in Robert Carter, "Boys Going Nowhere," The Strenuous Decade: A Social and Intellectual Record of the Nineteen Thirties, edited by Daniel Aaron and Robert Bendiner (Garden City, New York: Anchor Books, Doubleday & Company, Inc., 1970), pp. 44–52, quoted at p. 44.

19. Kenneth C. Davis, Don't Know Much About History—Everything You Need to Know about American History but Never Learned (New York: HarperCollins, 2003), p. 346 (quoted). (20) Louis-Ferdinand Celine's Journey to the End of Night (1932) was translated into English in 1934; Death on the Installment Plan (1936) was translated into En-

glish in 1938. Compare Halliburton's world view as interpreted by Jonathan Root, p. 216.

Chapter 10

1. For the sampling of activities in 1933 see *RHL*, pp. 344–347, quoted at p. 346. Also see *RHL-P*: Gavin (April 4), Pulitzer (May 1), Walter Futter (May 18), Memphis trip (June 1), Fox (June 13), Roosevelt (June 13) [quoted], Lowell Thomas and Boy Scouts (April 23), parents to Europe (January 9).

2. For the Chicago trip see *RHL*, p. 347. Also see *RHL-P*, July 20, 1933 (Leo and his friend) and September 1, 1933.

3. For the Columbian Exposition, see Forrest Wilson, "It Seems Only Yesterday ... The Great World's Fair of 1893," *Cosmopolitan*, July, 1933, pp. 26–27, 157–160 (quoted at pp. 26 and 27).

4. For the 1933 "Century of Progress World's Fair," see the *Official Guide—Book of the Fair–1933*, op. cit. For the theme of the fair, see p. 11. The Fair officially opened on May 27 and the initial season ended on November 1, 1933. See p. 8. Cf. Emmett Dedman, *Fabulous Chicago* (New York: Random House, 1953), pp. 333–334. See in general Allen Weller, "Lorado Taft, the Ferguson Fund, and the Advent of Modernism," *The Old Guard and the Avant Guard Modernism in Chicago–1910-1940*, edited by Sue Ann Prince (Chicago: University of Chicago Press, 1990), pp. 39–57, at 46. For Robert Ripley's participation see Bob Considine, *Ripley–The Modern Marco Polo* (Garden City, New York: Doubleday & Company, 1961), pp. 140–142. Ripley's "Odditorium" was also featured at the San Francisco Exposition in 1939.

5. For more about World's Fairs see Burton Benedict et al., *The Anthropology of World's Fairs—San Francisco's Panama Pacific International Exposition of 1915* (London and New York: Lowrie Museum of Anthropology and Scolar Press, 1983), quoting Marcel Mauss *The Gift*, 1925 reprint edition (Glencoe, Illinois: The Free Press, 1959), p. 123. Also see Arnold Lewis, *An Early Encounter with Tomorrow—Europeans, Chicago's Loop, and the World's Columbian Exposition* (Urbana and Chicago: University of Illinois Press, 1997), pp. 167–194.

6. Paul's attitude towards technology was ambivalent. While he could marvel at skyscrapers and suspension bridges, he could wonder, as Jeffers, if "tamed nature" meant "dehumanized man."

7. Cf. Dedman, *Fabulous Chicago*, op. cit., pp. 336–337. Mary Louise "Texas" Guinan had a movie career which extended from *The Gun Woman* (1918) to *Broadway through a Keyhole* (1933); *Queen of the Night Clubs* (1929) seems her most aptly-titled role. See *Halliwell's Filmgoer's and Video Viewer's Companion*, edited by John Walker (HarperCollins, 1993, p. 343. According to Alexander, Texas Guinan was actually at the Fair when he was there, interview, April 6, 1997. Guinan toured the country in 1933 in a revue called *Too Hot for Paris* and performed at the

Chicago Century of Progress World's Fair. Confirmation of her owning or operating a restaurant there at the time of this writing is lacking. See Gilbert Maxwell *Helen Morgan—Her Life and Legend* (New York: Hawthorn Books, Inc., 1963), p. 163. For Guinan's career, see Traub, op. cit., pp. 71–77. Incidentally, Halliburton nemesis Burton Holmes photographed the Fair. See *The Man Who Photographed the World*, pp. 296–297.

8. See "Sven Hedin," *The Chinese Lama Temple—Potala of Jehol*, exhibition and ethnographical collections made by Dr. Gosta Montell, member of Dr. Sven Hedin's expeditions and donated by Vincent Bendix (A Century of Progress Exposition, Chicago: Chicago Lakeside Press, R.R. Donnelley & Sons Co., 1932), pp. 8–12, 13.

9. For information about Paul's stay in Chicago, I am indebted to John Scott, letter, August 30, 2003. For the photograph of Alexander (then Levy but unnamed) see title page, *Official Pictures*, photographs by Kaufmann and Fabry Co. (The Reuben H. Donnelly Corporation, 1933), probably the commonest of publications related to the Fair. Alexander emphasized his Jewishness more and more as he got older. Years later, as he recalled the Fair, he made it seem that he was the only Jewish person who attended it. Yet Jewish Day celebrations occurred; at one Chaim Weizmann, to become in 1948 the first president of Israel, was present, speaking on July 3, 1933. Programs containing lists of members belonging to Jewish support groups along with forums aimed at Jewish unity were issued, one for Jewish Day at A Century of Progress, July 3, 1933, "The Romance of a People," another for Jewish Day at A Century of Progress, July 27, 1934, "The Epic of a People," both, apparently, by R.H. Stone. For Sally Rand at this time see Studs Terkel, *Hard Times* (New York: The New Press, 2000), pp. 168–174.

10. Alexander (who incidentally never received a license to practice architecture in New York) is not mentioned in any published work of Wright's which I consulted. The "fireplace" Alexander said he helped build is pictured in Edgar Tafel, *Apprentice to Genius—Years with Frank Lloyd Wright* (New York: McGraw-Hill, Inc., 1979), pp. 112–113. In general see Edgar Tafel, *About Wright—An Album of Recollections by Those Who Knew Frank Lloyd Wright* (New York: John Wiley and Sons, 1993). The "Apprentices in Residence" program began in October 1932. Cf. Curtis Besinger, *Working with Mr. Wright: What It Was Like* (Cambridge: Cambridge University Press, 1995), p. 2. In general see Meryle Secrest, *Frank Lloyd Wright: A Biography* (New York: Alfred A. Knopf, 1992). Letters from the Wright Fellowship and Wright apprentice Edgar Tafel to Alexander date from November 4, 1933 and January 26, 1934, and are in my collection. There is also the draft of a letter, dated January, 1934, from Alexander to "Mr. Wright" which begins, "You may remember that I met you last summer at Taliesin, where I had hitch-hiked from New York, and where I secured an introduction to you through Edgar Tafel and Yen L'iang."

11. Fort Schuyler, established in 1856 and first garrisoned in January 17, 1861, when the Civil War commenced, was last garrisoned in 1934. Cf. Robert B. Roberts, *The Encyclopedia of Historic Forts—The Military, Pioneer, and Trading Posts of the United States* (New York: Macmillan Publishing Company, 1988), p. 579.

Chapter 11

1. For the Syndicate deal see *RHL-NS*, April 27 or 28, 1935 (quoted); also, *RHL*, p. 349. Also see Michael Blankenship, "A Fellow Traveler," op. cit., p. 43; cf. *JC*, p. 138. Quote is from the dust jacket of *Seven League Boots* (Garden City, New York: Garden City Publishing Company, 1935).

2. Later, with the two *Books of Marvels*, Mooney would again assist, though Halliburton would redo material that to him seemed *too* Mooney and *not enough* Halliburton. Cf. Blankenship, supra, p. 43. For cuts to the books, *PML-WA*, June 23, 1935. The "little gem" cut from the Romanoff story (I suspect) was anti–Semitism, as it overplayed the point that the assassins of the Czar's family were Jews. Paul thought it a "largely careless habit on Dick's part rather than maliciousness." Also see 271n9.

3. See "Straight Talk from Russia," *Seven League Boots*, op. cit., pp. 189–190 (quoted). Compare *RHL*, pp. 358–362.

4. Cf. *JC*, p. 143.

5. Halliburton lectured in the Washington area, and Paul may have accompanied him. Though little is devoted to this period in the published letters (*RHL*, pp. 374–375), among Halliburton's personal appearances was one at the Woodward and Lothrop department store, in Washington, D.C., in December, as an ad from the period indicates. Paul's letters usually bear a return address. Research into the "Cather" address, however, produced no solid leads. Willa Cather (1862–1947), born a year after James Mooney, had strong Nebraska connections, as did Mooney. For a time, in the 1880s, she lived in Red Cloud, Nebraska (named after Chief Red Cloud of the Oglala Tribe) and later attended the University of Nebraska in Lincoln. See James Woodress, "Red Cloud," *Willa Cather, A Literary Life* (Lincoln and London: University of Nebraska Press, 1987), pp. 44–63).

6. Originally from Richard, Virginia, John Treville Latouche, after winning a writing contest at age sixteen or so, arrived in New York in 1932 and for a time he attended Columbia University. A couple photographs, given to me by William Alexander for this research, show Latouche at the Chelsea; they are undated. A short biography of Latouche by Erik Haagensen appears on the Web at www.babydoe.org/latouche.htm. See mention of "Touche" in Virgil Thomson, *Selected Letters*, op. cit., p. 127. On John LaTouche and his circle of friends, which included composer Aaron Copland, see Christopher Sawyer-Laucanno, *An Invisible Spec-*

tator—A Biography of Paul Bowles (New York: Weidenfeld & Nicolson, 1989), pp. 153, 166–167, 181, and 205–208. Among others, LaTouche was a lyricist for Duke Ellington. For the Chelsea Hotel see Kathleen Hoover and John Cage, *Virgil Thomson*, op. cit., p. 111. Letter, 1935, from Paul Mooney to William Alexander from the Vanderbilt Hotel in New York.

7. Paul mentioned his mother's illness in letters to Alexander dated "Wednesday," probably March 1935 and "Sunday,"April 2, 1935. Anton Levandovsky clarified matters of locale. Letter to author, July 3, 2003.

8. *PML-WA*, (month uncertain), 1935.

9. Lenox had an art gallery which decades later exhibited abstract paintings by Paul's friend Leslie Powell who, by the 1960s was known to some as a "(Greenwich) Village painter." See Leslie Powell, op. cit., p. 13. For Paul's first mention of "Lenox," *PML-WA*, October 5, 1934. For "Lenox, Massachusetts," see Sarah Bird Wright, *Edith Wharton A to Z: The Essential Guide to the Life and Work* (New York: Facts on File, 1998), p. 151; for "The Mount" see pp. 172–175.

10. *PML-WA*, June 3, 1935 (quoted).

11. See Dell, *Homecoming*, op. cit., p. 251 (quoted). Consulted for *Waiting for Lefty—A Play in Six Scenes* was Richard Pack, "The Censors See Red," *New Theatre*, Herbert Kline, Editor, May 1935, *New Theatre*, pp. 5–7. Also consulted was *New Theatre*, February 1935, which contains the text of the play, pp. 13–20.

12. See Bodenheim, op. cit., p. 230 (quoted). *The Sleepwalkers*, probably the first American edition (1932), was among those in Paul's library. Letter from John Scott to author, April 29, 2003.

13. See Stuart Timmons, *The Trouble with Harry* (Boston: Alyson Publications, 1990), p. 112. For Dmitri Shostakovich see liner notes to *5th Symphony*, Leonard Bernstein—New York Philharmonic (1959), Great Performances, CBS Records, CD MYK 37218, pp. 4–5.

14. For immigrant communities in New York, see Stanley Nadel, *Little Germany—Ethnicity, Religion, and Class in New York City 1945-80* (University of Illinois Press, Urbana and Chicago, 1990), p. 6. Regarding some perceptions of FDR see Elizabeth Dilling, *The Roosevelt Red Record and its Background* (Kenilworth, Illinois: Self-published, 1936).

15. Alexander's political views, which he claimed were also those of Paul, appear scattered in his notes for an autobiography.

16. For Will Rogers' opinion on the Union of Soviet Socialist Republics, see Richard M. Ketchum, *Will Rogers—The Man and His Times* (New York: American Heritage Books, 1973), op. cit., pp. 344–345, 347–348 et passim.

17. Stuart Timmons, supra, pp. 59–60. Hay (1914–2002) reported to his biographer that he had "two or three affairs a day between 1932 and 1936," p. 63. Hay said he never had an affair with Paul, but found him attractive. For Hay's opinions in general, see Harry Hay, *Radically Gay—Gay Liberation in the Words of its Founder*, edited by Will Roscoe (Boston: Beacon Press, 1996). For Wiltshire Boulevard in the

present context see Mann, *William Haines*, p. 83. Also see Henry ("Harry") Hay, Jr. in Robert Aldrich, *Who's Who in Gay and Lesbian History*, op. cit., pp. 181–183. Under the name Donald Webster Cory, Hay wrote *The Homosexual in America* in 1951 and later the gay manifesto "The Call." See "Harry Hay, Early Proponent of Gay Rights, Dies at 90," *The New York Times*, Obituaries, Friday, October 25, 2002, A33. Also consulted was Steve Hogan and Lee Hudson, *Completely Queer—The Gay and Lesbian Encyclopedia* (New York: Henry Holt & Company, 1998), pp. 273–274.

18. Cf. Timmons, supra, p. 59.

19. For the Hirschfeld Institute, see Christopher Isherwood, *Christopher and His Kind 1929-1939* (New York: Farrar, Straus and Giroux, 1976; North Point Press paperback printing, 1996), pp. 14–19; on Paragraph 175 of the German Criminal Code, see p. 17. The questions Sinclair Lewis's *It Can't Happen Here* are quoted from a later paperback edition cover (New York: Triangle Books, 1939).

20. See Jack London, "How I Became A Socialist," and "What Life Means to Me," *The Portable Jack London*, edited by Earle Labor (New York: Penguin Books, 1994), pp. 458–461 and pp. 475–482. Quoted are p. 460 and p. 482. The photographs, from 1934, are in author's collection.

21. See Mary McCarthy, *Intellectual Memoirs—New York 1936-1938* with a foreword by Elizabeth Hardwick (New York: Harcourt Brace, 1993), pp. 1–2.

Chapter 12

1. A letter, dated February 27, 1935, notes that a "final editing" would precede Scribners' accepting the Ludecke manuscript, which suggests the project may have begun as early as 1934, even earlier. For Paul's fiances at the time, *PML-WA*, January 13, 1936.

2. See *RHL*, p. 257 (quoted).

3. Cf. Lothar Machtan, *The Hidden Hitler*, translated by John Brownjohn with notes translation by Susanne Ehlert (New York: Basic Books, c2001), p. 298. In general see Paul Maracin, *Night of the Long Knives: 48 Hours That Changed the History of the World* (New York: The Lyons Press, 2004). *Night of the Long Knives*, based on Paul Maracin's book, is also available on DVD from the History Channel, AAE-76829.

4. The full title of the 833-page book, with index and appendix, attributed to Kurt G.W. Ludecke, is *I Knew Hitler: The Story of a Nazi Who Escaped the Blood Purge*. That Kurt G.W. Ludecke (1890–1960) was also "Winfried Ludecke," author of *Secrets of Espionage—Tales of the Secret Service* (Philadelphia: J.P. Lippincott Company, 1929), is a possibility. Because espionage was the subject, the author's full identity was withheld, and the book's first readers were left to wonder who "Winfried Ludecke" really was. In the index to *I Knew Hitler* are

the names Gustav Adolf Hermann Ludecke and Hugo Emil Ludecke. The latter was an "International Spy." Both were said to be "confused with [the] author," but no "Winifred Ludecke" is mentioned, p. 811. The confusion with Hugo Emil Ludecke, Kurt Ludecke notes himself, p. 203. William L. Shirer refers to Kurt as "Karl," a "henchman" of Hitler's in the text of his *The Rise and Fall of the Third Reich—A History of Nazi Germany* (Greenwich, Conn.: Fawcett Publications, 1959), p. 170. A possible relative of Kurt G.W. Ludecke was Martin Ludecke, middle-weight wrestling champion of Central America in the 1920s. Mention of him is made in Earle Liederman (also the publisher), *The Science of Wrestling and the Art of Jiu-Jitsu* (1923), p. 223. For Kurt Ludecke's own background, see *I Knew Hitler*, pp. 292–294 et passim, quoted, p. 291 and p. 292. Also see Max Wallace, *The American Axis: Henry Ford, Charles Lindbergh and the Rise of the Third Reich* (New York: St. Martin's Press. 2003), pp. 49–50, 51–52, 64, and 126. Also see Machtan, supra, pp. 266–273. For his meeting celebrities, see *I Knew Hitler*, p. 294.

5. See Ludecke, *I Knew Hitler*, p. 311 (marriage to Mildred), p. 330 (move to Brookline), p. 328 (pro–Nazi cells), p. 329 (Count Luckner), p. 192 et seq. (Henry Ford), and pp. 191–194 (for Siegfried and Winifrid Wagner and sons). Compare Jonathan R. Logsdon, "Power, Ignorance, and Anti-Semitism: Henry Ford and His War on the Jews," *The Hanover Historical Review* 1999, Part Four, pp. 1–1, Ludecke, at pp. 2–3, paper, www.stockmasven.com/logsdon 99_.htm. For Ford's anti–Semitism, see Neil Baldwin, *Henry Ford and The Jews*, op. cit., and quoted characterization of Ludecke, see p. 182. Much of the Ford material in *I Knew Hitler* appears in a chapter cleverly entitled "Anti-Semitism: Motel T," pp. 191–218. For additional material on Von Luckner see Anthony G. Flude, http://homepages.ihug,co.nz/~tonyf/von/VonLuckner.html, 2001. Also see Lowell Thomas, *Count Luckner—The Sea Devil* (New York: Doubleday, Doran and Company, 1928).

6. Ibid., *I Knew Hitler*, dust jacket.

7. Ibid., *I Knew Hitler*, dust jacket. For the book itself see Machtan, supra, pp. 297–299.

8. Ibid., *I Knew Hitler*, dust jacket.

9. Ibid., *I Knew Hitler*, pp. 303–304.

10. Ibid., *I Knew Hitler*, p. 197 (quoted) et seq. Ludecke is pictured at the typewriter, in Neil Baldwin, op. cit, p. 183.

11. Ibid., *I Knew Hitler*, pp. 191–194 and 313–315 et passim; also see n. 5 above.

12. Ibid., *I Knew Hitler*, pp. 293–294 (quoted).

13. Ibid., *I Knew Hitler*, pp. 296–297 (quoted).

14. Ibid., *I Knew Hitler*, pp. 296–297 (quoted).

15. For Ludecke studying Indian life, see *I Knew Hitler*, p. 298.

16. *I Knew Hitler*, supra, p. 209 (quoted). For the book's authorship see Michael Blankenship, "A Fellow Traveler,"op. cit., p. 42.

17. Ibid., *I Knew Hitler*, p. 209 (quoted). For Ludecke preparing a manuscript see p. 298.

18. Paul's letters on this issue are dated February 27, 1935, June 23, 1935 and January 13, 1936 (quoted).

19. See *I Knew Hitler*, p. 523 (quoted).

20. Ibid., *I Knew Hitler*, p. 297.

21. For the Bach concert from Berlin, *PML-WA*, April 2, 1935 For Protestant fundamentalist preacher John Roach Straton (1875–1929) *PML-WA*, January 13, 1936. Through his radio broadcasts, Straton "denounced the moral revolution of the 1920s as the fruit of religious liberalism," *The Encyclopedia of New York City*, op. cit., p. 1127 (quoted).

22. *PML-WA*, May 25, 1935.

23. Ibid., May 25, 1935. For Halliburton's whereabouts at the time see *RHL*, pp. 366–369.

24. Ibid., May 25, 1935. For "Communists," *PML-WA*, June 3, 1935. "Us" refers to Paul himself and Francis "Fanny" Wellman, a female roving buddy of Mooney's at this time. An earlier "Lenox" letter, which mentions Wellman, is dated October 5, 1934. For financial straits, *PML-WA*, May 25, 1935.

25. *I Knew Hitler*, the dust jacket (quoted). For the rejected citizen application see *Time*, "People," December 18, 1939, p. 53 (quoted).

26. Ibid., *I Knew Hitler*, p. 91 (quoted). Another fine thumbnail sketch is of Gregor Strasser, p. 244. Cf. Anthony Read, *The Devil's Disciples—Hitler's Inner Circle*. (New York and London: W.W. Norton & Company, 2003), p. 115.

Chapter 13

1. For Halliburton's first murmurings of the "junk idea" see *RHL*, July 14, 1936, p. 381 (quoted). Also see *RHL-P*, May 15, 1937 for "junk idea." For the pre–Columbian commerce between China and Mexico, see *RHL*, p. 398 (quoted); also see p. 404 (quoted). For Dr. Margaret Chung, about whom more will be given later, see Gertrude Atherton, *My San Francisco—A Wayward Biography* (Indianapolis and New York: Bobbs-Merrill, 1946), pp. 272–277. For the 1407 Montgomery Address, see *RHL*, pp. 381–382. Near Coit Tower, the 1407 Montgomery Street building, built in 1870, still stands, and offers matchless views of the Bay, with views of Treasure Island a short walk away. Renovated since the 1930s, it is now condominiums. For another view of the origins of the *Sea Dragon* idea see *JC*, p. 150. Members of the Bohemian Grove might have told Halliburton, as an added source of inspiration, about rover Jack London who, thirty years before, had built a yacht called the *Snark* to sail around the world. See Daniel Dyer, *Jack London—A Biography* (New York: Scholastic Press, 1997), p. 467 et seq.

2. Consulted was *Ivanhoe—A Grove Play* by Charles G. Norris (San Francisco: Bohemian Club, 1936), signed by members of the cast and "Dick Halliburton, August 1936," in author's collection. Often he attended Bohemian Grove with friend Noel Sullivan and less so with pianist Henri Deering (who also signed said copy). See *RHL*, p. 382 and p. 386 (December 4, 1936).

3. *RHL-P*, November 3, 1936 (quoted); also,

RHL, p. 386. For soaring property values, *PML-WA*, February 27, 1936.

4. For hiring Alexander see *JC*; quoted at length is Richard's October 15, 1936 letter to his mother about building operations, pp. 151–152. In "Meanderings" Alexander indicates that Paul persuaded the anti–Semitic Halliburton to accept Bill as his designer and builder, noting "Jeremiah Disproved: or, How Levy Got the Job! Good!" For the Novarro house see Ellenberger, *Ramon Novarro*, op. cit., pp. 98–99; house is pictured on p. 98. Transcripts obtained by permission of Alexander from NYU indicate that he graduated in 1934. A letter Alexander received from the State Education Department, Albany, New York, addressed to Alexander Levy, 672 Parkway, Brooklyn, New York, and dated October 3, 1936, indicates that he had failed the examination. The letter noted that he could retake the examination on January 26 or January 27, 1937. Further investigation, including a telephone inquiry, confirmed that no Alexander Levy or William Alexander had received a license to practice architecture in the state of New York, and further explained that to do so would have been illegal. For agent bookings, see, for instance, *RHL-P*, June 25, 1938.

5. For the lecture agents see *RHL-P*, April 3, 1937, January 10, 1937, March 6, 1937 and April 18, 1937 (also notes Halliburton in Laguna, then San Francisco). For "house finances" and Paul's house management, see *RHL-P*, January 10, 1937. Prominently signed by Paul Mooney as the owner, the original deed for the Halliburton House was shown to me by William Alexander.

6. Pertinent letters are dated February 27, 1936 (quoted), and, January 13, 1936, *PML-WA*.

7. *PML-WA*, February 27, 1935. Compare Halliburton: "three hundred houses have gone up along the coast just below me, and a real estate combine is putting half a million dollars into the valley below." For the text see *JC*, pp. 151–153; *RHL* omits this information, pp. 383–384.

8. A letter, dated 1935, mentions the *Cosmopolitan* money and applying it to the cost of the house. For the surveyors, *PML-WA*, February 27, 1936 (quoted).

9. *PML-WA*, May 30, 1936, from Hollywood-Roosevelt Hotel. Alexander's business address appears on the reverse of an interior photograph of Hangover House. For the "tedium" of such a cross-country trip, *PML-WA*, February 27, 1936. For a view of the Dust Bowl, see Vance Johnson, *Heaven's Tableland—The Dust Bowl Story* (New York: Farrar, Straus and Company, 1947), p. 11.

10. Alexander recounts the trip in "Meanderings." Alexander recollected these first impressions of the West Coast in conversations with the author.

11. *PML-WA*, February 27, 1936.

12. Recounted in "Meanderings," and expanded in several conversations. For Major Powell and the Grand Canyon see Richard Halliburton, *The Book of Marvels—Occident*, pp. 34–36. Also see Corle, op. cit. (note 25), pp. 259–260.

13. Recounted in "Meanderings."

14. Quoted is a document from "Meanderings,"

dated October 16, 1936. Alexander identified it as his writing, though it is not typical of him to refer to himself in the third person.

15. Theses views are based on conversations with William Alexander, who used the phrase "men hungry for work." Together Alexander and the author visited Hangover House and the Laguna Beach community; part of the interview was taped for Rhodes College Halliburton Collection. In general see David Wyatt, *Five Fires—Race, Catastrophe, and the Shaping of California* (Menlo Park, California: Addison-Wesley Publishing Company, 1997), pp. 191–195. For Joe Lucas and Eiler Larsen (died in 1976), see *Who's Cooking in Laguna Beach*, compiled and annotated by Arlene Isaacs (Laguna Beach, California: Sun Box Press, 1980), pp. xvii–xviii. Also see Merle and Mabel Ramey, *First 100 Years in Laguna Beach 1876-1976* (Laguna Beach, California: Hastie Printers, 1976), p. 42 et passim. Bill Alexander, in "Meanderings," notes, "Paul and I would meet the newswriters and personalities who were Laguna's 'fixtures'—Poncho Barnes [and] ... the Danish greeter, bearded and reaching out at the bend of Center Street...."

16. This construction is based on conversations with William Alexander. For the place, the view, and the telephone number, PML-WA, June 23, 1935. Halliburton mentions that Paul and Alexander later moved into the house ("just camping") in a letter dated May 30, 1937 as he prepared for the lecture circuit, here en route from Vancouver to Banff, RHL-P, May 30, 1937. Their "camping out in the living room" is again noted in a letter dated June 12, 1937. Adds Halliburton, "Once I get there in July I'll make it homelike." Halliburton spent his first night there on August 18; though "completely empty," he found it "beautiful and satisfying even so," RHL-P, August 19, 1937. Pictures of Trapani, one of which shows him on the Hangover House site, are among the Mooney materials in author's collection.

17. For Toto Le Grand and Ramon Novarro see William J. Mann, *Behind the Screen—How Gays and Lesbians Shaped Hollywood 1910-1969* (New York: Penguin Books, 2001), pp. 96–97.

18. Paul quotes a letter from Halliburton in his own letter to Alexander, PML-WA, no date, but assigned by Alexander "1935." Halliburton's letters attest to Halliburton's hectic schedule, and often, his "voice was hoarse, after a strenuous week, and the travel killing." See RHL, p. 387, March 3, 1937. "Still stuck in New York," RHL-P, January 10, 1937. When he edited his son's letters, Wesley omitted as too dull to list all mention of his son's reported lecture stops. See, for instance, RHL-P, May 4, 1938. His "screen test" (now presumed lost) for "some adventure picture" never resulted in a movie contract; his enthusiasm for any such project fizzled in the congestion of his other activities. See RHL-P, October 6, 1937. Also see November 21, 1937. For the two *Books of Marvels* see RHL, pp. 287–293, January 21–October 17, 1937.

19. RHL, p. 376 (January 26, 1936).

20. For the San Francisco excursions, PML-WA, November, 1936. For "Tim Powers," PML-WA, Jan-

uary 13, 1936. Cliff House or the Legion of Honor seem other likely places where the photographs were shot, though the terrain and view better fit the Marin side.

21. For the art shows, PML-WA, September 26, 1937. "Meanderings" also mentions the Art Festival.

Chapter 14

1. Alexander told me that ill feelings between Paul and himself were reckless gossip and unfounded. Paul of course confessed that he was "temperamental as hell." See JC, p. 160. For the delays, WA-RH, February 22, 1937; "since [during this time] nothing could be accomplished," Paul and Alexander "went to see 'Frisco,—and the GOLDEN GATE." For rain delays, etc., RHL-P, March 6, 1937. For the "exasperating delays," RHL-P, April 3, 1937.

2. David Greggory's "Adventures of Richard Halliburton of Hangover House," op. cit. (quoted).

3. Alexander compared Paul with James Dean during our conversations.

4. See RHL-P, October 6, 1937.

5. In "Meanderings." For the division of labor and Paul's supervising see JC, p. 153.

6. In "Meanderings."

7. In "Meanderings" Alexander recounted the building of the house. The photographs of the workers were retrieved by the author. For changing contractors, William Alexander to Richard Halliburton, March 14, 1937. This letter also notes that Paul was busy putting together pictures of the work being done to send to Richard.

8. In "Meanderings."

9. The copy in question of *The Architectural Record* (October 1938) was given to me by William Alexander. Before delivering a lecture to a group of 3000 Jews in Chicago, Halliburton, a master of prudent omission, was asked that he not mention the death of the Russian Czar and his family because "everybody knows the assassins were Jews," RHL-P, October 29, 1937. For "Jewish audiences ahead," RHL-P, October 17, 1937. For a lecture before 500 Jewish women, "probably the richest group on earth," see RHL, p. 348.

10. WA-RH, January 26, 1937 (quoted). Also, RH-WA, June 30, 1937. For costs, WA-RH, January 26, 1937 and March 30, 1938.

11. Ibid., WA-RH, March 30, 1930.

12. Alexander's threat to walk off the job is noted in a postscript to a letter, RH-WA, June 30, 1937.

13. For Alexander keeping his client informed, RHL-P, March 6, 1937. For his wish to have Halliburton on hand, February 21, 1938. For Paul's wish to have Richard supervise, PML-WA, August 30, 1937. See January 10, 1937; also see RHL-P, August 30, 1937. For Paul continuing to supervise through winter, RHL-P, October 6, 1937.

14. For Halliburton's appraisal of Alexander and "house talk," RHL-P, April 18, 1937 (quoted). For

the other quoted materials, *RH-WA*, April 27, 1937, and *WA-RH*, May 9, 1937 (for "tetanus injections").

15. Cf. Timmons, supra, p. 62. *PML-WA*, "1935," but probably later. *PML-WA*, May 25, 1935 (quoted).

16. In "Meanderings" Alexander refers to the bar as "Mona's." Built in the 1920s by artist R. Clarkson Colman as his home and studio, the largest ever built in Laguna, it was later sold to another artist named Riddell and eventually to Mona Harris, who called it Mona's Studio Club. For Bing Crosby at the White House, see Isaacs, op. cit., p. xvii. Paul's popularity in the Laguna Beach community is noted in a letter written by real estate agent Alice M. Padgett. See *JC*, p. 168. For the art controversy and reference to himself as a "Lagunan," see PML-WA, September 8, 1937, which also clarifies Paul's brush with the law: "Grant Plumb spent a night in my old room at the jail—drunken driving," Paul wrote to Bill Alexander, "Bill Daniels the week before. Each got a far more severe fine & punishment than I did, so perhaps my priority was an advantage."

17. The "controversy about Airt" (sic) sprang from an editorial Paul wrote for the *Laguna Herald* in which he supposedly criticized the art work of one of its prominent citizens. A "mess" of a public relations nature resulted. The *Laguna Herald*, located at 264 Forest Avenue, no longer exists, and I have been unable to track down copies, let alone this particular copy, so the nature of the "mess" remains a mystery. Alexander himself remembered it having to do with the semi-clad discus thrower at the Laguna Art Fair. For the Tom Lewis incident, *PML-WA*, September 26, 1937.

18. For clashes between Paul and Bill Alexander see *JR*, p. 256 (quoted). Alexander later claimed they were exaggerated. For Paul's responsibilities including securing bank loans, PML-WA, September 26, 1937. For plumbing and electrical work, William Alexander to Richard Halliburton (citing Paul's requests), February 14, 1937.

19. *PML-WA*, September 8, 1937 (quoted).

20. The "gallery" connected the three bedrooms. The original glass bricks that make up the wall remain, *PML-WA*, November, Thursday, 1936. For furniture and inlays Halliburton brought in a "furniture-maker." On the back of a photograph of Halliburton's bedroom, the furniture maker is noted as Warren Sparks, *RHL-P*, June 25, 1938. For the flowers, *PML-WA*, "1937." The movies Paul and Richard attended are worth noting. Of films starring Clark Gable, *Mutiny on the Bounty* (1935) and *Test Pilot* (1938) would have appealed to Paul. See Warren G. Harris, *Clark Gable* (New York: Harmony Books, 2002) for both films. That Halliburton was a regular movie-goer is unclear from his letters. "Everyone says one of the characters [in *The Moon's Our Home* (1936), based on the Faith Baldwin novel, and starring Henry Fonda and Margaret Sullivan] is supposed to be me," he wrote, but whether he went to see the movie to discover for himself if this was so is not certain, *RHL-P*, May 13, 1936. Almost certainly, though, he and Paul saw the play version of *Victoria Regina* starring Helen Hayes and new talent Vincent Price. Halliburton notes that "we" went to see *Victoria Regina*,

and so on; I am presuming he meant Paul, though it could have been his friend "Noel" Sullivan. I suspect Halliburton saw *The Affairs of Cellini* (1934), a chuckler, starring Fredric March and Constance Bennett; he knew United Artists was filming it. See *RHL*, p. 351. RHL-P, October 11, 1936.

21. *PML-WA*, September 26, 1937 (quoted).

22. *PML-WA*, September 26, 1937.

23. Cf. *JR*, pp. 21–23 and 32–33. Also see *JC*, p. 152 and p. 133. For the "garden" see *RHL*, September 26, 1937, p. 392. Also see Halliburton letter to his mother Nelle, *JC*, pp. 151–152. See Nelle Halliburton's letter to her son Richard, *JC*, p. 159. For his intentions with the house, *RHL-P*, November 3–4, 1936, and November 27, 1936. As it takes form, the house's romantic and economic appeal join in Halliburton. For Laguna as a "boom town," *RHL-P*, November 27, 1936. For Halliburton's thoughts on the house's value, *RHL-P*, April 27, 1937 (quoted). For the relation between the marketability of the house and a road, *RHL-P*, October 6, 1937.

24. For Alexander's tours, see "Meanderings." For Halliburton's tour, *RHL-P*, August 17, 1937. Glenn Frank (1887–1940) had lately stepped down as president of the University of Wisconsin. He was, importantly, editor-in-chief of the University of Knowledge Incorporated (Chicago), and, in 1938, he would publish *Wonders of Modern Industry—The Story of the Machine Age*, which he co-edited with William Norman Mitchell. For Halliburton's view on visitors, *RHL-P*, September 4, 1937; for visitors distracting workers, April 18, 1937.

25. For party lines, *PML-WA*, "1937."

26. For Carrie Jacobs Bond's visit, *RHL-P*, October 17, 1937.

27. Alexander believed that the character of Howard Roark was modeled after himself, not after Frank Lloyd Wright. See in general "Orange County" Section, *Los Angeles Times*, September 3. 1989, p. 1 and 6. The published writings of Ayn Rand say nothing of a visit to Hangover House, though William Alexander insisted it was so. "Twenty places in the book are me!" he exclaimed to me. He called Rand "the gal who wrote the book about me—all about me. [She] used all the information I gave her in the two hour session in the house." He also insisted that the house appears in *The Fountainhead*. If so the Heller House (not the Enright House), of concrete, at "the top of a cliff where the steel hulk ... rose into a blue sky" and where "the great mats of the terraces hung over the silver sheet of water quivering far below," offers the closest match (I: 11, pp. 125–126, et seq.) From 1937 into 1938, Rand worked as a secretary in the architectural office of Ely Jacques Kahn to acquaint herself with the profession, and found in Kahn the anti–Roark antagonist Guy Francon. See *The Journals of Ayn Rand*, edited by David Harriman (New York: Dutton, Penguin Putnam, 1997), p. 143. William Alexander, Kahn's student at NYU, considered Kahn passé and resistant to new ideas. Rand considered Raymond Hood (1883–1934), also Alexander's teacher, a "prophet" and agreed with others that he was "the foremost modern architect in America."

Journals, p. 151. Also see pp. 149, 152 and 153. Alexander may have worked in Hood's drafting office as an apprentice, in 1933–1934.

28. See Tennessee Williams, *Selected Letters*, p. 173 (quoted). For Alexander's view see, offhand, Tony Denzer, "The Halliburton House and Its Architect, William Alexander," unpublished article, December 8, 1999, for Professor Thomas S. Hines, UCLA. For Avalon, see Frank Gruber, *Zane Grey—A Biography* (Roslyn, New York: Walter J. Black, 1969), shown opposite p. 114. Said to be fireproof, London's celebrated "Wolf House" near Bohemian Grove burned down before its completion in 1913. See Russ Kingman, *A Pictorial Life of Jack London* (New York: Crown Publishers, 1979), pp. 246–249.

29. See *RHL*, April 18, 1937, p. 389; April 27, 1937, p. 389; May 15, 1937, p. 390. For contexts see *JR*, p. 260; cf., *JC*, p. 156. For Halliburton's increasing skill, and addiction, to writing captions, see *RHL-P*, April 27, 1937, May 9, 1938, and May 24, 1938.

30. Halliburton's letter about his "mountain top in Laguna" is an apologia *pro sua vita*. *RHL-P*, September 18, 1937; compare *RHL*, pp. 385–386. For ⅓ time in Laguna, see *RHL-P*, November 27, 1936. The published version omits Halliburton's opinions about women and men, both of whose opinions bored him—but in different ways and to different degrees. For Halliburton's "torn sentiments" about the house, see *RHL-P*, September 18, 1937 (quoted). Also see *JC*, p. 156.

31. *RHL*, October 6, 1937, pp. 392–393 (quoted).

32. See Drohojowska-Philp, Hunter, "Historic Neighborhood: Whitley Heights—Preserving the Address of Hollywood's Early Royalty," *Architectural Digest*, April 1996, pp. 92–99, quotations from p. 92. "Topside" is pictured in the now rare booklet *Burton Holmes and the Travelogue—A Life Story* as told to Lothrop Stoddard, son of John L. Stoddard (Philadelphia: George F. Lasher Printing Company, 1939), unpaginated. The glamorous neighborhood which Holmes called a "Peter Pan suburb," was ready-made. In the garden to Topside, Holmes is pictured with Dolores Del Rio. In another picture, possibly on its porch, Holmes is pictured with Jean Harlow. Holmes also is pictured with "Jackie," a full-grown lion who seems to have lived on the premises. Holmes' first home, called "Nirvana," was located in New York and had a majestic view of Manhattan Towers; a third home, in fact, the Burton Holmes Films laboratory, was in Chicago, at 7510 N. Ashland Avenue. For the homes noted, see *The Book of Small Houses* (which Hangover House essentially is), by the editors of The Architectural Forum (New York: Simon and Schuster, 1936): Paul Pulliam House (pp. 126–127); Thorsten Sigstedt House (pp. 130–131); Anna Sten House (pp. 232–233); and Adobe House (pp. 236–237). For Hangover House itself, "Meanderings" includes the tally sheets of expenditures. Also, Alexander's correspondence with Halliburton contains progress reports including expenditures. Halliburton's mother, Nelle, suggested he keep information about the high costs a secret. See *JC*, p. 159.

33. For Captain Wallace Scott, see *JR*, pp. 275–276. Also recounted in "Meanderings."

34. See Michael Blankenship, "A Fellow Traveler," op. cit., p. 41.

35. For DeSola's condition, see *RHL-P*, December 4, 1936 and March 31, 1937. DeSola, his health somewhat restored, later visited Halliburton in San Francisco (apparently); the two visited Yosemite as a main event. *RHL-P*, June 19, 1936. The photograph taken by Ewing Garroway of two young men on Overhanging Rock, the photograph chosen as the frontispiece for the first *Book of Marvels*, is not of DeSola and Halliburton, though the standing figure resembles Halliburton. William Alexander wrongly thought the two figures were Paul Mooney and Halliburton. Subtitled "two climbers high above the Yosemite Valley," it appeared in *American Magazine*, September 1927, p. 53. For the Hindenburg disaster, *RHL-P*, May 15, 1937 (quoted). For the Earhart disappearance, *RHL-P*, August 1, 1938. Of course he continued to fly—and Paul picked him up at the airport (e.g., *RHL-P*, February 21, 1938); also see *RHL-P*, December 23, 1937 and February 21, 1938. Occupational hazards loomed large and small for the lecturer. In Grand Rapids, he "struck a blizzard—screaming winds and deep snow. The storm wrecked our audience. Even people with tickets wouldn't get there," *RHL-P*, March 3, 1937. For Halliburton's tachycardia, see *JR*, p. 41.

36. For Gay Beaman, see *RHL-P*, April 27, 1937, and others which follow. Beaman and wife Adelaide Beaman were Halliburton's "first house guests at the Laguna house," *RHL-P*, August 30, 1937. Halliburton's letters home indicate that he concerned himself in earnest about the property, and its disposal, from April 27 to April 30, 1937, property which, should he die, would pass to his parents but would be administered by the First National Bank; tax consequences would arise. Also of interest is his letter about the disposal of the property, should his parents die, dated July 25, 1938. For "joint property," and Princeton library provision, *RHL-P*, June 25, 1938 (quoted). For "the Mooney-DeSola policy," *RHL-P*, December 6, 1937. Toward an estimate of Halliburton's reported net worth, the house he appraised at $20,000, *RHL-P*, January 24, 1938. Also see April 27, 1937. A copy of the Last Will and Testament of Richard Halliburton, Deceased, filed October 12, 1939, is housed at Rhodes College's Barret Library.

37. *RH-WA*, June 30, 1937. Also, *PML-WA*, September 26, 1937.

38. For Paul "scouring Hollywood for a writing job," *RHL-P*, June 25, 1938. The regularity of this job search is unclear. In conversations, Alexander said a Muni confusion was possible.

39. For Paul's ill-luck finding a writing job and the "flying adventure," *RHL-P*, July 6, 1938. Paul did not communicate these activities himself, *PML-WA*, September 8, 1937. For the Tudor Apartments matter, same letter. For Alexander's departure, and the signed books, *RHL-P*, February 21, 1938.

40. For Richard Halliburton's view of women see "The Prince of Lovers Talks about Women," *The Illustrated Love Magazine*, op. cit., quoted on p. 41. Also see *RHL-P*, November 27, 1936. For Juliet's opinion of a marriage to Richard Halliburton, letter

from Juliet Halliburton Davis to William Short, curator, dated June 28, 1987. For house management duties in Halliburton's absence, RHL-P, September 8, 1938.

41. For junk plans, RHL-P, August 30, 1937. For Paul's initial reluctance, see Blankenship, "A Fellow Traveler," op. cit., p. 43. Root does not mention the Davises, though it is likely Mary Lou is one of the unnamed parties in the divorce action he mentions in which Halliburton was named co-respondent. See JR, p. 31.

42. RHL-WA, August 29, 1938. Author's collection.

Chapter 15

1. See RHL-P: two books from one, January 21, 1937; Taj Mahal, etc., March 26, 1938; junk and book promotion, May 15, 1937; Fort McHenry, July 26, 1937; sequels, July 26, 1937; "Royal Road to Romance in America," June 25, 1938, and RHL, p. 397; price of Marvels, January 21, 1937; for children's book, RHL, pp. 381–182. For circumstances of book see JC, pp. 150–152. Also see Blankenship, "A Fellow Traveler," p. 42.

2. For father's input see RHL-P, November 27, 1936 and March 6, 1937; his own rewriting, January 21, 1937; age-level, March 6, 1937; Chambers, April 3, 1937; for Chambers editing the captions, April 27, 1937; getting the book into the schools, August 30, 1937; tells parents to go to Jerusalem, etc., "all places they missed before," March 12, 1938.

3. For the carbons see RHL-P, October 17, 1937 and November 27, 1937. Root notes Mooney's help in the editing, JR, p. 258. Compare Cortese who writes, "He [Richard] apparently had to rewrite much of the Marvel book that Paul Mooney had done—too much Mooney instead of Halliburton—but he continued to work on it," JC, p. 154. Cf. Townsend, p. 5.

4. For San Francisco as a favorite city see Book of Marvels—The Occident, op. cit., p. 3. Chapters 1 and 2 are devoted to the Bay area. Also see, RHL, p. 392, and p. 379. Compare Kashmir, in northern India as also a "favorite place." See JR, p. 236.

5. By June 25, 1938, Halliburton has settled into the Chancellor Hotel. See RHL, p. 398. For San Francisco at this time see San Francisco—The Bay and Its Cities, compiled by Workers of the Writers' Program of the Work Projects Administration in Northern California (New York: Hastings House, 1940). See in general Jerry Flamm, Good Life in Hard Times—San Francisco's 20s and 30s (San Francisco: Chronicle Books, 1999). For the city's wide open appeal see Nan Alamilla Boyd, Jose Sarria, "Transgender and Gale Male Culture from the 1890s through the 1960s," Wide Open City—A History of Queer San Francisco to 1965 (Berkeley, Los Angeles, London: University of California Press, 2003), pp. 25–62, at pp. 52–61.

6. For the Halliburton picture see Book of Mar-

vels (1937), p. 17. For the Strauss poem, see Watkins, op. cit., p. 334.

7. Cf. Ed Reynolds, San Francisco Examiner, Section 1, Sunday, May 26, 1937.

8. Cf. JR, p. 258 et seq.

9. For the preparations see JR, pp. 263–264; also pp. 21–22. For applicants see p. 24. Zola Halliburton, hearing that John Potter planned to take a 60 foot sloop around the world, put him in touch with cousin Richard; Potter took on the assignment because he wanted "to purge [himself] of the wanderlust." Chase was "his college pal." Los Angeles Times, October 17, 1938 and November 29, 1938: Courtesy of Dartmouth College. When several Chinese businessmen offered the Sea Dragon plan their support, Halliburton considered forming the "Richard Halliburton Enterprise." See RHL, p. 394. These members of the "Chinese Six Companies" had invested heavily in the Exposition itself but decided the junk expedition too risky and so abandoned their support, leaving Halliburton somewhat in the lurch. Cf. JR, pp. 253–254. Kept out of the published version, the specific costs of the expedition appear frequently in Halliburton's later letters. Note RHL-P, August 1, 1938, August 31, 1938 (which mentions the need for a fourth young man to join the crew for an additional $4,000), and September 4, 1938. Vida Halliburton invested $2,500, and family friend Myrtle Crummer invested $4000. Cf., JC, pp. 158–159. For Potter, Torrey, et al., see JC, p. 22. For the withdrawal of the Chinese backers, RHL-P, April 20, 1938. For sponsorship see JR, pp. 258–259. Cf. Landsburg, op. cit., p. 20. Among the publicity agents for the Exposition was later television personality (House Party) Art Linkletter. See JR, p. 204 and p. 205. See JR, op. cit., pp. 258 and 259. Also see Art Linkletter and George Bishop, I Didn't Do It Alone—The Autobiography of Art Linkletter (Ottawa, Illinois, and Ossining, New York: Caroline House Publishers, Inc., 1980), pp. 118–119. "As Radio Director [of the Fair]," Linkletter wrote to me, "I and my associate, Clyde Vandeburg [now deceased] who was promotion manager for the Fair, originated the idea with Halliburton that he attempt to sail a junk from Hong Kong to San Francisco for the opening of the Fair on 2/18/39. We helped him with fund-raising which consisted principally of publicity about his search for crew members to accompany him on this adventure. Eventually about a dozen families came up with the money and we had a party for them, and you know the rest of the story. It was a sad and foolhardy trip." Letter to author, January 26, 1998. Dartmouth College was most helpful in providing additional information on crew members Chase, Potter and Torrey.

10. For Frank Buck a brochure from the New York World's Fair entitled "Frank Buck Jungleland at the World's Fair," 1939, was consulted. For Robert Ripley see 10, n. 4 above. For movie star Errol Flynn's entry into the world of sailor adventure, see his Beam Ends (Toronto and New York: Longman's, Green and Company, 1937).

11. See RHL-P, August 31, 1938 (quoted). It should now be clear that money figures ostensibly

as a motivating factor for Halliburton. Also see *RHL-P*, June 25, 1938. Attached to one of the form Bell letters Dr. Margaret Chung received was a note: "He [Richard] was to bring it [the *Sea Dragon*] over to take sightseers around the bay for the 1939 Worlds Fair." In private collection.

12. Cf. *JC*, p. 9. Consulted were the Bell letters. Quoted is a letter from John H. Halliburton to Michael Blankenship, July 8, 1986; copy of letter used by permission of William Alexander. Paul's deprecating remark on the *Book of Marvels—The Occident* is specifically aimed at the first ten chapters sent to the publisher, *PML-WA*, September 8, 1937.

13. See *JR*, p. 259.

14. Reference is from the *Indiana Evening Gazette*, March 13, 1928. Newspaper clippings of Halliburton's career, put together into scrapbooks by his father Wesley, reside at Rhodes College.

15. For the established pattern of Halliburton's professional life, see *RHL*, pp. 282–283. For details of the junk expedition, see *RHL-P*, July 14, 1938. Letter of July 21, 1938 (*RHL-P*) indicates Halliburton's last trip to Laguna Beach was July 4, 1938. For his eight days in Laguna see *RHL-P*, July 6, 1938. For Wilfred Crowell, "Fair people," Lloyd's and trips to Baton Rouge, etc., see *RHL*, pp. 394–395. For Crowell, also see *JR*, p. 22 et passim. For the "America book," see RHL, p. 398 (quoted), June 25, 1938; *RHL-P* version mentions disposition of property.

16. For mention of get-togethers, *RHL-P*, July 14 and July 21. Root notes, without expatiation, see the Atherton-Halliburton friendship, *JR*, p. 158. For Gertrude Atherton, see in general Emily Wortis Leider, *California's Daughter—Gertrude Atherton and Her Times*, op. cit. For references to Halliburton see p. 310 and p. 316. Halliburton elsewhere notes a dinner party hosted by a Mrs. Harvey for twelve people, including Gertrude Atherton, Noel Sullivan, and of course Halliburton. *RHL-P*, June 25, 1938.

17. For the meeting on Maiden Lane see Gertrude Atherton, *My San Francisco—A Wayward Biography* (Indianapolis and New York: Bobbs-Merrill Company, 1946), p. 276. For Greece and ruins, see Gertrude Atherton, *Adventures of a Novelist* (Liveright Publishers, 1932), p. 570 et passim; for Aspasia, p. 569 (quoted); for Van Vechten, p. 537; for Emperor Norton I and monkeys, pp. 3–4 (quoted). For Atherton (1857–1948), and PEN see Leider, op. cit., pp. 313–316. For Maxwell Aley, see pp. 313–314. For stories about husband George H.B. Atherton's death, see Leider, supra, p. 65.

18. For Chung's career, see Judy Tzu-Chun Wu, *Mom Chung of the Fair-Haired Bastards: A Thematic Biography of Dr. Margaret Chung (1889–1959)*, Ph.D. diss., Stanford, 1998. Also see, Atherton, *My San Francisco*, op. cit., pp. 272–277. For clipper information see Horace Brock, *Flying the Oceans: A Pilot's Story of Pan Am 1935–1955* (New York: Jason Aronson, 1978), pp. 110–111. Also see *Wings over Hong Kong—An Aviation History 1891–1998: A Tribute to Kai Tak* (Hong Kong: Odyssey Book, Pacific Century Publishers, 1998), p. 12 et seq. Dr. Chung's "Letters from the *Sea Dragon*" are addressed to 1407 Montgomery Street. Halliburton sent letters from

this address on July 1, July 14 and July 28, 1936. See *RHL*, pp. 381–382. Dr. Chung's office was at 752 Sacramento, several blocks away. See *San Francisco Exposition and Bay Counties Telephone Directory*, May 1939.

19. For Nelle Nance's arrival, the itinerary, and the party see *RHL-P*, September 10, 1938. Newspaper clippings in the notebooks kept in the Rhodes College Collection show Nelle Nance and Paul Mooney in San Francisco. For the Halliburtons' trip, which included stops in Athens, Constantinople, Budapest, and Vienna see *RHL-P*, August 31, 1938, and June 25, 1938; cf., *RHL*, p. 398. For mention of *The Summing Up* see *RHL-P*, August 1, 1938; for earlier mention see *RHL-P*, July 6, 1938 (unpublished); for his quoted opinion of the book see *RHL-P*, June 25, 1938. He read Atherton's book in Honolulu. *RHL-P*, October 7, 1938. Vida Halliburton, a contributor to the *Sea Dragon* expedition, was a prominent Los Angeles socialite. See *JR*, p. 22; also pp. 175–176. Vida was the wife and Zola was the daughter of wealthy oil-rigger Erle Halliburton, the nephew of Wesley Halliburton. Erle Jr., who had been chosen to be the *Sea Dragon's* radio operator, had to be ruled out after an eye operation sidelined him. See *RHL-P*, July 14, 1938.

20. See *RHL-P*, September 28, 1938 (quoted).

21. Cf., *JR*, p. 19. Quoted is a letter from Juliet Halliburton Davis to William Short, curator, dated June 28, 1987, op. cit., in which Davis recalled a conversation with her cousin Richard. For the different challenges Halliburton met in his life as an adventurer, see *JR*, pp. 18–19, 180–181. For Halliburton's disregard of danger and his focus on "his challenge and the glory beyond it," see p. 34. Halliburton compared the present project with the *Flying Carpet* one, which, though arduous, was a success. See *RHL*, July 6, 1938, p. 399.

22. For the 1848 junk voyage, and other early voyages, see Novaresio, op. cit., pp. 90–91.

23. For other junk voyages, see *RHL*, pp. 405–406. Later ventures include the 1999 voyage of Hodding Carter. Obsessed with Leif Erikson, Carter, and an "unlikely crew of adventurers," completed an epic journey from Greenland to North America, after a first failed attempt, in a square-rigged Viking cargo ship known as a *knarr*. For the voyage of the *knarr*, see Hodding Carter, *A Viking Voyage—In Which an Unlikely Crew of Adventurers Attempts an Epic Journey to the New World* (New York: Random House, 2000).

24. Slocum's adventures at sea are recounted in his *Sailing Alone around the World* and *Voyage of the Liberdade*.

25. For the 1875 expedition see RHL, pp. 404–405. Also see *JR*, p. 19. For the story of the HMS *Success* convict ship see the *San Francisco Chronicle*, February 4 and February 7, 1915.

26. The closest Halliburton ever came to captaining a ship was the Xpit adventure. See *New Worlds to Conquer* (Bobbs-Merrill, Indianapolis, 1929), pp. 64–76. For Halliburton's naval training see *JR*, p. 43. For his little knowledge of boats, see *RHL*, p. 411–412 (quoted).

27. For Paul, *RHL-P*, September 10, 1938 (quoted).

28. Nearly fifty years later, Gordon Torrey said that the junk "could have been heavy-lifted on the deck of a San Francisco bound freighter and carried across the Pacific and still have been a tremendous commercial success at the World's Fair." See *JC*, p. 178. For plans see *RHL-P*, June 25, 1938 (quoted). For money-making "concessions" at the Fair see *RHL-P*, August 31, 1938.

29. For the junk tours, *RHL-P*, May 15, 1937. For "lots of money," *RHL-P*, August 31, 1938. For the seven Bell letters, see RHL-P September 10, 1938. For arrival of crew members see *RHL*, p. 411 (November 10, 1938).

Chapter 16

1. *RHL-P*, September 28, 1938. Also see *RHL*, pp. 400–401 and pp. 408–409. See *JR*, p. 265; cf. *JC*, p. 159.

2. For Captain Welch see *JR*, p. 25. Cf. Weller, op. cit., p. 112. Also see *RHL*, p. 407. Also see *RHL-P*, August 1, 1938, which mentions Welch speaking Chinese. Regarding Welch's credentials I am indebted to Edward D. Howell, Jr., who made inquiries to T. McDonald, Captain of U.S. Coast Guard Reserve, Chief, Public Information Division, February 25, 1972. For Potter's remarks, see *JR*, p. 32. Also see p. 25 for Halliburton's and the crew's response to Captain Welch. Gordon Torrey evidently thought Welch capable enough. See Landsburg (who interviewed Torrey), op. cit., p. 23.

3. For Nell Nance's opinion see *JC*, p. 159.

4. See *RHL*, p. 407 (quoted). Also see Weller, op. cit., p. 112. For Paul mimeographing, see *RHL-P*, September 28, 1938. For his report writing see p. 192.

5. See the *Book of Marvels—The Orient* (Indianapolis and New York: Bobbs-Merrill, 1938), after p. 283. For weather conditions see *RHL*, p. 408 (quoted). For the Japanese presence and wartime blockade see Halliburton, *Letters*, pp. 402–403, 408–410, 421, 426–427. Also see *JR*, pp. 20–21. For pre-war Hong Kong see Snow, op. cit., pp. 1–52. Also see Christopher Isherwood in W.H. Auden and Christopher Isherwood, *Journey to a War* (New York: Random House, 1939), p. 29.

6. See *RHL*, p. 409. For peril also see Victor Purcell, *Chinese Evergreen* (New York: E.P. Dutton & Company, 1938), p. 18 et seq.

7. See *RHL*, p. 409.

8. See *RHL-P*, November 2, 1938. For Tommy Davis in Japan, for instance, see the *Book of Marvels—The Orient*, p. 295. As an adult Paul could compare Hong Kong and its mores, superficially at least, to various Chinatowns in America. For Los Angeles' Chinatown, see Richard Halliburton, "Half a Mile of History," *Readers Digest*, October 1937, pp. 70–73. Paul almost certainly co-wrote this feature on "Los Angeles' most colorful thoroughfare," Main Street.

9. For the British in Hong Kong, see Halliburton, *Letters*, p. 409. Also see W.D. Auden and Christopher Isherwood, *Journey to a War*, op. cit., p. 28; Nigel Cameron, *Hong Kong—The Cultured Pearl* (London: Oxford University Press, 1978), 166–167. Also see Victor Purcell, *Chinese Evergreen*, p. 37 et passim. For Halliburton's view of Hong Kong see *RHL-P*, November 2, 1938. For life on the Colony see Ted Ferguson, *Desperate Siege—The Battle of Hong Kong* (Garden City, New York: Doubleday & Company, Inc., 1980), p. 37 (quoted). Photographs offer scenes of the city at this time (opposite p. 84).

10. Various sources inform this picture of Hong Kong. Besides Halliburton's *Letters* (e.g., pp. 416–418), most helpful were Root's biography of Halliburton, Nigel Cameron (supra), G.B. Endacott and A. Hinton's *Fragrant Harbour—A Short History of Hong Kong* (Hong Kong: Oxford University Press, 1962), Gene Gleason, *Hong Kong* (New York: The John Day Company, 1963), *Time* (November 21, 1960), and others. For Westernization see Victor Purcell, *Chinese Evergreen*, supra, see p. 21 et passim. For the blending of cultures see *Wings*, supra, p. 19. For views see *A Selective Collection of Hong Kong Historic Postcards*, compiled by Tong Cheuk Man, David P.M. Toong, Alan S.K. Cheung and Mo Yu Kai (Hong Kong: Joint Publishing Company); the book contains colored postcard views of Hong Kong during the late-19th and into the 20th centuries and offers glimpses of Paul's and Richard's "last world" or the recent past that last world, of 1938–1939, drew upon. For Connaught Road, for instance, see p. 38, and for Ice House Street (the financial center), see p. 39; for Wellington Street ("a very busy thoroughfare with many shops"), see p. 43. Paul customarily sent postcards to friends and relatives; for this purpose, it is not unlikely that these early views, in some form, were available to him. Other views of this last world—many closer to the late 1930s, are to be found in *A Century of Hong Kong Roads and Streets* (Hong Kong: Joint Publishing Company, 2000); there is also the companion *A Century of Kowloon Roads and Streets* (Hong Kong: Joint Publishing Company, 2000). Photographs of these thoroughfares from the 1930s show panoramic street scenes as they might have looked to Paul. See, for instance, pp. 60 and 73. Also consulted was *The Encyclopedia Britannica* (14th edition, 1929), sv. "Hong Kong," vol. 11, pp. 718–721 (with plates).

11. To learn more about streets in Hong Kong see *A Century of Hong Kong Roads and Streets* (Joint Publishing Company, 2000) and the companion *A Century of Kowloon Roads and Streets*, supra. Mary A. Nourse, *A Short History of the Chinese* (New York: Bobbs-Merrill, 1942), provides contemporary views. Also see "Hong Kong" in Jim Antoniou, *Cities Then & Now (As They Are Today—As They Once Were)* (New York: Macmillan, 1994), pp. 128–133, which includes a transparent overlay showing the central district as it appeared in the 1920s superimposed over a color photograph of the same district as it appeared in the 1990s.

12. For Kowloon see *JR*, p. 20 and p. 30. For Nathan Road as "central artery" see Robert Burati and Harold Pettalkay, *Hong Kong* (Kodansha Inter-

national, Tokyo, Japan & Palo Alto, California, 1970), p. 16. For the "boarding house" (possibly the Kowloon Hotel), *RHL-P*, November 2, 1938. See *JR*, p. 23. For conditions there see *RHL*, p. 411. For the Hong Kong Club, see Purcell, p. 23 et seq.

13. For the Hong Kong Hotel and the "maritime population" that gathered there, possibly offering valuable information (as well as negative predictions) about navigation, see *JR*, p. 20. For another reference to the Hong Kong Hotel, see *Hong Kong* (New York: Vintage Books, 1989), pp. 174–175. Also see Cameron, pp. 36, 67, 68, 153 and *A Century of Kowloon Roads and Streets* (Hong Kong: Joint Publishing Company, 2000), pp. 49 and 63. Also see *Wings over Hong Kong—An Aviation History 1891–1998*: A Tribute to Kai Tak (Hong Kong: Pacific Century Publishers, 1998), p. 19 (where the hotel is also photographed). For the Clock Tower, see Cameron, pp. 65–66, and p. 158. On p. 65 is Pedder Street as it appeared in 1880. The Hotel was situated along three main roads, Des Voeux Road Central, Queen's Road Central and Pedder Street. In 1926 fire destroyed the part of the building facing Des Voeux Road Central; unaffected was that part of the building facing Queen's Road and Pedder Street. My gratitude is extended to Hong Kong historian Ricky Yam of Hong Kong, who has studied the Hong Kong newspapers of the period. For the Japanese in Hong Kong see Philip Snow, *The Fall of Hong Kong—Britain, China and the Japanese Occupation* (New Haven and London: Yale University Press, 2003), p. 36. Yamishita was at the Hong Kong Hotel from 1929; it is not certain if he was there in 1939.

14. For Paul's spare eating habits, I am indebted to William Alexander. For Halliburton at the American Consulate, *RHL-P*, November 2, 1938. For what food was eaten see *RHL*, p. 415. For the condition of the refugees, compare *JR*, p. 17.

15. See *Nellie Bly's Book—Around the World in 72 Days*, edited by Ira Peck (Brookfield, Connecticut: Twenty-First Century Books, 1998), p. 89. For the Ferry see Purcell, op. cit., p. 38 et seq.

16. For the junks at Gin Drinker's Bay see *RHL*, pp. 409–410. For Fat Kau see *RHL*, p. 414 et seq. For the shipyard site, see *RHL*, p. 414 (quoted). Also see *JR*, pp. 20 and 21.

17. For the building of the junk, which began with the keel, then the ribbing, see *RHL*, pp. 414–418. For loose work habits and labor organization compare Purcell, p. 94 et seq.

18. For the parties, see *RHL*, pp. 417–418 (quoted).

19. For Welch as "dictatorial" see *RHL-P*, November 2, 1938. For Paul's opinion, which seemed to grow towards higher pitches of animosity, see *JC*, p. 160. For Potter's opinion, see *JC*, p. 180 (quoted). For Henry Von Fehren, Bell letter #1 (part of which is omitted in *RHL*). For Paul and the mimeographing see *RHL-P*, September 28, 1938. For Paul as an "experienced seaman," see Bell letter #1. Paul had at best been a cabin boy on his trip to Constantinople; still, he had functioned on a ship.

20. *RHL-P*, January 23, 1939 (quoted).

21. *RHL-P*, November 2, 1938. See *JC*, p. 160.

Also see above, note #2. For Captain Welch as a cause for some worry, see *JR*, p. 23 et seq.

22. For the gifts, "Xmas presents [sent] to everybody," a "suitcase full," *RHL-P*, November 11, 1938. Several of Paul's figurines—one of a Chinese philosopher, another of a dragon, and a third of a man in prayer—are owned by John M. Scott.

23. For Kai Tak see *Wings Over Hong Kong*, op. cit. For it as Kai Tek Aerodrome, see Purcell, op. cit., p. 47.

24. For the Bell *articles* see *RHL*, p. 401 et seq. For origin see *JR*, p. 25. Quoted in Bell *letter* #1. Fact change example: While "Number Four Wife" receives job money in Bell *article* (*RHL*, p. 417), "Fat Kau's second wife" receives it in Bell *letter* #2.

25. Halliburton's own letters during the *Sea Dragon* expedition, often hurriedly written, are relatively few in number; November 21, December 12, January 1, January 23, February 10, February 23 and March 3 are major letters sent home during the final months. Quoted is Bell letter #1, 1938.

26. For the itinerary see *RHL*, p. 402. For route information, *RHL-P*, September 10, August 1, 1938 (for Pan Am and Navy okay), and December 12, 1938. For route changes once at sea, see *RHL*, pp. 432–433. For Halliburton's contacts with Pan-Am pilots, see Horace Brock, op. cit., pp. 110–111. For Captain Dale Collins, letter to Edward T. Howell, Jr., May 7, 1946 (quoted). (27) For Captain Welch's "30 degree latitude" idea, *RHL-P*, September 28, 1938.

28. Halliburton, or Paul, wrote about the evacuation of Canton in "Letters from the Sea Dragon," January 27, 1939, unpublished. For the places Paul and Richard had been in China, besides Hong Kong, see *RHL*, pp. 408–409, 414–415. For Paul as "journalist" (uncut in published version) see *RHL*, p. 406. Paul's skills as "an inexperienced seaman ... crack photographer," and a "journalist" are noted in Bell letter #1. Also see *RHL-P*, November 2, 1938. What pictures Paul took during the *Sea Dragon* expedition were either sent home or lost when the *Sea Dragon* perished.

29. See *JR*, p. 23. For expected (and evident) arrival times, see *RHL*, pp. 411–412. Potter later noted that he, Torrey and Chase—Barstow isn't named, arrived in November. See *JC*, p. 179. In the original of the letter to his parents dated November 21, 1938, Halliburton heavily inked out a number of lines, though the context and a few legible words and phrases suggest his annoyance, before he relented, over the boys' early arrival. For living arrangements see *JR*, pp. 22–23.

30. See *RHL-P*, November 2, 1938. Halliburton noted that, on the ship, "we all [i.e., Paul, himself and Captain Welch] have separate rooms and see each other rarely." For turns to the worse once all the crew were gathered see *RHL-P*, January 1, 1939. Cf. *RHL*, pp. 406–407 from the Bell letters. For Torrey's assessment see *JC*, p. 178. For the Sligh incident see *JR*, p. 32.

31. See *JC*, Mooney letter, p. 160 (quoted). The date of the letter depends upon the dates provided in the letter Richard Halliburton wrote on Novem-

ber 10. There it is indicated that Gordon Torrey and George Barstow would arrive in Hong Kong on December 1 and the others, almost certainly John Potter and Robert Chase, would arrive on December 15. The boy fresh from Dartmouth, presumably a graduate thereof, could have been Torrey. Paul may not have met Chase (the Dartmouth senior) as yet. See RHL, p. 411.

32. Ibid., p. 160 (quoted).

33. See RHL-P, January 1 (quoted). For Potter's remarks see JC, p. 181 (quoted). For the Bell letter, see RHL, p. 407 (quoted).

34. See RHL-P, August 31, 1938 (quoted). Bell Letter #1 (quoted). "Letters from the Sea Dragon," #1, quoted. "Bertha Barstow" is noted in a letter Halliburton wrote home dated September 26, 1937; she is also mentioned in a letter dated June 12, 1937. Bell letter #2 offers additional information on the crew.

35. See JC, Mooney letter, p. 160 (quoted). For spies and informers see JR, p. 20.

Chapter 17

1. See Jean Cocteau, Round the World Again in 80 Days (New York: Tauris Parke Paperbacks, 2000), p. 141 (quoted).

2. See RHL, p. 408 (quoted); cf. RHL, p. 402.

3. For the Sea Dragon as a "rich prize," see RHL, p. 421. For guns see RHL-P, January 1, 1939; also RHL, p. 421. For supplies see RHL-P, January 23, 1939.

4. For the "evolution" of the junk, see RHL, pp. 411–412 (quoted), December 12, 1938. For all of Hong Kong coming out to see the junk, RHL-P, January 1, 1939.

5. See RHL, p. 413 (quoted). For a description of the junk see RHL, pp. 420–421 (quoted).

6. For "poetry ship" see RHL, p. 426.

7. See RHL, p. 421 (quoted). For Ripley see www.staugustine-ripleys.com/about/bio.php.

8. For the variety of junk types see Paolo Novaresio, The Explorers—From the Ancient World to the Present (New York: Stewart, Tabori & Chang, 1996), pp. 90–91. Also see Robert F. Fitch, "Life Afloat in China—Tens of Thousands of Chinese in Congested Ports Spend Their Entire Existence on Boats," National Geographic, SI, no. 6, June 1927, pp. 665–686. Also see Purcell, p. 209 et seq.

9. RHL-P, September 23, 1938. For mixed reactions by onlookers see JR, p. 26.

10. Reference is to the Potter-Torrey film.

11. See Johnson's Dictionary—A Modern Selection, by E.L. McAdam, Jr. and George Milne (New York: Pantheon Books, 1963), p. 373 (quoted). A Johnson Reader, edited by McAdam and Milne (New York: Pantheon Books, 1964), p. 461 (quoted). For Sir Francis Drake see George Sanderlin, The Sea Dragon—Journals of Francis Drake's Voyage around the World (New York, Evanston and London: Harper and Row Publishers, 1969).

12. For the dragon as a land creature, see JR, p. 34. For other views of the dragon in Chinese culture

see Tao Tao Liu Sanders, Dragons, Gods & Spirits from Chinese Mythology (New York: Schocken Books, 1980), pp. 48–59. For the Dragon Boat Races see Nigel Cameron, Hong Kong—The Cultured Pearl, op. cit., p. 229. Also see Bruce Chatwin, "The Dragon-Lines," Hong Kong—True Stories of Life on the Road (San Francisco: Traveler's Tales Inc., 1997), pp. 50–57, at 52–53. See Dorothy Perkins, The Encyclopedia of China, Essential Reference to China, Its History and Culture (New York: Facts on File, 1999) for "dragon," (p. 155), "junk," (p. 250), "fen shui" (also under "dragon, pp. 131–132), and other pertinent terms. For the views of China that persisted well into his time see Colin Mackerras, Western Images of China (Hong Kong: Oxford University Press, 1989), pp. 70–87.

13. Cf. JR, p. 26–28. For the junk's difficulties in performance, see JC, 180–181 (text of letter from John Potter, quoted at p. 181); (tiller), p. 180.

14. Cf. JR, pp. 26–28. For the engine RHL, pp. 419–420. For the espionage William Alexander noted in conversation only that they were theories.

15. For the horoscope, RHL-NS, February 11, 1928. For Halliburton's belief in "Occidental gods," based on a letter to Crowell, see JR, p. 32. For the Wenchow junk, RHL, p. 419–420. Also, RHL-P, November 21, 1938. For Lloyd's see JR, p. 26.

16. RHL-P, November 11, 1938; also RHL-P, January 1, 1939.

17. RHL-P, January 1, 1939.

18. RHL-P, January 23, 1939 (quoted). For the crew see RHL p. 421; also pp. 425–426. For the passenger hopefuls see JR, p. 33. The giant (baby) panda—"prospective mascot for the Sea Dragon"—is pictured with Halliburton in RHL (opposite p. 371). Also see RHL, p. 412 (November 21, 1938).

19. Cf. JR, pp. 25–26. Root does not specify a source for this information, though Gordon Torrey is a likely candidate, as is Captain Charles Jokstad. A photograph shows Halliburton, back turned, in white shirt and dress pants, overseeing the building of the Sea Dragon; to his right is a young man who fits the description of this Portuguese young man (possibly Patrick Kelly). It was Captain Charles Jokstad who carefully inspected the junk and warned against the voyage. See JR, pp. 269–270. For Jokstad and Torrey as sources for Root's biography of Halliburton, see Acknowledgments, p. 7. For Patrick Kelly, whose seasickness during the trial run forced his resignation from the expedition, see RHL, p. 425, 428, and 430. Halliburton thought Kelly, a "dark-skinned Latin" born in Canton, was actually named Miguel or Manuel, p. 425. For the "Gripps" see Phillip Snow, The Fall of Hong Kong, op. cit., p. 51. For Torrey's notes on Halliburton, see JC, p. 177 (quoted). For Potter's see JC, p. 180 (quoted).

20. For the ceremony based on Bell Letter #4, see JC, p. 161 (quoted). For the Chinese girl and "demons" see RHL, p. 402.

21. See RHL, p. 427 (quoted). For Potter's remarks, see JC, p. 181.

22. See RHL, pp. 428–429. See JR, pp. 28–29; cf. JR, pp. 161–162. For radio communication see RHL, p. 424.

23. See *RHL*, p. 429. Potter (quoted in text) later reported, "Actually I had sustained a smashed rib and a few strained muscles when the boom of the staysail struck me while the ship was yawing." John Potter, Letter (unpublished) to Edward T. Howell, Jr., January 15, 1946. For Potter's and Torrey's physical afflictions, see *JC*, pp. 29 and 32; cf. *JC*, pp. 177 and 179.

24. See *RHL*, p. 429.

25. See *RHL*, p. 430. Also see *JR*, pp. 29–30.

26. For Kelly, and others, see *RHL*, p. 430 (quoted). For Davis see p. 425. For Torrey's views see *JC*, pp. 177–179 (quoted at 179). For Halliburton's preoccupations including his being "named co-respondent in a divorce action brought by a Los Angeles physician and bibliophile," see *JR*, p. 31. For Barstow see *RHL-P*, February 10, 1939. For Halliburton and seasickness, which he called "mal de mer," see *The Royal Road to Romance*, p. 369.

27. For "sickly amateurs," and Scandinavians, *RHL-P*, February 10, 1939 (quoted). For "better crew now," see *RHL-P*, March 3, 1939; also February 23, 1939. For Fitch see "City Youth on Missing Junk, Navy Searching for Lost Halliburton Ship," *Minneapolis Star*, March 31, 1939.

28. For Paul's attitude see *JR*, p. 33 (quoted), from a letter Paul wrote to "a friend in Los Angeles." Evidently Paul was not an indifferent correspondent. He wrote "long, newsy letters" (now presumed lost) to his mother, reported the *Washington Star* (May 16, 1939), "while the crew of 11 (sic) was journeying through war-torn China."

29. For "skin itch" see *RHL-P*, February 23, 1939. For the "eczema," see *JR*, p. 22. Root notes that the case of nerves kept Halliburton in bed at the Kowloon Hotel during the month of January, while the *Sea Dragon* was moored at Main Wharf. For financial expectations see *RHL-P*, March 3, 1939.

30. For Halliburton's attitude, see *RHL*, pp. 425–426 (quoted), February 10, 1939. For Crowell, see *RHL*, pp. 431–432 (March 3, 1939).

31. For the fin-keel and other adjustments, see *RHL*, pp. 430–431. Cf. *JR*, pp. 26–30 (quoted); for an "18-inch fin keel," see p. 30; for the concrete ballast, see pp. 26–27. After inspecting the junk, Captain Charles Jokstad recommended that ten more tons be added. For the fin-keel *not* being installed, an issue still debated, see Lieutenant D.E. Collins, "The Royal Road Across the Pacific," *U.S. Naval Institute Proceedings*, April 1940, pp. 501–512, p. 506.

32. For Paul's remarks see Landsburg, op. cit., pp. 24–25.

33. See *RHL*, p. 421 (quoted). For Halliburton's last letter from Hong Kong, see *RHL*, p. 432 (March 3, 1939); for facsimile copy see opposite p. 430.

Chapter 18

1. These are reconstructed images, but are consistent with Paul's known role, dress and manner.

2. See *JC* pp. 163 and 164 (quoted). Also see *JR*, pp. 266 and 268.

3. See *RHL*, p. 406 (quoted). Cf. *JR*, p. 266.

4. For the route see Amos L. Wood, *Beachcombing the Pacific* (West Chester, Pennsylvania: Schiffer Publishing Ltd., 1987), p. 209.

5. See *RHL*, pp. 432–433.

6. See *RHL*, p. 427 (quoted). For the S.S. *Coolidge* see Michael McFayden, "S.S. *Coolidge*: A Short History" (Michael McFayden, Scuba Diving Website—History Page). In 1937 it had made a run from Yokohama to San Francisco in 9½ hours. A model of the ship resides at the San Francisco Maritime Museum.

7. For the S.S. *Coolidge*, and the report (evidently) of its captain, K.A. Ahlin, see *JR*, pp. 266–267. The S.S. *Coolidge* was reportedly the largest passenger ship ever constructed in the United States: 654 feet, 3 inches long with a waterline of 615 feet and a gross water displacement of 21,936 tons. Cf. McFayden, op. cit; the ship's sinking in World War II is also covered here. Earlier, on March 6, 1937, the ship ran into the oil tanker *Frank H. Buck* near the Golden Gate Bridge and suffered serious damage to its stern, which required ten days to repair. For Welch's final messages, *JC*, pp. 163–164. Cf. *RHL*, pp. 432–433. Also see Landsburg, p. 25.

8. See *JC*, p. 164 (Collins' report is quoted here).

9. For dating of messages see *JC*, p. 164. Cf. *JR*, pp. 266 and 267. For the time of day when the *Sea Dragon* met its fate see *JR*, p. 266 and p. 108. Also consulted was the U.S. Navy Hydrographic Bulletin, April 5, 1939 and a letter from Helene Philibert, head of special research projects, U.S. Navy Department, to Edward T. Howell, Jr., dated September 20, 1946, which summarizes Lieutenant D.E. Collins, "The Royal Road Across the Pacific," *U.S. Naval Institute Proceedings*, April 1940, pp. 501–507. The time was "0500" according to Dale E. Collins, commanding officer of the S.S. *President Coolidge*, which brought Halliburton to China. Letter to Halliburton enthusiast Edward T. Howell, Jr., dated May 7, 1946.

10. *Morning Post* (April 1939), based on report in *San Francisco Examiner* (March 30, 1939). Clipping from the *Morning Post* was tucked in the pages of William Alexander's "Meanderings."

11. See Amos L. Wood, op. cit., p. 209.

12. Cf. *JR*, p. 267. See also *JC* (Collins' report), p. 164.

13. Joseph Conrad, *Typhoon* (any edition).

14. Cf. *JR*, pp. 266–267.

15. The (so-called) sighting of the *Sea Dragon* by the *Tai Ping* was noted in an item William Alexander clipped from a newspaper and placed in his "Meanderings." For the *Jefferson Davis* see *JR*, p. 267. For the Beaufort report see *JC*, pp. 163–164. Possibly the force of the storm grew from a force six. Cf. *JC*, op. cit., p. 164.

16. For the Beaufort Scale (as quoted here) see Richard Henderson, *Sea Sense—Safety Afloat in Terms of Sail, Power, and Multihull Boat Design, Construction Rig, Equipment, Coping with Emergencies, and Boat Management in Heavy Weather* (Camden, Maine: International Marine Publishing Company, 1972), p. 296. A more recent study is Scott Huler's *Defining*

the Wind, op. cit., especially the 1906 Table II, Met Office Publication No. 180, p. 78, aims of the Beaufort Scale, p. 79, and "The Beaufort Scale, and Who Wrote It, in a General Way," Chapter 3, pp. 69–92. Also see "Preparations for Sea and Safety Equipment," pp. 80–103; "Handling Emergencies," pp. 104–156; and "Weather, Waves, and General Storm Strategy," pp. 157–179.

17. For Torrey's opinion see *JC*, p. 178 (quoted).

18. For Dr. E. A. Petersen, see *JC*, p. 165 (quoted). Also see *JR*, p. 268. For the S.S. *Coolidge*, see McFayden, op. cit. For crew relationships see Tim Severin, *The China Voyage—Across the Pacific by Bamboo Raft* (Reading, Massachusetts: Addison-Wesley Publishing Company, 1994), pp. 85–86; also, p. 95.

19. *The Royal Road to Romance* (Indianapolis: Bobbs-Merrill, 1925), pp. 395–396 (quoted).

20. See "Even Death Was a Stirring Adventure to Halliburton," *Click*, October 1939, pp. 28–29 (quoted at page 28).

21. For enchanted isles see *The Glorious Adventure* (Indianapolis: Bobbs-Merrill, 1927), p. 357. For the *Gold Shell* and Shelley, see *The Royal Road to Romance*, p. 149 and 151 (quoted). For the train crash, *RHL-P*, February 13, 1936.

22. See Willa Cather, "Paul's Case," op. cit., pp. 260–261 (quoted).

23. For Halliburton's earlier trip to Japan, on the S.S. *President Madison*, see *The Royal Road to Romance*, pp. 373–397, quoted at p. 375 and p. 395. For the mail pouches, see p. 367 et seq.

Chapter 19

1. *Time*, April 10, 1939, p. 62.

2. *Washington Post*, April 1939.

3. For the U.S.S. *Astoria* search see *JC*, p. 176. Also see Joanne and Annie Chris, www.glenalpine. com/chris/astoria/official_history.htm. For this, and other searches, see *JR*, pp. 268–269. Root notes that four seaplanes were used in the search. The *Washington Star* notes "three," June 16, 1939; clippings from William Alexander's "Meanderings."

4. *Washington Star*, May 17, 1939; June 16, 1939 (quoted)

5. Letter, unpublished, Alicia Mooney to William Alexander, April, 1939.

6. Thanks are extended to Mark Stevens (1940–2005) for his help as well as to William Alexander, who clarified the nature of Paul's holdings in Laguna Beach. In a letter to Alexander, dated February 2, 1955, shortly after Ione Mooney's death, Alicia Mooney emphasized that she wanted the "California land ... to disappear from the lives of my sisters and brother," and no longer be the burden it had been for her mother. The Maryland property apparently was purchased about 1922, shortly after James Mooney's death.

7. For Alice M. Padgett's letter see *JC*, p. 168. Information on the jury hearing, which involved the issue of insurance, appears here and in a press release

from Memphis about October 5. Alicia Mooney, in a letter to William Alexander, dated June 21, 1978, discussed the insurance policies. The letter, dated February 2, 1955, supra, mentioned the "financial burden" of the "California land." For the "premature" verdict of death, see Landsburg, p. 26.

8. For the financial information, *RHL-P*, the "Mooney-Desola policy"; disposal of Laguna property should Richard himself die, June 25, 1938; "If Paul and I [sink?] together," January 23, 1939; "tough summer" and "once at sea," September 4, 1938, and January 23, 1939. For property values escalating, letter (unpublished) from Wallace Scott to William Alexander, dated March 16, 1947. Author's collection.

9. For tenancy see *JR*, p. 275 (quoted). William Alexander also talked about the tenants in various conversations, and made some references to them in "Meanderings."

10. A newspaper item (undated), among William Alexander's clippings, indicates Van Johnson's interest in the house. For Johnson's dating Henie at this time see Raymond Strait and Leif Henie, *Queen of Ice—Queen of Shadows: The Unsuspected Life of Sonja Henie* (Boston: Scarborough House, 1985), pp. 204–295. A letter (unpublished) from Wallace Scott to William Alexander, dated March 16, 1947, notes the belief that Johnson lived at the house.

11. The clipping that refers to Captain Jokstad's sighting, a press release from "San Francisco," bears the date "7-6-40." On the earlier sighting of debris see *JR*, p. 274; *Boston Post*, "Believe Wreck Sighted Is Junk Seadragon [sic]," January 6, 1940; letter (unpublished), Dale E. Collins to Edward Howell, May 7, 1946, p. 2. Also see Langsburg, op cit., p. 22. Jack Denton Scott in *Passport to Adventure* writes of having rented out "an orange and green forty-foot teakwood three-masted sailing junk" (called the *Sea Dragon*) that was "eighteen tons" and "equipped with a diesel engine" said to be "identical with the craft, so I am told, in which Richard Halliburton sailed away, never to be seen again," p. 151.

12. See Amos L. Wood, op. cit., pp. 208, 209, and 210 (quoted). Wartime preoccupations prevented a verification of the keel as an authentic part of the *Sea Dragon*. "Assuming that the original woods (used at the Hong Kong shipyards in 1939) were identified," notes Wood, parts of the *Sea Dragon* could still turn up (if they have not already). As locations he suggested the coast of British Columbia (notably Cox Bay), "isolated beaches in Alaska or Baja, Mexico," p. 210. More credible is Captain Jokstad's 1940 sighting from aboard a steamer going from Yokohama to Honolulu of a heavily barnacle-infested "rudder" and "other timbers" which, having once inspected the *Sea Dragon*, he believed from the junk. See Captain Charles Jokstad, *The Captain and the Sea* (New York: Vantage Press, 1967), p. 190.

13. Dana, *Two Years Before the Mast*, op. cit., VI, p. 31.

14. See Gertrude Atherton, *My San Francisco*, op. cit., p. 276.

15. Tennessee Williams, *Selected Letters*, op. cit., p. 173. The Hart Crane lines from "Legend" appear

as an inscription in Williams' play *Sweet Bird of Youth* (New York: New Directions, 1959). For theories of Halliburton's survival, see Landsburg, for instance, pp. 26–27. Also see *The New York Times*, June 11, 1939, about Halliburton "one day rescued from a South Sea Island with a new book written entirely on tapa cloth with ink made from the juice of the sea urchin." Landsburg also quotes the item, p. 26. Following his essay on Halliburton, Landsburg focuses on the life and disappearance of Colonel Percy Harrison Fawcett (1867–1925), a dreamer and romantic like Halliburton, who with his son Jack and friend Raleigh Rimmel disappeared in the Brazilian jungles while searching for "Z" or "Shangri-La" and sightings of whom continued until the mid–1960s when it seemed unlikely he could still be alive, pp. 30–48. For Hangover House as haunted see Hal McClure, "The Ghost of Laguna's Hangover House," Associated Press, *Orange County Tribune*, Sunday, January 20, 1957.

16. The words "phantom ships" and "souls of long-drowned sailors" begin J.M. Hiatt's and Moye Stephens' "Ghosts of the Air," op. cit., p. 176.

17. *Time*, July 8. 1940, p. 69–71.

18. *The Glorious Adventure*, op. cit., p. 131.

19. Alexander always referred to it as the "Halliburton chest." The translation of the passage from Confucius' *Analects* carved on the chest, Alexander told me, came with the chest and appeared to be in Alicia's hand.

20. *Burton Holmes: The Man Who Photographed The World—Travelogues 1892-1938*, with introduction by Irving Wallace and selected and edited by Genoa Caldwell (New York: Abrams, 1977), p. 319 (quoted).

21. For the dates of the Fair see Gladys Hansen,

San Francisco Almanac (Chronicle Books, San Francisco, 1995), p. 185. For the opening of *Gone with the Wind* see McGill's *Survey of the Cinema—English Language—First Series* (New York: Salem Press, 1980), p. 657. The "1940 San Francisco Concerts" are available on four compact disks through Music and Arts, CD 971. Did a splinter survive? See Amos L. Wood, op. cit., pp. 208–210. For the Laguna arts event a Program of the Festival of Arts for 1939 was consulted.

22. Elly Beinhorn, or Elly Rosemeyer-Beinhorn, wrote her husband's biography *Mein Mann der Rennfahrer—Der Lebensweg Bernd Rosemeyers* which appeared in 1938 (Berlin). On Bernd Rosemeyer(s) (1909–1938) "idol of the masses," see, for instance, weltchronik.de/bio/cethegus/r/rosemeyer.htm. Also see Cyril Postumus, "Bernd Rosemeyer," *Great Racing Drivers*, edited by David Hodges (New York: Arco Publishing Company, Inc., 1966), pp. 129–133.

23. *Washington Post*, B6, Sunday, September 24, 1995.

24. My thanks to Dartmouth College for permitting me to use clippings from their files; (for Torrey) *The Quoddy Times*; (for Potter) *Darien County News Review*, January 16, 1997; (for Chase), *The New York Herald Tribune*, April 30, 1939 and *The Boston Herald*, March 26, 1941.

25. For Douglas Fairbanks see, for instance, The Douglas Fairbanks Sr. Museum, "Douglas Fairbanks—The King of Silent Hollywood," douglasfairbanks.org/douglasfairbanks/bio.htm.

26. For *The Wizard of Oz*, production and premier, see Gerald Clarke, *Get Happy—The Life of Judy Garland* (New York: Random House, 2000), pp. 102–103.

Bibliography

Adams, William T. ("Oliver Optic"). *Northern Lands; or Young America in Russia and Prussia: A Story of Travel and Adventure.* Boston: Lee and Shepard Publishers; New York: Lee, Shepard and Dillingham, 1872.

Adler, Alfred. "The Homosexual Problem." n.p., 1917.

Aero Digest, November 1929.

Air Travel News 3, no. 12 (December 1929).

Aldrich, Robert, and Garry Wotherspoon, eds. *Who's Who in Gay and Lesbian History—From World War II to the Present Day.* New York and London: Routledge, 2001.

Alexander, William. "Meanderings" or "The Many Faces of William Alexander" (unpublished manuscript). Author's collection.

Allan, Tony. *The Glamour Years—Paris 1919-1940.* New York: Gallery Books, 1977.

Amelia Earhart. Video documentary. "The American Experience." Written, produced, and directed by Nancy Porter. 1993.

Anderson, Patrick, and Alistair Sutherland, eds. *Eros: An Anthology of Male Friendship.* New York: Citadel Press, 1963.

Antoniou, Jim. *Cities Then & Now (As They Are Today—As They Once Were).* New York: Macmillan, 1994.

Appignanesi, Lisa. *The Cabaret.* Rev. ed. New Haven, Conn.: Yale University Press, 2004.

Architectural Forum, eds. *The Book of Small Houses.* New York: Simon & Schuster, 1936.

Architectural Record, Building News. "House for Writer Affords Privacy and Spectacular View," Alexander Levy, B. Arch., October 1938, pp. 47–51.

The Art Digest. Article on Donald Forbes in exhibition program. 1 February 1942.

Atherton, Gertrude. *Adventures of a Novelist.* New York: Horace Liveright, 1932.

_____. *Can Women Be Gentlemen?* Boston: Houghton Mi·in Company, 1938.

_____. *My San Francisco—A Wayward Biography.* New York: Bobbs-Merrill Company, 1946.

Aubrey, John. *Aubrey's Brief Lives.* Edited by Oliver Lawson Dick. Ann Arbor: University of Michigan Press, 1957.

Auden, W.H., and Christopher Isherwood. *Journey to a War.* London: Faber & Faber, 1939.

Austen, Roger. *Genteel Pagan—The Double Life of Charles Warren Stoddard.* Edited by John W. Crowley. Amherst: University of Massachusetts Press, 1991.

Avery, Gillian. *Behold the Child—American Children and Their Books, 1621-1922.* London: The Bodley Head, 1994.

Bahti, Tom. *Southwestern Indian Ceremonials.* Las Vegas, Nevada: KC Publications, 1970.

Balakian, Anna. Preface to *Babylon,* by René Crevel. Translated by Kay Boyle. San Francisco: North Point Press, 1985.

Baldwin, Neil. *Henry Ford and the Jews—The Mass Production of Hate.* New York: Public Affairs, 2001.

Batache, Eddy. *La Mysticité charnelle de René Crevel.* Paris, 1976.

Baum, Timothy. *Man Ray's Paris Portraits: 1921-1939.* Washington, D.C.: Middendorf Gallery, 1991.

Beaton, Cecil. *The Wandering Years: Diaries 1922-1939.* Boston: Little, Brown & Company, 1961.

Beebe, William. "Adventures in Exploration at the World's End." *The Mentor,* April 1925, 3–22.

Beinhorn, Elly. *Flying Girl.* London: Geoffrey Bles, 1935.

_____. *Mein Mann der Rennfahrer—Der Lebensweg Bernd Rosemeyers.* Berlin: n.p., 1938.

"Believe Wreck Sighted Is Junk Seadragon." *Boston Post,* 6 January 1940.

Benedict, Burton, et al. *The Anthropology of World's Fairs—San Francisco's Panama Pacific International Exposition of 1915.* London and New York: Lowrie Museum of Anthropology and Scholar Press, 1983.

Benstock, Shari. *Women of the Left Bank.* Austin: University of Texas Press, 1986.

Bercovici, Konrad. *Around the World in New York.* New York: D. Appleton-Century Company, 1938.

Bergman, David. "Ethnography." glbtq. An Encyclopedia of Gay, Lesbian, Bisexual, Transgender & Queer Culture. http://www.glbtq.com/literature/ethnography.html

Berkhofer, Robert F., Jr. *The White Man's Indian.* New York: Vintage Books, 1978.

Besinger, Curtis. *Working With Mr. Wright: What It Was Like.* Cambridge: Cambridge University Press, 1995.

Black, Stephen. *Eugene O'Neill—Beyond Mourning and Tragedy.* New Haven, Conn.: Yale University Press, 1999.

Blanch, Lesley. *Pierre Loti—The Legendary Romantic.* New York: Carroll & Graf Publishers, 1983.

Blankenship, Michael. "A Fellow Traveler." *The Advocate: The National Gay and Lesbian Newsmagazine* 18 (July 1989), 38–43.

_____. *Central High Alumni Record.* Entry for James Mooney, graduating class of 1922–1923). (Washington, D.C.: Central High School, 1990).

Bly, Nellie. *Nellie Bly's Book—Around the World in 72 Days.* Edited by Ira Peck. Brookfield, Connecticut: Twenty-First Century Books, 1998.

Bodenheim, Maxwell. *My Life and Loves in Greenwich Village.* New York: Bridgehead Books, 1954.

Bowling, Lance. Recording notes. *American Classics* (includes Charles Wakefield Cadman's "Piano Trio in D Major"). Naxos 8.559067. Compact disc.

Boyd, Nan Alamilla. *Wide Open Town—A History of Queer San Francisco to 1965.* Berkeley: University of California Press, 2003.

Boyle, Kay, and Robert McAlmon. *Being Geniuses Together—1920–1930.* Garden City, N.Y.: Doubleday & Company, 1968.

Bradbury, Malcolm, ed. *The Atlas of Literature.* London: De Agostini Editions, 1996.

Brandon, Ruth. *Surreal Lives—The Surrealists 1917–1945.* New York: Macmillan, 1999.

Breashears, David, and Audrey Salkeld. *Last Climb: The Legendary Everest Expeditions of George Mallory.* Washington, D.C.: National Geographic Society, 1999.

Brimmer, Frank E. "Billions for Scenery." *American Motorist,* March 1928, 9–10, 30–31.

Briody, Dan. *The Halliburton Agenda: The Politics of Oil and Money.* Hoboken, New Jersey: John Wiley & Sons, Inc., 2004.

Broch, Hermann. *The Sleepwalkers.* Translated by Willa and Edwin Muir. San Francisco: North Point Press, 1985.

Brock, Horace. *Flying the Oceans: A Pilot's Story of Pan Am, 1935–1955.* New York: Jason Aronson, 1978.

Bronner, Stephen Eric. *Rosa Luxemburg—A Revolutionary for Our Times.* University Park: Pennsylvania State University Press, 1997.

Brooke, Rupert. *Letters from America.* Preface by Henry James. New York: Charles Scribner's Sons, 1916.

_____. *The Poetical Works.* Edited by Geoffrey Keynes. London and Boston: Faber & Faber, 1985.

Brown, Eva. *The Plaza, 1907–1967: Its Life and Times.* New York: Van Rees Press, 1967.

Brown, Joseph Epes. *The Spiritual Legacy of the American Indian.* Pendle Hill Pamphlet, no. 135. Philadelphia: Pendle Hill, 1964.

Buot, Francois. *Crevel.* Paris: Bernard Grasset, 1991.

Burati, Robert, and Harold Pettalkay. *Hong Kong.* This Beautiful World series. Tokyo: Kodansha International, Ltd., 1970.

Burlingame, Margaret R. "The Laguna Beach Group." *The American Magazine of Art* 24, no. 4, 259–266.

Burnett, Frances Hodgson. *The Secret Garden.* Edited by Alison Lurie. New York: Penguin Books, 1999.

Byington, Robert. "Interviews with Virgil Thomson, Eugene MacCown, Quentin Bell, and Hugh Ross Williamson." In *A Sacred Quest: The Life and Writings of Mary Butts,* edited by Christopher Wagstaff. Kingston, N.Y.: McPherson & Company, 1995.

Byron, Lord George Gordon. *His Very Self and Voice—Collected Conversations of Lord Byron.* Edited by Ernest J. Lovell. New York: Macmillan, 1954.

Cabell, James Branch. *Jurgen.* New York: Dover Publications, 1977.

"Cadmus Tars under Fire at the San Francisco Fair." *Newsweek,* 19 August 1940.

Caldwell, Genoa, ed. *Burton Holmes: The Man Who Photographed the World—Travelogues 1892–1938.* New York: Abrams, 1977.

Cameron, Nigel. *Hong Kong—The Cultured Pearl.* Oxford and Hong Kong: Oxford University Press, 1978.

Cantarella, Eva. *Bisexuality in the Greek World.* New Haven, Conn.: Yale University Press, 2002.

Cardozo High School (subject). www.exploreedu.
org/index.php?id=308.

"Career highlights" [of Richard Halliburton]. *Indiana Evening Gazette*, 13 March 1928, clipping in scrapbooks, Rhodes College Collection, Memphis, Tenn.

Carman, Bliss. *More Songs from Vagabondia*. Boston: Small, Maynard & Company, 1911.

_____. *Pipes of Pan, Number One, From the Book of Myths*. Boston: L.C. Page & Company, 1902.

Carroll, David. *The Matinee Idols*. New York: Arbor House, 1972.

Carter, Hodding. *A Viking Voyage—In Which an Unlikely Crew of Adventurers Attempts an Epic Journey to the New World*. New York: Random House, 2000.

Carter, Robert. "Boys Going Nowhere." In *The Strenuous Decade: A Social and Intellectual Record of the Nineteen Thirties*, edited by Daniel Aaron and Robert Bendiner. Garden City, N.Y.: Anchor Books, Doubleday & Company, 1970.

Cather, Willa. *Collected Short Stories—1892–1912*. Edited by Virginia Faulkner. Lincoln: University of Nebraska Press, 1970.

Céline, Louis-Ferdinand. *Journey to the End of the Night*. New York: New Directions Publishing, 1983.

_____. *Death on the Installment Plan*. New York: New Directions Publishing, 1971.

A Century of Hong Kong Roads and Streets. Hong Kong: Joint Publishing Company, 2000.

A Century of Kowloon Roads and Streets. Hong Kong: Joint Publishing Company, 2000.

Chambers, David Laurance. *The Meter of Macbeth: Its Relation to Shakespeare's Earlier and Later Work*. New York: A. H. S. Press, facsimile reprint of edition, 1972.

Champney, Lizzie W. *Three Vassar Girls Abroad—Rambles of Three College Girls on a Vacation Trip Through France and Spain for Amusement and Instruction with Their Haps and Mishaps*. Boston: Estes and Lauriat, 1883.

Chandler, Anna Curtis. *Pan the Piper and Other Marvelous Tales*. New York: Harper, 1923.

_____. *Stories for Children Based upon Rare Objects at the Metropolitan Museum*. New York: Harper, 1929.

_____. *Dragons on Guard—An Imaginative Interpretation of Old China in Stories of Art and History*. New York: J.B. Lippincott Company, 1944.

Chandler, Arthur. "Empire of the Republic: The Exposition Coloniale Internationale De Paris, 1931." *World's Fair Magazine*, 8, no. 4.; also *Contemporary French Civilization*, Winter/Spring 1990; expanded and revised version, 2000. http:/charon.sfsu.edu/PARIS EXPOSITIONS/1931EXPO.html.

Chatwin, Bruce. *Hong Kong—True Stories of Life on the Road*. San Francisco: Traveler's Tales, 1997.

Chauncey, George. *Gay New York—Gender, Urban Culture and the Making of the Gay World 1890–1940*. New York: Basic Books, 1994.

Chisholm, Anne. *Nancy Cunard—A Biography*. New York: Alfred A. Knopf, 1979.

Chris, Joanne, and Annie Chris. www.glenal pine.com/chris/astoria/official_history,htm.

Churchill, Allen. *The Literary Decade—A Panorama of the Writers, Publishers, and Litterateurs of the 1920s*. Englewood Cliffs, N.J.: Prentice-Hall, 1971.

_____. *The Improper Bohemians—A Re-Creation of Greenwich Village in Its Heyday*. New York: E.P. Dutton, & Company, 1959.

Clark, Francis E. *Our Journey around the World*. Includes Harriet E. *Clark's Glimpses of Life in Far Off Lands As Seen Through a Woman's Eyes*. Hartford, Conn.: A.D. Worthington & Co., 1895.

Clarke, Gerald. *Get Happy—The Life of Judy Garland*. New York: Random House, 2000.

Clayton, Douglas. *Floyd Dell : The Life and Times of an American Rebel*. Chicago: Ivan R. Dee, 1994.

Click, September 1939.

Cocker, Mark. *Loneliness and Time—The Story of British Travel Writing*. New York: Pantheon Books, 1993.

Cocteau, Jean. *Round the World Again in 80 Days*. New York: Tauris Parke Paperbacks, 2000.

Colby, William. "Routes to Rainy Mountain: A Biography of James Mooney, Ethnologist." Ph.D. diss., University of Wisconsin, 1977.

Cole, Robert. *A Traveler's History of Paris*. Brooklyn: Interlink Books, 1998.

Collins, Dale E. Letter (unpublished) to Edward Howell, 7 May 1946.

Conaway, James. *The Smithsonian—150 Years of Adventure, Discovery, and Wonder*. New York: Alfred A. Knopf, 1995.

Connell, Evan S. *A Long Desire*. Berkely, Calif.: North Point Press, 1979.

_____. "The Last Great Traveler." *Oxford American: The Travel Issue*, March/April 2001, 124–129.

Conover, Anne. *Caresse Crosby—From Black Sun to Roccasinibalda*. Santa Barbara, Calif.: Capra Press, 1989.

Considine, Bob. *Ripley—The Modern Marco Polo*. Garden City, N.Y.: Doubleday & Company, 1961.

"Controlled Recklessness and Frida Kahlo Images." *New York Times*, 11 November 1995, Section C, 13, c. 1.

Cook, Thomas. *A Golden Jubilee Cruise around the World, or Around the World–A De Luxe Cruise.* Photo-brochure. New York: Thos. Cook & Sons, 1922.

Corle, Edwin. *The Grand Canyon–A Panorama of the Southwest.* New York: Duehl, Sloan & Pierce, 1945.

Cortese, James. *Richard Halliburton's Royal Road.* Memphis: White Rose Press, 1989.

Cousins, James Henry. *The Bardic Pilgrimage.* New York: Roerich Museum Press, 1934.

Crane, Hart. *The Complete Poems and Selected Letters and Prose of Hart Crane.* Edited by Brom Weber. New York: Boni & Liveright, 1966.

Crevel, René. *Detours.* Paris: G. Aubart, Editions de la Nouvelle Revue Francaise, 1924.

_____. *Correspondence de René Crevel à Gertrude Stein.* Traducion, presentation et annotation par Jean-Michel Devesa. Paris: L'Harmattan, 2000.

_____. *Difficult Death.* San Francisco: North Point Press, 1989.

_____. *Lettres de desir et de souffrance.* Paris: Libraire Artheme Fayard, 1996.

_____. *Putting My Foot in It.* Translation by Thomas Buckley. Dalkey Archive Press, 1992.

Crisler, Jane. "George Moore's Paris." In *George Moore in Perspective,* edited by Janet Egleson Dunleavy. Totowa, N.J.: Barnes & Noble Books, 1983.

Crosby, Caresse. *The Passionate Years.* New York: The Dial Press, 1953.

Crouch, Tom D. *Wings–A History of Aviation from Kites to the Space Age.* Washington: Smithsonian National Air and Space Museum/W.W. Norton, 2003.

Cunard, Nancy. *Grand Man–Memories of Norman Douglas.* London: Secker & Warburg, 1954.

_____. *GM: Memories of George Moore.* London: Hart-Davis, 1956.

_____. *These Were the Hours–Memories of My Hours Press, Reanville and Paris, 1928–1931.* Edited by Hugh Ford. Carbondale, Ill.: Southern Illinois University Press, 1969.

Cunard, Nancy, ed. *Negro–An Anthology.* London: Wishart & Company, 1934.

The Cunarder. Magazine of the Cunard Steam Ship Company, Ltd. Various issues.

Current, Richard Nelson, and Marcia Ewing Current. *Loie Fuller–Goddess of Light.* Boston: Northeastern University Press, 1997.

Curzon, Lord George Nathaniel. *Travels with a Superior Person.* Edited by Peter King. London: Sidgwick & Jackson, 1985.

Curwood, James Oliver. *The Ancient Highway.* New York: Grosset & Dunlap, 1925.

Curwood, James Oliver (subject). Shiawassee District Library. www.sdl.lib.mi.us/curwood.htm.

Dana, Richard Henry. *Two Years Before the Mast–A Personal Narrative of Life at Sea.* New York: Signet Classic, 1964.

"Dancing through Life—Jerome Robbins in a 'Proustian' mood." *Newsweek,* 6 March 1989, 56.

Daniels, Edwin, and JD Challenger. *Ghost Dancing–Sacred Medicine and the Art of JD Challenger.* New York: Stewart, Tabori & Chang, 1998.

Davies, William H. *The Autobiography of a Super-Tramp.* New York: Alfred A. Knopf, 1917.

Davis, Juliet Halliburton, letter to William Short, curator, Halliburton Collection, Rhodes College, Memphis, Tenn., June 28, 1987.

Davis, Kenneth C. *Don't Know Much About History–Everything You Need to Know About American History but Never Learned.* New York: HarperCollins, 2003.

Dayton, Dorothy. "Richard Halliburton, 'Prince of Lovers,' Talks about Women and Love." *The Illustrated Love Magazine,* March 1930, 36–41.

De Acosta, Mercedes. *Here Lies the Heart.* New York: Reynal & Company, 1960.

_____. *Streets and Shadows.* New York: Moffat, Yard & Company, 1922.

Dedman, Emmett. *Fabulous Chicago.* New York: Random House, 1953.

DeFaa, Chip. "On the Trail of Richard Halliburton '21: A Young Alumnus Searches for the Man Behind the Legend." *Princeton Alumni Weekly,* 13 May 1973.

Delany, Paul. *The Neo-Pagans–Rupert Brooke and the Ordeal of Youth.* New York: The Free Press, 1987.

Dell, Floyd. *Homecoming–An Autobiography.* New York: Farrar & Rinehart, 1933.

_____. "Robinson Crusoe." In *Intellectual Vagabondage.* New York: George H. Doran Company, 1926).

_____. "Shell-Shock and the Poetry of Robinson Jeffers." *Modern Quarterly III,* September–December 1926.

DeMallie, Raymond. Introduction to the Bison Book Edition of *The Ghost-Dance Religion and the Sioux Outbreak of 1890* by James Mooney. Lincoln: University of Nebraska, 1991.

Dilling, Elizabeth. *The Roosevelt Red Record and its Background.* Kenilworth, Illinois: self-published, 1936.

Dodson, Howard, Christopher Moore, and Roberta Yancy. *The Black New Yorkers: The Schomberg Illustrated Chronology of 400 Years of African American History.* New York: John Wiley & Sons, 2000.

Drohojowska-Philp, Hunter. "Historic Neighborhood: Whitley Heights—Preserving the

Address of Hollywood's Early Royalty." *Architectural Digest*, April 1996, 92–99.

Dunford, Penny. "Concetta Scaravaglione." In *Biographical Dictionary of Woman Artists in Europe and America since 1850*. Philadelphia: University of Pennsylvania Press, 1989.

Dunleavy, Janet Egleson, and Gareth W. Dunleavy. *Douglas Hyde–A Maker of Modern Ireland*. Berkeley: University of California Press, 1991.

Dunning, A.J. *Extremes–Reflections on Human Behavior*. New York: Harcourt Brace Jovanovich, 1993.

Durozoi, Gerard. *History of the Surrealist Movement*. Translated by Alison Anderson. Chicago: University of Chicago Press, 2002.

Dyer, Daniel. *Jack London–A Biography*. New York: Scholastic Press, 1997.

Edmiston, Susan, and Linda D. Cirino. *Literary New York: A History and Guide*. Boston: Houghton Mifflin company, 1976.

Ellenberger, Allan R. *Ramon Novarro–A Biography of the Silent Film Idol, 1899-1968*. Jefferson, N.C.: McFarland & Company, 1999.

Ellis, Simone. *Santa Fe Art*. North Dighton, Mass.: World Publishing Group, 2004.

Elmendorf, Dwight L. "Natural Wonders of America." *The Mentor, A Wise and Faithful Guide and Friend* 1, no. 7 (March 31, 1913).

Endacott, G.B. *A History of Hong Kong*. 2nd ed. New York and Oxford: Oxford University Press, 1973.

Endacott, G.B., and A. Hinton. *Fragrant Harbour–A Short History of Hong Kong*. Oxford and Hong Kong: 1962.

Ernst, Robert. *Weakness Is a Crime–The Life of Bernarr MacFadden*. Syracuse: Syracuse University Press, 1991.

Evans, Charles M. *War of the Aeronauts–A History of Ballooning in the Civil War*. Mechanicsburg, Pa.: Stackpole Books, 2002.

Fairbanks, Douglas, Jr. *The Fairbanks Album, Drawn from the Family Archives*. New York: New York Graphic Society, 1975.

Fass, Paula S. *The Damned and the Beautiful*. New York and Oxford: Oxford University Press, 1977.

Ferguson, Ted. *Desperate Siege–The Battle of Hong Kong*. Garden City, N.Y.: Doubleday & Company, 1980.

Fergusson, Erna. *Our Southwest*. New York: Alfred A. Knopf, 1940.

Fielding, Daphne. *Emerald and Nancy–Lady Cunard and her Daughter*. London: Eyre & Spottiswoode, 1968.

Fitch, Robert F. "Life Afloat in China—Tens of Thousands of Chinese in Congested Ports Spend Their Entire Existence on Boats." *National Geographic* 51, no. 6 (June 1927), 665–686.

Fitzgerald, F. Scott. *Correspondence of F. Scott Fitzgerald*. Edited by Matthew J. Bruccoli and Margaret M. Duggan. New York: Random House, 1980.

Flanner, Janet. *Paris Was Yesterday, 1925-1939*. Edited by Irving Drutman. New York: Harcourt Brace Jovanovich, 1988.

Fleming, Paula Richardson, and Judith Luskey. *The North American Indians in Early Photographs*. London: Calmann & King, 1986.

Fletcher, Richard. "Faith to Faith—When Worlds Collide." *History Magazine* 4, no. 4 (April 2003), 37–39.

Flude, Anthony G. http://homepages.ihug, co.nz/~tonyf/von/VonLuckner.html,.

Flynn, Errol. *Beam Ends*. Toronto and New York: Longman's, Green & Company, 1937.

Fone, Byrne. *Homophobia–A History*. New York: Metropolitan Books/Henry Holt & Company, 2000.

Ford, Hugh, ed. *Nancy Cunard: Brave, Poet, Indomitable Rebel, 1896-1965*. New York: Chilton Book Company, 1968.

Fortune, June 1934, 81–89.

Franck, Harry A. *All About Going Abroad*. New York: Brentano's Publishers, 1927.

_____. *Marco Polo, Junior*. New York: The Century Company, 1929.

_____. *Vagabond Journey Around the World*. Garden City, N.Y.: Garden City Publishing Company, 1910.

Franck, Rachel Latta. *I Married a Vagabond–The Story of the Family of the Writing Vagabond*. New York: D. Appleton-Century Company, 1939.

Frank, Glenn. *Wonders of Modern Industry–The Story of the Machine Age*. Edited by William Norman Mitchell. n.p., n.d.

Frappier-Mazur, Lucienne. *Writing the Orgy–Power and Parody in Sade*. Translated by Gillian C. Gill. Philadelphia: University of Pennsylvania Press, 1996.

Frazier, Ian. *Great Plains*. New York: Farrar, Straus, Giroux, 1989.

Friedman, Richard, and Harold Wellman. *The Fellowship–The Untold Story of Frank Lloyd Wright and the Taliesin Fellowship*. New York: HarperCollins Publishers, 2006.

Gaddusek, Robert E. *Hemingway's Paris*. New York: Charles Scribner's Sons, 1978.

Gale, Robert L. *Charles Warren Stoddard*. Western Writers Series no. 30. Boise: Boise State University, 1977.

Gardner, Erle Stanley. *The Hidden Heart of Baja*. New York: William Morrow & Company, 1962.

Garner, Bess Adams. *Mexico—Notes in the Margin*. Boston: Houghton Mi·in Company, 1937.

Garner, Phillipe, and David Alan Mellor, eds. *Cecil Beaton—Photographs 1920-1970*. New York: Stewart, Tabori & Chang, 1995.

Gelernter, David. *1939—The Lost World of the Fair*. New York: The Free Press, 1995.

Gerhard, Peter, and Howard E. Gulick. *Lower California Guidebook*. Glendale, Calif.: The Arthur H. Clark Company, 1956.

Gilfoyle, Timothy F. "Policing of Sexuality." In *Inventing Times Square—Commerce and Culture at the Crossroads of the World*, edited by William R. Taylor. Baltimore: John Hopkins University Press, 1991.

Gilliam, Ronald."Around the World in the Flying Carpet." *Aviation History*, vol. 14, issue 5 (May 2004), 22–60.

_____. "Moye Stephens Piloted More Than 100 Types of Aircraft and Flew Around the World in The Flying Carpet." *Aviation History* vol. 9, issue 6 (July 1999).

Gillman, Peter, and Leni Gillman. *The Wildest Dream: Mallory—His Life and Conflicting Passions*. London: Headline Book Publishing, 2001.

Gleason, Gene. *Hong Kong*. New York: The John Day Company, 1963.

Glyn, Elinor. *Romantic Adventure*. New York: Dutton, 1937.

Golway, Terry. *Irish Rebel—John Devoy and America's Fight for Ireland's Freedom*. New York: St. Martin's Press, 1998.

Gordimer, Nadine, "Introduction: The Empire of Joseph Roth." In *The Radetsky March*, by Joseph Roth. Woodstock, N.Y.: The Overlook Press, 1995.

Gould, Stephen Jay. *Questioning the Millennium: A Rationalist's Guide to a Precisely Arbitrary Countdown*. New York: Harmony Books, 1995.

Graham, Stephen. *The Gentle Art of Tramping*. New York: D. Appleton & Company, 1926.

_____. *New York Nights*. New York: George H. Doran Company, 1927.

Grant, R.G. *Flight—100 Years of Aviation*. New York: Dorling Kindersley Publishing, 2002.

Grass: A Nation's Battle for Life. Film. Directed by Merian C. Cooper and Ernest B. Schoedsack, 1925.

Gray, George W. "Up Where the Blue Begins." *American Magazine*, September 1927, 52.

The Great Air Race of 1924. Video documentary. "The American Experience." Produced by David Grubin. AMEX-201-DAE4. 1989.

Greenberg, David F. *The Construction of Homosexuality*. Chicago: University of Chicago Press, 1988.

Greggory, David. "Adventures of Richard Halliburton of Hangover House." Unpublished screenplay.

Gruber, Frank. *Zane Grey—A Biography*. Roslyn, N.Y.: Walter J. Black, 1969.

Guardian, 25 September 1995, 11.

Haagensen, Erik. www.babydoe.org/latouche.htm.

Hahn, Emily. *Times and Places*. New York: Thomas Y. Crowell Company, 1970.

Hale, Keith, ed. *Friends and Apostles: The Correspondence of Rupert Brooke and James Strachey 1905-1914*. New Haven, Conn.: Yale University Press, 1998.

Halliburton, Richard. *The Royal Road to Romance*. Indianapolis and New York: Bobbs-Merrill, 1925.

_____. *The Glorious Adventure*. Indianapolis and New York: Bobbs-Merrill, 1927.

_____. *New Worlds to Conquer*. Indianapolis and New York: Bobbs-Merrill, 1929.

_____. "The place where the sun is tied." *Ladies Home Journal*, June 1929.

_____. "The place where the sun is tied." *Ladies Home Journal*, July 1929.

_____. "The place where the sun is tied." *Ladies Home Journal*, September 1929.

_____. Letter to Richard Pitcairn (unpublished), 4 November 1930, author's collection.

_____. *The Flying Carpet*. Indianapolis and New York: Bobbs-Merrill, 1932.

_____. *Seven League Boots*. Indianapolis and New York: Bobbs-Merrill, 1935.

_____. "I've Eaten Christmas Dinner All around the World." *Cosmopolitan*, January 1936, 111.

_____. *Book of Marvels—The Occident*. Indianapolis and New York: Bobbs-Merrill, 1937.

_____. "Half a Mile of History." *Readers Digest*, October 1937, 70–73.

_____. *Second Book of Marvels—The Orient*. Indianapolis and New York: Bobbs-Merrill, 1938.

_____. "Letters from the Sea Dragon," the Richard Halliburton Trans-Pacific Chinese Junk Expedition—Hong Kong to Treasure Island San Francisco, California, 1939. Prospectus.

_____. *His Story of His Life's Adventure As Told in Letters to His Mother and Father*. New York: Bobbs-Merrill Company, 1940.

_____. Letters (unpublished portions), Halliburton Collection, Princeton University Library.

_____. Letters to Noel Sullivan and Gertrude Atherton, University of California, Bancroft Library.

_____. Letters (unpublished) to William Alexander, William Alexander Collection.

"Halliburton: Adventurer's Legend, Mansion Are All But (Forgotten)." *Los Angeles Times*, Orange County, Part II, September 3, 1989.

Halpern, Katherine Spencer. "Women in Applied Anthropology—The Early Years." In *Hidden Scholars—Women Anthropologists and the Native American Southwest*, edited by Nancy J. Parezo. Albuquerque: University of New Mexico Press, 1993.

Haneman, H.W. *In the Facts of Life—A Book of Brighter Biography Executed in the Manner of Some of Our Best or Best-Known Writers, Scriveners & Scribes*. New York: Farrar & Rinehart, 1930.

Hansen, Gladys. *San Francisco Almanac*. San Francisco: Chronicle Books, 1995.

Hardwick, Joan. *Addicted to Romance: The Life and Adventures of Elinor Glyn*. London: Andre Deutsch Limited, 1994.

Harkens, John E. *Metropolis of the American Nile: An Illustrated History of Memphis and Shelby County*. Oxford, Miss.: The Guild Bindery Press, 1982.

Harrington, Mildred. "Dick Halliburton Has Followed the Royal Road to Romance." *The American Woman's Magazine*, October 1926, 26–28, 218, 220, 224.

Harris, Warren G. *Clark Gable*. New York: Harmony Books, 2002.

Harrison, Helen A., and Constance Ayers Denne. *Hamptons Bohemia—Two Centuries of Artists and Writers on the Beach*. San Francisco: Chronicle Books, 2002.

"Harry Hay, Early Proponent of Gay Rights, Dies at 90." *New York Times*, 25 October 2002, A33.

Hart, James D. *The Popular Book—A History of America's Literary Taste*. Berkeley: University of California Press, 1961.

Hawthorne, Hildegarde. *Romantic Cities of California*. New York: Appleton-Century Crofts, 1940.

Hay, Harry. *Radically Gay—Gay Liberation in the Words of Its Founder*. Edited by Will Roscoe. Boston: Beacon Press, 1996.

Hayes, Jarrod. *Queer Sites*. Chicago: University of Chicago Press, 2000.

Hefmann, Jim, ed. *20s All-American Ads*. Cologne, Germany: Taschen, 2004.

Hegemann, Elizabeth Compton. *Navajo Trading Days*. Albuquerque: University of New Mexico Press, 1963.

Hemingway, Ernest. *Ernest Hemingway—Selected Letters—1917-1961*. Edited by Carlos Baker. New York: Charles Scribner's Sons, 1981.

Henderson, Helen W. *A Loiterer in New York—Discoveries Made by a Rambler through Obvious Yet Unsought Highways and Byways*. New York: George W. Doran, 1917.

Henderson, Richard. *Sea Sense—Safety Afloat in Terms of Sail, Power, and Multihull Boat Design, Construction Rig, Equipment, Coping with Emergencies, and Boat Management in Heavy Weather*. Camden, Maine.: International Marine Publishing Company, 1972.

Hendrick, Burton J. *The Lees of Virginia—Biography of a Family*. Boston: Little, Brown & Company, 1935.

Heppenheimer, T.A. "Howard Hughes, the Innovator, the Method Before the Madness." *Invention & Technology* 14, no. 3, 36–46.

Herndon, Booton. *Mary Pickford and Douglas Fairbanks: The Most Popular Couple the World Has Known*. New York: W.W. Norton, 1977.

Hesse, Herman. *Herman Hesse and Romain Rolland: Correspondence, Diary Entries, and Reflections, 1915 to 1940*. Translated by M.G. Hesse. London and New Jersey: Oswald Wolff & Humanities Press, 1978.

———. *Demian—The Story of Emil Sinclair's Youth*. Translated by Michael Roloff and Michael Lebeck. New York: Bantam Books, 1966.

Highland, Monica. *Greetings from Southern California—A Look at the Past through Postcards*. Portland, Ore.: Graphic Arts Center Publishing Company, 1988.

Hoare, Philip. *Oscar Wilde's Last Stand—Decadence, Conspiracy, and the Most Outrageous Trial of the Century*. New York: Arcade Publishing, 1998.

Hodge, Frederick Walter. *The Handbook of American Indians North of Mexico*. 2 vols. Washington, D.C.: U.S. Government Printing Office, 1907, 1912.

Hodgson, Barbara. *No Place for a Lady—Tales of Adventurous Women Travelers*. Berkeley, Calif.: Ten Speed Press, 2002.

Hoffer, Peter T. *Klaus Mann*. Boston: Twayne Publishers, 1978.

Hogan, Steve, and Lee Hudson. *Completely Queer—The Gay and Lesbian Encyclopedia*. New York: Henry Holt & Company, 1998.

Holiday in Hong Kong 2, no. 10 (1–10 April 1959), 16.

Holmes, Burton, and Lothrop Stoddard. *Burton Holmes and the Travelogue—A Life Story*. Philadelphia: George F. Lasher Printing Company, 1939.

Holmes, Richard. *Sidetracks—Explorations of a Romantic Traveler*. New York: Vintage Books, 2000.

Homer. *The Odyssey*. Translated by A.T. Murray. Cambridge, Mass.: Loeb Classical Library/ Harvard University Press, 1934.

"Hong Kong." *The Encyclopedia Britannica*. 14th ed. New York and London: Encyclopedia Britannica, 1929.

Hoover, Kathleen, and John Cage. *Virgil Thomson—His Life and Work*. New York: Sagamore Press, 1959.

Hoover, Robert A. *Forever Flying.* New York: Pocket Books, 1996.

Horne, Alistair. *Seven Ages of Paris.* New York: Alfred A. Knopf, 2002.

Horticultural Exhibition Souvenir Book. Chicago: Century of Progress Exhibition, 1934.

"The House That Richard Halliburton Built ... And Never Lived In." *Look Magazine,* 19 December 1939, 64–65.

Huddleston, Sisley. *Paris Salons, Cafes, Studios.* Philadelphia: J.B. Lippincott & Company, 1928.

Huler, Scott. *Defining the Wind—The Beaufort Scale and How a Nineteenth Century Admiral Turned Science into Poetry.* New York: Crown Publications, 2004.

Hurewitz, Daniel. *Stepping Out—Nine Walks through New York's Gay and Lesbian Past.* New York: Henry Holt & Company, 1997.

Isaacs, Arlene. *Who's Cooking in Laguna Beach.* Laguna Beach, Calif.: Sun Box Press, 1980.

Isherwood, Christopher. *Christopher and His Kind (1929-1939).* New York: Farrar, Straus & Giroux, 1976.

_____. *Diaries, I, 1939-1960.* New York: HarperCollins Publishers, 1997.

_____. *Lost Years—A Memoir.* Edited by Katherine Bucknell. New York: HarperCollins Publishers, 2000.

Jackson, Kenneth T., ed. *The Encyclopedia of New York City.* New Haven, Conn.: Yale University Press, 1995.

Jeffers, Robinson. *The Selected Poetry of Robinson Jeffers.* New York: Random House, 1938.

Jenkins, Rolland. *The Mediterranean Cruise: An Up-to-date and Concise Handbook for Travelers.* New York: G.P. Putnam's Sons, 1923.

Jessen, Gene Nora. *The Powder Puff Derby of 1929—The True Story of the First Women's Cross-Country Air Race.* Naperville, Ill.: Sourcebooks, Inc., 2002.

Johnson, Douglas, and Madeleine Johnson. *The Age of Illusion: Art and Politics in France—1918-1940.* New York: Rizzoli International Publications, 1987.

Johnson, Paul E. *Sam Patch, The Famous Jumper.* New York: Hill & Wang, 2003.

Johnson, Samuel. *A Johnson Reader.* Edited by E.L. McAdam and George Milne. New York: Pantheon Books, 1964.

_____. *Johnson's Dictionary—A Modern Selection.* Edited by E.L. McAdam and George Milne. New York: Pantheon Books, 1963.

Johnson, Vance. *Heaven's Tableland—The Dust Bowl Story.* New York: Farrar, Straus & Company, 1947.

Jones, Robert Edmond. *The Dramatic Imagina-tion—Reflections and Speculations on the Art of the Theatre.* New York: Theatre Arts Books, 1941.

Josephson, Matthew. *Life among the Surrealists.* New York: Holt, Rinehart & Winston, 1962.

Sylvester, Charles, ed. *Journeys through Bookland.* 10 vols. Chicago: Bellows-Reeves, 1909.

Jowitt, Deborah. *Jerome Robbins—His Life, His Theatre, His Dance.* New York: Simon & Schuster, 2004.

Juvenal and Persius. Translated by G.G. Ramsay. Cambridge, Mass.: Loeb Classical Library/Harvard University Press, 1929.

Karman, James. *Robinson Jeffers—Poet of California.* Rev. ed. Ashland, Ore.: Story Line Press, 2001.

Katz, Jonathan, comp. *Gay American History: Lesbians and Gay Men in the U.S.A.* New York: Thomas Crowell & Company, 1976.

Keller, James Robert. *The Roles of Political and Sexual Identity in the Works of Klaus Mann.* Vol. 56 in *Studies on Theses and Motifs in Literature,* edited by Horst S. Daemmrich, New York: Peter Lang Publishing, 2001.

Kelly, Gretchen. "Richard Halliburton—In Search of Adventure." *Metrosource,* spring, 1998, 38–42.

Kennedy, Rod, Jr. *Hollywood in Vintage Postcards.* Salt Lake City: Gibbs Smith, 2003.

Kershaw, Alex. *Jack London—A Life.* New York: St. Martin's Press, 1997.

Kessler, Lauren. *The Life and Times of Pancho Barnes.* New York: Random House, 2000.

Ketchum, Richard M. *Will Rogers—The Man and His Times.* New York: American Heritage Books, 1973.

Kiki. *Kiki's Memoirs.* Edited by Billy Kluver and Julie Martin. New York: Ecco Press, 1996.

Kingman, Russ. *A Pictorial Life of Jack London.* New York: Crown Publishers, 1979.

Kirstein, Lincoln. *Paul Cadmus.* New York: Imago, 1984.

Kleeblatt, Norman L., and Susan Chevlowe, eds. *Painting a Place in America: Jewish Artists in New York, 1900-1945.* New York: The Jewish Museum, 1991.

Kluver, Billy, and Julie Martin. *Kiki's Paris—Artists and Lovers, 1900-1930.* New York: Harry N. Abrams, 1989.

Kochno, Boris. *Diaghilev and the Ballet Russes.* Translated by Adrienne Foulke. London: The Penguin Press, 1971.

Koestenbaum, Wayne. *The Queen's Throat—Opera, Homosexuality, and the Mystery of Desire.* New York: Poseidon Press, 1993.

Kolb, Ellsworth L. *Through the Grand Canyon from Wyoming to Mexico.* New York: Macmillan, 1936.

Kriegsman, Alan M. "Dancing on the sunny side:

Master Choreographer Jerome Robbins." *Washington Post*, 4 March 1979.

Kyvig, David E. *Daily Life in the United States, 1920-1939: Decades of Promise and Pain*. Westport, Conn.: Greenwood Press, 2002.

Lambert, Gavin. *Nazimova*. New York: Alfred A. Knopf, 1997.

Landsburg, Alan. *In Search of Missing Persons*. New York: Bantam Books, 1978.

LaTouche, John Treville. *The Congo*. Brussels: Elsevier, 1949.

Lawrence, D.H. *Mornings in Mexico*. New York: Alfred A. Knopf, 1927.

Lawrence, Greg. *Dance with Demons: The Life of Jerome Robbins*. New York: G.P. Putnam's Sons, 2001.

Leddick, David. *Intimate Companions—A Triography of George Platt Lynes, Paul Cadmus, Lincoln Kirstein, and Their Circle*. New York: St. Martin's Press: 2001.

Leider, Emily Wortis. *California's Daughter—Gertrude Atherton and Her Times*. Stanford, Calif.: Stanford University Press, 1991.

Leland, John. *A Guide to Hemingway's Paris with Walking Tours*. Chapel Hill, N.C.: Algonquin Books, 1989.

Lengyel, Emil. *Turkey*. New York: Random House, 1941.

Leverich, Lyle. *Tom—The Unknown Tennessee Williams*. New York: New Directions, 1995.

Lewis, Arnold. *An Early Encounter with Tomorrow—Europeans, Chicago's Loop, and the World's Columbian Exposition*. Urbana and Chicago: University of Illinois Press, 1997.

Lewis, Daniel. *The Illustrated Dance Technique of José Limon*. New York: Harper & Row, 1984.

Life, 6 September 1937.

Life, 13 February 1939.

Life, 6 March 1939.

Life, 11 August 1958.

Limon, José. *An Unfinished Memoir*. Edited by Lynn Garafola. Middletown, Conn.: Wesleyan University Press, 1999.

Lindbergh, Charles. "To Bogota and Back By Air—The Narrative of a 9,500-Mile Flight from Washington, Over Thirteen Latin-American Countries and Return, in the Single—Seater Airplane 'Spirit of St. Louis.'" *National Geographic*, 53, no. 3 (May 1928), 529–602.

Lindsay, Vachel. *Golden Whales of California*. New York: Macmillan, 1920.

Linkletter, Art, and George Bishop. *I Didn't Do It Alone—The Autobiography of Art Linkletter*. Ottawa, Ill., and Ossining, N.Y.: Caroline House Publishers, 1980.

_____. Letter to author (unpublished), 26 January 1998.

Lewis, D.B. Wyndham. *Francois Villon—A Documentary Survey*. Garden City, N.Y.: Garden City Publishing Company, 1928.

Littlefield, William H. *Falmouth Enterprise*, 12 August 1966.

Littlewood, Ian. *Sultry Climates—Travel & Sex*. New York: Da Capo Press, 2002.

Logsdon, Jonathan R. "Power, Ignorance, and Anti-Semitism: Henry Ford and His War on Jews." The Hanover Historical Review, 1999, 1–11, www.stockmaven.com/logsdon99_D.htm.

London, Jack. *The Portable Jack London*. Edited by Earle Labor. New York: Penguin Books, 1994.

_____. *John Barleycorn*. New York: Modern Library, 2001.

Londraville, Janis, and Richard Londraville. *The Most Beautiful Man in the World: Paul Swan from Wilde to Warhol*. Lincoln and London: University of Nebraska Press, 2006.

Longford, Elizabeth. *Byron's Greece*. New York: Harper & Row, 1975.

Look, 29 March 1938.

Loughery, John. *The Other Side of Silence: Men's Lives and Gay Identities: A Twentieth-Century History*. New York: Henry Holt & Company, 1998.

Loussier, Jean, and Robin Langley Sommer. *Lost Europe—Images of a Vanished World*. New York: Crescent Books, 1997.

Love, Brenda. *Encyclopedia of Unusual Sex Practices*. Greenwich Editions, 2000.

Loy, Mina. *The Last Lunar Baedeker*. Edited by Roger L. Conover. New York: Farrar, Straus & Giroux, 1996.

Ludecke, Kurt G.W. *I Knew Hitler: The Story of a Nazi Who Escaped the Blood Purge*. New York: Scribners, 1937.

Ludecke, Winifred. *Secrets of Espionage—Tales of the Secret Service*. Philadelphia: J.P. Lippincott Company, 1929.

Lynes, George Platt, Monroe Wheeler, and Glenway Wescott. *When We Were Three: The Travel Albums of George Platt Lynes, Monroe Wheeler, and Glenway Wescott*. Texts by Anatole Pohorilenko and James Crump. Santa Fe, N.M.: Arena Editions, 1998.

MacCarthy, Fiona. *Byron: Life and Legend*. New York: Farrar, Straus & Giroux, 2002.

MacCown, Eugene. *The Siege of Innocence*. New York: Doubleday & Company, 1950.

MacDonogh, Giles. Translator's Preface to *The Hitler Book—The Secret Dossier Prepared for Stalin from the Interrogation of Hitler's Personal Aides*, edited by Henrik Eberle and Matthias Uhl. New York: Public Affairs, 2005.

MacFadden, Mary, and Emile Gauvreau. *Dumbbells and Carrot Strips—The Story of Bernarr Mac-*

Fadden. New York: Henry Holt & Company, 1953.

Mackerras, Colin. *Western Images of China*. Oxford and Hong Kong: Oxford University Press, 1989.

MacManus, Seumas. *The Story of the Irish Race*. New York: Devin-Adair Company, 1921.

Machtan, Lothar. *The Hidden Hitler*. Translated by John Brownjohn with notes and translation by Susanne Ehlert. New York: Basic Books, 2001.

Mademoiselle: The Magazine for Smart Young Women, October 1938.

Mails, Thomas E. *The Cherokee People—The Story of the Cherokees from Earliest Origins to Contemporary Times*. Tulsa, Okla.: Council Oak Books, 1992.

Mann, William J. *Behind the Screen—How Gays and Lesbians Shaped Hollywood, 1910-1969*. New York: Penguin Books, 2001.

_____. *Wisecracker—The Life and Times of William Haines, Hollywood's First Openly Gay Star*. New York: Viking, 1998.

Maracin, Paul. *Night of the Long Knives: 48 Hours That Changed the History of the World*. New York: The Lyons Press, 2004. The DVD of the same title is available from the History Channel, AAE-76829.

Markham, Edwin, ed. *The Real America in Romance*. 13 vols. New York and Chicago: William H. Wise & Company, 1914.

Marks, Carole, and Diana Edkins. *The Power of Pride—Stylemakers and Rulebreakers of the Harlem Renaissance*. New York: Crown Publishers, 1999.

Martin, John. "Dance" reviews. *New York Times*, various, early 1930s.

Martin, Robert K. *The Homosexual Tradition in American Poetry*. Austin: University of Texas Press, 1979.

Marvel, Ik (Donald Grant Mitchell). *Dream Life—A Fable of the Seasons*. New York: Charles Scribner's, 1852.

Mauss, Marcel. *The Gift*. Glencoe, Illinois: The Free Press, 1959.

Mautz, Carl. *Biographies of Western Photographers—A Reference Guide to Photographers Working in the 19th Century American West*. Nevada City, Calif.: Carl Mautz Publishing, 1997.

Max, Gerry. "Many Mansions." Unpublished monograph. Aldo Magi Materials in Thomas Wolfe Collection at University of North Carolina, Chapel Hill.

_____. "Richard Halliburton and Thomas Wolfe: When Youth Kept Open House." *North Carolina Literary Review* no. 5 (1996), 82–93.

Maxwell, Gilbert. *Helen Morgan—Her Life and Legend*. New York: Hawthorn Books, 1963.

McAllister, Hugh. *The Flight of the Silver Ship, or Around the World in a Giant Dirigible*. Akron, Ohio: Saalfield Publishing Company, 1930.

McAnally, D.R., Jr. *Irish Wonders*. New York: Gramercy Books, 1996.

McCarthy, Mary. *Intellectual Memoirs—New York 1936-1938*. New York: Harcourt Brace, 1993.

McClure, Hal, "The Ghost of Laguna's Hangover House." Associated Press, Los Angeles, Orange County, 20 January 1957.

McConnell, Curt. *Coast to Coast by Automobile—The Pioneering Trips, 1899-1908*. Stanford, Calif.: Stanford University Press, 2000.

McDonald, T. Letter (unpublished) to Edward T. Howell, 25 February 1972.

McFayden, Michael. "S.S. *Coolidge*: A Short History," http://www.michaelmcfadyenscuba.info/news.php

McGloin, John Bernard. *San Francisco—The Story of a City*. San Rafael, Calif.: Presidio Press, 1979.

Menpes, Mortimer, with Dorothy Menpes. *Brittany*. London: Adam and Charles Black, 1912.

Meyer, Philippe. *A Parisian's Paris*. Paris: Flammarion, 1999.

Meyers, Jeffrey. *The Wounded Spirit: T.E. Lawrence's Seven Pillars of Wisdom*. New York: St. Martin's Press, 1989.

Mileck, Joseph. *Herman Hesse—Life and Art*. Berkeley: University of California Press, 1978.

Milhaud, Darius. *My Happy Life—An Autobiography*. Translated by Donald Evans, George Hall, and Christopher Palmer. London and New York: Marion Boyars, 1995.

Modern Screen 5, no. 4 (March 1933).

Mintz, Steven. *Huck's Raft—A History of American Childhood*. Cambridge, Mass.: Belkamp Press/Harvard University Press, 2004.

Moll, Albert. *Perversions of the Sex Instinct—A Study of Sexual Inversion*. Translated by Maurice Popkin. Newark, N.J.: Julian Press, 1931.

Mooney, Ione Lee Gaut. Genealogy (unpublished). Records Request #106225. Daughters of the American Revolution (microfiche).

Mooney, James. *The Ghost Dance*. Reprint of Part 2 of the 14th Annual Report of the Bureau of Ethnology to the Secretary of the Smithsonian Institution. North Dighton, Mass.: JB Press, 1996.

_____. *History, Myths, and Sacred Formulas of the Cherokees: Containing the Full Texts of Myths of the Cherokee (1900 and the Sacred Formula)*. Fairview, N.C.: Bright Mountain Books, 1992.

Mooney, Alicia. Letters (unpublished) to William Alexander, William Alexander Collection.

Mooney, Paul. Letters (unpublished) to William Alexander, William Alexander Collection.

_____. Letter (unpublished) to Evelyn Mooney, Anton Levandowsky Collection.

_____. *Seven Poems*. New York: Ramapo Printers, 1927.

Morris, Jan. *Hong Kong*. New York: Vintage Books, 1989.

Morris, Michael. *The Many Lives of Natacha Rambova*. New York: Abbeville Press, 1991.

Moses, Lester George. *The Indian Man: A Biography of James Mooney*. Urbana and Chicago: University of Illinois Press, 1984.

Nadel, Stanley. *Little Germany—Ethnicity, Religion, and Class in New York City, 1945-80*. Urbana and Chicago: University of Illinois Press, 1990.

New Theatre, February 1935.

New Theatre, May 1935.

The New Yorker, 28 September 1929.

The New York Times, 6 November 1932, 6.

The New York Times, 11 June 1939.

Nichols, Roger. *The Harlequin Years—Music in Paris, 1917-1929*. Berkeley: University of California Press, 2002.

Norris, Charles G. *Ivanhoe—A Grove Play*. San Francisco: Bohemian Club, 1936.

Nourse, Mary A. *A Short History of the Chinese*. Indianapolis and New York: Bobbs-Merrill, 1942.

Novaresio, Paolo. *The Explorers—From the Ancient World to the Present*. New York: Stewart, Tabori & Chang, 1996.

"Nudist Life," *The Nudist*, November 1933.

O'Connor, Patrick. *Josephine Baker*. Boston: Bulfinch Press, 1988.

O'Donnell, Thomas J. *The Confessions of T.E. Lawrence*. Athens, Ohio: Ohio University Press, 1979.

Official Pictures. Chicago World's Fair, 1933. Photographs by Kaufmann and Fabry Co. The Reuben H. Donnelly Corporation, 1933.

Official William Beebe Website. http://home town.aol.com/chines6930/mw1/beebe1.htm

O hEithir, Breandan. *A Pocket History of Ireland*. Dublin: O'Brien Press, 2000.

Olds, Elizabeth Fagg. *Women of the Four Winds—The Adventures of Four of America's First Women Explorers*. Boston: Houghton Mi·in, 1985.

O'Neil, Paul. *Barnstormers and Speed Kings*. Alexandria, Va.: Time-Life Books, 1981.

O'Neill, Eugene. *Beyond the Horizon*. In *Four Plays by Eugene O'Neill*. New York: Signet, 1998.

"Organized Motorist." *American Motorist*, March 1928, 22–23, 33.

Ottley, Roi. *New World a Coming—Inside Black America*. Boston: Houghton Mi·in, 1943.

Pacific Dreams—Currents of Surrealism and Fantasy in California Art, 1934-1957. Los Angeles: UCLA/Armand Hammer Museum of Art and Cultural Center, 1995.

Pakenham, Thomas. *The Year of Liberty—The Great Irish Rebellion of 1798*. London: Weidenfeld & Nicolson, 1997.

Palmer, Rose A. *The North American Indians—An Account of the American Indians North of Mexico, Compiled From Original Sources*. Washington, D.C.: Smithsonian Scientific Series, 1929.

Parkman, Francis. *The Oregon Trail*. Edited by David Levin. New York: Penguin Books, 1982.

Parrot, Nicole. *Mannequins*. Paris: Calona, 1982.

Paul, Elliot. *The Last Time I Saw Paris*. New York: Random House, 1942.

Perkins, Dorothy. *The Encyclopedia of China, Essential Reference to China, Its History and Culture*. New York: Facts on File, 1999.

Perrottet, Tony. *Route 66 A.D.—On the Trail of Ancient Roman Tourists*. New York: Random House, 2002.

Petronius. *Satyricon*. Translated by Michael Heseltine. Cambridge, Mass.: Loeb Classical Library/Harvard University Press, 1997.

Philibert, Helene. Letter (unpublished) to Edward T. Howell, 20 September 1946.

"The Pioneers and Aeromodelling-Independent Evolutions & Histories: Elly-Beinhorn-Rosemeyer."www.ctie.monash.aw/hargrave/beinhorn.htm.

Poetry—A Magazine of Verse 38, no. 3 (June 1926) and 41, no. 2 (November 1932).

Polk, Milbrey, and Mary Tiegreen. *Women of Discovery—A Celebration of Intrepid Women Who Explored the World*. New York: Clarkson Potter Publishers, 2001.

Pollock, Barbara, and Charles Humphrey Woodford. *Dance Is a Moment: A Portrait of Jose Limon in Words and Pictures*. Pennington, N.J.: Princeton Book Company, 1993.

Porter, Eliot. *Down the Colorado: John Wesley Powell's Diary of the First Trip Through the Grand Canyon*. New York: Arrowood Press, 1988.

Post, Wiley, and Harold Gatty. *Around the World in Eight Days—The Flight of the Winnie Mae*. Introduction by Will Rogers. New York: Rand McNally, 1931.

Postumus, Cyril. "Bernd Rosemeyer." In *Great Racing Drivers*, edited by David Hodges. New York: Arco Publishing Company, 1967.

Powell, Leslie. "Painting from a Life's Journey." n.p., 1967.

Purcell, Victor. *Chinese Evergreen*. New York: E.P. Dutton & Company, 1938.

Rabate, Jean-Michel. "On Joycean and Wildean Sodomy." In *Quare Joyce*, edited by Joseph Valente. Ann Arbor, Mich.: University of Michigan Press, 2000.

Raitz, Karl, ed. *The National Road*. Baltimore: John Hopkins University, 1996.

Ramsey, Merle, and Mabel Ramsey. *First 100*

Years in Laguna Beach, 1876–1976. Laguna Beach, Calif.: Hastie Printers, 1976.

Rand, Ayn. *The Fountainhead.* New York: Signet Books, 1963.

_____. *The Journals of Ayn Rand.* Edited by David Harriman. New York: Dutton/Penguin Putnam, 1997.

Rankin, Nicholas. *Dead Man's Chest—Travels after Robert Louis Stevenson.* London: Phoenix Press, 1987.

Raspe, R.E., and others. *Singular Travels, Campaigns and Adventures of Baron Munchausen.* New York: Dover Publications, 1960.

Read, Anthony. *The Devil's Disciples—Hitler's Inner Circle.* New York: W.W. Norton, 2003.

Reed, John. *Daughter of the Revolution and Other Stories.* Edited by Floyd Dell. New York: Vanguard Press, 1927.

_____. *Ten Days That Shook the World.* New York: Modern Library, 1934.

Reese, Betsy. *The Life and World of Henry Hamilton Bennett.* Wisconsin Dells, Wisc.: H.H. Bennett Studio, 1975.

Revue des Folies Bergere, La Folie du Jour, Quatrieme Album, 1926–1927. Paris: Editions Artistiques de Paris.

Richardson, Russell. *Europe from a Motor Car.* Chicago and New York: Rand McNally & Company, 1914.

Ripley, Robert (subject). www.staugustine-ripleys. com/about/bio.php.

Roberts, Mary Louise Roberts. *Disruptive Acts—The New Women in Fin de Siecle France.* Chicago: University of Chicago Press, 2002.

Roberts, Robert B. *The Encyclopedia of Historic Forts—The Military, Pioneer, and Trading Posts of the United States.* New York: Macmillan, 1988.

Robinson, Paul. *Gay Lives—Homosexual Autobiography from John Addington Symonds to Paul Monette.* Chicago: University of Chicago Press, 1999.

Rogers, Betty. *Will Rogers—The Story of His Life.* Garden City, N.Y.: Garden City Publishing, 1941.

Root, Jonathan. *Halliburton—The Magnificent Myth.* New York: Coward-McCann, 1965.

Rosario, Vernon A. *The Erotic Imagination.* New York and Oxford: Oxford University Press, 1997.

Roth, Joseph. *Report from a Parisian in Paradise—Essays from France 1925–1939.* Translated by Michael Hofmann. New York: W.W. Norton, 1999.

San Francisco—The Bay and Its Cities. Compiled by Workers of the Writers' Program of the Work Projects Administration in Northern California. New York: Hastings House, 1940.

San Francisco Exposition and Bay Counties Telephone Directory, May 1939.

San Francisco Exposition Concerts—The fabled 24 September 1940 San Francisco Concerts. Music and Arts, CD 971. 4 compact discs.

Sanderlin, George. *The Sea Dragon—Journals of Francis Drake's Voyage around the World.* New York: Harper & Row, 1969.

Sanders, Tao Tao Liu. *Dragons, Gods & Spirits from Chinese Mythology.* New York: Schocken Books, 1980.

Sandor, Gluck. Obituary. *The New York Times,* 11 March 1978, Sec. 2, 2.

Sassoon, Siegfried. *Collected Poems 1908–1956.* London and Boston: Faber & Faber, 1961.

Sawyer-Laucanno, Christopher. *An Invisible Spectator—A Biography of Paul Bowles.* New York: Weidenfeld & Nicolson, 1989.

Scaravaglione, Concetta. Obituary. *The New York Times,* 6 September 1975.

Scharff, Virginia. *Taking the Wheel: Women and the Coming of the Motor Age.* New York: The Free Press, 1991.

Schmidt, Michael. *Lives of the Poets.* New York: Alfred A. Knopf, 1999.

"Schools & Colleges." *Harper's Magazine* no. 627 (August 1902).

Scott, Jack Denton. *Passport to Adventure.* New York: Random House, 1966.

Schultz, Barbara Hunter. *Pancho: The Biography of Florence Lowe Barnes.* Lancaster, Calif.: Little Buttes Publishing Company, 1996.

Schwartz, David M. "On the Royal Road to Adventure with 'Daring Dick.'" *Smithsonian,* March 1989, 159–178.

Secrest, Meryle. *Frank Lloyd Wright: A Biography.* New York: Alfred A. Knopf, 1992.

A Selective Collective of Hong Kong Historic Postcards, compiled by Tong Cheuk Man, David P.M. Toong, Alan S.K. Cheung and Mo Yu Kai. Hong Kong: Joint Publishing Company, n.d.

Severin, Tim. *The China Voyage—Across the Pacific by Bamboo Raft.* Reading, Mass.: Addison-Wesley Publishing, 1994.

Seward, Desmond. *Caravaggio—A Passionate Life.* New York: William Morrow & Company, 1998.

Seymour-Smith, Martin. *Who's Who in Twentieth Century Literature.* New York: McGraw Hill, 1977.

Shand, Alexander Innes. *Old Time Travel—Personal Reminiscences of the Continent Forty Years Ago Compared with Experiences of the Present Day.* London: John Murray, 1903.

Sheean, Vincent. *Personal History.* Garden City, N.Y.: Doubleday, Doran & Company, 1936.

Shinkman, Paul. *So Little Disillusion—An American Correspondent in Paris and London, 1924–1931.* Edited by Elizabeth Benn Shinkman. McLean, Va.: EPM Publications, 1983.

Shirer, William L. *The Rise and Fall of the Third Reich—A History of Nazi Germany.* Greenwich, Conn.: Fawcett Publications, 1959.

Shostakovich, Dmitri. *5th Symphony. Great Performances.* New York Philharmonic: Leonard Bernstein. CBS Records, CD MYK 37218. 1959. Compact disc.

Sibalis, Michael D. "Paris." In *Queer Sites*, edited by David Higgs. New York and London: Routledge, 1999.

Silber, Evelyn, and David Finn. *Gaudier-Brzeska— Life and Art.* New York and London: Thames & Hudson, 1996.

Simenon, Georges. *Inquest on Bouvet.* Translated by Eugene MacCown. London: Hamish Hamilton, 1958.

Sinclair, Upton. *Cup of Fury.* Great Neck, N.Y.: Channel Press, 1956.

Slocum, Captain Joshua. *Sailing Alone around the World.* New York: Dover Publications, 1956.

_____. *Voyage of the Liberdade.* New York: Dover Publications, 1998.

Smith, Edward H. *Around a Round World—Journeyings of a Traveler.* Oshkosh, Wisc.: Press of Castle-Pierce Company, 1922.

The Smithsonian Experience. Washington, D.C.: The Smithsonian Institution, 1977.

Snow, Philip. *The Fall of Hong Kong—Britain, China and the Japanese Occupation.* New Haven, Conn.: Yale University Press, 2003.

Sontag, Susan. "Homage to Halliburton." *Oxford American: The Travel Issue,* March/April 2001, 120–122.

Sprawson, Charles. *Haunts of the Black Masseur— The Swimmer As Hero.* New York: Pantheon Books, 1992.

Spring, Justin. *Paul Cadmus—The Male Nude.* Chesterfield, Mass.: Chameleon Books, 2002.

Springer, Arthur. *Red Wine of Youth—A Life of Rupert Brooke.* New York: Bobbs-Merrill, 1952.

Stansell, Christine. *American Moderns—Bohemian New York and the Creation of a New Century.* New York: Henry Holt & Company, 2000.

Stefoff, Rebecca. *Women of the World—Women Travelers and Explorers.* New York and Oxford: Oxford University Press, 1992.

Stegner, Wallace. *Beyond the Hundredth Meridian— John Wesley Powell and the Second Coming of the West.* New York: Penguin Books, 1992.

Stelzig, Eugene L. *Herman Hesse's Fictions of the Self—Autobiography and the Confessional Imagination.* Princeton, N.J.: Princeton University Press, 1988.

Stephens, C.A. *The Knockabout Club Alongshore— The Adventures of a Party of Young Men on a Trip from Boston to the Land of the Midnight Sun.* Boston: Estes & Lauriat, 1882.

Stephens, Moye, with J.M. Hiatt. "Ghosts of the Air." In *100 Ghastly Little Ghost Stories,* edited by Stefan R. Dziemianowicz, Robert Weinberg, and Martin H. Greenberg. Totowa, N.J.: Barnes & Noble, 1993.

Sterling, George. *Ode on the Opening of the Panama-Pacific International Exposition.* San Francisco: A.M. Robertson, 1915.

_____. *Robinson Jeffers—The Man and the Artist.* New York: Boni & Liveright, 1926.

Stevens, Alden, and Marion Stevens. *The Stevens America—A Traveler's Guide to the United States.* Boston: Little, Brown, & Company, 1950.

Stewart, Desmond. *T.E. Lawrence: A New Biography.* New York: Harper & Row, 1977.

Stewart, Jeffrey C., ed. *Paul Robeson, Artist and Citizen.* New Brunswick, N.J., and New York: Rutgers University Press and The Paul Robeson Cultural Center, 1999.

Stewart, Omer C. *Peyote Religion—A History.* Norman, Okla.: University of Oklahoma Press, 1987.

Stoddard, Charles Warren (subject). glbtq. An Encyclopedia of Gay, Lesbian, Bisexual, Transgender and Queer Culture. http://www.glbtq.com/literature/stoddard_cw.htlm.

Stoddard, Charles Warren. *Poems of Charles Warren Stoddard.* Compiled by Ina Coolbrith. New York: John Lane Company, 1917.

_____. *South-Sea Idyls.* New York: Charles Scribner's Sons, 1892.

Stoddard, John L. *Scenic America—Beauties of the Western Hemisphere—Containing a Rare and Elaborate Collection of Photographic Views of the United States, Canada, Mexico, Central and South America.* n.p. [19th century.]

Stovall, Tyler. *Paris Noir—African Americans in the City of Light.* Boston and New York: Houghton Mi·in, 1996.

Strait, Raymond, and Leif Henie. *Queen of Ice—Queen of Shadows; The Unsuspected Life of Sonja Henie.* Boston: Scarborough House, 1985.

Supf, Peter. *Airman's World—A Book about Flying.* Translated by Cyrus Brooks. London: George Routledge & Sons, 1933.

Swanton, John R. "James Mooney." *American Anthropologist,* 24 (1922), 209–214.

Tafel, Edgar. *About Wright—An Album of Recollections by Those Who Knew Frank Lloyd Wright.* New York: John Wiley & Sons, 1993.

_____. *Working with Mr. Wright: What It Was Like.* Cambridge and New York: Cambridge University Press, 1995.

Tarpa Topics, the Retired Trans World Airline Pilot's Magazine, April 1996.

Tate, Grover Ted. *The Lady Who Tamed Pegasus—The Story of Pancho Barnes*. Bend, Ore.: Maverick Publications, 1986.

Taylor, Colin. *Myths of the North American Indians*. Totowa, N.J.: Barnes & Noble, 1995.

Taylor, John. *Travels through Stuart Britain—The Adventures of John Taylor, The Water Poet*. Edited and selected by John Chandler. Phoenix Mill, England: Sutton Publishing, 1999.

Taylor, Pamela. Review. *The Siege of Innocence* by Eugene MacCown. *The Saturday Review of Literature*, 4 May 1950, 30.

Terkel, Studs. *Hard Times*. New York: The New Press, 2000.

Theroux, Paul. Introduction to *The Best American Travel Writing*. Boston: Houghton Mi∙in, 2001. Audio recording. 5 compact discs.

_____. *Chicago Tribune*, December 11, 1995.

Thomas, Lowell. *Count Luckner—The Sea Devil*. New York: Doubleday, Doran & Company, 1928.

_____. *Seven Wonders of the World*. Garden City, N.Y.: Hanover House, 1956.

Thomson, Virgil. *Selected Letters of Virgil Thomson*. Edited by Tim Page and Vanessa Weeks Page. New York: Summit Books, 1988.

_____. *Virgil Thomson*. New York: Alfred A. Knopf, 1966.

Thurston, J.S. *Laguna Beach of Early Days*. Culver City, Calif.: Murray & Gee, 1947.

Time, May 30, 1927.

Time, September 23, 1929.

Time, November 17, 1930.

Time, April 4, 1932.

Time, June 20, 1932.

Time, January 16, 1933.

Time, January 29, 1934.

Time, January 28, 1935.

Time, August 5, 1935.

Time, August 29, 1938.

Time, April 10, 1939.

Time, December 18, 1939.

Time, July 8, 1940.

Time, August 4, 1958.

Time, November 21, 1960.

Timmons, Stuart. *The Trouble with Harry*. Boston: Alyson Publications, 1990.

Tinniswood, Adrian. *The Polite Tourist—Four Centuries of Country House Visiting*. New York: Harry N. Abrams, 1989.

Tip Top Weekly no. 699 (4 September 1909).

Tommasini, Anthony. *Virgil Thomson—Composer on the Aisle*. New York: W.W. Norton, 1997.

Tottel, Richard. *Tottel's Miscellany (1557–1587)*.

Edited by Hyder Edward Rollins. Cambridge, Mass.: Harvard University Press, 1966.

Townsend, Guy. "Richard Halliburton: The Forgotten Myth." *City of Memphis* 2, no. 5 (August 1977), 33–37.

Traub, James. *The Devil's Playground—A Century of Pleasure and Profit on Times Square*. New York: Random House, 2004.

Travel, August 1932.

Tuchman, Barbara W. *Stilwell and the American Experience in China, 1911–1945*. New York: Macmillan, 1970.

Turner, Andy. "The Royal Road to Carolina." *North Carolina Literary Review* no. 5 (1996), 88–89.

Turner, Elizabeth Hutton. *Americans in Paris (1921–1931)*. Washington, D.C.: Counterpoint, 1996.

Unterecker, John. *Voyager—A Life of Hart Crane*. New York and London: Liveright, 1969.

U.S. Navy Hydrographic Bulletin to Edward T. Howell, 5 April 1939.

Uys, Errol Lincoln. *Riding the Rails—Teenagers on the Move During the Great Deparession*. New York: TV Books, 1999.

Vaill, Amanda. *Everybody Was So Young*. Boston and New York: Houghton Mi∙in, 1998.

_____. *Somewhere—The Life of Jerome Robbins*. New York: Broadway Books, 2006.

Van Vechten, Carl. *Parties: Scenes from Contemporary New York Life*. New York: Alfred Knopf, 1930.

_____. *The Splendid Drunken Years—Selections From the Daybooks, 1922–1930*. Edited by Bruce Keller. Urbana and Chicago: University of Illinois Press, 2003.

Verrill, A. Hyatt. "Dances and Ceremonials." In *The American Indian—North, South and Central America*. The New Home Library, 1927.

Volta, Ornella. *Erik Satie*. Paris: Editions Hazan, 1997.

Von Krafft-Ebing, Richard. *The Psychopathia Sexualis*. Translated by Franklin S. Klaf. New York: Stein & Day, 1965.

Walker, Stanley. *The Night Club Era*. Baltimore: Johns Hopkins University Press, 1999.

Wallace, Max. *The American Axis: Henry Ford, Charles Lindbergh and the Rise of the Third Reich*. New York: St. Martin's Press, 2003.

Wallis, Michael. *Route 66—The Mother Road*. New York: St. Martin's Press, 1990.

Ware, Caroline Farrar. *Greenwich Village, 1920–1930*. Berkeley: University of California Press, 1994.

Walsh, James P., and Timothy O'Keefe. *Legacy of a Native Son—James Duval Phelan and Villa Montalvo*. Los Gatos, Calif.: Forbes Mill Press, 1993.

Watkins, T.H. *The Great Depression—American in the 1930s*. Boston: Back Bay Books/Little, Brown & Company, 1993.

Weller, Allen. "Lorado Taft, the Ferguson Fund, and the Advent of Modernism." In *The Old Guard and the Avant Guard Modernism in Chicago—1910-1940*, edited by Sue Ann Prince. Chicago: University of Chicago Press, 1990.

Weller, George. "The Passing of the Last Playboy." *Esquire*, April 1940, 58.

Westermarck, Edward. *The Future of Marriage in Western Culture*. London: Macmillan & Company, 1936.

_____. *The Origin and Development of Moral Ideas*. London: Macmillan & Company, 1906.

Western Flying, August 1929.

Wetzsteon, Ross. *Republic of Dreams—Greenwich Village: The American Bohemia, 1910-1960*. New York: Simon & Schuster, 2002.

Whitaker, Rick. *The First Time I Met Frank O'Hara—Reading Gay American Writers*. New York: Four Walls Eight Windows, 2003.

Wickes, George. *The Amazon of Letters—The Life and Loves of Natalie Barney*. London: W.H. Allen, 1977.

Williams, Esther. *The Million Dollar Mermaid*. New York: Simon & Schuster, 1999.

Williams, Tennessee. *The Selected Letters of Tennessee Williams, Volume 1—1920-1945*. Edited by Albert J. Devlin and Nancy M. Tischler. New York: New Directions, 2000.

_____. *Sweet Bird of Youth*. New York: New Directions, 1959.

Wilson, Colin. *The Mammoth Book of the History of Murder*. New York: Carroll & Graf Publishers, 1990.

Wilson, Forrest. "It Seems Only Yesterday ... The Great World's Fair of 1893." *Cosmopolitan*, July 1933, 26-27, 157-160.

Wilson, James Grant, and John Fiske, eds. *Appletons' Cyclopedia of America Biography*. New York: D. Appleton & Company, 1887-1888.

Wineapple, Brenda. *Genet—A Biography of Janet Flanner*. New York: Tichnor & Fields, 1989.

Wings Over Hong Kong—An Aviation History 1891-1998: A Tribute to Kai Tak. Hong Kong: Pacific Century Publishers, 1998.

Witzel, Michael Karl. *Route 66 Remembered*. St. Paul, Minn.: MBI Publishing Company, 1996.

Wolfe, Thomas. *The Notebooks of Thomas Wolfe*. Edited by Richard S. Kennedy and Paschal Reeves. 2 vols. Chapel Hill, N.C.: University of North Caroline Press, 1970.

_____. *The Party at Jack's*. Edited by Suzanne Stutman and John L. Idol, Jr. Chapel Hill, N.C.: North Carolina Press, 1995.

Wood, Amos L. *Beachcombing the Pacific*. West Chester, Pa.: Schiffer Publishing Ltd., 1987.

Wood, Clement. *Bernarr MacFadden: A Study in Success*. 1929. Reprint, New York: Beekman Publishers, 1974.

Woodress, James. *Willa Cather, A Literary Life*. Lincoln, Neb.: University of Nebraska Press, 1987.

Worster, Donald. *A River Running West—The Life of John Wesley Powell*. New York and Oxford: Oxford University Press, 2001.

Wu, Judy Tzu-Chun. "Mom Chung of the Fair-Haired Bastards: A Thematic Biography of Dr. Margaret Chung (1889-1959)." Ph.D. diss., Stanford University, 1998.

Wyatt, David. *Five Fires—Race, Catastrophe, and the Shaping of California*. Menlo Park, Calif.: Addison-Wesley Publishing, 1997.

Xantus, John. *Travels in Southern California*. Translated and edited by Theodore Schoenman and Helen Benedek Schoenman. Detroit: Wayne State University Press, 1976.

Yeager, General Chuck, and Leo Janos. *Yeager—An Autobiography*. New York: Bantam Books, 1985.

Yingling, Thomas. *Hart Crane and the Homosexual Text—New Thresholds, New Anatomies*. Chicago: The University of Chicago Press, 1990.

Zailian, Marian. "Robbins' Band of Merry Musicals—Broadway Legend's work lights up San Francisco." *San Francisco Chronicle*, 11 August 1991, 18.

Index